Options for Aged Care in China

DIRECTIONS IN DEVELOPMENT
Human Development

Options for Aged Care in China

Building an Efficient and Sustainable Aged Care System

Elena Glinskaya and Zhanlian Feng, Editors

WORLD BANK GROUP

1 2 3 4 21 20 19 18

ISBN (paper): 978-1-4648-1075-6
ISBN (electronic): 978-1-4648-1076-3
DOI: 10.1596/978-1-4648-1075-6

Cover photo: © Li Wenyong. Used with permission. Further permission required for re-use.
Cover design: Debra Naylor, Naylor Design, Inc.

Library of Congress Cataloging-in-Publication Data has been applied for

Contents

Boxes

Figures

Tables

Foreword

Older people make up a growing proportion of the populations in many middle- and high-income countries, which presents new challenges for growth and development. Whereas the degree and pace vary by country, falling fertility rates and longer life expectancies mean there is a declining proportion of young people and an increasing proportion of the elderly. Such population aging has major economic implications and raises concerns about increased health care costs, the sustainability of pension systems, and the availability of care services for the elderly.

China is experiencing one of the most rapid transitions to an aging society ever witnessed. It will move from being an aging to an aged society by 2027; in just 25 years, 14 percent of China's population will be 65 and older, up from 7 percent in 2002. This transition took 115 years for France, 45 years for England, and 69 years for the United States. The aging process in China is projected to accelerate further in the coming decades, with growth of the elderly population being especially pronounced between 2015 and 2040. By 2050, 26 percent of China's population is expected to be 65 or older, and about 8 percent will be 80 years or older.

Such rapid aging is putting pressure on China's current informal and formal arrangements for aged care. Traditionally, the family has been the primary source of care for the elderly in China. However, changes in family structure, economic development, and migration are eroding the easy availability of informal care for the elderly. The Chinese government recognizes the need to strengthen formal aged care provisions and expand access to services, but it faces numerous challenges to developing an efficient and sustainable approach to aged care, including fulfilling its new role as a "steward" (rather than direct provider) of formal aged care services.

This report was prepared at the request of the China National Development and Reform Commission to support the government in tackling these challenges. The objective is to help the government move from the broad strategic directions for aged care captured by the 13th Five-Year Plan and other government plans toward a concrete and coherent policy framework. Specifically, this report describes the current landscape and challenges for aged care in China, looking at both supply and demand for services; it reviews international experiences in aged care provision and assesses their relevance to China; and it proposes policy options based on evidence and best practices.

The key message of this report is that China should build a balanced mix of services across home, community, and institutional settings that can best meet older people's preferences and needs. Although continued government support is needed for those elderly who have limited functional ability and who are poor and vulnerable, the most effective and sustainable approach would be to leverage resources and complementary capacities from both the public and private sectors to create a functioning market for elderly care across income groups and across urban and rural areas. The report highlights three priority areas for China going forward:

- Build the government's stewardship capacity and develop relationships with private sector providers;
- Empower consumers by shifting subsidies toward services and care recipients, not beds and providers; and
- Extend long-term care financing in a systemic yet sustainable way.

The aged care systems of Organisation for Economic Co-operation and Development countries and other developed economies in the East Asia region provide useful examples in all three of these areas. In the end, however, policy makers in China must develop a system that best suits the Chinese cultural, socioeconomic, political, and health care contexts.

We hope this report will contribute to a deeper and more informed policy dialogue on how to best develop China's aged care system and that it helps the government translate its strategies for aged care into concrete reforms that will result in effective, equitable, and sustainable support for China's elderly.

Bert Hofman
Country Director
China, Mongolia and Korea
The World Bank

Michal Rutkowski
Senior Director
Social Protection and Jobs
Global Practice
The World Bank

Acknowledgments

This book was put together by Elena Glinskaya (World Bank) and Zhanlian Feng (RTI International), based on contributions from a team of researchers and practitioners in the aged care field from all over the world. The book, which consists of an overview and ten chapters, was prepared at the request of the China National Development and Reform Commission (NDRC). Overall guidance for the work was provided by Bert Hofman,Jehan Arulpragasam, and Philip O'Keefe, (all from the World Bank).

The overview was written by Elena Glinskaya (World Bank) and Zhanlian Feng (RTI International). The ten chapters of the book were written by Jan M. Bauer (Copenhagen Business School), Xinxin Chen (Peking University), Lizzy Feiler (Consultant), Zhanlian Feng (RTI International), John Giles (World Bank), Elena Glinskaya (World Bank), Yuqing Hu (World Bank), Qinghua Li (RTI International), Yvonne Li (International China Ageing Industry Association), Chang Liu (ACCESS Health International/Duke-NUS Graduate Medical School), Du Peng (Renmin University), Gong Sen (Development Research Center, State Council), Jin Song (Chinese Academy of Social Sciences), Charlie Wang (International China Ageing Industry Association), Dewen Wang (World Bank), Joshua M. Wiener (RTI International), Heather Wong (International China Ageing Industry Association), Jiahui Zhang (Development Research Center, State Council), Shuo Zhang (World Bank), Yaohui Zhao (Peking University), and Nan Tracy Zheng (RTI International). Lizzy Feiler (consultant), Jin Song (Chinese Academy of Social Sciences), Rui Liu (World Bank), and Yang Huang (World Bank) provided invaluable inputs to the overview and the rest of book.

The authors are grateful to Philip O'Keefe (World Bank), Marzena Breza (European Union), Jiadi Yu (International Finance Corporation), Victoria Levin (World Bank), Ana Maria Boudet (World Bank), Changqing Sun (World Bank), and Xiaoyuan Dong (University of Winnipeg), for serving as peer reviewers for this book. The authors also thank Aleksandra Posarac, Veronica Silva Villalobos, Aparnaa Somanathan, Josefina Posadas, Yang Huang, Lansong Zhang, and Erkin Mamadaliev—all from the World Bank—for their valuable comments and feedback during the preparation and review process.

The authors thank Tianxiu Kang, Xuan Peng, Tao Su, and Anqi Li for providing excellent administrative support for preparation of this work.

List of Abbreviations

ADL	Activities of daily living
CCRC	Continuing care retirement community
CHARLS	China Health and Retirement Longitudinal Study
CPC	Communist Party of China
DOCA	Departments of Civil Affairs
DRC	Development Research Center of the State Council
EDR	Elderly dependency ratio
EU	European Union
GDP	Gross domestic product
IADL	Instrumental activities of daily living
ICAIA	International China Ageing Industry Association
ICT	Information and communication technology
LTC	Long-term care
MOF	Ministry of Finance
MOCA	Ministry of Civil Affairs
NCA	National Committee on Aging
NCD	Noncommunicable disease
NDRC	National Development and Reform Commission
NGO	Nongovernmental organization
NPO	Nonprofit organization
NRCMS	New Rural Cooperative Medical Scheme
NRPS	National Rural Pension Scheme
OECD	Organisation for Economic Co-operation and Development
PCIC	People-centered integrated care
PWLF	Public Welfare Lottery Fund
RMB	Renminbi
URPS	Urban Resident Pension Scheme

Glossary of Terms

Commissioning	A set of interrelated tasks that need to be undertaken to turn policy objectives into effective social services. Effective commissioning is fundamental to well-functioning social services. Commissioning organizations need to make informed, deliberate choices about which service model is the best match for the defined population or client group. They should consider objectives, needs, cost effectiveness, funding, pricing, risk management, quality, eligibility, performance measurement, information flows, provider-market sustainability, and interactions with other services (New Zealand Productivity Commission 2015).
Contestability	The characteristic of situations in which providers, whether public or private, face a real prospect that alternative providers will replace them if their performance is persistently unsatisfactory (New Zealand Productivity Commission 2015).
Effective demand	Effective demand refers to the demand that consumers are willing to and have the ability to purchase (Hu et al. 2010).
Informal or familial care	Care provided by family members, friends, and volunteers, usually unpaid (Genet et al. 2012).
Long-term care	Long-term care (LTC) refers to the range of services designed to support people who are unable to perform physical and cognitive functions, measured through ability to perform activities of daily living (ADLs) and instrumental activities of daily living (IADLs). Individuals may need LTC due to limited functional ability, chronic conditions, trauma, or illness that limit their ability to carry out basic self-care or personal tasks that must be performed each day. LTC refers to family-based care in the home- and community as well as institutional care. It is quite distinct from health care, in that while health care services seek to change the health condition (from unwell to well), LTC services seek to make the current condition (unwell) more bearable.

Long-term care expenditures	Based on the definition in the 2012 Joint Health Accounts Questionnaire (JHAQ) of the System of Health Accounts (SHA), long-term care expenditures comprise long-term (health) care and the social services of long-term care. The health component of LTC spending relates to health and nursing care for patients who need assistance on a continuing basis due to chronic impairments and a reduced degree of independence and activities of daily living (ADL). The following items are included in LTC (health): (i) palliative care; (ii) long-term nursing care; (iii) personal care services (assistance with ADL restrictions); and (iv) services in support of informal (family) care. The social component of LTC includes (i) home help (help with IADLs); (ii) residential (care) services; and (iii) other social services provided in an LTC context.
Market for social services	A market is a setting in which parties voluntarily undertake exchanges. The market for social services refers to the provision of social services in exchange for payment. Funding could come from a government agency or another organization (for example, a philanthropic trust). In some cases, clients partly or fully fund the service. The provision and purchase of social services meets the economic definition of a market, yet it has complex and distinctive features that make it different from simple markets (New Zealand Productivity Commission 2015).
Needs assessment	Systematic exploration of the physical and financial possibilities of a person living independently, according to specified rules (Genet et al. 2012).
NPO	Nonprofit organization
Nursing care	Activities of nurses that are of a technical, supportive, or rehabilitative nature (see rehabilitative nursing, supportive nursing, technical nursing) (Genet et al. 2012).
Out-of-pocket payment	The total amount of their own money that individuals spend on both medical expenses and nonmedical expenses (for example, transport, home care) related to care processes pertinent to health care (http://www.biomedcentral.com/1471-2458/14/1008). In the LTC sector, this represents the share of expenses that the individual party must pay directly to the care provider, without a third party.
Palliative care	Palliative care is an approach that improves the quality of life of patients and their families facing the problems associated with life-threatening illness (WHO definition).

Purchasing The purchasing process identifies and selects non-government providers and agrees on terms of supply through a contract. It includes calling for expressions of interest to supply social services, evaluating proposals from potential providers, completing due diligence, negotiating the terms of the contract, and awarding the contract (New Zealand Productivity Commission 2015).

Personal care services Providing assistance with dressing, feeding, washing, and toileting, and getting in or out of bed (also known as PADL) (Genet et al. 2012).

Respite care Short-term care (for example, help with ADLs) aimed at relieving informal caregivers, that is, providing the caregiver with time away from the patient (Genet et al. 2012).

***San wu* senior citizens** "*San wu*" or "Three No's" are people who have lost the ability to work, who have no source of income, and who have no legal guardians to support them (State Council Information Office 2006). Historically, the term Three No's simply meant "no children, no income, and no relatives." Despite the updated definition, the term remains essentially the same.

Stewardship An overarching responsibility for the monitoring, planning, and management of resources in such a way as to maintain and improve system performance. Relevant activities include monitoring system performance, identifying barriers to and opportunities for beneficial change, and leading the wider conversations required to achieve that change (New Zealand Productivity Commission 2015).

***Wubao* senior citizens** In rural areas, the term "Three No's–Five Guarantees" (*wubao*) denotes elderly people who are guaranteed food, clothing, housing, medical care, and burial expenses by the local government.

Overview

Elena Glinskaya and Zhanlian Feng

Introduction

China is aging at an unprecedented rate. Improvements in life expectancy and the consequences of the decades-old family planning policy have led to a rapid increase in the elderly population. According to the United Nations' World Population Prospects, the proportion of older people age 65 and over will more than double from 2010 to 2030, and the elderly will account for over one quarter of the total population by 2050.[1] Population aging will not only pose challenges for elder care but also have an impact on the economy and all aspects of society (World Bank 2016a).

Traditionally, care for the frail elderly has been the responsibility of the family, prescribed by the Confucian norm of filial piety. But this practice is increasingly coming under strain. Particularly in urban China, a new "4–2–1" family structure is emerging which consists of four grandparents: two parents (both without siblings); and one single child, who would be expected to shoulder the major responsibility for caregiving. Even though China has recently (in late 2015) ended the one-child policy to allow all couples to have two children, the demographic impact of this policy change is predicted to be limited and the aging of the population will continue unabated in the coming decades.[2] Rural China faces even more challenges in elder care as the population there is aging more rapidly than in urban areas, and the mass migration of rural youth to the cities for employment opportunities has left behind many elderly parents in the villages. This situation is aggravated by the generally lower level of income security, pensions, health care, and an infrastructure of social support and services for the elderly in rural areas, as compared to urban areas. Together, these have created a situation in which the tradition of filial piety alone—even though it remains

Elena Glinskaya is a Lead Economist and Program Leader for Human Development for China, Mongolia, and the Republic of Korea at the World Bank. Zhanlian Feng is a Senior Research Analyst at RTI International.

strong today—cannot be relied upon to serve the needs of a burgeoning elderly population in China.[3]

Given these demographic and socioeconomic trends, a large gap is emerging between the demand for aged care and its supply. Public opinion polls show that Chinese citizens expect the government to step up to fill this gap. In one recent study, for example, about 60 percent of those surveyed expect the government to provide retirement income, and over 80 percent expect the government to facilitate aged care services and invest in care and rehabilitation facilities for the elderly (World Bank 2016b).

The government faces a number of challenges in developing aged care policies to facilitate the supply of formal elderly care services. Responding to the revealed private demand alone will not allow a market to develop, as formal aged care services are expensive. There is a wedge between the *private demand* (also called effective demand) and the *need* (determined by the degree of individuals' limited functional ability or impairment) for care, with the latter usually exceeding the former. Without government subsidies, only high-income individuals will be able to afford purchasing services produced in the market. Because the poor who qualify as welfare recipients are covered by public resources, and the rich are able to pay for privately produced services, it is the broad middle class that, in the absence of government intervention, will not have access to the services they need and will therefore have to rely on informal provision for aged care. As this outcome is not desirable (nor is it acceptable to China's government), one of the government's roles, therefore, is to foster market development by subsidizing services more broadly to allow for a broad consumer base. The key is to design and administer subsidies that are efficient and equitable.

The government has additional stewardship roles in the aged care market, because in most economies the providers of services are primarily private entities and public agencies rarely provide services directly (this is also the trend seen in China's evolving aged care market). Stewardship functions (in addition to financing) include ensuring the quality and safety of the services provided. Some specific features of the aged care market pose additional challenges for government stewardship. First, similar to the health care market, there is a large informational asymmetry between providers and consumers, making competition and consumer choice difficult. Second, where the government is not a major provider or financier (and does not set prices) it needs to find ways of influencing service quality and the pricing strategy of private providers (which would otherwise be driven by profit maximization in a noncompetitive market). Finally, while private insurance could have been a vehicle for aged care financing, there has been little development of private insurance for aged care around the world. One major reason is that private insurance for aged care is expensive and beyond the means of most people. Even if affordability is less of an issue, individuals tend to be myopic, and when they are young they do not believe that they will need aged care in later years. There also exists moral hazard: if aged care insurance is private and voluntary, those who know that they are at a high risk of limited functional ability and needing care will be most likely to purchase insurance, so that the pool will be composed of high-cost individuals and increasing premiums for all. In addition, since the package of aged care services typically includes services that are valued generally (e.g., housekeeping, meal preparation), otherwise healthy individuals would also want to qualify for those services. Certainly for publicly financed services, the government needs to exercise the "gate-keeping" role to ensure that those services meet minimum quality standards and reach individuals who have the most need.

The government is aware of the need to develop an efficient and sustainable approach to aged care. To this end, the General Office of the State Council issued the *12th Five-Year Plan for the Development of Aged Care Services in China* and the *Development Plan for a System of Social Services for the Aged (2011–2015)*. In March 2017, the State Council released the *13th Five-Year National Plan of Undertakings on Aging and Development of an Aged Care System*, which further elaborates and strengthens the roadmap for 2016 to 2020. The National Development and Reform Commission (NDRC) helped draft these plans and is now leading the development of policy measures for the provision of social services for the elderly.

This volume has been prepared to support the translation of the broad ideas on aged care provision expressed in the 12th and 13th Five-Year Plans and other government plans into reality and to help the government tackle the challenges described above. It strives to identify a policy framework that fits the Chinese context and can be put in place gradually. Specifically, it aims to provide an up-to-date understanding of the evolving aged care landscape in China; review international experiences in long-term care provision, financing, and quality assurance and assess their relevance to China's current situation; discuss implications of current developments and trends for the future of aged care in China; and propose policy options based on available evidence and best practices.

This volume is organized following a simple "demand and supply" framework. On the demand side, factors that drive the need for aged care include demographics (e.g., age structure of the population, family structure and dynamics), health-related needs (e.g., physical and cognitive/mental impairments), and income and assets (which determine the effective demand for formal or paid care). The supply side mainly involves the availability and mix of formal (i.e., paid) services across home, community, and institutional (residential) care settings. The availability of informal care (i.e., unpaid and voluntary care by family members, friends, or others), which remains the dominant source of care for most elderly people in need of care, is driven primarily by demand-side factors but can also be influenced by the supply of formal services. The government's aged-care policies can have a direct impact on the supply of formal care and, to a lesser degree, on the demand for such care. Together, all these factors determine the range, depth, and quality of aged care provision.

The content of this volume is as follows. The overview summarizes key trends and findings from chapters 1–10 and some additional sources. It consists of two parts: Part I describes the current landscape (including the role played by the private sector) and highlights the challenges for aged care, and Part II proposes policy options for further developing the aged care system in China.

Chapter 1 describes the factors and forces that drive the demand for aged care, such as demographic shifts, trends in the health status of the elderly, changing social values, and diminishing intergenerational support amid rapid socioeconomic transition, urbanization, and increased population mobility. While both public and private financial resources available to the elderly (their own or spouse's savings and earnings, and adult children's contributions) underlie the demand for aged care, this demand will also be influenced heavily by government policies on ongoing pension and health insurance reforms. Availability of informal care from family members is a major factor in the demand for formal care, and it will largely depend on living arrangements and labor supply decisions of family members.

Chapter 2 outlines the policy framework for aged care in China. It covers the institutional and regulatory framework currently in place.

Chapter 3 provides an update on the current supply of aged care services in China, recent policy initiatives to increase supply, and emerging models of service provision in selected provinces and municipalities across the country. It highlights the importance of planning and developing an optimal mix of services that meet consumer needs and preferences and that are delivered in the least restrictive settings where independence, autonomy, dignity, and quality of life are valued and maximized. The chapter is informed by a review and analysis of international experiences in the provision of long-term care services. These international experiences provide historical precedents and lessons that Chinese policy makers can use to guide the development of a viable aged care system for China.

Chapter 4 describes the role that the private sector currently plays in the provision of aged care services in China across home, community, and institutional (residential) care settings and its potential for growth. It discusses policy actions and measures needed to increase private sector participation in the care delivery system. The discussion is aided by findings from selected case studies that highlight examples of successful or promising business models, both domestic and from abroad.

Chapter 5 presents a review of existing long-term care financing systems in developed economies, with a focus on key issues and design options facing policy makers in those economies, and discusses their implications for China. This is followed by a description of the current aged care financing situation in China, which is characterized by the dominance of private payments and limited public support for both service users (welfare recipients and other eligible vulnerable elders) and providers (in the form of subsidies for construction and operating costs). The chapter highlights the importance of establishing a systematic and sustainable financing mechanism that makes aged care services widely affordable for those in need.

Chapter 6 discusses "commissioner-provider" relations in the provision and delivery of aged care services, drawing on experiences from Europe where most economies have moved away from public provision of long-term care services to engaging private sector providers for market-based solutions, guided by the so-called New Public Management framework. It discusses the implications of these international experiences for China, where policy makers have come to realize that the government needs to shift its role from being a direct supplier and provider of aged care services to being a purchaser and regulator of services which are to be provided increasingly by the private sector.

Chapter 7 addresses regulatory oversight and quality assurance for aged care services. The chapter begins with a review of international experiences in long-term care quality assurance, which provide useful lessons for Chinese policy makers in developing an effective regulatory framework and quality assurance system. This is followed by a description of recent initiatives for aged care quality assurance in China, both nationally and in selected provinces and municipalities. It concludes by highlighting key policy challenges in this area and suggesting future directions and potential strategies to meet those challenges.

Chapter 8 focuses on the coordination and integration of services, both within the long-term care sector and between medical/health care and long-term care services, drawing primarily on a review of international experiences. Even in economies with well-developed long-term care systems, the fragmentation of services and lack of coordination across service providers remain common problems. The chapter also discusses the main challenges and constraints China faces in building an integrated care system for the elderly at this early stage of development, particularly in the long-term care sector.

Chapter 9 discusses the aged care workforce and approaches to addressing the shortage of skilled care workers. It begins with a brief overview of aged care workforce issues in the Organisation for Economic Co-operation and Development (OECD) and Asian economies that face challenges similar to those found in China. It then discusses China's challenges in developing its long-term care workforce, including frontline caregivers (in both institutional and home- and community-based settings) as well as health care professionals and social workers. The chapter concludes by proposing some priority areas for strengthening China's long-term care workforce and ensuring that they provide quality services that can meet the country's growing demand for elder care.

Chapter 10 explores how China may benefit from policy learning from other countries and from its own experiences for better formulation of its aged care policies. Based on the European experience, a toolbox for policy learning and exchange is provided that can improve policy making on the national and local levels, which entails an information infrastructure and government structures amenable to policy learning and exchange. It concludes with a set of recommendations specific to the Chinese context.

Of note, a glossary of essential terms used in this report is provided in the front matter. The terms "long-term care (LTC)" and "aged care" are used in this report interchangeably—aged care is defined as LTC for the elderly. Overall, LTC refers to the range of services designed to support people who are unable to perform physical and cognitive functions, measured through ability to perform activities of daily living (ADLs) and instrumental activities of daily living (IADLs) (Norton 2000). Individuals may need LTC due to frailness, limited functional ability, physical injury, a chronic condition, or a mental health problem which limits their ability to carry out basic self-care or personal tasks that must be performed each day. LTC is quite distinct from health care; while health care services seek to change the health condition (from unwell to well), LTC services seek to make the current condition (unwell) more manageable, slow down the decline in functioning, and help individuals maintain the highest practicable physical, mental, and psychosocial well-being.

Current Landscape and Challenges of Aged Care in China

Demand for Elderly Care

The demand for long-term care in China is shaped by demographic trends and affected by a range of socioeconomic factors. To gain a better understanding of current and future long-term care needs in China, this section highlights some of the main factors affecting the demand for long-term care. Consistent with international evidence, it shows that in addition to demographic trends, the main factors include the health conditions of the elderly and the availability of informal care (Chawla, Betcherman, and Banerji 2007). Informal care, in turn, is related to the labor participation of informal care providers as well as the residency patterns and migration of potential care providers (adult children).

Demographic Trends and Elderly Patterns of Limited Functional Ability

China's demographic transition is among the most rapid ever witnessed. China became an "aging" society in 2002 and will become an "aged" society (from having 7 percent of the population over 65 years of age to 14 percent) in just 25 years, by 2027. In comparison, this transition took 115 years for France, 45 years for England, and 69 years for the United States. Both rising life expectancy and the sharp fall in total fertility rate to approximately 1.5 have driven an increase in the old age dependency ratio (ratio of population aged 65+ per 100 population 20–64), and UN Population Projections suggest that it will continue to rise at an unprecedented rate in the coming decades. By 2030, 25.3 percent of China's population is projected to be over age 60, which is almost the projected level for the OECD (27.5 percent). Furthermore, the share of China's population over age 80 (the "oldest old") will increase rapidly, from 1.6 percent in 2015 to a projected 11 percent by 2060 (chapter 1; World Bank 2016b).

Trends in population aging vary significantly across different areas of China. Rural areas are aging more rapidly than urban areas: the proportion of population age 60 and over was 7.8 percent in rural areas, and 7.1 percent in urban areas in 1982, and it rose to 13.7 percent and 12.1 percent, respectively, by 2005. The disparity between rural and urban areas; can be attributed mainly to rural-to-urban migration, as migrants tend to be younger than those remaining in rural areas (World Bank 2010). In 2005, Chongqing, Sichuan, and Shanghai (metropolitan areas) had the highest proportions of elderly population. The proportions of elderly population increased most rapidly in Chongqing, Sichuan, Hubei, and Anhui Provinces (metropolitan areas), in large part due to the migration of young and middle-aged populations from central and western areas to the east coast areas (NBS 2006). Currently, the number and proportion of the elderly population are higher in the east coast areas compared to the central and western areas.

The need for long-term care is greatly influenced by the prevalence of functional and cognitive limitations, and in China as elsewhere in the world, this prevalence is strongly associated with age.[4] Results from the China Health and Retirement Longitudinal Study (CHARLS), which is representative of the population over 45 years of age and their co-resident partners, show that 9 percent of women ages 65–69 have an ADL limited functional ability, and this proportion rises to 30 percent among those over age 80. Similar patterns hold for men, but for each age group over 65, the share of men with an ADL limited functional ability is lower than the share for women (chapter 1).[5]

Forty-year projections of future limited functional ability rates for the population over age 45 show that the share of elderly having ADL and IADL disabilities will continue to increase, driven by population aging. Under the assumption that five-year cohorts will have similar disability rates through 2050, figure O.1 shows future limited functional ability functional ability rates of the population over age 45, projected on the basis of current ADL and IADL limited functional ability rates. Both the increase and share of individuals with disabilities will be higher for women: by 2050, it is projected that 15 percent of women over age 45 will have at least slight ADL disabilities, compared to 8 percent for men.

Data show that older men and women with high school education or more have significantly lower rates of limited functional ability than elderly with low

Figure O.1 Projected ADL and IADL Disabilities of the Population over Age 45, by Gender and Urban and Rural Location in China

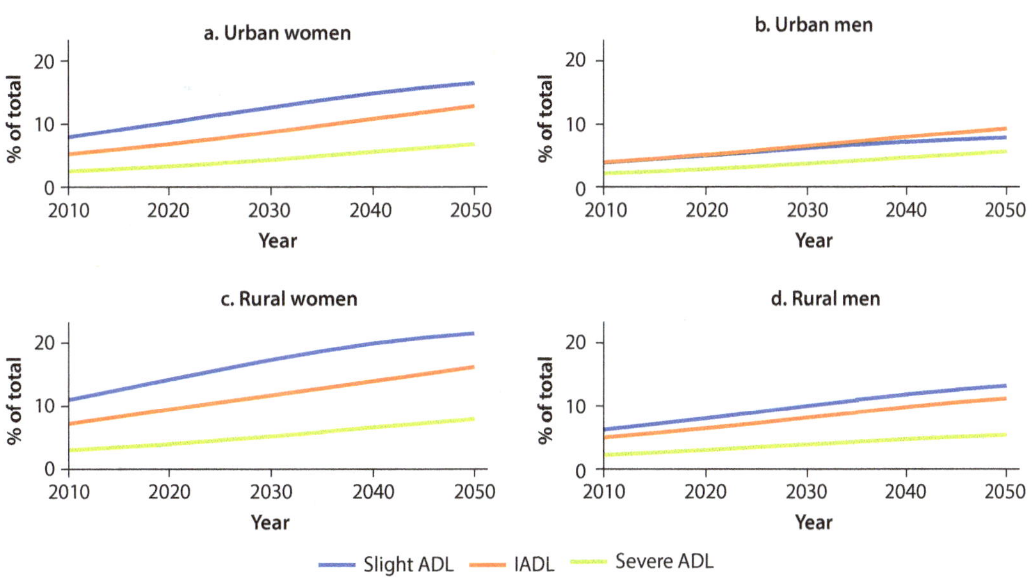

Sources: Giles et al. 2016a using data from CHARLS 2011; United Nations Population Division, World Population Prospects.

levels of education. The age cohorts in their 30s and 40s today have completed more school, had better nutrition as children, and are less likely to be working in physically taxing activities, all of which raise the prospect that rates of limited functional ability may decline in the future. With economic development and the transition to the service economy, individuals will have had better nutrition over their lifetimes, and a greater share of the population will be working in less physically demanding jobs.[6]

At the same time, an epidemiological transition in terms of a shift in morbidity and mortality from communicable to noncommunicable diseases (NCDs) may have the opposite effects on limited functional ability. The population cohorts entering their 70s and 80s in the next two decades may have been more exposed to NCD-related risks in middle age than previous cohorts, making them more vulnerable to disabilities in old age. As a consequence of increased longevity, a higher share of the elderly may suffer from NCDs toward the end of life. Increased incidence of diabetes and high blood pressure, in particular, may predict increases in long-term care needs.

Projected ADL and IADL limited functional ability rates for rural and urban China show that higher levels of limited functional ability in rural China follow from higher rates of population aging (figure O.1). By 2050, limited functional ability rates are likely to be highest for rural women, with more than 20 percent projected to have a limited functional ability. In contrast, the projections suggest that nearly 15 percent of urban women will have a limited functional ability, compared to only 8 percent of urban men. This is similar to the recent projections of the Elderly Dependency Ratios (EDRs) from Cai et al. (2012), which highlight the possibility that EDRs will be much higher in rural areas than in urban areas. If current migration and urbanization patterns persist, poorer elderly living in rural areas may face greater long-term care needs.

These projections underscore the likely direction of change and the importance of thinking about future long-term care arrangements, although actual realizations of limited functional ability will likely differ. Both population and limited functional ability predictions face considerable uncertainty in terms of realized fertility and mortality rates, and incidence of ADLs and IADLs could increase or decrease with China's continued development and epidemiological transition.[7]

China has also witnessed significant increases in mental health problems. The general consensus is that mental health problems are rising in China, but the driving forces behind this rise are not well understood since mental health remains a closeted topic. The WHO's Global Burden of Disease Study predicts a constant increase in the prominence of mental illness, to account for 17.4 percent of all illnesses in China by 2020.[8] This trend has been attributed to several factors, including the dismantling of familial and traditional safety networks, rising numbers of individuals involved in risky economic activities, and increasing work-related pressure and stress (Phillips, Liu, and Zhang 1999).

The prevalence of dementia and Alzheimer's disease and the associated cognitive impairment and problems with carrying out ADLs and IADLs are also high in China (Li et al. 2014; National Population Aging Response Strategy Research

Team 2014). The Chinese Longitudinal Healthy Longevity Survey, conducted by Peking University, indicates that the proportion of elders with dementia is on the rise in China (Yin and Du 2012). China had more than 6 million elderly patients with dementia as of 2010, and some estimates suggest that this number could rise to 22.5 million by 2040 (Cao 2014).

Patterns of Informal Care Provision

Around the world, the majority of elder care is provided by informal caregivers at home (Colombo et al. 2011). Similarly in China, spouses and/or adult children are the most significant source of care for infirm elderly remaining at home. Estimates based on CHARLS data show that among those receiving assistance with daily living, over three-quarters reported that their spouse, adult child, or a combination of the two were the primary source of care. Less than 1 percent of respondents reported that care was provided by a hired elder care nanny. One out of eight elderly in urban areas and one out of seven in rural areas reported that they needed care but had no care provider (Giles et al. 2016a).

In terms of the gender of informal care providers, women are more likely to provide care in urban areas. The gender difference in the likelihood of elder care provision is most pronounced at ages 45–49, when women are more likely than men to report providing care (34 percent versus 28 percent), see table O.1. This difference is significant and is most likely explained by the fact that blue-collar women may take early retirement and exit from work at age 45. In rural areas, men and women are equally likely to provide care. As the majority of co-resident husbands and wives in rural areas work on their own farms or in self-employed activities, provision of care for an elderly parent may be readily shared.[9]

In terms of the gender of informal care recipients, men primarily receive care from spouses, while women—who tend to outlive their spouses—are far more likely to receive care from adult children or other providers. In 2011, seven out of ten of infirm men received care from a spouse, while husbands were care providers for five out of ten of infirm women. Adult children are a considerably more important source of assistance for women than for men: 26 percent of women and 14 percent of men received care exclusively from adult children

Table O.1 Incidence and Time Spent Caring for Elderly Parents and Parents-in-Law

	Proportion of older adults providing care				*Hours per week spent providing care*			
	Urban		*Rural*		*Urban*		*Rural*	
Age	*Men*	*Women*	*Men*	*Women*	*Men*	*Women*	*Men*	*Women*
Overall	0.14	0.17	0.12	0.12	16.6	17.9	19.4	17.8
45–49	0.28	0.34	0.25	0.26	15.1	17.0	20.4	20.4
50–54	0.27	0.29	0.22	0.21	13.3	17.5	16.0	14.5
55–59	0.18	0.20	0.14	0.14	15.1	16.5	12.6	16.6
60–64	0.10	0.07	0.08	0.06	26.5	20.9	32.2	20.0
65+	0.03	0.02	0.03	0.02	23.8	32.9	24.7	14.9

Source: Giles et al. 2015 using data from CHARLS 2011.
Note: Sample is weighted by individual weights with household nonresponse adjustment.

in 2013. While spouses may already be out of their peak earning years, the use of adult children for provision of care may lead to substitution away from employment or other activities.

Informal care provision is not meeting all care needs of the infirm elderly. The greatest unmet need is for assistance going to the bathroom. For both genders and in both urban and rural areas, unmet needs in using the toilet are consistent with patterns of declining co-residence at older ages: only 50 percent of urban women and 56 percent of urban men who required help reported having assistance; and in rural areas, the comparable shares were 58 and 52 percent. The higher frequency of unmet needs using the toilet suggests that those elderly lacking a spouse and relying on non-resident children and others for assistance may not have all needs sufficiently met. Roughly 80 percent of the elderly with each of the other ADL disabilities reported having assistance (with the exception of urban women who require help bathing, at only 60 percent).

Gender differences in unmet needs are also notable, with nearly 90 percent of urban men needing help with household chores receiving assistance, compared to only 80 percent of urban women. Similar to earlier patterns, this highlights the difference in access to support for women who outlive their husbands and the potential benefits of community-based facilities that can provide assistance to the elderly for some of these basic activities.

Co-Residence Patterns, Migration, and Labor Supply

The elderly in China have long co-resided with the family of at least one of their adult children, a living arrangement that has often facilitated mutual support. At younger ages, the healthy elderly often provide care to grandchildren and assistance with other household chores. The shift toward support of the elderly by younger generations often proceeds gradually and often not before age 80 and beyond. Elderly with relatively minor disabilities and no urgent needs for medical care tend to receive help from co-resident or nearby adult children, and only move on to more formal arrangements or even residence in assisted living facilities as their care needs escalate over time.

Changes in family structure and economic development are eroding the availability of care from co-resident family members. In particular, two important changes are taking place. First, the likelihood of aging parents at younger ages (between ages 45 and 60) living with adult children has increased, which reflects an implicit transfer of support from parents to adult children who face higher housing costs than younger adults of the past. Second, for those aging parents over age 65, the share of elderly living with adult children fell from close to two-thirds in the early 1980s to roughly two-fifths by 2011. This decline was likely driven by increased migration over the last 30 years as well as by preferences for privacy among urban children and parents who can afford to live separately.[10] These patterns indicate that informal family-based support for elderly with disabilities is also coming under pressure with changes in living arrangements.

Both increasing migration and decreasing family size will reduce the likelihood that adult children live with or in close proximity to elderly parents.

In the absence of co-residence or residence within close proximity, adult children are less likely to be well-informed about the well-being and care needs of their elderly parents. Evidence from other surveys suggests that many current seniors worry that there will be no one taking care of them. The 2010 Sampling Survey of the Aged Population in Rural/Urban China indicates that 39.8 percent of elderly people worried about having no one to take care of them when needed, of which 23.6 percent were "Somewhat Worried" and 16.2 percent were "Very Worried."

For those planning to migrate, the need to provide long-term care to elderly parents carries a high and potentially increasing opportunity cost. Prior research has found evidence that serious illness of an aged parent influences the decision to work as a migrant. For example, Giles and Mu (2007) used parent mortality in the subsequent two years as a measure of current serious illness, as death in the near future is a proxy for current infirmity, and found a significant negative association between near-term mortality and migration. Many elderly may be disabled for considerably longer periods of time before passing away, so return migration in response to care needs might only occur after an elderly parent has been frail for a considerable period of time. As it becomes more likely that the elderly will live into their 80s, periods of limited functional ability longer than one or two years are likely to become more prevalent.

Opportunity costs are also incurred for those who have to combine market work and care responsibilities. Estimates of the relationship between the labor supply of adults 45–65 years old and care supply show substantial negative effects of caregiving on the labor supply of rural men and women, and declines in hours worked of women in both urban and rural areas (Giles, Chen, and Zhao 2016b and chapter 1). These findings are consistent with earlier research that found that care provision has negative consequences for female labor supply (Ettner 1995; Jacobs et al. 2014; Liu, Dong, and Zheng 2010; Meng 2011; Van Houtven, Coe, and Skira 2013), and suggest a negative relationship between care provision and labor force participation of rural women aged 45–65. Maurer-Fazio (2011), on the other hand, found evidence consistent with an "added worker effect": the presence of an elderly parent or in-law over age 75 in the household is associated with an increased likelihood that prime-age women are in the labor force.

The absence of an observable effect of caregiving on urban women's labor force participation may be explained by their early retirement. In fact, mandatory retirement for workers in civil service and formal sector jobs occurs at an early age in urban China, and this age differs by gender and occupation. Blue collar women retire at 50, white collar women at 55, and men at age 60. While 50 and 55 are quite young, it is possible to retire even earlier. Since the economic restructuring in the late 1990s, workers have been able to apply for early-retirement five years before their mandatory retirement age.[11] Results from the CHARLS survey show that by age 51, nearly 38 percent of urban women are receiving a pension, and only 40 percent are still in the labor force. Retirement before mandatory ages can be seen among both men and women. Nearly 20 percent of urban men are receiving a pension by age 57, when male labor force participation has dropped to 65 percent from 80 percent at age 45 (more in chapter 1). Expectations of work as caregivers may be a significant obstacle to raising the retirement age for women. If, however, the retirement age is increased, the relationship between the labor supply of women 45–65 years old and their care supply is likely to change.

Going forward, families with frail elderly will be weighing the costs of providing informal care, taking into account both the direct monetary cost of hiring care at home or placing an elderly relative into a facility and the opportunity costs of migration and work. Having the choice and ability to purchase care in the market is desirable and conducive to the well-being of both care recipients and family caregivers. The government needs to guide and foster the development of a system of formal care provision that offers meaningful and affordable services to families. In OECD economies, formal private and public arrangements for provision of long-term care emerged with the shift in living arrangements. China's system needs to keep pace with ongoing changes in demographic and co-residence patterns.

Policy Framework and Institutional Setup for Developing Formal Elderly Care

The Chinese government recognizes the need to develop an efficient and sustainable approach to aged care. Developing the elderly care sector is an integral element of complex public policies which influence the daily lives of millions of Chinese citizens. Aged care policies interact with other social policies—including social assistance, welfare, child care, health, education (including curriculum development for colleges and universities, specialized courses, and professional trainings), housing, and labor market policies. All these influence market opportunities of caregivers and also affect the development of related industries through production of goods and services consumed primarily by the older population. This section highlights key elements of China's aged care policy framework that have been developed through a series of government directives, laws, and regulations concerning the provision of elderly care services.

Policy Framework in China

Compared with developments in the areas of health insurance and pensions, the aged care system in China is at a nascent stage. China has achieved expansion of its health insurance system at a speed that has few precedents globally: from coverage of only about 55 percent of the urban population and 21 percent of the rural population in 2003, urban and rural health insurance coverage soared to 89 percent and 97.5 percent, respectively, by 2011. Significant increases in government subsidies for health insurance have helped reduce out-of-pocket (OOP) spending, which is a major cause of impoverishment, and insurance benefits have also been expanded gradually. The New Rural Cooperative Medical Scheme (NRCMS), which covers the rural population, has become more comprehensive, incrementally adding outpatient benefits while including coverage for specific chronic diseases (e.g., certain types of cancer, diabetes).

The expansion of pension coverage has also proceeded at an unprecedented rate. China established the National Rural Pension Scheme (NRPS) in September 2009 and introduced the Urban Resident Pension Scheme (URPS) in July 2011. Both schemes were rolled out rapidly, and by the end of October 2012, the URPS had 229 million contributors with a coverage rate of 65.4 percent, and the NRPS had 325 million contributors with a coverage rate of 76.7 percent.

Further reforms are planned in both health insurance and pensions. For health insurance, future reforms are expected to expand coverage of chronic diseases that are more prevalent among the elderly. Both for health insurance and pensions, future reforms will aim to unify coverage for rural and urban residents, following the government's decision to merge urban and rural resident schemes. As coverage expansion has been prioritized to date, albeit with shallow financial protection, going forward, pension and health systems are facing the challenges of balancing coverage, adequacy, and sustainability. Nonetheless, with the development of universal medical insurance and a pension system approaching universal coverage, China has made a tremendous step forward.

Meanwhile, the Chinese government acknowledges the need to develop a sustainable and innovative aged care system. To meet the pressing challenge of aged care, the government has adopted a range of strategies and policies specifically for aged care (chapter 2). Key national policy milestones in the form of policy documents and directives issued over the past 20 years are summarized in figure O.2 and discussed below. Provincial-level action plans to aid the implementation of these policies are also discussed.

While the earlier laws and directives focused on the rights of the elderly and industry promotion, several milestone documents issued by the State Council in the last decade are: the *12th Five-Year Plan for the Development of Aged Care Services in China* (2011), the *Development Plan for a System of Social Services for the Aged (2011–2015)* (2011), the *Opinions on Accelerating the Development of Services for the Aged* (2013) and most recently in 2017, the 13th Five-Year Plan for the Development of Elder Care Services and Building of Elderly Care System. In addition, there are more general laws or policy documents such as "*Some Opinions on Promoting the Development of a Health Care Industry.*" In 2014, the Ministry of Commerce and Ministry of Civil Affairs (MOCA) issued Announcement No. 81 on *Encouraging Foreign Investors to Establish For-Profit Elderly Care Institutions in China.*

Looking more closely at the four recent milestone documents, the *12th Five-Year Plan for the Development of Aged Care Services* envisages a system with three tiers, and with home-based care as its bedrock, supported by community-based care and underpinned by institutional care. In particular, it sets targets for a 90-7-3 structure—that is, 90 percent of the elderly should receive home-based care, 7 percent community-based care, and 3 percent institutional care. This means that the family has primary responsibility for elderly care, community-based services provide support with the advantage of geographical proximity to the elderly, and institutional care fills the gap to meet the needs of elders for intensive care.

The 13th Five-Year Plan for the Development of Elder Care Services and Building of Elderly Care System makes clear that private provision and private

Figure O.2 Key Policy Papers on Aged Care in China

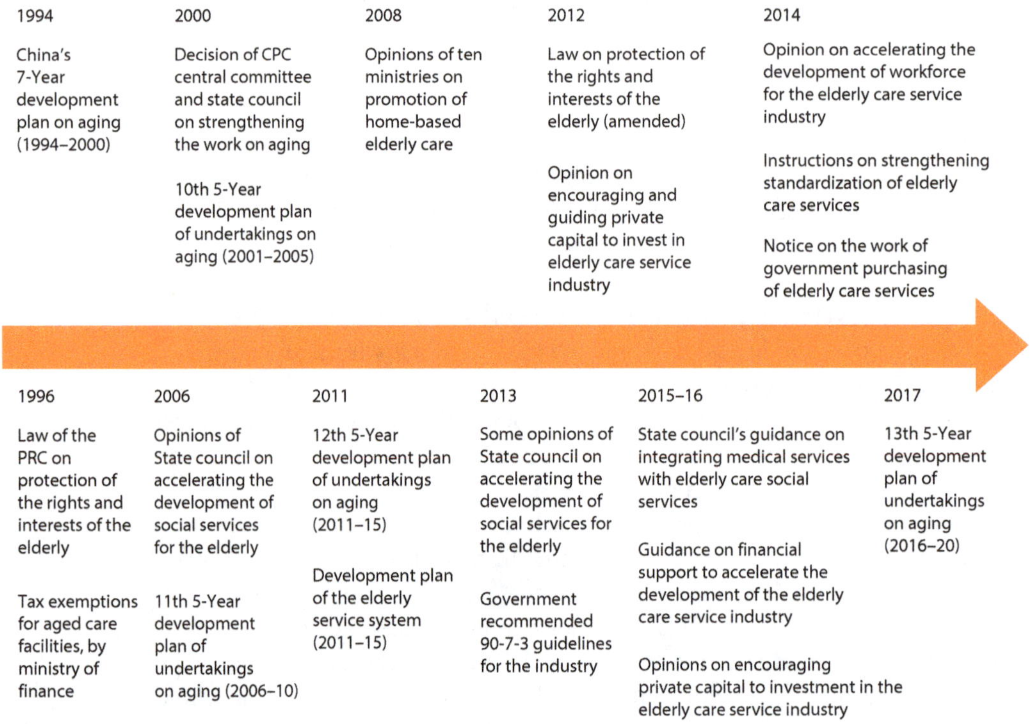

Source: Compilation based on various government documents. See chapter 2 for further details.
Note: CPC = Communist Party of China; PRC = People's Republic of China.

(self) payment will play the main role in the elderly care system going forward, while the government will continue to allocate funding to cover services for selected low-income and vulnerable groups. It also strongly signaled that the government will devote an increasing amount of public resources—over 50 percent of the 'Welfare Lottery Fund'—to support elderly care services and will continue to develop policies to stimulate the market for private provision. It also signaled its readiness for stewardship of the elderly care market and its commitment to start piloting the long-term care insurance (both social and private insurance); it encouraged integration between medical and social services; and it called for strengthening workforce training where aged care services are delivered, in facilities of higher learning, and in business schools. The specific monitorable targets set for the 13th Five-Year Plan period include the development of private provision, increasing nursing care, expanding geriatric services in hospitals, securing allocations from the 'Welfare Lottery Fund', and expanding social grassroots participation of the elderly.

The *Development Plan for a System of Social Services for the Aged (2011–2015)* builds on this premise and calls for the development of a new mechanism for elder care, learning from international experiences, and exploring and piloting innovative approaches to financing, service provision, and quality assurance, among other measures. Developing an aged care workforce with adequate technical and managerial skills is also key to growing the aged care sector.

According to the State Council's *Opinions on Accelerating the Development of Services for the Aged* (2013), local governments should encourage the establishment of aged care institutions in both rural and urban areas by simplifying administrative and bureaucratic procedures such as registration, licensing, standardization, and information disclosure. The policy directive guides local governments to encourage investors, both domestic and foreign, to set up home-based care services and large-scale service providers. Publicly financed institutions will focus on providing free or low-cost services for "vulnerable elders." The management of all public social welfare homes will be shifted gradually to private hands, while the government will retain the ownership rights for assets and supervise the quality of services. Integrating medical services into aged care institutions will be achieved by encouraging medical establishments to create separate wards for elderly patients, conducting home visits and wellness checkups by health personnel, signing medical contracts with elder care institutions, providing health consultations, and encouraging telehealth care.

Accelerating the Development of Services for the Aged sets targets of having at least one professional aged care facility in every prefectural-level city and 30 beds per 1,000 elderly persons by 2015.[12] The document calls for measures to promote private long-term care insurance as well as accident insurance, especially those designed for the elderly. The document also includes a number of supplementary measures such as those concerning barrier-free houses, physical fitness, and community participation (e.g., encouraging volunteer work and safeguarding the rights and interests of older people, as promoted in the *Silver Action* or *Golden Sunshine Action* programs).

Consistent with these milestone documents, several provincial authorities have issued Action Plans to boost the development of aged care services. As an example, box O.1 below provides detailed information on the Action Plan

Box O.1 Action Plan of the Anhui Provincial Government to Boost Aged Care Services

Mix of services and eligibility targeting. Community-based services should be key for aged care provision, and further development of community-based services should be prioritized. Each newly built residential area should allocate appropriate space in the neighborhood for aged care services. Service providers (including venture capitalists and small businesses) should be encouraged to engage in home-based care and to provide aged care in their neighborhoods. Public residential care facilities should be strengthened but serve as providers of last resort for elderly with physical or mental impairments. Public resources should be allocated to social welfare institutions and nursing facilities that serve the poor and severely disabled elderly.

box continues next page

Box O.1 Action Plan of the Anhui Provincial Government to Boost Aged Care Services *(continued)*

Cooperation at the local level. The aged care system should be aligned with local needs, harnessing the potential of senior citizens' associations to serve neighborhoods and local communities. In rural areas with appropriate population density, residential care facilities should be part of rural community service centers or other public facilities. Rural communities should encourage the development of "mutual help" in aged care facilities. Just as in urban areas, residential care facilities should be providers of last resort for those in need of intensive care.

Financing and procurement of services. More than half of local Welfare Lottery Fund revenues should be used to finance aged care. Governments at different levels (prefecture and county) should jointly finance public aged care facilities. Local authorities should develop innovative funding methods and increase the cost-efficiency of services. Authorities need to strengthen efforts to set up procedures for public procurement of aged care services from the private sector. They should use contracting and contract management as the main policy tools for interacting with private providers, including direct purchasing of services and outsourcing of the management and operation of publicly owned aged care facilities to the private and non-government sectors—a so-called "mixed model." To this end, the relevant authorities should develop service catalogues and contract standards as part of coherent and well-documented procurement strategies. Local governments have the leeway to either select or assign a service provider or to organize a public tendering process. Public procurement of services may involve either direct purchasing of services or contracting out the management and operation of publicly owned aged care facilities to the private and non-government sectors. Particular attention is given to a service model in which government funds are used to construct aged care facilities, while the private sector is invited to operate the facilities for service provision. In this model, a publicly owned aged care facility could use its property or equipment as equity to develop and operate aged care services together with private investors. (This will lead to the emergence of aged care facilities with mixed ownership.) Every county/district has to establish an asset management plan for all public aged care facilities. To promote this model, management strategies for privately operated public facilities must be developed, including a clear delineation of the government's role in the process.

Government subsidies for aged care should be made available to both public and private, domestic and foreign providers of residential care or home-based services. The subsidy amount should be linked to the level of limited functional ability or impairment of the person served. Private sector service providers may receive a one-time subsidy to cover construction costs and regular subsidies for operational costs, including a subsidy for loan interest and a service subsidy. Prefectural and county governments are required to provide an operation subsidy of RMB 200 per resident per month for aged care facilities. The subsidy amount varies by the type of service provided. For the care of the disabled or residents with dementia, the operation and service subsidy increases by 50 percent, 100 percent, and over 200 percent for those with mild, moderate, or severe limited functional ability, respectively. The government sets prices for paying customers in government-owned facilities, while private service providers can charge market prices.

box continues next page

Box O.1 Action Plan of the Anhui Provincial Government to Boost Aged Care Services *(continued)*

Building a market of service providers. To facilitate market entry, private sector providers are allowed to operate multiple residential care sites with one single business license. If they have a business license, they are also allowed to operate without an operation permit while in the process of seeking an operation permit. The minimum registered capital requirement should be eliminated, and the procedures for obtaining an operation permit should be streamlined. Operators who rent public properties to operate non-profit aged care facilities are eligible for a three-year rental payment exemption. Service providers registered as "non-profit" are allowed to use a proportion of their earnings to reward investors, and after five years of operation, these facilities can be transferred to others.

Regulations, standards, monitoring and evaluation. Filing requirements for community-based organizations should be relaxed. Overall, all policies noted for aged care facilities are also applicable to community-based residential facilities that are funded by private capital. Local governments should be empowered to develop quality assurance for aged care provision as well as rules to regulate market entry and exit. Local governments should develop an evaluation system for aged care that is evidence-based and includes an assessment of needs and eligibility criteria for receiving public subsidies. In fact, it is required that all beneficiaries of public subsidies and the services they receive be subject to a needs assessment and a service quality evaluation. Among other functions, a monitoring and evaluation system will support information sharing among different service providers (aged care facilities, community-based services, housekeeping services, health care, and nursing services). Such a system would underpin and facilitate regular professional evaluation of aged care services.

Ensuring integrated services. The integration of medical and social services features prominently in the Action Plan. It suggests that health care facilities should consider needs for elder care in their capital planning. It encourages combining home care and residential facilities with nursing and rehabilitation care. Smaller aged care facilities (those with fewer than 100 beds) could apply for a permit to operate a clinic. Likewise, health facilities that registered aged care facilities as legal entities and still operate them can enjoy the same preferential policies granted to any private service providers engaged in aged care service provision. At the same time, aged care facilities can apply to be a designated health services provider under health insurance (schemes for urban workers, urban residents, or rural residents) for providing health care that meets the standards and criteria for reimbursement. For primary health services, the Action Plan also requires that health facilities provide health management services, establish health records for the elderly in their catchment area, and create primary care packages of preferential services for the elderly.

Source: Authors' compilation from Anhui's DOCA plans for accelerating the development of the aged care industry.

proposed by Anhui Province. The plan lays out the short-term objective (by the end of 2020) of putting in place "a fully functional aged care system with reasonable layout and appropriate dimension that covers both rural and urban areas, well aligned with local needs" and also sets the quantitative targets as "the availability of 45 residential aged care facility beds per 1,000 people age 65 or older;

universal coverage of community-based residential care facilities in cities, and near-universal coverage of community-based service facilities in towns (90 percent) and rural areas (80 percent)." The Action Plan calls on local authorities to exercise stewardship over the public and private segments of service provision, and it covers key aspects such as increasing service supply and extending access; financing and procurement of services; growing a market of service providers and encouraging private sector engagement in service provision; strengthening regulations, standards, monitoring, and evaluation; and promoting service integration and coordination.

Administrative Responsibilities and Institutional Setup

The responsibility for planning, coordinating, and guiding aged care services nationwide lies with the *China National Committee on Ageing*, established by the State Council. The Committee formulates strategies and policies for aged care, coordinates the relevant departments and guides them to implement development plans, and supervises implementation at local levels. The current director of the *China National Committee on Ageing* is a vice-premier of the State Council. The Committee is comprised of 32 ministries, with each ministry represented by one vice-minister. Each territorial authority (provinces, provincial-level autonomous regions, and municipalities directly under the central government; prefectural-level cities or leagues; counties and county-level cities or districts; and towns, townships, or urban communities) maintains an office for the Committee on Aging for daily administration and implementation of policies. Specialized staff are allocated to the committees. This structure ensures a strong network for turning policies into practice, from the central to the local level.

The administrative responsibility at the national level lies with MOCA. Under the jurisdiction of the State Council, MOCA is responsible for domestic social affairs, which include social welfare and services for the aged, disabled, veterans, and other specific target groups. Within MOCA, the national regulatory authority over aged care services rests with the Division of Social Welfare for the Elderly and Disabled, under the Department of Social Welfare. The Ministry defines the national policy and is responsible for regulations and standards, and it is also involved in the development of national training curricula and accreditation of training programs for aged care workers.

The local Departments of Civil Affairs (DOCA) are in charge of turning policies into practice at the provincial and local levels, in line with the laws and regulations. They set the rules for market entry and exit of aged care providers, ensure quality control and adherence to management standards, and may impose sanctions on providers for breaching rules or disregarding standards. Not-for-profit service providers are required to register with their local DOCA, while for-profits must register with the Industrial and Commercial Administration Department (ICAD). To obtain an operating license for social care delivery, a provider applies to DOCA; to deliver skilled nursing or medical services, the provider applies to the Department of Health (DOH). Providers need to go through qualification reviews to obtain the relevant licenses. DOCAs also coordinate the work of different partners involved in services for the aged, disabled, veterans, and other specific groups in need of support. They supervise, monitor, and evaluate the development of the aged care sector and promote research on innovative and good practices.

Community organizations are expected to play an active role in delivering aged care in both urban and rural areas. Many community-based services and programs are administrated by the Urban Residents' Committee or the Rural Villagers Committee or are delivered in cooperation with the Committees. Acting at the neighborhood level, these Committees are quasi-governmental organizations that perform various administrative functions as mandated by the local government. Over the past two decades, these Committees have been gradually taking on new responsibilities, pooling community resources, and developing and implementing a wide range of programs such as services for the elderly (Xu and Chow 2011).

The Ministry of Finance (MOF) is responsible for allocating financial resources to the development of publicly supported aged care services and setting prices for such services. Other line ministries (education, food and drugs, industry and commerce, housing, taxation, price setting) share responsibilities according to their mandates. The institutional structure that governs aged care policies and service provision at the national and subnational levels is illustrated in figure O.3.

Figure O.3 Institutional Setup for Aged Care at National and Local Levels

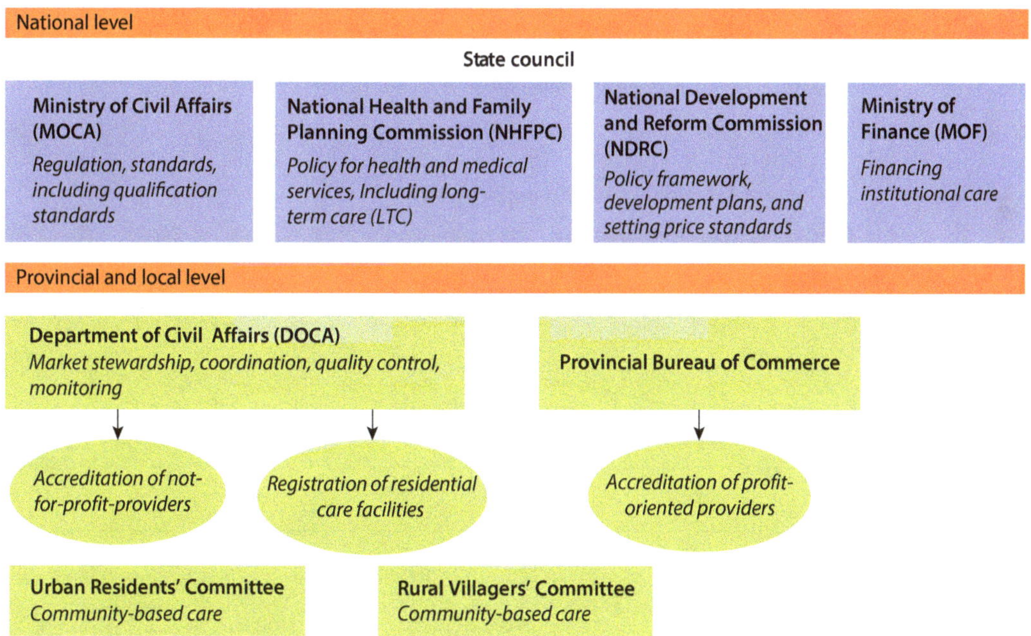

Source: Based on various government documents.

Public Financing

Much of the government funding for aged care comes from the Public Welfare Lottery Fund (PWLF). MOCA reports that between the mid-1980s and 2010, about three-fifths of national elderly welfare-related expenditures were funded from the PWLF, while local government contributed about one-quarter of spending, and other sources accounted for about 15 percent (MOCA 2015). Money for the PWLF is derived from the proceeds of the Welfare Lottery and the Sport Lottery. Total revenues from these two lotteries more than doubled in nominal terms between 2010 and 2014, with the Welfare Lottery receiving RMB 206 billion and the Sports Lottery about RMB 175 billion in 2014 (figure O.4).

The allocation of lottery funds is complex. After deducting lottery prizes (about half of all revenues) and administrative costs (around 15 percent of revenues), the remaining 35 percent is placed in the PWLF. Accordingly, the estimated amount retained in the PWLF in 2014 amounted to approximately RMB 133 billion. The funds in the PWLF are shared equally between the national and provincial authorities. Funds retained at the provincial level are required to be spent on public welfare, and about half of Welfare Lottery fund (not the Sports Lottery fund) is directed toward various elderly welfare projects and activities. In 2014, the provincial authorities appropriated an estimated RMB 18 billion nationwide from the PWLF for elderly welfare. From the proceeds retained at the national level, elderly-welfare-related expenditures are estimated at 1-1.5 percent of the PWLF or RMB 0.9 billion in 2014.

These calculations place the amount of public expenditures on elderly care in China at 0.02–0.04 percent of gross domestic product (GDP). In addition, some forms of care for the frail elderly (health care, rehabilitation, nursing care) are covered by the health insurance system and the health budget, but there are no reliable estimates of these expenditures attributed to long-term care for the elderly (Lorenzini, Morgan, and Murakami 2015).

Figure O.4 Lottery Sales Volume, 2010–15

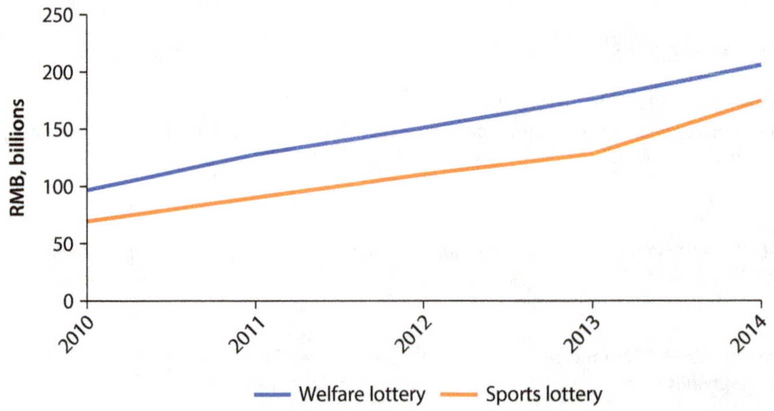

Sources: MOCA, Various years; General Administration of Sport, Various years

Between the mid-1980s and 2010, PWLF funds appropriated for elderly welfare by the provincial authorities were spent at the provincial level (about 40 percent of total, on average), prefecture level (about 40 percent), and district/county level (about 20 percent). In recent years, there has been a trend to increase the proportion of total PWLF spending executed at the prefecture and county level, with a relative decline of the provincial-level share.

Overall, about 90 percent of all PWLF funds are spent on infrastructure, with the share of non-infrastructure being higher at the provincial and prefecture levels and lower at the district/county level. Non-infrastructure expenditures include various subsides to the elderly and other activities. By the end of 2014, 18 provinces had used PWLF resources to launch the subsidy policies for elderly age 80 and above, 22 provinces had launched subsidies for elderly in economic difficulties, and 4 provinces had launched subsidies for nursing care targeting elderly with mental impairments and economic difficulties (MOCA 2015). Although there has been a trend in recent years to increase the share of non-infrastructure spending at all levels, PWLF expenditures are still mostly for financing various types of infrastructure, including new construction, reconstruction, or expansion of existing facilities such as nursing homes, rural old people's homes, honor homes (for veterans), as well as cultural, recreational, and activity centers for the elderly.

Eligibility for Publicly Subsidized Aged Care

Government guarantees for subsidized support and social services (typically in government-run welfare homes) are extended to a small number of welfare recipients. In urban areas, they are referred to as "Three No's" (*san wu*)—people who have lost the ability to work, have no source of income, and have no legal guardians to support them. In rural areas, people who qualify as "Three No's–Five Guarantees" (*wubao*) are elders for whom the local government guarantees food, clothing, housing, medical care, and burial expenses. At the same time, other "vulnerable seniors" are entitled to free or low-cost publicly financed care and services. According to government statistics, China had 76,000 *san wu* in urban areas and 5.29 million *wubao* recipients in rural areas nationwide in 2014 (MOCA 2015). Altogether, these welfare recipients accounted for less than 2.5 percent of the total population age 60 and over in China in 2014.

Within these broad guidelines, the entitlement to fully or partly subsidized elderly care is determined at the local level. In Anhui, for example, the official implementation plan for accelerating the development of the aged care industry stipulates that the government will fund aged care services for vulnerable elders who are incapable of working, have no source of income, and have no one to support them. Furthermore, low-income and childless seniors shall have access to aged care services with lower charges. Chengdu city (capital of Sichuan Province) adopts the principle of "*guarantee the ones mostly in need, give preference to those moderately in need, be transparent and fair, coordinate and balance.*" The needy elderly are divided into three groups: the Three No's who are guaranteed government support; elders who are considered a special group (i.e., those with severe limited functional ability, those who lost their only child; and those who are recognized as having made major contributions to society); and the rest of the elderly. Public sector service providers guarantee support for people in the first group, covering housing needs and all other expenses. People in the second and third groups need to contribute OOP payments for prices determined by the county-level government and typically have to queue for services. Similar guidelines exist in other provinces.

At the same time, practically all government-funded welfare facilities now also take elders who are willing to pay for care. Prices in government-funded facilities tend to be significantly lower than those in private facilities (chapter 5). In fact, in urban public facilities, the majority of residents now pay privately, availing themselves of subsidies provided to government-run facilities implicitly. In contrast, the vast majority of residents in rural facilities are still welfare recipients, although this is starting to change (Feng et al. 2014).

Recently, there has been a nationwide move to expand and focus the beneficiary group to include elders with physical or mental disabilities and the "oldest old," those age 80 and above. Provincial DOCAs instruct public aged care facilities to prioritize resources for disabled beneficiaries and direct subsidized home-based care to them and to the "oldest old." This entails commensurate increases in subsidies for those with higher degrees of limited functional ability.

The Mix of Publicly Subsidized Services

The mix of aged care services that is provided free or at subsidized rates to eligible beneficiaries is determined locally. Within the broad guidelines set at the national and provincial levels (as described above and in chapter 2), local municipal or county governments are responsible for optimizing the service mix to suit local needs. For services provided in residential facilities, the *Basic Standards for Social Welfare Institutions for the Elderly* (2001) set out general rules for meals, personal care, rehabilitation, and psychosocial services. Quality and service mix provided in the residential facilities vary widely, with municipal-run facilities typically having better equipment and a more attractive array of services compared with facilities run by lower-level (e.g., district, county, township) governments.

Current practices in home-based and community care vary as well. Guidelines for the home care service package and community-based services are provided in the *12th Five-Year Plan for the Development of Aged Care Services* and the *Opinions on Accelerating the Development of Social Services for the Aged*. These suggest that the home care service package should include medical care, housekeeping, legal services, spiritual services, emergency aid, rescue services, and so on. For community-based services, the policy documents foresee the inclusion of adult day care centers, home visits, emergency aid, health and wellness clinics, and recreational activities. Typically, home-based services include preparation of meals, basic cleaning, assistance with caring for bedridden seniors, and some respite services. Community stations typically organize social activities, basic diagnostic health checks, rehabilitation through basic exercise and rehabilitation equipment, assistance with personal tasks, companionship, and services referrals. In Hefei city (capital of Anhui Province), for example, individuals age 70 or older are entitled to receive home-based services valued at up to RMB 100 per month.

Current Supply of Aged Care

Aged care generally takes three basic forms: home-based care, community-based care, and institutional care. Home care (also called domiciliary care) can be provided by informal caregivers (family members, friends, or neighbors) or formal, professional caregivers, or a combination of both. Clients of home- or community-based care live in their own domicile. Residential care facilities (also called institutional care) provide a wider range of aged care support and may also include nursing or medical care.

The current aged care landscape and mix of services in China (described in box O.2 below) have resulted in part from government policies but are also shaped by tradition, a surge in consumer demand, and strong commercial

Box O.2 Current Landscape of Aged Care Services in China

Institutional care: Broadly, China has three main types of institutional care facilities today, differentiated by target clientele, source of revenues, and levels of care provided: (1) public social welfare facilities, (2) nursing homes, and (3) residential care facilities and retirement communities.

Public social welfare facilities (welfare homes and public nursing homes) have been around for decades and used to exclusively serve welfare recipients such as childless elders, orphans, and developmentally disabled adults without families. Many such facilities, mostly in urban areas, have recently expanded to also take in non-welfare individuals who pay for their care privately and who constitute the majority of current residents. The services and amenities available in public social welfare facilities depend to a large extent on which level of government owns and runs the facility. Municipal government-run facilities, many of which are known to keep a long waitlist of interested clients, typically are better-equipped and offer a more attractive array of services than facilities run by lower-level (e.g., district, county, township) governments.

Skilled nursing homes are public or private facilities that have professional staff (e.g., nurses, therapists, physicians) available to provide skilled nursing, rehabilitation, or medical services.

Residential care facilities and retirement communities, mostly developed and operated by the private sector, include senior apartments, assisted living facilities, and retirement communities that provide various levels of personal care assistance and professional services.

With regard to ownership, facilities could be broadly characterized as: government-built and government-operated, government-built and privately operated, and privately built and privately operated. The latter two are among the various *modi operandi* the government has been promoting to encourage private sector engagement in the development of institutional aged care services. The government-built and privately operated mode is called a mixed

box continues next page

Box O.2 Current landscape of aged care services in China *(continued)*

model and is viewed as a public-private partnership (PPP) model in which the government contracts with a competent private sector entity that delivers the desired services and manages the daily operations of the facility while receiving public subsidies (e.g., below market-value rental, discounted utility rates).

Community-based and home-based care: Broadly, China has two types of *community centers*. The first type is the physical community center, which provides cooked meals, organization of social activities, basic diagnostic health checks, rehabilitation through basic exercise and rehabilitation equipment, assistance with personal tasks, companionship, and services referrals. These services are provided during the day, and some centers may also set up beds for seniors to stay overnight. Services are provided free of charge to eligible seniors, while other seniors are offered services below market prices. Payment systems differ depending on the local circumstances. The second type of community center is the virtual center, in which services are offered through an information network that links community services to the seniors.

Home-based care typically includes social services such as assistance with daily living (e.g., bathing, feeding, household chores) and medical care services (e.g., nursing, rehabilitation). Non-government providers operate the majority of community centers and provide home-based care.

With regard to commissioner-provider relations for home- and community-based services, the majority of services are commissioned by the local government at various levels. Under the government-contractor model, resources for organizing in-home care services are allocated by various levels of government, including districts, sub-districts, and local communities. The services are provided to the eligible elderly residing in these settings, with various levels of government initiating, funding, and supervising these services. The providers are typically engaged through a government procurement process. Most of them are non-profit organizations, as the reimbursement rates are low. Home- and community-based services in private retirement communities are typically commissioned by the real estate developers.

Sources: Chapters 3 and 4.

interests in the senior care market. Overall, the development of home- and community-based services has been limited, while residential care facilities are booming. This trend may have been induced by the targets set by the government to increase residential care capacity to at least 30 beds per 1,000 elderly people (age 60 and above) by 2015 (target met, per current government statistics). By the end of 2015, China had a total of 6,727,000 residential care beds or 30.3 beds per 1,000 people ages 60 and older (MOCA 2016). The *2014 Report on Development of Aging Service Industry in China* indicates that 87 percent of all residential institutions provided basic accommodations and services, 10 percent offered some nursing services, and the remaining 3 percent provided integrated social and medical services, including hospice services (chapter 3).

Against this backdrop, a new sector of formal elderly care services has started emerging in China to meet the needs of frail and disabled elders who can no longer be cared for adequately by family caregivers. This nascent sector is evolving across the country, catalyzed by government policies and private-sector initiatives. Currently, formal services—both publicly and privately provided—are available to the general population and require private payment. Private facilities charge higher prices than the public facilities, and those public facilities that are better-equipped and offer an attractive array of services keep a waitlist for interested clients. Free services are available to *san wu* and *wubao* senior citizens and are typically provided in public residential facilities that receive funding from the government budget (from various levels of government).

A Booming Residential Care Sector

Historically, residential (or institutional) elder care in China was rare and limited to a small number of publicly supported welfare recipients, such as those qualifying as Three No's. As such, this institutional care for the poor elderly (most of them childless) was more of a welfare and anti-poverty measure than a long-term care option.

In the mid-1990s, China implemented reforms to decentralize the operation and financing of state welfare institutions. Since then, these institutions have shifted their financial base from reliance on public funding to more diversified revenue sources, including privately paying individuals. In response to growing demand for elder care services, residential care facilities have expanded significantly in both the public and private sectors. In cities (where clients have more purchasing power), private providers are at the forefront.

The national and local governments of China have strongly promoted and incentivized the construction of new residential care facilities for the elderly. Incentives such as lump-sum subsidies for investments (new construction) and regular subsidies for each occupied bed are motivating private sector providers to enter the senior care industry. This has led to considerable growth in institutional elder care in recent years (Feng et al. 2014). Residential care facilities are increasing in size; while the number of care facilities decreased from 44,304 facilities in 2012 to 33,043 in 2014 (figure O.5), the total number of beds increased from 4.2 million in 2012 to 4.9 million in 2013, and 5.8 million in 2014 (figure O.6 and table O.2). The target of 30 beds per 1,000 people age 60 and above by 2015 was reached in that year at 30.3 beds per 1,000 elders, which is still lower than in most OECD economies.

The most common types are public residential care facilities in rural areas (*jing lao yuan*), public social welfare homes in urban areas, and private residential care or nursing facilities, mostly in urban areas. The majority (roughly three-quarters) of existing residential care facilities are rural homes for the aged (*jing lao yuan*), which are financed and managed by local governments (chapter 2, cited from National Bureau of Statistics, *China Social Statistics Yearbook (2010–2014)*. Privately run Continuing Care Retirement Communities (CCRCs), which target seniors with high incomes and provide a full range of services, are still rare. China also has senior apartments with limited services, which are more of a housing option than long-term care.

Figure O.5 China: Number of Residential Aged Care Facilities in China, 2010–04

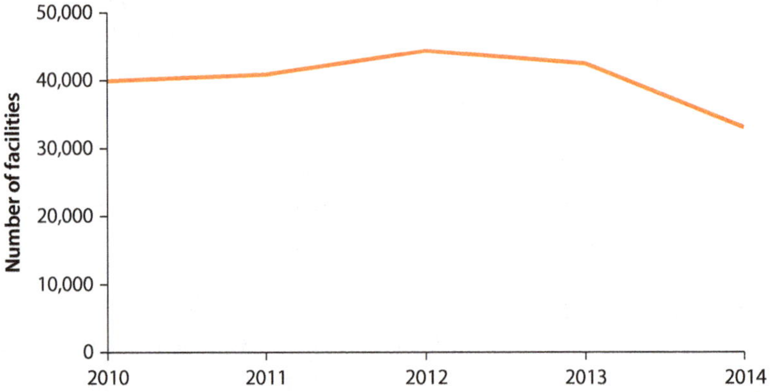

Source: NBS 2011~2015.

Figure O.6 China: Number of Beds in Residential Aged Care Facilities in China, 2010–14

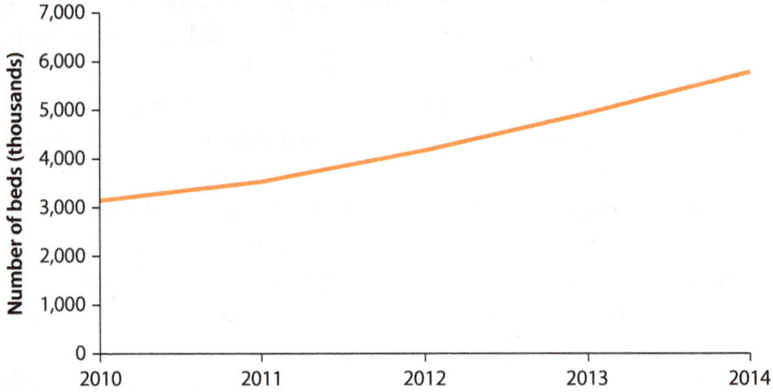

Source: NBS 2011~2015.

Table O.2 Number of Beds for Elderly Care in China, 2009–13 (10,000 Beds)

Year	*2009*	*2010*	*2011*	*2012*	*2013*
Total beds	289.0	307.3	343.2	416.5	493.7
Urban institutions	49.3	56.7	63.0	78.2	97.1
Rural institutions	208.8	224.9	242.1	261.0	272.9
Social welfare homes	22.8	24.5	27.2	30.9	34.6
Community institutions	4.5	1.2	10.9	19.8	64.1

Source: NBS 2011~2015.

Facility types also differ in terms of the ownership of fixed assets (the premises), facility management, and service provision, such as government-built and government-operated facilities, government-built and privately operated facilities, and privately built and privately operated facilities. The government is promoting the latter two types to encourage private sector engagement in the senior care industry. For government-built and privately operated care facilities, subsidies are provided in the form of free or below-market-value rentals.

The rapid growth of China's residential aged care sector in recent years have been driven, for the most part, by rising consumer demand. It has also been spurred by increased government subsidies for bed construction and facility operating costs. Internationally, there were many similar precedents in the early growth of institutional care fueled by public financing. In the United States, for example, the late 1960s and early 1970s witnessed a nursing home boom immediately following the passage of Medicare (1965) and Medicaid (1966) programs, which began to provide public funding for post-acute care (through Medicare) and long-term care (through Medicaid) for eligible individuals (Smith and Feng 2010).

Limited Coverage of Home- and Community-Based Services

Although home- and community-based elder care programs have emerged and expanded in recent years, they are largely concentrated in major metropolitan areas (Wu et al. 2005; Yang 2013). Nationally, community-based adult day care centers covered nearly 50 percent of urban communities and 20 percent of rural communities in 2014. The target set by the central government was to cover 60 percent by 2015. Urban community-based social services are typically managed and organized by local governments and are delivered primarily by nongovernmental organizations (NGOs) and other private small business service providers and volunteers (Xu and Chow 2011).

Community-based services have two broad channels of funding: public welfare assistance funds; and other sources such as individual and corporate contributions, and contributions from schools, hospitals, etc. Those that are funded by public assistance funds target low-income groups such as the *dibao* beneficiaries (government-provided, minimum living guarantee for the needy), and are usually available to the intended beneficiaries free or for a minimal charge. Those that receive external financing fund a broader set of services, encompassing adult day care centers, in-home care, community-sponsored meals programs, community kitchens, recreational centers, and mutual aid networks. These services require payment and therefore are affordable only to elders who have the ability to pay. The subsidy amounts for provision of these services depend greatly on local funding, availability of good-quality staff, and the enthusiastic participation of the community. Some community centers may maintain a small number of beds as an additional service for partially dependent or fully dependent seniors who need overnight or short-term stays. The government encourages community centers to set up beds by providing a bed construction subsidy (chapter 4).

More recently, a new type of home-based elder care model, dubbed Virtual Elder Care Home or Elder Care Home without Walls, has gained popularity in China. It features home care agencies providing a wide range of personal care and homemaker services in elders' homes. Services are initiated by phone calls to a local-government-sponsored information and service center, which then sends a qualified service provider to the elder person's home. Participating providers contract with the local government and are reimbursed for services purchased by the government on behalf of eligible care recipients, the majority of whom are Three No's or otherwise vulnerable. Since its inception in 2007 in the city of Suzhou in Jiangsu Province, the Virtual Elder Care Home model has spread to many parts of the country, including Gansu Province in northwest China (Feng et al. 2012).

Initiatives to accelerate the development of home- and community-based aged care services have been launched across other major cities in China. Various programs and service models are being developed and tested under these initiatives, such as community stations that provide day care and temporary services (Chengdu, Sichuan Province), respite care and services that provide temporary relief to family caregivers (Hangzhou, Zhejiang Province), and adult day care centers that provide temporary nursing services (Tianjin). In Beijing, Wenzhou, and Hangzhou, home services include housecleaning, personal care, basic nursing care, rehabilitation exercises, health education, companionship, and counseling services.

In rural areas, an emerging community-based elder care model called Happiness Homes (*xing fu yuan*) builds on rural cooperatives, where groups of rural elders live together in village housing. No service staff are employed; instead, the elders support each other. The villages provide housing and utilities for free. Living expenses for *wubao* elders are covered by the government, while others must pay for their expenses privately (themselves or by family members). Happiness Homes originated in Hebei Province and were first established in 2012. By 2014, they covered about 12 percent of villages. Gansu Province has set up rural Happiness Homes for the elderly; in Heilongjiang Province, five villages and towns were selected in 2010 to be rural aged care system pilot areas. The pilot aimed at expanding the target group of people for aged care services in rural areas. There are also initiatives involving Time Banks being piloted across the country.

Private Sector Involvement

A strategic shift in policy direction has recently occurred in China, with the government shifting from the role of direct supplier and provider to the role of purchaser and regulator of services. The government recognizes that it is no longer able to respond to the pressing need for aged care services without enlisting the private sector. Accordingly, it has issued a series of national policy directives over the last decade to speed up private sector development of social services for the aged (as described above and in chapter 2). These directives make it clear that private provision and private (self) payment will play the main role in the elderly care system going forward, while the government will continue to allocate funding to cover services for selected vulnerable groups.

Currently, the private aged care services sector in China consists of two types of organizations: nonprofit organizations (NPOs) and commercial for-profit organizations (chapter 4). NPOs—which include domestic civil society, faith-based organizations, and community-oriented organizations—tend to provide affordable services and earn modest financial returns. They usually target the lower-middle and low end of the market and serve seniors who can make modest payments. In contrast, for-profit commercial organizations tend to target the mid- to high-end price range of the market, with the goal of earning substantial financial returns on their investments while striving to provide high-quality services. However, virtually all private sector residential care facilities in China are currently registered as non-profit, non-enterprise entities (chapter 4).

Although institutional care services in China are provided mainly by public senior care facilities and social welfare homes operated by local governments, private senior care facilities have proliferated across major Chinese cities in recent years and are playing an increasing role in providing institutional care for the elderly. These facilities vary in the mix of services provided, fees charged, and residents served.

To incentivize private companies to provide a wide array of aged care services, the government employs subsidies and preferential policies, including free or subsidized land, supporting infrastructure, per-bed construction subsidies, subsidized loans for equipment investment, and utility subsidies (virtually free water and gas). Some localities also offer subsidies on a per-bed basis to cover recurrent costs of operation. Many localities then require that a number of beds are available to seniors on welfare at prices equal to the cost of care, thus alleviating the need for the government to develop and manage new public aged care facilities. Both NPOs and for-profit firms are encouraged to develop and manage skilled nursing facilities.

In the past few years, local and foreign real estate firms, operators, and Chinese institutional investors have targeted wealthy Chinese seniors for assisted living facilities, nursing homes, and CCRCs, with only a few planning to enter the mid-tier market in the future. The high-end facilities are relatively few in number, are of varying quality, and are too expensive for most elderly people (Zhan et al. 2006). One example of a high-end facility is the Gonghe Garden facility in Beijing, a 270-unit complex providing a full range of care and services at a monthly price ranging from RMB 7,000 to RMB 17,000. In comparison, an average wage in the formal sector in Beijing is reported to be around RMB 6,000, and the average monthly pension of state enterprise retirees in Beijing is around RMB 3,500.[13] The company operating Gonghe Garden believes such facilities cater only to the top 0.1 percent of the market (Caixin Online 2013). Many high-end facilities are operating far below full capacity, due in large part to the lack of effective demand.

Chinese real estate and insurance companies are actively entering the senior housing market, targeting seniors with mid to high incomes. Examples include

Cherish Yearn in Shanghai and Langdent and Sun City in Beijing. Vanke, one of China's largest real estate developers, launched senior housing projects in Hangzhou and is now developing a 10-year elderly care expansion strategy for the firm. Greentown launched its senior housing project combined with an elderly university in 2013. Union Life launched the first genuine United States–based CCRC, a 3,000-bed facility in Wuhan, in 2014. In 2015, Taikang Life's CCRC project opened its 258-unit senior retirement facility in Changping.

Companies from the United States, Japan, and France have entered China's institutional care market through partnerships with Chinese firms. In 2011, Japan's Long Life Group opened its first high-end nursing home in Qingdao and expected to expand the number to 100 in ten years. Another Japanese firm, RIEI Co., set up its wholly owned subsidiary in Beijing in 2011 and cooperated with Shanghai Sieton Group to open a for-profit nursing home in Shanghai in 2013. Sino Ocean Land initially partnered with Emeritus Senior Living, a U.S. senior living company, in its Beijing Yizhuang Project and has now collaborated with Meridian Senior Living, another U.S. senior living operating firm, in its Shanghai Cascade Project. Chinese conglomerate Fosun partnered with U.S. Fortress, a senior housing investment specialist fund, to develop the Starcastle brand and senior retirement projects in Shanghai. In 2014, several French care providers, including Colisee, Orpea, and Domus Vi—also entered China's market. Colisee will open a nursing home that provides skilled nursing care and memory care in Nanjing. Orpea signed a contract with Nanjing Drum Tower Hospital to reconstruct a rehabilitation nursing home of 180 beds. Orpea's other three projects will be located in Shenzhen, Chengdu, and Kunming. In these joint-venture projects, Chinese companies usually provide funds, land, and facilities, while their foreign partners are responsible for operation, management, and training.

Starting in 2012, the national and local governments began to encourage the development of a "mixed model." The central government has recognized the gap in skilled nursing facilities for medium-income seniors, and since 2013, it has encouraged the private sector's engagement in the mid-tier market through outsourcing the operation of publicly owned facilities to the private sector. In 2013, MOCA started a pilot reform of public aged care facilities, requiring at least one public facility to be outsourced for private sector operation in each province. By September 2014, 124 public aged care facilities in 28 provinces had been selected to participate in the pilot. In the reform, private operators are selected to manage the public facilities, following the appropriate procurement procedures.

Local governments are experimenting with various modalities of a "mixed model," and a number of commissioning models are currently being developed in China (table O.3). At present, management contracts and leasing are the two most common types of public-private partnerships in institutional elder care in China. Anecdotal evidence suggests that the private for-profit sector is reluctant to bid for the public nursing home management contracts unless operators are chosen based on the "price-quality" combination, rather than on price alone.

For-profit companies are more likely to operate specialized-skilled nursing facilities that tend to be located in large cities and predominantly serve the

Table O.3 Types of Public-Private Partnerships in Institutional Care

Type	*Description*
Procurement	Local municipality purchases beds from the private nursing home.
Management contracts	Private nursing home operators assume management responsibilities (e.g., staffing, supplies, training) for public nursing homes.
Leasing	Operation and management of public nursing homes by private operators. Private operators bear all risks and retain profits but do not assume ownership of nursing homes.
Service contract	Public nursing homes outsource a set of services, such as housekeeping, catering, and laundry, to the private sector.
Shareholdings	The ownership structure of public nursing homes is changed by selling shares to a private investor.

Sources: ICAIA 2014; Yu 2014.

middle and upper classes. To attract and retain a demanding and educated clientele, they generally provide a broader and higher level of care that might not be available in public senior care facilities. The data show that 10 percent of the private senior care facilities provide rehabilitation services, and 3 percent provide hospice care (chapter 4). According to statistics from the Ministry of Health, in 2012, 155 out of 301 rehabilitation hospitals in China were private facilities.

The numbers of private elderly care facilities vary from province to province depending on local regulatory policies, income levels of seniors, and the elderly demographic. In Beijing, private senior facilities accounted for 49 percent of all available beds in 2014.[14] In contrast, private nursing facility beds accounted for only 28 percent of the total number in Hebei Province in 2013.[15] In Jilin Province, the private sector accounted for 60 percent of facilities and 47 percent of all beds in 2014.[16] Since 2013, local Civil Affairs Bureaus have published data that include the number of private elder care facilities on their websites, an indication of the increasing importance of private sector engagement in the senior care industry.

Most for-profit providers focus on community care services commissioned by real estate developers targeted at middle- to high-income seniors and their families. Foreign companies provide home-based care targeting middle- to high-income seniors, with a focus on major cities. For example, Singapore-based "Active Global Ageing" is providing home care delivered by trained nurses, U.S. "Right At Home" delivers caregiving and housekeeping services through university graduate caregivers, and Pinetree offers at-home skilled caregiving to seniors who are semi- or fully dependent.

Public institutions receive substantial implicit subsidies from the government (free rent, workforce, and salaries) and are passing these subsidies on to consumers through lower prices. It is a common perception therefore that this gives them a competitive advantage over private sector facilities. High capital investments, uncertainty regarding effective demand, and difficulties in obtaining land manifest themselves in low returns on capital that continue to deter private sector investors and operators from entering the low and middle end of the institutional care market (chapter 4).

Main Challenges for China's Aged Care System

Is China on the right path to creating an aged care system that can meet the current and future needs of its ever-growing elderly population? At the national level, a broad contour of a three-tiered aged care system has been laid out in the 12th Five-Year Plan and other national policy directives. The guiding principle of this planned system, which emphasizes home-based care as its bedrock, supported by community-based care and underpinned by institutional care, is sound and consistent with prevailing international practice.

A universal preference for home- and community-based services rather than institutional care is seen across economies, despite cultural differences. Home care services range from assistance with daily chores to personal care, meal preparation, transport assistance, and equipment. In economies with a strong welfare tradition and a high rate of female labor participation, home- and community-based care is mainly provided by professional caregivers and is based on formal needs assessment. In Europe, the professional care sector is an important job creator for many domestic and migrant workers.

As the needs of clients change over time—either temporarily or permanently—a care continuum with the proper mix of services is needed to meet these changing needs. The mix of services provided across home, community, and institutional settings may vary, and there may not be direct correspondence between the level of limited functional ability or the needs of the elderly and the form of care provided. Services provided at home can range from domestic aid and personal care to supportive services and health services. Community-based services can include social and recreational services as well as rehabilitation and some nursing services. Institutional care can include assisted living, food and accommodations, supervision of medical care, specialized care (e.g., dementia care), and hospice services. Ideally, a continuum of aged care services encompasses an optimal and flexible service mix to respond to the diverse needs of the elderly.

In terms of the type of service providers, there is a predominance of private service providers across OECD economies. Relatively few economies maintain public provision of residential care (e.g., Sweden). NPOs like charities play a large role in aged care service delivery in some economies (e.g., Australia), following a long tradition of such practices in those economies.

In the OECD and in virtually all developed economies, public resources are typically used to pay for most or a substantial share of total long-term care costs for eligible recipients (European Commission 2014). Governments channel public financing to long-term care for two reasons: (1) because long-term care services are not affordable for the vast majority of elderly people and (2) to relieve the informal care work of family members, which is difficult to combine with labor market participation of the caregivers. Therefore, in most developed economies, formal long-term care is financed primarily through general taxation and obligatory social security contributions (Colombo et al. 2011). For example, in the United States, over 75 percent of nursing home residents have their care paid for by government-administered programs (Kaiser Family Foundation 2013). Three main parameters explain the differences in aged care spending in OECD countries: the source of finance, the rules defining eligible target groups and the forms and mix of care and services provided to them, and the forms of payment for service provision.

Especially in recent years, OECD economies increased the use of a range of policies to encourage home care. These include a mix of demand- and supply-side interventions, such as direct expansion of home care supply (e.g., Canada, Ireland, New Zealand, Poland, Sweden), regulatory measures, and financial incentives. Non-institutional care enables older people to continue living in their own homes and to live independently, which can also be cost-efficient.

China's government is also moving in the right direction by encouraging and supporting the private sector in the development of aged care services and increasing its financial support for the development of elderly care. However, as is typical of many national policy guidelines issued by the central government, there is a lack of specific and enforceable measures to turn the broad policy visions into reality. Ultimately, it trickles down to the subnational and local governments to develop and implement those measures that best suit local needs and resources. To this end, numerous constraints, unmet needs, and programmatic challenges must be addressed. Three pressing issues are highlighted below.

Nurturing the Stewardship Capacity of the Government

As the role of the government firmly shifts from direct provider and supplier to purchaser and regulator, the government needs to assume responsibility for fostering, monitoring, and regulating the entire senior care market—public, private, and mixed, and all sub-sectors of this market (home-based, community-based, and all forms of residential care). This entails capacity building and the establishment of institutional arrangements at many levels and across many agencies. It also requires training and maintaining a professional workforce in both the public and private sectors, which is currently lacking.

Fragmentation across Regulatory Bodies. Social welfare homes, public nursing homes, and private not-for-profit residential care facilities are currently under the supervision of MOCA. Private for-profit residential care facilities, nursing homes, and retirement communities register through the Ministry of Industry and Commerce and its subordinate departments or bureaus at the local level; they are not supervised by civil affairs agencies at the same level. Skilled nursing homes and rehabilitation facilities are under the supervision of the National Health and Family Planning Commission, because nursing and therapy care are regarded as health care skills. Compliance with building codes and safety issues is under the supervision of the fire departments. The different regulatory bodies' oversight of different parts of the aged care industry results in uncoordinated and inadequate supervision of the industry, overlapping services, and inconsistent regulations. Furthermore, there have been very limited financial inducements to encourage the development of private nursing homes because most of the government funding and subsidies for the aged care industry sit within MOCA.

Weak Regulatory Oversight and Monitoring, Especially of the Private and Mixed Sectors. The primary regulatory mechanism deployed by the government in engaging private sector providers is to require registration and licensing for market entry to ensure that providers have the minimum capacity needed to deliver services. In order to provide elder care services, registered providers then need to obtain operating licenses. There is no unified information system that collects and keeps data on both public and private providers. There are some checks of the services provided that are commissioned by public agencies, but the government lacks a robust system to hold these external providers accountable for the services they deliver.

Currently, regulatory oversight and other strategies to ensure adequate quality are lacking and remain a relatively low priority on the policy agenda. While media stories about poor quality of care and safety concerns in the residential care sector occasionally surface, there is little data with which to assess the quality of existing and new services. The government also needs to set up a management and evaluation system for home- and community-based care organizations, where quality monitoring is more difficult, given the wide range of services provided in varied settings. The system should enable monitoring of the care needs of elderly people and produce data that can be used for quality improvements.

Lack of A Uniform-Needs Assessment. A needs assessment, typically on the levels of physical and mental impairments or disabilities, should be used to determine both eligibility for publicly supported services and the most appropriate and cost-efficient mix of services that fit individual needs. This is a common practice in all countries with developed long-term care systems. China does not have a regular, universal system of needs assessment in place and can build on international practices and local pilots. Encouragingly, some good practices exist at the local level. For example, Shanghai piloted a universal needs assessment toolkit (modeled after the international InterRAI instrument) in two districts in 2014 and is now expanding this assessment tool into a citywide policy.

Limited Capacity to Gauge and Forecast Care Needs. This limitation relates to both the current demand and supply of elderly care services. On the demand side, in order to plan and help grow aged care services, reliable data are needed to gauge the needs and effective demand for services on a regular basis. However, such data are difficult to obtain, partly due to the lack of a well-developed and working information infrastructure. There are some national data sources, including the decennial census data and several nationally representative sample surveys that gather demographic, socioeconomic, and health data for the elderly population in China (chapter 10). However, such data have not been fully utilized to understand current care needs and to forecast future needs of the elderly population. Lack of transparency and barriers to timely and widespread access to these data for the research community aggravate this situation. As a result, the knowledge and evidence base that can be used to inform aged care policy making is weak.

Improving the Allocation of Public Financing for Long-Term Care

Currently, China spends about 0.02–0.04 percent of its GDP on elderly care, and this limited public financing is mainly geared toward subsidies for the construction of residential care facilities. In fact, public subsidies are directly linked to the number of beds in care homes. Although more and better services for frail older people are undoubtedly needed, this "institutional bias" in subsidizing residential care beds leads to an unbalanced service mix. Financing upfront investments in residential care contributes necessary inputs for service provision but may not necessarily improve provider performance or quality of services. Home- and community-based services receive little funding and are not consistently promoted, despite the general preference for such services among the elderly.

While the supply of residential care beds has increased rapidly, partly fueled by government subsidies for bed construction, the available data show that existing facilities in both the public and private sectors have many empty beds. In urban areas, government facilities generally have higher occupancy rates than private facilities. In Nanjing, for instance, the average occupancy rate (share of occupied beds out of total available beds in a facility) as of 2009 was 69 percent in private sector facilities, compared to 83 percent in government facilities. In Tianjin, the averages as of 2010 were 76 percent and 91 percent in private and government facilities, respectively (Liu, Feng, and Mor 2014). The lower occupancy rates in private sector facilities could be the result of high pricing (beyond the means of many elders and their families), lack of services, and poor quality of care.

Lack of systematic financing for long-term care, contributing to low effective demand for care. The need for long-term care is undoubtedly substantial and will continue to grow as the aging of the Chinese population accelerates, but the effective demand for care services does not simply reflect the need for care (chapter 1). Thus, the question is: to what extent can the need for care be turned into effective demand and satisfied successfully?

Public financing for aged care is currently granted only to the most disadvantaged elderly—those who qualify as *san wu* or *wubao*—and there is a big financing gap for the vast majority of older people who do not have sufficient means to pay for needed care and services. Although China has established a three-pillar pension system, the replacement rate in the national pension system is low, and the role of corporate annuity and private commercial insurance is limited (chapter 4). Given the low pensions for most people, it is unlikely that many people can afford formal long-term care. With access enabled primarily by the ability to pay, it is the affluent and the privileged who can afford high-quality care and services. Without the broad-based effective demand, providers will find it hard to expand their business.

Little "Demand-Side" Financing, Hindering the Emergence of Efficient Providers. Without putting resources in the hands of consumers to increase effective demand, direct subsidies to providers do not necessarily encourage the emergence of efficient providers. The government is the most significant and powerful financier of community services for the elderly, but it is difficult to fulfill its functions of ensuring quality and efficiency of spending without putting money in the hands of consumers. With the exception of wealthy people, the elderly population does not have the purchasing power to buy professional care services, and therefore little market competition is fostered. The solution is a system of direct cash transfers or service vouchers, which in turn would require a needs assessment to determine who should be eligible for these transfers (in addition to satisfying means test eligibility criteria).

Public Resources Not Targeted at People Most in Need of Care. Publicly financed or subsidized aged care needs to be targeted at those who are most in need of care: those who have physical and mental impairments and need assistance with their daily activities. The current public system tilts toward supporting residential accommodations for the poor and lonely elderly, regardless of their physical condition and care needs. This bias stems from historical practices—for years, the government has funded and operated care facilities such as urban social welfare homes and rural older people's homes to support welfare recipients.

Publicly run facilities have recently expanded to accept privately paying individuals, who now constitute the majority of current residents of welfare homes in urban areas (residents of rural older people's homes are still almost exclusively welfare recipients). Many publicly run facilities house seniors who are in need of shelter but not care, as the managers of those facilities (who face excess demand) tend to accept healthy and able seniors over those who are impaired and heavily dependent. Under this regime, the implicit public subsidies provided to the social welfare homes accrue to the healthy, self-paying customers. It is encouraging that the government is now requiring that 50 percent of new public beds built be made available to seniors with care needs. However, whether this requirement is enforceable in actual practice remains a question.

As in other countries, adequate and sustainable public financing is essential for broadening aged care coverage in China. In addition, the mechanism of public financing—where the money comes from, how it is spent, and how providers are reimbursed—matters because providers are often driven by and respond to financial incentives built into the public reimbursement system. Devising a systemic and sustainable financing system should be given higher priority on the policy agenda. Options for a coherent strategy for long-term care financing are explored below and in chapter 5 in greater detail.

Strengthening the Capacity of Service Providers

China's delivery system for institutional aged care increasingly depends on private sector service providers, but the capacity of these providers in an emerging market is still weak.

Lack of "Level Playing Field" Impeding the Growth of Private Sector Service Providers. Fair and transparent rules are needed to enable the market entry and survival of private providers. Research shows that in major cities like Tianjin and

Nanjing, government-owned and operated elder care facilities have significantly higher occupancy rates (which are vital to the financial well-being of the facility) than private sector facilities. However, as mentioned earlier, their residents tend to be healthier and have fewer functional impairments than those in private sector facilities (Feng et al. 2012; Liu, Feng, and Mor 2014). These case-mix differences are likely the result of selective or discriminatory admission policies that favor relatively healthy residents, more so in government facilities than in private sector homes. Private sector facilities seem to be more willing to admit functionally impaired residents. One study reported that government-owned care homes are often reserved for the upper class or wealthy families and retired government cadres, whereas poorer, sicker elders have fewer options and choices (Zhan et al. 2006).

As China's aged care development moves forward, government-run aged care facilities should reconsider their admission policies and target services at the disabled, frail, and otherwise vulnerable elders who are most in need of publicly supported institutional care. Government-owned and operated facilities enjoy a multitude of advantages over their private sector counterparts, such as public financing; generous subsidies on rents, utilities, and operating costs; and greater integration with local communities and professionals. By virtue of their public ownership, government-run facilities should customize and target their services to older people who are most in need of care, but the finding of a greater number of healthier and presumably low-need residents in government-owned facilities than in private sector homes indicates the opposite.

As further described later in this overview, the aged care system in most countries is a "quasi market," and its functioning depends to a large extent on public financing as well as transparent rules and standards. These rules and standards pertain to the services as well as accreditation of providers and public procurement procedures. One concern is that in the absence of effective regulatory oversight, the shift of service provision to the private sector in the Chinese senior care market might compromise the quality of care (Feng et al. 2014; Liu, Feng, and Mor 2014).

Lack of a Well-Trained Workforce and Low Capacity of Caregivers. As in other economies, China has a shortage of qualified and skilled care workers. The lack of adequately trained staff—among many other factors such as weak regulatory oversight—is a major barrier to quality improvements in institutional elder care in China (chapter 9). A recent review points out that staff in Chinese residential care facilities are older and have lower educational levels than their counterparts in western economies, and few facilities use established qualification standards to prepare staff for their roles in the facility (Song et al. 2014). In urban facilities, most direct-care staff are migrant workers from nearby rural areas or locals who were laid off from state-run enterprises in the process of public sector reform and restructuring (Feng et al. 2011; Song et al. 2014). The organizational and technical capacity of service providers needs further development and strengthening in both the public and private sectors and across all care settings.

In order to respond to future demand and address challenges that the fledgling system will encounter along the way, China will need to adopt an appropriate approach to aged care that reflects its demographic realities and fiscal possibilities, as well as its broader vision for social services and cultural preferences. The second part of this overview presents a conceptual framework for the aged care governance and delivery system and draws on international experiences and current practices in China to propose some practical solutions for putting in place various components of this framework.

Implications for the Future of Aged Care in China

Mounting pressures resulting from rapid demographic shifts and socioeconomic developments in China underscore the urgent need to develop an aged care system, and these pressures will only intensify going forward. The characteristics of the elderly population in China will also change: future seniors will be better educated, more likely to live in urban areas, and have fewer children and family caregivers. More of them will be covered by medical insurance and old age insurance (pensions and retirement incomes), and many (especially urban seniors) will have real estate property. With increased purchasing power, Chinese seniors will demand a variety of services of good quality.

It is not feasible to forecast the forms and types of care and amount of services that future seniors would prefer and demand; instead, China needs a coherent policy framework and corresponding institutions to monitor ongoing socioeconomic changes and continue to expand social investments that better match the needs and demands for aged care services and their supply. Given the complexity of the aged care sector and the large scale of needs, an efficient governance system for policy making, enabled by coordinated institutional support across government agencies, is required. Some elements of this governance system exist already, but there is still an unfinished agenda of defining the governance framework and translating it into a well-functioning care delivery system.

A conceptual framework for developing the aged care governance and delivery systems in China is depicted in figure O.7 and described in this section. The key points of this framework are articulated based on considerations that combine international experience in aged care provision and the current realities in China.

Strengthening Policy Formulation

The implementation of a comprehensive long-term care system requires an agile government that can benefit from the advancements of other more developed long-term care systems by testing and adapting those ideas in the Chinese context. This approach can only be mastered by a government structure that is designed to learn and willing to do so. This requires the collection of information and government structures to foster policy learning.

A governance system with a clear division of roles and responsibilities for all partners at the national, regional, and local levels and a well-communicated

Figure O.7 A Conceptual Framework for Aged Care Governance and Delivery Systems

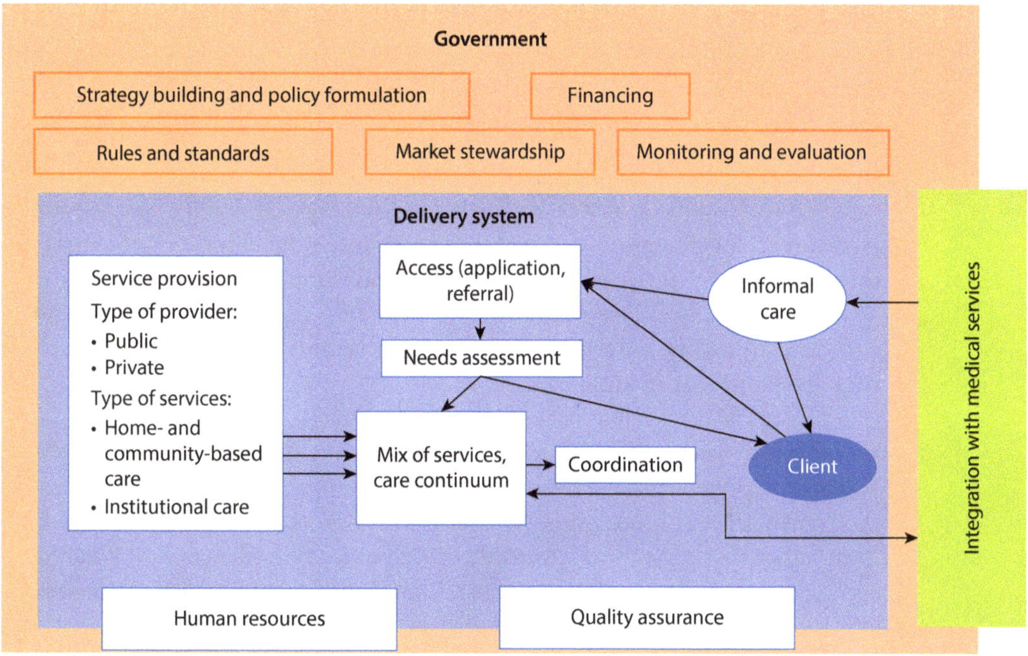

regulatory framework are also needed. The national government has a key role in designing—and reforming, if necessary—rules and standards for aged care as well as ensuring compliance and implementation. The government of China has already adopted a range of policy documents for the long-term care sector, as described earlier, and now faces the challenge of putting them into practice. An assessment of the coherence of policy papers and an identification of gaps in the current regulatory framework may be an important first step toward a coherent and effective aging policy.

A number of key issues on policy learning and formulation in China are highlighted below. More detailed discussion of these issues, including international experiences, is presented in chapter 10.

Division of tasks and responsibilities, and cooperation between national and subnational governments[17]

The roles of the national, provincial, and local governments should be defined clearly, supported by the commensurate financial resources. A core task of the national government with its line ministries and specialized agencies is to define a coherent strategy to develop, update, and implement the regulatory framework with a basic set of rules and standards for the aged care sector. Provincial and local authorities are expected to develop action plans with specific measures that fit local circumstances but are also consistent with the basic set of rules and standards mandated by the central government.

They should exercise oversight of aged care services and organize the provision of vocational training for care workers in close cooperation with care providers.

On macro-level policy planning, the State Council is responsible for issuing national plans on aging, and local governments are responsible for local planning and annual programs according to the national plans. For specific system building, the State Council and relevant ministries set standards for elderly care service facilities, service practitioners, and service quality. Local governments at all levels should make plans to guarantee the elderly's right to access to basic medical services and encourage and support the private sector to provide home-based care and develop community services. Local governments also need to incorporate the construction of senior care facilities into urban-rural development planning.

Exchange of experiences and good practices across China

Valuable experiences have been gained in implementing aged care programs at the provincial and local levels. Mutual learning from good practices as well as from failures would push forward the development of efficient and sustainable aged care policies and services across China. To benefit from these experiences, existing good practices should be evaluated by independent researchers.

Better information for an improved evidence base

A nationwide information system with comparable data that is regularly collected and analyzed would provide the necessary evidence base for developing and implementing coherent aged care policies. The national authority should define the minimum information that local authorities must gather and report on regularly, which should include key indicators on inputs (cost, manpower), performance, and outcomes. Although outcomes of social services and long-term care may be difficult to define and measure, some process indicators should be developed to describe the changes and benefits resulting from care activities.

To expand a demand-driven, long-term care industry, the government needs better data and statistical tools. Indeed, the creation of a platform for collecting and analyzing information on the elderly is outlined in the 12th Five-Year Plan. Existing sources should be complemented with new data to assess current supply as well as local needs and demands. China's National Committee on Aging recently announced a survey of more than 200,000 elderly,[18] and multiple data sources that might be helpful in understanding remaining gaps between supply and demand of care services are available.[19] To the extent possible, these data sets can be matched with market or even provider information to estimate the relationship between supply and demand of care services. Such knowledge would be essential in allocating funds to local governments and would help ensure the efficient use of public money.

In terms of institutional arrangements, the Office of the China National Committee on Aging could serve as a helpful point of contact for international exchange and national knowledge creation. In addition, many non-governmental institutions have become involved in the research on aging and provide policy consultations. These institutions include universities and both government and non-government think-tanks, whose expertise can be tapped to inform and improve policy making.

Given the many stakeholders involved, effective national coordination is needed for several reasons. The aged care system is interconnected with health care, social services, and pensions, which are administered by different government bodies. National guidelines and quality standards need to be developed to harmonize the activities of local governments. National statistics require consistent data collection to monitor and evaluate overall sector performance. Consulting local governments and fostering exchanges between different stakeholders can provide important information for efficient policy formulation.

Focusing on outcomes of aged care

A national-level research institution should publish key data and analysis on outcomes of care services at the local and national levels on a regular basis. The "Adult Social Care Outcomes Framework" applied in the United Kingdom may serve as an example of good practices.[20] This framework, launched in 2011, sets out how data collected annually are combined to measure users' quality of life, independence, and care experience. The outcomes are designed to compare the performance of care systems between local authorities.

In China, local authorities should have oversight for aged care in their region. This includes tools and approaches to hold all providers accountable for care quality and outcomes. They should monitor outcomes and challenge providers if planned outcomes are not met. In terms of care quality, data collection and evaluation should become part of local commissioning, guided by national standards. This information is vital for monitoring providers but also allows comparison of local government performance at the national level.

To the extent feasible, data should be collected with broad coverage. As this is costly for providers, they may have little incentive to collect and transmit such data to the government. Therefore, quality assessment should become part of the procurement contracts or a requirement for receiving a long-term care provider license. An alternative option is the collection of data from the public side through regular quality inspections. If feasible, an automated data collection routine is preferable. Different indicators could be useful in measuring home-based and residential care, but research should test the validity of international examples for application in China.

Developing a system of needs assessment at the policy and service delivery levels

Projections of demand and needs assessments are necessary at the macro level for policy planning and at the micro (or service delivery) level for determining eligibility and care planning. For mid- and long-term policy making, a macro-level approach—an evidence-based system of projecting and foreseeing future needs—is needed. At the micro level, assessment of individual needs is necessary to target resources at those who need care, thereby achieving care quality and cost-efficiency.

Many OECD countries have both macro- and micro-level systems of needs assessment. At the macro level, some government agencies in these countries (e.g., the Congressional Budget Office and the Office of the Assistant Secretary for Planning and Evaluation of the Department of Health and Human Services in the United States) conduct mid- and long-term projections on government spending on various public programs, including those that cover long-term services and supports for the elderly based on current prevalence and trends of limited functional ability in the older population. At the micro level, many of these countries have developed and implemented systems of strict needs assessment on levels of functional impairment (both physical and cognitive) and assessments of income and wealth at the individual level. The assessments are used to determine eligibility and benefits and also to make individualized care plans.

One important component of China's National Aged Care Information System, recently launched by MOCA, is a database of older people who receive aged care and those who need care, for which the use of a standardized individual-level assessment tool to collect health, function, self-care ability, and other useful information is crucial. The Ability Assessment for Older Adults, which is largely based on interRAI, was posted by MOCA in 2013 to solicit public comments. The assessment tool was tested among 581 seniors with varying degrees of dependency in six facilities in Beijing, Guangzhou (capital city of Guangdong Province), and Suzhou (in Jiangsu Province). Based on the testing results, the tool was revised and re-tested in ten facilities in Beijing (MOCA 2013). The tool was tentatively posted as a recommended (but not required) standard.

Several cities, such as Beijing, Shanghai, Nanjing, and Guangzhou, have begun using standardized tools similar to the Ability Assessment for Older Adults to assess the function and self-care ability of seniors who apply for aged care services. The primary goal of individual assessment is to determine care needs and thus appropriately allocate resources. The assessment varies across regions but provides a foundation for potential standardized data collection that could also be used for quality assurance in the future.

Optimizing the Match between Aged Care Demand and Supply

Strengthening preventive measures to prolong independent living and health

Aging has a strong impact on the overall economic and social development of a country, and many OECD countries have realized that the sole focus on senior care problems is a passive way of tackling the issue (DRC 2014). Preventive measures taken in the earlier years of life can improve health in old age and help reduce the need for—and costs of—care. Besides behavioral interventions and lifestyle changes that contribute to healthy aging at the individual level, public policies also play an important role. For instance, tightening up tobacco controls in both public and private spaces may help reduce the prevalence of chronic obstructive pulmonary disease, which is among the most common and burdensome chronic diseases in the older population. Urban and spatial planning may also have an impact on the living conditions and care needs of the elderly.

China can also draw on its own experience in health care delivery from the 1960s to mid-1990s, which emphasized basic primary health care for all, preventive medicine, and health promotion strategies to curb infectious diseases and improve the overall health profile of China's population. Now China, like many other developing economies, faces the challenge of coping with the rising burden of chronic or NCDs as the population is aging rapidly. In many respects, this is a more difficult kind of challenge to tackle than that posed by infectious diseases. The efficacy for older people of preventive care and health promotion earlier in life are cumulative over many years, so the benefits of ongoing preventive measures may not be evident immediately. Nevertheless, both the government and the public should raise awareness of the importance of preventive care and actively engage in encouraging healthy aging of the population.

Rebalancing the mix of services.

The government's policy framework for a three-tier long-term care system aptly emphasizes home- and community-based services, but current policies and resource allocations incentivize institutional care more than home- and community-based services (Feng et al. 2012). With government policies that have input-related targets, such as number of beds (and sometimes number of staff, as well), there is a danger that the emerging aged care system in China may become biased toward institutional care rather than giving the highest priority to home care. Building facilities and beds (physical infrastructure) is also easier than providing home- and community-based services, and since care homes are widely visible whereas home-based care is difficult to show, local authorities may prefer the former. However, the focus on residential care neglects the preference of most elderly people for aging in place. This may be a factor behind the large number of empty beds in existing and newly built facilities—a waste of resources that could be better used to support older people at home or in the community where they prefer to be.

A more comprehensive national strategy and approach that give priority to home- and community-based care may be needed. The overarching goal should be to enable older people to remain independent in their own homes for as long as possible to prevent unnecessary health care utilization (such as potentially preventable hospitalizations and emergency department visits) and to avoid or delay institutionalization. According to international experience, well-organized home care is more cost-efficient than residential care. Home care systems can also be adapted to changing needs and help contain long-term care expenditures.

Rebalancing the long-term care system and reallocating resources accordingly require a strategy based on needs assessments at the individual, local, and national levels. The strategy should combine informal and formal care for home- and community-based services. Policy makers can use available policy instruments (e.g., tax exemptions, subsidies, and other financial incentives) to help build a balanced mix of services that reflect older people's preferences and best meet their needs.

However, professional home- and community-based long-term care services are relatively rare, except in a few major cities like Shanghai. The few services that do exist at the neighborhood and village levels show that there is high potential for supporting older people to live in their homes and age in place. These services may include a visiting service and home delivery of meals. Community senior activity centers may be incorporated into programs to facilitate support at the local level. Further development of community-based service models would require close cooperation among municipal, district, and street/neighborhood authorities.

The current senior care delivery system in China consists of providers with various types of ownership and structures. This mixed delivery system, which needs strict oversight and quality control, could be used to test different operational models for service development and delivery, such as state-built and operated, state-built and privately run, privately operated with government support, government subsidies for construction and operating costs, and government purchasing of services from the private sector. It remains to be seen which model would produce the best results.

In addition, the availability of medical services is one of the most important considerations for elders who choose a care facility (chapter 4). Many prioritize the availability of full-time physicians and timely provision of medical services. Therefore, facilities in proximity to large medical institutions or staffed with professional medical service personnel are more desirable to the elderly. Having no one to resort to in times of illness concerns the elderly who live at home the most (chapter 9). However, few of the existing senior care facilities in China have medical practitioners, nurses, and allied health professionals.

Financing Aged Care

Key Considerations and International Experience

An adequate system of financing is a precondition for translating the need for care and services into effective demand. The design of a financing model has three main elements: (1) the source of finance, (2) the rules defining eligible target groups and forms of care services provided, and (3) the system of payment for service provision, which is linked with the delivery system (table O.4).

Spending levels for elder care services vary greatly within Europe. For medical and social care combined, public spending in European Union (EU) countries ranges from 4.5 percent of GDP in Denmark to 0.2 percent in Cyprus, with an average of 1.8 percent. For social care alone, spending ranges from 0.02 percent of GDP in Latvia to 0.7 percent of GDP in the Netherlands (European Commission 2013, based on data from the 2012 *Ageing Report*). The northern and Western European countries have higher shares of public financing. Expenditures for long-term care are relatively small compared to general health services and public pension systems.

Table O.4 Elements for Designing a Model of Financing for Aged Care

Source of finance	• Tax-based (Nordic European countries) • Public, compulsory long-term care social insurance models (Germany, the Netherlands, Luxembourg, Japan, and the Republic of Korea) • Co-payment by clients (a common requirement in many countries which may vary by care setting)
Eligible target group	• Universal coverage • Means-tested, based on strict income or asset tests to set financial thresholds for eligibility for publicly funded care • Level of need according to needs assessment
Forms of services	• Home care • Community care (day care centers) • Institutional (residential) care
Payment for service provision	• To eligible clients: cash payment or in-kind services, vouchers • To service providers: payment for time, services, or outcomes

Source: Authors, based on Colombo et al. 2011.

The financing approaches vary significantly across the OECD countries. Overall, the main sources of financing for aged care services in OECD countries are general taxation, obligatory social security contributions, voluntary private insurance, and OOP payments directly made by users. At one extreme is universal coverage within a single program, in which long-term care coverage is provided through a single system (e.g., tax-based models in Nordic countries; public long-term care insurance models in Germany, the Netherlands, Luxembourg, Japan, and the Republic of Korea; and personal care and nursing care through health coverage in Belgium). At the other end of the spectrum are means-tested safety net schemes in which strict income or asset tests are used to set financial thresholds for eligibility for publicly funded long-term care services and benefits targeting the needy (e.g., England, the United States).

As long-term care services are expensive and unaffordable without some third-party coverage for most people throughout the developed world, especially for older people with disabilities, the state plays an active role in financing. However, there are also limits to taxpayers' willingness to contribute to the cost of long-term care through higher taxes. All countries with a public long-term care coverage scheme require some cost sharing by care recipients, especially for room and board in institutional settings (Colombo et al. 2011), regardless of the specific financing mechanisms used. For co-payments, the purchasing power of clients is typically increased through transfers such as cash benefits or vouchers. Co-payments from clients (OOP payments made directly to the provider) can be fixed rates or be means-tested (free for the poor or full payment for the rich).

Private payments on the part of care users are a general feature of all publicly financed care systems. Private financing accounts for one-third of total long-term care expenditures in Germany, around 26 percent in Slovenia, 22 percent in the United States (Kaiser Family Foundation 2013), and 17 percent in Austria

(European Commission 2014, based on OECD Health Database and national sources). The most frequent form is OOP payment, while private insurance for elder care services is not very common due to a range of limiting factors—for example, adverse selection, in which people at greater risk of needing care will buy insurance while people with "good risks" will not, thus driving premium prices higher. OOP payments are often capped; an upper limit (with annual adjustment) for individuals' private contributions was introduced in the United Kingdom with the Care Act 2014.[21] Two other important parameters of individuals' financial capacity are whether their assets are considered for co-payment and whether their relatives are obliged to make financial contributions.

For eligibility determination, countries operating means-tested programs (e.g., England, New Zealand, and the United States) limit public benefits to people who are poor (usually a definition that takes into account both income and assets) or who become poor due to the high costs of medical and long-term care. The philosophical premise behind means-tested programs is that the primary responsibility for care of older people and younger persons with disabilities rests with individuals and their family and that government should act only as a payer of last resort for those unable to provide for themselves. Other countries (e.g., Germany, Japan, the Netherlands, Sweden, and Korea) opt for universal coverage following the philosophical approach that the government should take the lead in ensuring that all people with disabilities, regardless of financial status, should be eligible for the long-term care services they need. In this type of system, social solidarity is highly valued, and the right to long-term care is viewed similarly to the right to medical care. Regardless of the financing model used, eligibility for public benefits requires meeting specified limited functional ability criteria based on needs assessment.

In terms of payment systems, methods for paying providers include fixed (negotiated) budgets or fee for services (per time unit, number of visits, number of care packages, care intensity). Payment by results or outcomes is less frequent but is a basic feature of social impact bond models. As results or outcomes are difficult to measure and adverse incentives should be avoided, a combination of payment by results and input or process indicators would be desirable. In many countries, publicly supported long-term care is provided in the form of in-kind services rather than cash benefits, although there are notable exceptions in Germany, Italy, Austria, and a few other countries. Public payments and subsidies for long-term care typically go to service providers rather than directly to care recipients.

Spending levels also depend on the efficiency of the delivery system. Most countries have partly or totally out-contracted aged care services to private nonprofit or for-profit organizations, while few countries rely on public services. For historical reasons, spending levels also depend on the form or mix of publicly funded services, which vary greatly across home, community, and institutional care settings. Policies in many countries strive to transform care models from historically institutional to home- and community-based care as part of the deinstitutionalization movement because institutional care is more expensive than care provided at home or in the community (Feiler et al. 2016). Expenditure levels are contained by supporting informal caregivers and less cost-intensive home- and community-based services.

Currently, the main challenge in most OECD countries is that needs and demands are increasing while the availability of funds is decreasing. Due to changing demographics and labor market characteristics, the provision of informal care by family members is becoming a less feasible option. Meanwhile, long-term care services are not affordable for the vast majority of people with disabilities and elderly people with lower income levels. A mix of public and private financing is the rule, with the common principle that individuals contribute to the cost of care unless they cannot afford to do so, in which case the state pays.

There is no "silver bullet" available to ensure sustainable financing of long-term care. Each of the different approaches has its advantages and disadvantages (table O.5). Any discussion of the sustainability of long-term care must also consider the need to influence the demand side (i.e., the needs of an aging population) through prevention, rehabilitation, and adaptations to the living environment (European Commission 2014).

Implications for China

Experience from OECD countries demonstrates that, historically, the amount of public financing for long-term care largely depends on how much a society can rely on informal care. Factors having a long-term impact on the need for elder care and expenditure levels are the ratio of elderly to working-age population, disease prevention and health promotion, household structure, female labor force participation, and migration patterns.

In China, the role of the government as "commissioner and regulator of aged care services" (versus direct supplier or major financier) has materialized in the low level of funds allocated to aged care. To further stimulate private sector development of services for older people, in March 2016, five Chinese ministries

Table O.5 Advantages and Disadvantages of Financing Approaches to Aged Care

Approach	*Advantages*	*Disadvantages*
Mandatory social insurance (Germany, Korea, Rep., Japan)	Entitlement to benefit Affordable contribution (if income-related)	Limited tax base Rigidity in benefits awarded Implicit debt
Tax-based, universal systems	Broader tax base	No direct link between revenues and benefits Less transparency in benefit allocation Implicit debt
Private insurance	Theoretically neutral for the public budget	If voluntary: • Not affordable for people with low, insecure income • Adverse selection (If mandatory, may require subsidies for people with low incomes)

Source: European Commission 2014.

(including the People's Bank of China, MOCA, the China Banking Regulatory Commission, the China Securities Regulatory Commission, and the China Insurance Regulatory Commission) announced the establishment of an inter-ministerial working group to help develop innovative financing and insurance products. However, few of these measures are intended to address the financing of long-term care for individual consumers.

Public finance is a pre-condition for building a service market with wide coverage that is accessible for all clients in need and where consumers can exercise their choices. In OECD countries, long-term care is based on stable public financial resources (either tax-based or social insurance–based). Financial pressure has led to gradual adjustments, but the basics of wide coverage of quality services have been maintained. To increase the coverage and quality of aged care services in China, an effective and sustainable public financing system needs to be established. A mix of public and private payments should be designed and implemented. An important issue in the development of a robust public financing system in China would be the division of responsibilities for financing among the different layers of government.

In the short run, a tax-based system with eligibility based on need (defined as a combination of severity of limited functional ability and resources) may be appropriate for China, but a social insurance–based system would be most appropriate in the long run. In particular, China may wish to start with a broader but means-tested, public, long-term care financing system that is less restrictive than the current system, which focuses narrowly on the Three No's. A logical next step would be for the government to widen the safety net to cover a greater number of elders most in need of long-term care and direct public resources to them.

Changing public support for the aged care system in China from supporting providers through subsidies to supporting them by procuring their services through competitive bidding will greatly improve the efficiency of the system and of public expenditures, in particular. Increasing the purchasing capacity of specific groups and needy elderly persons will also serve two goals: equity and efficiency. In fact, there are various experiences at the local level in which the government has started to support individuals with limited allowances, either in cash or vouchers for eligible services. The support has been targeted at specific groups such as very old, frail, and isolated persons without consistent application of a needs assessment. While the funds are barely enough to cover significant amounts of long-term care, they do improve the financial position of people who are at a high risk of needing long-term care.

In terms of spending on long-term care relative to GDP, public spending is expected to increase in order to improve the depth and quality of care coverage.

Building a Regulatory Framework and Improving Quality Assurance

International Experience and Key Considerations

The stewardship role of the aged care market is typically centered in the government but is more than the formal government authorities—it joins together all actors at vertical levels (national, provincial, and local) and at the horizontal level (health, social policy, infrastructure, economy) that need to cooperate for a well-functioning aged care system. In addition to the government and care providers, a complex system like long-term care also requires specialized support structures, with specialized agencies, researchers, and networkers functioning as the interface between policy making and policy implementation (chapter 7).

The cornerstone of a well-functioning aged care system is a concise regulatory framework with rules and standards for both the supply and demand sides in rural and urban areas and for all social groups in need. With a regulatory framework, the government gets control over the achievement of policy goals and the level of public spending. The pillars of the regulatory framework are:

- accreditation of suppliers, ensuring that suppliers have the necessary managerial and technical capacity and resources;
- public procurement rules and procedures;
- eligibility rules and systems of needs assessment to determine the quantitative and qualitative needs of clients;
- service standards and quality assurance;
- qualification system for different types of care workers; and
- reporting and monitoring system.

Internationally, the most common approach to ensuring quality of long-term care is regulation—that is, ensuring that providers meet quality standards established by government agencies in order to be licensed to operate or to receive government funding. The role of government regulation in long-term care quality assurance is critical because long-term care consumers and their families are typically too disabled and vulnerable—physically, mentally, and/or socially—to change providers when they receive suboptimal care and thus cannot effectively use their exit from the provider to motivate improvements in quality. Moreover, in many countries, supply constraints mean that consumers have difficulty changing providers even if they are unhappy with the quality of the care they are receiving, as alternative providers are not available.

Accreditation of Service Providers. Most countries have established procedures for provider accreditation, and some have established specialized government agencies (e.g., the United Kingdom, Australia). This enables regulatory oversight of minimum standards for professional and organizational capacities and resources of care facilities, staff-client ratios, and skills requirements for care staff. Regular inspections (scheduled or unscheduled) are also a common practice.

In the United States, nursing homes and home health agencies are licensed by the states but must comply with federal quality standards in order to receive federal funding. Federal regulatory requirements cover a wide range of items, from inputs and structural capacity to care processes such as initial and periodic assessments for nursing home residents and home health consumers (Centers for Medicare and Medicaid Services 2015).

In the United Kingdom, providers have to register with the national Care Quality Commission and meet minimum quality standards in six key areas (see chapter 7 for details). The Care Quality Commission also conducts inspections of care providers. It has changed the practice of annual inspections and moved to a risk-based approach in which providers rated as requiring improvement or being inadequate are inspected more frequently than those with a good or outstanding rating. The regulatory framework has recently been amended, with a new Care Act coming into force in two steps (2015 and 2016).[22]

Australia requires residential and home care providers to be formally accredited by the Aged Care Standards and Accreditation Agency,[23] which is also a condition for receiving public funding. There are five basic standards (management system, staffing and organizational development, health and personal care, care recipient lifestyle, and physical environment and safety), each with principles and expected outcomes.

Accreditation of residential and home care providers is also mandatory in Japan. The prefectures are entrusted with certifying providers, and the municipalities are in charge of supervision and auditing. The standards for certification relate to staffing, complaints handling procedures and elder protection, management and administration, and services provided (chapter 7).

Eligibility Rules and Needs Assessment. Another important field of regulation concerns the processes of determining who is eligible for support and how to assess care needs. Usually, the national government defines the rules and standards and mandates local authorities, government agencies, or medical doctors (general practitioners) to carry out the assessment with the individual person.

As discussed earlier, there are two basic options concerning eligibility: a universal system open to all, and a means-tested system in which only people below a defined income level are eligible. Accordingly, assessment may take into account levels of limited functional ability and functional limitations as well as income levels.

Monitoring and Evaluation and Quality Assurance. A precondition for effective monitoring and quality assurance is a regulatory framework with defined quality standards and a national strategy with defined goals and measurable targets. Another precondition for monitoring and evaluation is the availability of reliable data regularly collected across China, which makes regulatory oversight possible. Common problems in most countries are data gaps and incoherent data. Monitoring standards and uniform reporting requirements also need to be in place.

As mentioned earlier, outcomes in social care are difficult to define and measure. With exceptions such as rehabilitation, most of long-term care aims to manage ongoing conditions to slow the decline of health and functioning rather than improve or cure them. All local authorities need to identify the outcomes that care services aim to achieve. Service contracts are frequently time- or task-based rather than outcome-based. They generally do not incentivize providers to rehabilitate or improve user independence. Moving to outcomes-based commissioning is not easy, and some local authorities need to develop their commissioning skills and capacity (Feiler et al. 2016).

It should be emphasized that quality assurance may be difficult without a robust public financing system to enforce sanctions for poor quality. Financing for providers, such as subsidies for new construction and operating costs and discounted charges for utilities, are not appropriate instruments for enforcing quality standards or building a market with fair competition.

Current Situation in China and Key Priorities

Formalizing the Regulatory Framework. In China, the regulatory framework for aged care is still at an early stage but progressing. China currently has three sets of national standards: the *Code for the Design of Buildings for Elderly Persons* (1999), *Basic Standards for Social Welfare Institutions for the Elderly* (2001), and *National Occupational Standards for Aged-Care Workers* (2002). To further formalize the licensing process, MOCA issued two new regulations, *Procedures for Licensing Senior Care Facilities* and *Measures for the Management of Senior Care Facilities*, both promulgated in 2013. Several additional sets of national standards governing senior care services are in the pipeline. These national standards are general principles and provide local governments with the flexibility to establish enforceable standards under the national principles. In 2014, MOCA, the Ministry of Commerce, and several other government agencies co-issued a policy document entitled *Guiding Opinions on Promoting the Standardization of Senior Care Services*, which states that comprehensive standards on a whole range of institutional and home- and community-based senior care services should be established by 2020.

To regulate and enhance human resource development and qualification standards, the government has adopted *National Occupational Standards for Aged Care Workers* (revised 2011). A minimum of 180 hours of training is required to get a basic certification for care work, and there are opportunities for higher qualification. According to a recent survey (China Philanthropy Research Institute 2015), more than 300,000 formal care workers are engaged in aged care, but less than one-third of them have formal qualifications. Given that 200,000 have participated in training in recent years, it appears that trained care workers are leaving the sector. The shortage of skilled workers, ranging from basic professional care workers to specialized staff such as nurses, dietitians, rehabilitation therapists, and psychologists, is a critical concern.

The *National Occupational Standards for Aged Care Workers* (2002) regulate the human resources of the aged care sector. Legal provisions for accrediting and managing service providers—*Procedures for Licensing Senior Care Facilities* and *Measures for the Management of Senior Care Facilities*—were adopted in 2013. These are general national standards that allow local governments to further specify the rules. Examples of provincial quality standards and rules can be found in the provinces of Zhejiang and Heilongjiang or the cities of Tianjin and Shanghai, where standards have been set for home care as well as for residential care (chapter 7).

The Government of China also made provisions to develop a comprehensive National Aged Care Information System (2011). This information system is designed to include a facility assessment system, a consumer assessment system, a service quality monitoring and management system, a query for regular facility inspections, a complaint management system, and a professional training system. A core element of the system is a database of aged care recipients and those in need of care, with a standardized needs assessment tool for individuals, the "Ability Assessment for Older Adults." The ambitious objective of the information system is to provide all levels of government with tools and data to regulate the care industry as well as to make information accessible for the wider public.

Enhancing Regulatory Oversight. Regulatory oversight should be the primary approach to quality assurance for aged care in China, moving toward a more uniform approach that builds upon successful regional and local experiences. Most of the recent developments in quality assurance were initiated by provincial and municipal governments under the overall guidelines from the central government. While this approach promotes innovation and provides opportunities for provinces and cities to learn from each other's experiences, there is considerable variation across geographic areas, and some areas may have inadequate standards and enforcement. Greater uniformity could strengthen the national quality assurance system and help eliminate geographical disparities in quality.

However, since formal long-term care services in China are still at an early stage of development, very strict regulations may not be advisable for two reasons. First, it can be too costly to be financially feasible or appealing to policy makers. This is particularly so in the current policy environment in which the main goal is to increase supply and build service capacity quickly, which seems to sideline concerns over quality assurance and regulatory oversight (Feng et al. 2014). Second, it may have the unintended effect of stifling private sector initiatives to further the growth of the industry. Instead, the current regulations should be made consistent and transparent, which would appeal to investors and facilitate their entry into the aged care market. The government could then gradually implement tighter regulations and stronger enforcement.

The review of international experiences in long-term care quality assurance highlights the importance of building a standardized information system for measuring, monitoring, and improving quality of care. This kind of information infrastructure can foster an evidence-based approach to policy making, quality improvements, and regulation. It entails the periodic collection of good-quality information on long-term care providers and service users.

However, China has little publicly available information on the characteristics of and quality of care provided by senior care service providers to aid quality monitoring or inform consumer choices (Feng et al. 2014). As in other countries, it would be more feasible to start with collecting such information from institutional care providers and their residents, then expand the data collection to home- and community-based service providers and their customers. Standardized tools to assess aged care providers (both institutional and home- and community-based) nationwide need to be developed and implemented.

It will also be important to further develop and implement standardized individual assessment tools to regularly assess seniors, particularly aged care recipients' function and other health-related conditions. The *Ability Assessment for Older Adults* proposed by MOCA and similar tools adopted by several provinces and cities provide a solid foundation for further development of a standardized tool. The National Commission on Aging and 24 national government agencies issued the *Opinions on Promoting Preferential Treatments for Seniors* in 2013, which requires that all health care institutions build health records for seniors age 65 years or older in their service regions and provide free annual physical exams and health consultations for them. These requirements provide opportunities for standardized assessment of seniors which may generate valuable data useful for quality assurance.

Given the importance of the skills and competencies of aged care professionals in delivering high-quality care, policies supporting aged care as a profession could have a profound impact on quality of care. In addition to the policies adopted by a few provinces and cities to subsidize aged care training and award caregivers who remain in the profession, further raising compensation (higher pay and better benefits) will attract more people with better education to enter this profession. This would improve the social status of people working in this industry, which in turn would improve the reputation of the profession, thereby creating a virtuous circle for the growth of aged care professionals.

Better compensation for the aged care industry will not only attract more people to become trained caregivers but will also attract more clinicians to work in aged care. Based on provincial reports in response to *Several Opinions of the State Council on Accelerating Development of the Aged Care Industry* (2013), 14 provinces view the shortage of caregivers capable of providing skilled care services as one of the main issues faced by the aged care industry (China Philanthropy Research Institute 2015). In particular, aged care facilities face shortages of clinicians such as medical staff, skilled nurses, social workers, dietitians, rehabilitation therapists, and counseling psychologists. Home- and community-based service agencies face the same challenge; most of them only focus on non-skilled services such as homemaking and meal delivery.

Finally, policy makers in China could act more forcefully on the "power of the purse" which, if used creatively, could be effective in incentivizing providers in regulatory compliance and quality improvements. The review of international experiences revealed that quality assurance for aged care is particularly challenging where public financing of such care is limited and the government thus has little stake or incentive to strengthen regulatory oversight and where providers have little reason to comply with government requirements. Therefore, the more the Chinese government has at stake (with increased public financing in the aged care service sector), the better positioned it will be to demand greater quality assurance and more effective regulatory oversight.

Building a Market of Private Service Providers and Developing Commissioner-Provider Relations

Key Considerations and International Experience

In recent decades, most OECD countries turned to nongovernmental, private organizations to implement or deliver social human services. Most European countries have well-developed social economy sectors ("third sector," NGOs, charities), and in some countries, they are major providers of elder care. In many Western European countries, the Red Cross or Caritas are large providers of residential and nursing home care. In the United Kingdom, Age UK is a big provider of day care, and organizations such as Anchor provide sheltered housing. These NGOs are equally financed with public funds as commercial providers.

Nonetheless, the role of the government in designing policies, ensuring financing, and overseeing service implementation remains. This new paradigm with shared tasks between public and private actors—often labeled the "New Public Management approach" (chapter 6)—ought to improve social services in various ways: making the delivery system more innovative, flexible, and responsive to clients' needs while making social services more cost-efficient.

Outsourced service provision creates a "quasi-market" with a triangle system consisting of a public contractor, a private service provider, and the individual to be served (figure O.8). Different from conventional markets, there is a split between the public contractor and the provider system, which may include private as well as public and not-for-profit organizations. Various service providers are selected and contracted by a public contractor then chosen by clients who are free to choose their preferred service providers (or who at least have a voice in expressing their satisfaction with service quality), creating market competition (Feiler et al. 2016).

A typical problem of a quasi-market like the aged care service sector is market imperfection. A public contractor acts on behalf of the clients but pursues

Figure O.8 Service Provision Triangle in Aged Care: a "Quasi-Market"

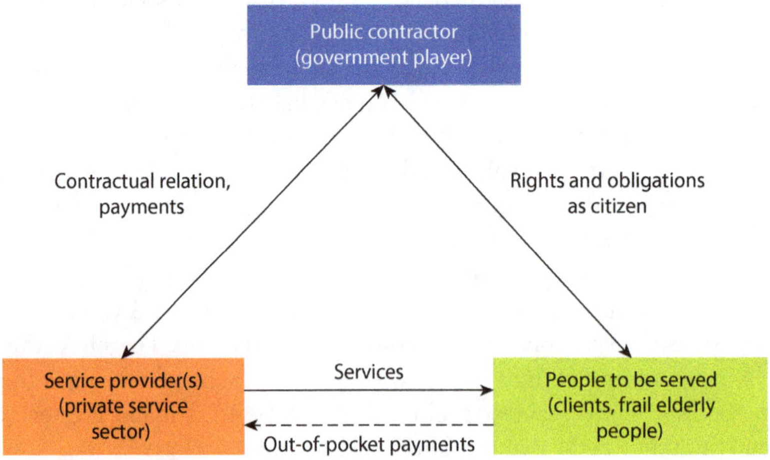

multiple objectives (e.g., quality of care, cost containment) and does not have full information. Clients of aged care services also tend to lack information and rarely have the opportunity to choose freely among different providers.[24] Free choice and the possibility of changing providers is more feasible in the case of home care services but rather limited in the case of residential care, as the move from one facility to another can be a challenging endeavor. To overcome the pitfalls and risks of market failures, governments apply instruments to regulate markets, such as commissioning (contracting) rules, accreditation of providers, service standards, and monitoring (chapter 7). Users can be empowered to choose their preferred providers or even be given purchasing power with cash transfers or vouchers (Feiler et al. 2016; Le Grand 2011).

In a transparent and flexible market with an enabling regulatory framework that is enforced, new providers can enter the market, good performers can grow, and bad performers will exit the market. A network of different types of private providers—large and small, profit-oriented and NPOs—ensure that consumer needs and demands can be met in urban as well as in more remote rural areas.

An explicit commissioning strategy of the government is a set of tools to define the characteristics of the elderly care delivery system and address its specific objectives, including quality improvement, integrated service provision, encouragement of innovative approaches, ensuring national standards, equity of service delivery, and containment of expenditures (Feiler et al. 2016). As cooperation in the "quasi market" is as important as competition, it also needs to avoid trade-offs (chapter 6). The commissioning of social care involves collaboration not only between local authority commissioners and independent providers but also among different public agencies to ensure a service continuum with integrated health and social services.

Executing a coherent commissioning strategy requires the continuing development of capacities and capabilities. It entails more than organizing public procurement, starting from shaping and defining the market, to stewardship of the market, and ending with monitoring and improving overall service performance. All stages of the process require actions on the part of the government.

Implications for the Current Situation in China

China can benefit from advancements in the service commissioning literature and the experience of other countries while adapting the approach to China's unique culture and social context. Following international trends and the New Public Management (NPM) approach, efficient care provision will depend on the successful implementation of a transparent and flexible care market. The market design must reward good providers and allow them to grow, while bad providers must be held accountable for poor performance and ultimately exit the market. However, in the context of long-term care, these important market mechanisms must act within a regulatory framework and require government oversight and sufficient funding to ensure an adequate supply of high-quality care for the population. Stages of a government commissioning strategy are presented in figure O.9, and its application to China is discussed below.

Figure O.9 Stages of a Governmental Commissioning Strategy

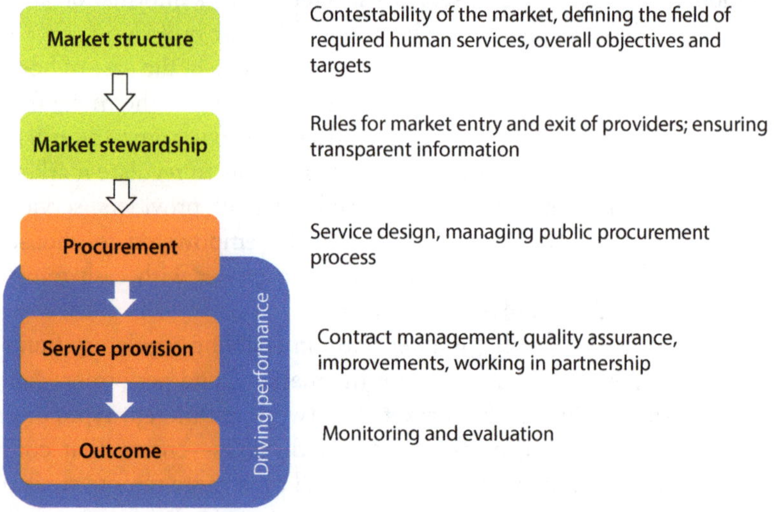

Source: Based on Gash et al. 2013.

Market Structure. The design of the market structure is a core government task and requires a debate on the overall policy goals of the long-term care market and the general market structure needed to achieve those goals. As highlighted in the 2011 *12th Five-Year Plan for the Development of China's Undertakings for the Aged,* the government aims at "establishing a basic strategic framework to deal with ageing; formulating and implementing medium and long-term plans for the development" that provides "universal coverage of basic old-age security" in urban and rural areas. More specifically, long-term care should be focused on home-based services and promote family and voluntary involvement. The government also plans to increase beds in residential care places by 3.42 million over the five years. To reach those goals, the private sector may be incentivized by preferential policies. In addition, the government will "formulate policies with regard to the purchase of services for elderly people with special needs by the government." While these regulations provide a broad framework for a long-term care industry and generally follow the direction of international developments, there is little emphasis on user choices, and public funding is mostly provided to the supply side of the market.

Market Stewardship. Against this backdrop, the national government needs to execute market stewardship to ensure that these goals are reached. To date, reality still lags behind many of the aspirations. For example, despite the emphasis on home care, most financial resources have been used to increase residential care capacity (Feng et al. 2012). In addition, the way public funding is allocated to providers often lacks competition, and many private providers face uneven competition with well-funded state providers (Wu, Mao, and Zhong 2009). Such issues are related to a lack of sufficient government oversight and unclear responsibilities that hinder the performance of the sector.

Good stewardship is challenging and requires a specific set of capabilities, which include understanding of the policy environment and market dynamics and knowledge of finance and business. Efficient oversight also requires a high level of professionalism in the government to manage the complex interplay among all stakeholders. A successful long-term care market in which the public sector commissions non-state providers to offer a broad range of services to the elderly relies on professional government activity at every stage of the process, from the national to the local level. The government needs to acknowledge this challenge and promote the change in responsibilities and tasks in all participating public entities. Commissioning bodies should be professional, and the responsible individuals require adequate training (Gash et al. 2013). For example, England has established a Commissioning Academy that aims to train public employees who work on defining policy, shaping public service provision, or allocating resources for services to citizens.

Because regulatory oversight requires a clear understanding of the market and all parties involved, the government should implement an information system to gather statistics on care demand and ensure consistent data collection across all regions. For the allocation of funds and proper capacity planning, the government not only needs to understand current demand but should also anticipate future developments. The government should also engage with all stakeholders, such as users, various types of providers, and local authorities, to improve the understanding of the market and incorporate different perspectives into decision making, as oversight requires knowledge of both the demand and the supply sides of care (Gash et al. 2013).

The government should also enable consumer choice by providing them with sufficient information about service quality and prices to help with rational decision making. Countries like Germany, England, and the United States have set up rating websites that support the elderly and their family members in finding the right provider. If different choices are available, such evaluation systems enable consumers to execute an important market function by choosing the best providers. Particularly in home care markets, experience has shown that consumers who are "voting with their feet" can positively affect service quality. Ultimately, the goal of social service provision is to increase consumer well-being, so consumers themselves should be viewed as an important part of a successful market.

Failure in social service provision and public oversight is often related to lack of accountability and unclear responsibilities among different players, so the national government needs to assign clear roles and structure the public entities accordingly. A well-designed accountability system also includes monitoring and enforcement. The Community Care Act in England entrusts local authorities to ensure a working care market. This decentralization of responsibility provides some leeway for innovation, with local governments having the opportunity to cooperate with providers to create new solutions which can be scaled up if successful.

Sufficient funding should be provided to the commissioning entities based on local demand. Excessive budget pressure on commissioners or providers usually leads to a deterioration in service performance and can reduce user choices (Gash et al. 2013). One way to reduce budget pressure is to implement some sort of means testing, which allows the use of less public funds for people with better ability to pay. As shown in the case of Hong Kong SAR, China, if public subsidies are given to providers (rather than to consumers) this might be more difficult to achieve (Chui 2011).

Even though market mechanisms should ultimately crowd out bad service providers, control mechanisms are needed to ensure the health and dignity of service users. Virtually all care systems reviewed here rely on some sort of accreditation or licensing to ensure a minimum level of quality. To ensure long-term compliance, a neutral entity should monitor providers and report misconduct to the government. However, monitoring efforts should be suitable and not too costly for small providers (Irish, Salamon, and Simon 2009).

Procurement. To ensure equal opportunities, procurement practices should be specified at the national level to guide local procurement activities (NDRC 2015). Although procurement of long-term care services is regulated under the *Law of Government Purchasing of the People's Republic of China*, the available legislation is vague and provides an insufficient framework which is not properly enforced. Successful public procurement requires an appropriate legal framework in order to be sustainable, with rules that are transparent and properly enforced to ensure that the best candidate is able to make the best offer. Commissioning entities need to provide sufficient information and increase communication with providers to remove information asymmetries. A clear understanding of the procurement item is needed on both sides to improve the efficiency of the process and ensure the service performance of successful providers. In addition, service contracts should include incentive arrangements to encourage cost savings, efficiency, and effectiveness (Irish, Salamon, and Simon 2009).

If the Chinese government wants to increase service quality, procurement should go beyond the common practice of construction and operation subsidies based on beds provided (NDRC 2015). In addition, public procurement is often too focused on price rather than quality. Particularly in the case of long-term care, measuring the quality of the service is difficult. However, if contracts are only awarded to the lowest bidder, this is often associated with a race to the bottom in quality. Good commissioning drives innovation by influencing providers to achieve better overall outcomes (Gash et al. 2013). The review of long-term care systems shows that commissioners use multiple instruments to transfer public funding to providers. Particularly in light of China's continued efforts to expand health insurance among the population, commissioners can, for example, create incentives that foster integrated services and prevention within residential homes. An example from the United States shows that such services are often underdeveloped in a free market but can lead to better health for the elderly and lower costs for the health sector (Grabowski et al. 2015).

Service Provision. Commissioning non-state companies for service provision poses a certain risk for the government as it separates the responsibility for high-quality services from the actual provision, making it important to ensure that the companies have the necessary capabilities. This inherent principal-agent problem is usually addressed with contracts and competition, although some countries like Germany engage in a cooperative partnership with private providers and build a relationship of trust. Nonprofit organizations (NPOs), in particular, share common goals with the local government as they usually have no desire for rent seeking. However, strong government involvement in the daily management of many NPOs hampers competition in the public bidding process.

As the history of private NPOs is relatively short in China, those institutions often lack professionalism and sufficient financial means to invest. Shortage of skills is still a common issue for providers of long-term care in Western countries, which can lead to low service quality and high staff turnover. The government should invest in such institutions to develop their innovative potential and help them grow to become independent and capable partners in the provision of long-term care services (NDRC 2015; Teets and Jagusztyn 2013). In many European countries, regulation fosters government collaboration with non-state institutions and requires incorporating welfare corporations into large parts of the planning and design of service provision (Irish, Salamon, and Simon 2009).

To ensure a broad range of services, the government needs to give adequate incentives to the market and provide sufficient and transparent funding to providers. Providers must be able to at least recover their full costs, and low government funding is linked to higher user fees. If the government wants to expand access to long-term care services to the less affluent who can only afford low user fees, sufficient funding must be provided. Only large financial incentives provide the government with enough leverage to influence user fees.

Outcomes. The long-term care market is prone to market failures, and despite substantial efforts, no country has found a best-practice solution yet. All care systems reviewed suffer from dangerously escalating costs and require regular adjustments. The development of a service market with non-state provision requires much "learning by doing" and constant adaptation and improvement. However, measuring long-term care performance is a difficult endeavor.

To achieve the desired outcomes, it will be important to ensure careful monitoring of the progress and performance of the long-term care system. Internationally, performance measures have shifted from outputs (e.g., beds available) to outcomes. In England, for instance, measures include users' quality of life, independence, and experience of care. A systematic, continuous, and independent evaluation of outcomes allows the government to assess provider performance, helps ensure comparable service quality between local governments, and allows the objective evaluation of local innovation. Easily accessible information that is available in a timely manner helps ensure service supply and allows for quick action if needed.

Service Integration—Dovetailing Social Care with Health Services

Aged care services have two elements: health and social. Ensuring coordination of and continuity in medical care and long-term care is necessary as it enhances the quality of care and patient experience and is more cost-effective.

International Experience

A common challenge in many countries' health care and long-term care delivery systems is the lack of integration of different services across different programs or settings, both within long-term care and across acute medical care and long-term care. This leads to fragmented care for older people for whom both types of care may be necessary. The fragmentation of programs, services, and benefits for long-term care recipients often contributes to misaligned incentives such as cost shifting between payers and providers and also increases the cost to the individuals and to society (chapter 8).

Coordinating social care and health care services is especially challenging because in most countries, the health care system is separate from the provision and regulation of long-term care, even though the lines are not always clear-cut. Health and social care are usually under totally different regulatory frameworks, have different organizational structures, are provided by different professionals, and use different financing and payment models. Among the few countries that offer public long-term care insurance (Germany, Japan, and Korea), long-term care insurance is operated separately from the health insurance system.

Integration of different kinds of services is no easy task in several respects. First, the necessary services and manpower must be available. Second, these services should be connected somehow through both physical and informational links and financial incentives. Third, systematic and normative goals and values are necessary so that important system engineering can be implemented.

Care coordination increasingly dominates the service delivery landscape in many OECD countries (chapter 8). It consists of a mix of measures that link professionals and organizations at all levels of the health system, emphasize patient-centered care integration, manage patient referrals through the delivery system, and promote follow-up care as well as the continuity of long-term service provision.

The concept of care coordination is often based on the strong role of primary care as the driver of coordination functions, including gatekeeping. Such a model anticipates and shapes patterns of care according to the projected health and medical needs of the population while placing considerable emphasis on strengthening the role and raising the quality of primary care. It considers changing demands such as the aging of the population, the rapid increase in chronic diseases, significant strengthening of community-focused care, the vertical and horizontal integration of facilities (physical, as well as in areas of information and communication) to provide comprehensive services along a continuum or chain of care, and using primary care as the point of entry into the system.

Recent OECD experience suggests an emerging delivery model in which considerable emphasis is placed on primary care (as a gatekeeper and "case manager"), defined links among providers, and specialized outpatient and day surgical treatment, which reduces the need for inpatient beds. The international trend is toward the transfer of services currently provided in hospitals to community-based ambulatory centers or telemedicine clinics. Rapid advances in information and communication technology (ICT) are facilitating this trend (Leichsenring and Alaszewski 2004). Several East Asian economies have also launched initiatives to integrate health and long-term care for the elderly. More specifically:

- One community-based care program present throughout the region is the Republic of Korea-Association of Southeast Asian Nations (ROK-ASEAN) Home Care Program, supported by HelpAge International. This program, which builds on the success of a home care model involving volunteers in Korea, has been implemented in ASEAN economies with adaptations to the local context (ROK-ASEAN Cooperation Fund 2013).
- Older people's groups (or "senior citizens' clubs") operate or are planned in Brunei, Japan, and Thailand and can offer support networks, health information dissemination, and fitness activities (Kasim 2013; UNFPA and HelpAge International 2011).
- The Japanese government is trying to integrate long-term care and health care with a primary emphasis on community-based care, and a general practitioner's assessment is required as part of the long-term-care triage process.
- In Singapore, the Agency for Integrated Care was created in 2009 to bring about a patient-focused integration of primary, intermediate, and long-term care. It is operating at all levels—patient, provider, and system—and it works to have providers at all levels coordinate their efforts on behalf of the patient (AIC 2015).
- Thailand has piloted a "home health care" scheme through 26 local hospitals, targeted at older people living at home, with services including health promotion, treatment, and rehabilitation. Thailand has also piloted service models that integrate health and social care—the "Bangkok 7 Model" and the "Community-Based Integrated Services of Health Care and Social Welfare" for Thai Older Persons, which involve collaboration among local authorities, volunteers, and older people. (HelpAge International 2015 provides further references.)

Implications for the Current Situation in China

Continuity of care, a major tenet of coordinated care, is still in its infancy in China. There is still very limited cross-referral across the three tiers of health facilities to ensure that health conditions are managed at the most appropriate and cost-effective level. Competition among hospitals for revenues provides few incentives to coordinate care with primary care units or other hospitals, contributing to "disintegrated" behaviors such as lack of referrals and follow-up care. The well-recognized poor quality of primary care providers also leads patients to seek care in hospitals.[25]

Another major challenge in the health sector that is relevant to care coordination is China's existing bias in spending toward hospitals relative to OECD countries.[26] This bias appears to be intensifying, and the system is becoming increasingly "top heavy," which will increase costs and contribute little to improving health outcomes. Despite the massive expansion of grassroots facilities and beds in both urban and rural areas, recent government data show that hospitals continue to gain an increasing share of both outpatient visits and inpatient admissions. Of special concern is that expensive tertiary public hospitals are registering the most growth in both inpatients and outpatients compared to lower-cost first- and second-level hospitals. Since 2005, the bed-to-population ratio has increased 56 percent, and admission rates have more than doubled. This tendency toward more beds and admissions runs counter to international trends: in the OECD, the bed-to-population ratio and admission rates are rapidly declining as countries shift to more cost-effective ambulatory care models and adapt new technologies that reduce hospital use.[27]

The fundamental health care reform initiated in 2009 is a realignment of the health delivery system away from the current hospital-centric model to one which manages care across levels of the system, with primary care providers playing the key role in care coordination. Three key elements of health reforms include: reorienting the delivery system with a greater emphasis on primary and preventive care, reforming health financing and incentive systems, and deepening reforms of the hospital system.

In 2015, the Chinese central government issued national guidelines for integrating medical and social care. The guidelines set an ambitious goal of making all elder care facilities capable of providing medical/health care by 2020 and outline a number of important steps, including: establishing and completing collaborative models between the health care and social aged care sectors; supporting aged care facilities to provide health care services; pushing health care services to the community and to the households; incentivizing the private sector to develop integrated health and social service projects; encouraging the development of facilities that provide both health and social services; implementing preferential tax and land policies to cultivate the private sector; and supporting the development of manpower and human resources. These reforms are necessary to meet the challenges of population aging, the increasing burden of chronic diseases, and the rising demand for both health care and long-term care. If successful, these reforms will put China on a solid path toward establishing an integrated and coordinated care delivery system.

However, there will be many systematic and operational challenges at both the national and local levels in implementing these guidelines. For example, one major problem is that most elder care facilities have so little medical/health care available currently. While building the infrastructure and providing the necessary devices may not be difficult, the challenge is to find and retain qualified medical professionals (physicians and non-physician practitioners). Without substantial financial incentives or career advancement opportunities, diverting health professionals to non-hospital settings is extremely difficult. Another challenge concerns financing and regulation: as mentioned above, social and health care services are generally regulated by different governmental functions and under different insurance/public funding schemes. Whether health care and elder care financing can be coordinated effectively has important implications for how well the services can be integrated.

To achieve higher care quality and efficiency in the aged care system, the large gaps in coordination of services—both within long-term care and across medical care and long-term care—need to be addressed. To be affordable and sustainable, the development of aged care services should proceed in close coordination with the ongoing reforms that shape health services provision and utilization. At the same time, health care reforms should take into account expected demographic changes and the fact that the increasing share of elderly in the population will lead to increasing demand for health services.

Strengthening the Aged Care Workforce

Maintaining an Adequate Long-Term Care Workforce Is a Common Challenge in All Economies

An adequate long-term care workforce includes workers and professionals with a range of skills and credentials. In all countries, the majority of them are frontline workers who provide hands-on help with basic ADL such as eating, dressing, bathing, and toileting. They are typically women who are certified nurse aides, home health care aides, and home or personal care workers. They are generally low-skilled workers requiring minimal training in most countries. The long-term care workforce also includes long-term care facility administrators and licensed health professionals, including registered nurses, licensed practical or vocational nurses, social workers, physical therapists, occupational therapists, and physician assistants or aides. Relatively few in numbers, these skilled professionals usually assume supervisory or managerial responsibilities rather than providing direct, hands-on care (Stone and Harahan 2010). In only a few countries (such as the Netherlands), physicians are directly involved in the provision of long-term care (chapter 9).

Many countries face a chronic shortage of long-term care workers, especially of well-trained and skilled workers. Recruiting and retaining direct-care workers in long-term care settings is particularly challenging due to many factors, including demanding working conditions, low wages, low job prestige, few fringe benefits, and limited career options and career paths. Often viewed as dead-end jobs, these positions are characterized by high turnover, low retention, and high job dissatisfaction. These workforce challenges are common across OECD countries (Colombo et al. 2011). Despite numerous policy efforts aimed at addressing these challenges, unfortunately there are few successes that can be readily shared and replicated in different countries.

The skills shortage is a particularly acute issue. Private providers in a competitive service market are challenged to develop not only the technical and social skills of their care workers but also state-of-the-art managerial skills. The development of social service markets tends to trigger a process of voluntary professionalization and NPOs to embrace ethical principles and guidelines, compliance standards, staff training and advisory services for partners, and quality assurance procedures. However, these voluntary efforts toward professionalism may take a long time to materialize.

Training requirements for formal aged care workers vary from country to country. In the United States, federal law requires a minimum 75 hours of training or passing a certification exam for a certified nurse aide, and some states may have additional requirements. European countries often have more extended qualification requirements. Formalized initial and continuous training is in place for personal home care in 60 percent of European countries and for domestic helpers in 25 percent of the countries (Feiler et al. 2016). In Thailand, a training course over three months leads to formal qualification of care assistants.

From a policy perspective, potential solutions to tackle the long-standing workforce issues in the long-term care sector include establishing and enforcing occupational standards (job descriptions), ensuring adequate wages, and mandating initial and continuous staff training. Working conditions may be improved by offering supervision (coaching) and making use of ICT tools to support and supplement personal care (e.g., the use of telecare). For example, alarm systems are common in most European countries, where GPS tracking and video communications are also being tested in various aged care settings.

The Shortage of a Well-Trained Aged Care Workforce in China

China lacks a qualified long-term care workforce, and skilled care workers are particularly lacking. Although there are national occupational standards for aged care workers in place and formal training is organized by MOCA, the Ministry of Labor, and other government-approved organizations, enforcement of those standards is at the local level, and the effectiveness of the training is limited. As a result, a large skills gap and the shortage of trained care workers persist, especially in rural areas. It is estimated that the elder care industry in China needs 10 million care workers, of which a great majority would work in institutional care facilities. However, by 2015, the industry only had 1 million care workers, of which merely 20,000 had undertaken some official training (chapter 9). The shortage of nurses in China's residential care facilities, which have about 3.1 million occupied beds, is estimated to reach 600,000 (DRC 2015).

In urban areas, the majority of skilled care workers are employed in elder care institutions, while home- and community-based services are provided mainly by non-professional staff. In rural areas, there are very few skilled care workers even in elder care homes, much less in home- and community-based care settings.

The development of elder care in rural areas lags far behind that in urban areas, and in general, family care remains the dominant form of elder care. The concentration of skilled care workers in urban residential aged care facilities mirrors the pattern of health care professionals concentrated in county- or higher-level hospitals rather than in lower-level primary health care facilities.

Elder care workers in China are predominantly middle-aged females who have low levels of education, are mostly from rural areas, and are highly mobile (chapter 9). Few of them have received professional training, so their jobs are limited to simple tasks such as housekeeping, purchasing necessities, delivering meals, basic personal care, companionship, and chatting with the elderly. Many of them are not trained to provide professional care for disabled elders needing specialized care.

In addition, China does not have enough qualified social workers, who can play a critical role in elder care. Only a small number of care homes in major cities have social workers. Moreover, professional social workers in elderly care institutions and communities are generally young, and while they have a passion for work and a good reserve of theoretical knowledge, they often lack the ability to translate theory into practical skills (chapter 9).

Physicians and other health care personnel such as physical or occupational therapists and professional nurses are rarely available in current senior care facilities in China. The shortage of health care professionals has critical implications for elder care institutions, which need medical support. While some urban elder care institutions are staffed with professional medical personnel, home- and community-based service providers as well as rural elder care homes rely mainly on existing medical resources within the locality, which are often inadequate.

Barriers to Further Growth of the Aged Care Workforce

One of the main concerns for the aged care industry in China is the low pay and lack of job security for its workforce. Wages for care workers are generally low, although there are large regional differences, and their working conditions are precarious. Only 65 percent of elder care workers have formal labor contracts (chapter 9). Domestic care workers are not covered by labor market regulations in China so labor laws do not apply to them, and they are not organized in trade unions.

Social attitudes are also unfavorable toward elder care workers, who generally have low social status in China. The job of elder care workers is to serve others in need, and according to traditional notions, such service jobs are not "decent." Furthermore, taking care of the elderly is arduous, especially taking care of those who are unable to function independently.

Low wages for care workers are partly related to the fact that it is difficult to raise service fees and charges for elder care. Given the meager retirement income for most urban retirees (about RMB 2,000 per month on average), they are very sensitive to the amounts charged by elder care institutions. Some believe that public elder care institutions should not charge too much. To maintain social stability, local governments are also reluctant to increase charges for elder care in public facilities. In addition, home- and community-based service providers, which are currently less popular among elders due to the limited availability and narrow coverage of services, tend to lower prices to attract more customers, which in turn restricts pay raises for care workers.

The medical staffs of elder care institutions, in particular, suffer from poor compensation and lack of stability. Attending physicians in residential care homes may earn only half of what those working in hospitals earn, while nurses earn one-third of what their hospital counterparts earn (chapter 9). Thus, residential care homes in general lack appeal to physicians and licensed nurses. Moreover, medical practitioners working in elder care facilities may also face greater constraints in career advancement and have low professional self-identity and sense of satisfaction. However, some public elder care institutions can often provide permanent staff status (and thus more stability) and even household registration (*hukou*) and higher social status, which are attractive to specialized technicians. Few private institutions offer such advantages.

Supporting and Upgrading the Aged Care Workforce

To address the shortage of high-quality workers in long-term care, stabilizing and elevating the status of elder care workers is a critical priority going forward. To retain and incentivize the current aged care workforce, Chinese policy makers should focus on finding sustainable ways to raise the wages of these workers, and local governments must eventually increase minimum wages for elder care workers. Another labor-related need is *hukou* reform, which would allow more workers to migrate from low-income areas to cities where they can learn caregiving skills and serve the growing ranks of senior citizens.

More medical staff and social workers also need to be brought into the elder care sector. In particular, the industry needs to create a good environment for nurses, raise their pay level, and encourage them to be case managers and managers of nursing homes. Along with retired doctors, Chinese nurses must be empowered to become nursing home managers to meet the need for skilled professionals.

At the same time, informal caregivers should be given more support. This could be accomplished through strengthening professional instruction for family members and community volunteers, providing appropriate subsidies to family members and community volunteers for their services, and increasing supervision of the market for live-in nannies and housekeeping services.

Increasing Investment in Education and Training

China's 12th Five-Year Plan for the Development of Aged Care Services and Undertakings on Aging stipulates that the training of elder care professionals shall be accelerated, especially the training of elder care paramedics and elder care managers. In 2011, MOCA issued the "National Civil Affairs Professionals Mid- and Long-Term Development Plan (2010–2020)," aimed at strengthening human resources. In 2014, the Ministry of Education, MOCA, and seven other ministries jointly issued "Opinions on Accelerating the Training of Elderly Care Professionals."

Many initiatives are being undertaken to increase and improve training availability at the local level. For example, Henan Province has set up training courses in several colleges and vocational schools and is adopting distance learning methods. The local government of Shandong requires that all aged care providers train their staff. Providers with a certification rate of their staff below 85 percent do not receive public subsidies. Luzhou city in Sichuan Province trains aged care workers in courses offered by colleges and technical schools. Shizuishan city (in Jingxia) has set up aged care training at the Shizuishan Social Welfare Institute, which provides a 21-day training course and issues the national entrance-level aged care provider certificate.

Investment in education and training of new and experienced personnel is essential to build a high-quality workforce. Care workers need to be professionalized to raise their status and to equip them with the skills necessary to respond to a wide range of needs, including not only nursing skills but also social care skills. To this end, the formal system of education for elder care needs to be reformed. An evaluation and assessment of the effectiveness of teaching and training programs and schools is needed. Courses and curricula should be structured such that more emphasis is placed on practice rather than theory and on how care can be delivered in homes and communities. The quality of education also depends to a large extent on the faculty, so the government could look into expanding incentives (particularly financial incentives) to recruit high-quality teachers and staff who are equipped to impart the knowledge and skills needed to produce well-trained elder care providers.

At the same time, education and technical support is needed for all providers along the care continuum to help them improve the quality of care and meet established government standards. Funding for new training institutes may be needed. Policies to promote training for service staff must be encouraged and employment with proper certification made mandatory.

Even for professionals such as doctors and nurses, it will be important for them to gain knowledge of gerontology and other special needs care in order to provide better services for the elderly. Special needs care includes areas such as dementia care, rehabilitation, mental and physical rehabilitation combined through psycho-motor therapy, and traditional Chinese medicine for health management. The government could promulgate policies that allow public hospital doctors to provide services in private practices and even at home. Such forms of training for nurses, caregivers, and other specialists could be added to curricula at universities, vocational schools, or online education.

Training could also be geared toward improving the management of elder care services. The care manager, still a relatively new concept in China, is responsible for doing a needs assessment and helping to coordinate among health and other services, which is vital to delivering the appropriate products and services to the elderly. Although most institutions do not have such positions, China can prepare early by educating a new generation of care plan managers now.

In summary, investment in education and training for professional care workers is crucial for delivering efficient and quality services. Training curricula need to be practice-relevant and lead to formal qualifications. Qualified and experienced teachers are needed. Courses and curricula should be structured in a way that more attention is given to practice rather than to theory and to care in home- and community-based settings. Continuous training of care staff should be made mandatory. Training in the specific skills and competencies required to care for patients with multiple chronic problems, dementia, and those at the end of life are needed. Training policies should also include administrative and managerial staffs. Last but not least, training opportunities should also be available for informal caregivers.

Sequencing, Priorities, and the Interplay with Other Key Reforms

The social compact for publicly financed elderly care will evolve in China as the country progresses toward upper-middle-income status. The success of the Chinese economy and the pace of social sector reforms (health and pensions) have created rising expectations from citizens that coverage and quality of services will continue to deepen at the same pace as in recent years. China will, however, inevitably face the dilemma seen in many OECD countries of setting a sustainable level of entitlement. The social compact regarding aged care is key in deciding how to apply international experience in the aged care industry to develop efficient and sustainable options for China.

Related to this, ensuring the availability of the aged care continuum should not be viewed as yet another big expenditure item or an entitlement that cannot be afforded. The view on aging needs to be positive: seeing it as a sign of progress and an opportunity for innovation, not as a crisis. How China prepares itself for an aged society will help the government respond to the needs of its citizens. It will also help shape much of its future service industry and market and offer a major source of domestic consumption.

In China as in other counties all over the world, most older people prefer "aging in place"—to live in their own homes for as long as possible. Chinese policy makers should be careful to avoid an institutional bias in the country's fledgling long-term care system. Instead, they should use available policy instruments (e.g., tax exemptions, subsidies, and other financial incentives) to help build a balanced mix of services across home, community, and institutional settings that reflect older people's preferences and best meet their needs.

While the government should continue to support public provision of aged care targeting needy and vulnerable elders, the best approach would be to leverage resources and complementary capacities from the public and private sectors to create a functioning market for elderly care. The government should continue to encourage greater participation of the private sector while strengthening its stewardship capacities and commissioner-provider relationships.

While the aged care landscape in China is evolving rapidly, government regulatory oversight remains weak. The review of international experiences revealed that quality assurance for aged care is challenging where public financing of such care is minimal, as providers have little incentive to comply with government requirements. The more the Chinese government has at stake (with increased public financing in the aged care service sector), the better positioned it will be to demand greater quality assurance and more effective regulatory oversight.

While China is still at an early stage of developing its aged care sector, ensuring care coordination and continuity both within and across the medical care and long-term care systems is a crucial consideration. Integrated care for the elderly and person-centered care put the clients in the central role and asks what they need in order to remain at home and autonomous and to raise the quality of their lives. This is a fundamental shift from current practice in which care systems tend to operate in their own interest and in ways that are most convenient for the service provider rather than the service user. This enhances the quality of care and patient experience and is more cost-effective than the current segregated aged care systems.

At present, the lack of a qualified and professional workforce in long-term care is an urgent issue in China. The majority of direct care workers are inadequately trained and poorly paid. However, inadequate training for direct care workers is not the only impediment. Professional clinical and management staff are also needed to ensure a transition to a modern, information-based long-term care delivery system. Chinese policy makers should prioritize education and training to develop a professionalized long-term care workforce.

An added challenge in China is that policy makers need to think about the distinctly different features of aged care provision and delivery in urban and rural areas, which are sharply divided (as they have always been) and characterized by considerable inequalities and disparities, economically and socially. In particular, in urban areas, demand is characterized by higher purchasing power of consumers, availability of more skilled labor, and the proximity of medical resources. There are also economies of scale in service provision in densely populated urban areas. Under a conducive policy regime, the development of viable business models in urban areas is therefore feasible. In contrast, rural areas experience a major outflow of prime-aged individuals and thus are deprived of both informal care and formal workers. Considerably lower purchasing capacity, coupled with lower population density, makes market development in rural areas particularly challenging. Public role in both aged care financing and provision will remain critical in rural areas and should focus on supporting innovative and promising new models of care for all in need of care (as opposed to continued focus on residential care facilities for *wubao* and *san wu* elders only). The magnitude of the rural challenge depends on *hukou* reform, which if it proceeds would allow the migration of entire families to urban areas. If those currently in their 40s and 50s can move to urban settings with their adult children, it could help facilitate the meeting of care needs as they age.

Although the review of international experiences in long-term care policy and practice as presented in this volume provides useful guidance, policy makers in China ultimately need to develop a viable aged care delivery system that best suits the Chinese cultural, socioeconomic, political, and health care contexts. Starting with a relatively blank slate, this system is still in the early stage of development. Many important components of this system need to be developed soon, with potentially competing demands for limited resources.

In terms of prioritization, three critical priority areas emerge from the analysis of aged care issues presented in this report:

- Urgently build up government stewardship capacities and develop the relationship with private sector providers;
- Empower consumers by shifting subsidies toward services and care recipients, not beds and providers; and
- Extend long-term care financing in a systemic yet sustainable way.

As reforms of China's aged care sector are implemented, the reform parameters will need to be adjusted in line with those in other related sectors and with broader socioeconomic developments in China. Trends and outcomes in several closely related areas—such as the availability of fiscal resources, the directions of pension and health systems reforms, the *hukou* system, and labor market participation of women—will be critical determinants of the demand for aged care and the supply of informal care. Interdependencies between different policy and reform areas and their impact on the evolving aged care sector need to be considered and anticipated. More specifically:

- The health care sector in China is currently undergoing a wave of profound reforms. One of the major reform goals is to shift medical resources and health care utilization away from hospitals to community-based clinics and health centers, thereby strengthening the role of primary care providers. Other goals include reforming public hospitals and encouraging the private sector to enter the health care market. More broadly, the reform seeks to reorient the medical system to a people-centered integrated care (PCIC) delivery model that is organized around the health needs of individuals and families. The bedrock of a high-performing PCIC model is a strong primary care system that is integrated with secondary and tertiary care through formal linkages and has good data, information sharing among providers and between providers and patients, and active engagement of patients in their care. These health sector reforms may create opportunities for the aged care sector, in which a new model to integrate medical care and long-term care is being actively promoted by government and service providers.[28] If the PCIC model for health care delivery succeeds in China, home- and community-based aged care will become a piece in the mosaic of the overall chain of integrated care.
- China is reforming its *hukou* system. In fact, the target set forth in the 13th Five-Year Plan is to increase the proportion of population with an urban *hukou* from 37 percent in 2014 to 45 percent by 2020. This means that an additional 100 million rural migrants will obtain urban *hukou* by 2020 and hence social benefit coverage. The 13th Five-Year Plan also promotes nationwide implementation of a resident permit scheme entitling non-*hukou* residents to basic public services coverage. These reforms will have a

strong impact on the demand and supply of aged care by allowing adult children, who are the main providers of informal care, to bring their parents (and grandparents) with them when they move to the cities. There will then be less need for aged care services in rural areas and more informal care available in urban areas. Urban community-based social support services would also be needed, but these are easier to develop given the concentration of private providers in urban areas and economies of scale in service provision. During their healthier years, the elderly will likely be expected to provide child care services in their households, which may increase the propensity for intergenerational co-residence.

- Raising the retirement age is high on China's pension reform agenda. Mandatory retirement for workers in civil service and formal sector jobs occurs at an early age in urban China, with blue-collar women retiring at age 50, white-collar women at age 55, and men at age 60. While 50 and 55 are quite young, it is possible to retire even earlier by applying for early retirement five years before the mandatory retirement age. The results presented in this volume and some other work show that early retirement facilitates care for the elderly, and the anticipation of care provision may be behind some exits from work.[29] Therefore, incentivizing longer working lives may prove difficult if women (and some men) view care for elderly parents (and grandchildren) to be their responsibility. One way of meeting care needs and raising the participation of older women in work may be to train highly motivated, young retirees to be care providers both for their own parents and for other elderly living in the community. This may be arranged through community centers or other means of outreach.

Notes

1. United Nations, *World Population Prospects, the 2015 Revision*, http://esa.un.org/unpd/wpp/.
2. Population Reference Bureau, 2015, China Abandons One-Child Policy, http://www.prb.org/Publications/Articles/2015/china-ends-onechild-policy.aspx.
3. Traditionally, adult children in China were expected to support and care for their parents; at the same time, older people were expected to maintain their parental duties into old age and to care for and educate their grandchildren (Chow 2006; Yue 2005).
4. The elderly are characterized as healthy or unhealthy. Unhealthy elderly may be sick and in need of medical care or may be frail and in need of LTC. Some elderly who are recovering from illness may require LTC to support their recovery.
5. A common approach to measuring functional and cognitive limitations is through self-reported responses to questions on ability to perform ADLs and IADLs. These ADLs/IADLs are then used to characterize limited functional ability patterns among the elderly and corresponding long-term care needs. Values of ADLs/IADLs are based on a series of questions from the household surveys. In the case of China, for the purposes of describing aged care needs, the CHARLS survey is used, which specifically identifies individuals who have difficulties with physical ADLs or cognitive

function IADLs. In particular, the ADLs collected in CHARLS are: dressing, including taking clothes out of a closet, putting them on, buttoning up, and fastening a belt; bathing or showering; eating, including cutting up food; getting into or out of bed; and using the toilet, including getting up and down. The IADLs collected are: doing household chores; preparing hot meals; shopping for groceries; making phone calls; and taking medications. The response choices are: (1) No, I don't have any difficulty; (2) I have difficulty but I can still perform the activity; (3) Yes, I have difficulty and need help; and (4) I cannot perform the activity. Other approaches to measuring limited functional ability among the elderly vary from direct self-report (e.g., "do you have a limited functional ability?") to narrow or broad diagnostic-based disabilities.

6. The possibility that these factors will contribute to a decline in limited functional ability is evident when examining the socioeconomic gradients for physical functioning; see World Bank 2016b.
7. World Bank (2016b) highlights the differences between long-term projections from the UN's World Population Prospects and subsequent updates.
8. See WHO: http://www.who.int/healthinfo/global_burden_disease/en/.
9. The frequency of caring for the elderly is not as high as the frequency of caring for grandchildren. Table A1 in the appendix of Giles et al. (2016b), for example, shows that the overall share of urban women providing care to grandchildren is nearly twice as high as the share providing elder care, with care provision being particularly significant between ages 55 and 65. There is also a larger and more significant gender gap, as women are far more likely to be providing care to grandchildren.
10. This is also consistent with global evidence from developing economies (Evans and Palacios, 2013), which finds both declining co-residence as economies get richer and lower co-residence among richer elderly across economies (median co-residence in a sample of 61 developing economies in the mid-2000s was over 83 percent for people age 60+ in the poorest quintile but fell to only 64 percent for the richest quintile).
11. Early retirement was initially a means of easing some workers out of state owned enterprise (SOE) jobs during restructuring efforts of the late 1990s (Giles et al. 2006). As a practice, however, it did not end with the period of restructuring.
12. According to statistics from the National Development and Reform Commission, the latter target has been achieved: by 2015, there were 30.3 residential care beds per 1,000 people over the age of 60, which represents a 70 percent increase from 2010 (http://www.shanghaidaily.com/national/Chinas-nursing-home-beds-rise-to-67-mln-in-2015/shdaily.shtml).
13. Data on the average monthly wage and pensions in Beijing are cited from http://www.ecovis.com/focus-china/chinas-social-security-system/ and (http://www.chinanews.com/sh/2015/03-13/7128422.shtml).
14. Source: Beijing Statistical Information Net.
15. Source: Hebei BCA.
16. Source: Jilin BCA.
17. Three main approaches to division of responsibilities across national and subnational authorities are observed in OECD countries: (1) the centralized type, with a dominant role for the national government, detailed regulation at the national level, and a mere operational role for regional and local governments (examples can be found in smaller European, Nordic countries but also in France); (2) the decentralized or so-called 'framework type,' with an important role for private sector providers and

regional and local governments while the national government only sets the broad regulatory framework (examples include the United Kingdom and the Netherlands); and (3) the *laissez-faire* type, with a minimum of national government vision and coordination, and the government having responsibility only for the poorest (typical for some ex-communist countries like Bulgaria and Romania).

18. http://www.chinadaily.com.cn/china/2015-07/29/content_21438901.htm.
19. Several data sources based on nationally representative, population-based sample surveys are particularly useful for policy relevant analysis, including: Sampling Survey of the Aged Population in Urban and Rural China, China Health and Retirement Longitudinal Study (CHARLS), Chinese Longitudinal Healthy Longevity Survey (CLHLS), and China Longitudinal Aging Social Survey (CLASS). See chapter 10 for more details.
20. Adult Social Care Outcomes Framework. https://www.gov.uk/government/publications/adult-social-care-outcomes-framework-2014-to-2015.
21. Care Act 2014, http://www.legislation.gov.uk/ukpga/2014/23/contents/enacted.
22. Care Act 2014, http://www.legislation.gov.uk/ukpga/2014/23/contents/enacted.
23. See https://www.aacqa.gov.au/for-providers/accreditation-standards.
24. This situation is commonly referred to as "information asymmetry." There are many markets with goods that possess this quality (e.g., health care, used cars).
25. A literature review of health service delivery in China concluded that a key quality of care issue was lack of qualified staff at the lower levels.
26. In 2010, nearly 50 percent of total public health spending was on hospitals.
27. Average fees per hospital discharge increased by 27 percent between 2005 and 2010.
28. See World Bank. 2016c for more on the health sector reforms and the PCIC, in particular.
29. In fact, focus group interviews show that discussions about raising the retirement age are frequently greeted with strong protests, and one frequently heard claim is that raising women's retirement age will complicate the provision of care to grandchildren and elderly parents. In a poll reported in *China Youth Daily*, 94.5 percent of respondents oppose raising the retirement age. Of these, 27 percent oppose because it will complicate provision of care to grandchildren and elderly (*China Youth Daily*, August 29, 2013).

References

AIC (Agency for Integrated Care). 2015. "Singapore Programme for Integrated Care for the Elderly (SPICE)." http://www.aic.sg/page.aspx?id=782.

Cai, Fang, John Giles, Philip O'Keefe, and Dewen Wang. 2012. *The Elderly and Old Age Support in Rural China: Challenges and Prospects*. Washington, DC: World Bank.

Caixin Online. 2013. "Blues for Gray Hair: What's Wrong with China's Elder Care Section." March 6. http://english.caixin.com/2013-06-03/100536498.html.

Cao, Yuling. 2014. "Analysis on Demands and Provision of Elderly Care Services in China—Based on Empirical Research in Dalian and Nantong." *Population Journal* (03).

Centers for Medicare and Medicaid Services. 2015. *Nursing Home Data Compendium, 2015 Edition*. Baltimore, MD: Centers for Medicare and Medicaid Services. https://www.cms

.gov/Medicare/Provider-Enrollment-and-Certification/CertificationandComplianc /Downloads/nursinghomedatacompendium_508-2015.pdf.

Chawla, Mukesh, Gordon Betcherman, and Arup Banerji. 2007. *From Red to Gray: The "Third Transition" of Aging Populations in Eastern Europe and the Former Soviet Union*. Washington, DC: World Bank.

China Philanthropy Research Institute. 2015. "老年照护服务需求巨大，亟待政策完善与行动力" (accessed May 9, 2015). http://www.pubchn.com/news/show.php?itemid =84761.

Chow, N. 2006. "The Practice of Filial Piety and Its Impact on Long-Term Care Policies for Elderly People in Asian Chinese Communities." *Asian Journal of Gerontology & Geriatrics* 1 (1): 31–35.

Chui, Ernest Wing-Tak. 2011. "Long-Term Care Policy in Hong Kong: Challenges and Future Directions." *Home Health Services Quarterly* 30 (3): 119–32. http://doi.org/10 .1080/01621424.2011.592413.

Colombo, F., A. Llena-Nozal, J. Mercier, and F. Tjadens, 2011. *Help Wanted? Providing and Paying for Long-Term Care*. Paris: OECD Publishing.

DRC (Development Research Center of the State Council). 2014. "China's Elder Care System—Progress, Existing Problems and Reform Ideas." Department of Social Development, World Bank TCC5 Project.

———. 2015. *Research on Government Procurement of Services from Social Organizations*. DRC.

Ettner, Susan L. 1995. "The Impact of 'Parent Care' on Female Labor Supply Decisions." *Demography* 32 (1): 63–80.

European Commission. 2013. "Long-Term Care in Ageing Societies—Challenges and Policy Options." *Social Investment Package.* SWD 41 final.

———. 2014. "Peer Review in Slovenia: Long-Term Care—The Problem of Sustainable Financing." European Commission.

Feiler, Lizzi, Ulrich Hoerning, Drew von Glahn, Elena Glinskaya, and Dewen Wang. 2016. "Paying for Social Goods: Involving the Private and Non-Profit Sector in Delivery of Social Services." Informal, Beijing office.

Feng, Z., X. Guan, X. Feng, C. Liu, H. Zhan, and V. Mor. 2014. "Long-Term Care in China: Reining in Market Forces through Regulatory Oversight." In *Regulating Long-Term Care Quality: An International Comparison*, edited by V. Mor, T. Leone, and A. Maresso, 409–43. Cambridge, U.K.: Cambridge University Press.

Feng, Zhanlian, Chang Liu, Xinping Guan, and Vincent Mor. 2012. "China's Rapidly Aging Population Creates Policy Challenges in Shaping a Viable Long-Term Care System." *Health Affairs* 31 (12): 2764–73. doi:10.1377/hlthaff.2012.0535.

Feng, Z., H. J. Zhan, X. Feng, C. Liu, M. Sun, and V. Mor. 2011. "An Industry in the Making: The Emergence of Institutional Elder Care in Urban China." Journal of American Geriatrics Society 59(4): 738–44.

Gash, Tom, Nehal Davison, Sam Sims, and Louisa Hotson. 2013. *Making Public Service Markets Work*. Institute for Government. http://www.instituteforgovernment.org .uk/sites/default/files/publications/Making_public_service_markets_work_final _0.pdf.

General Administration of Sport. Various years. Notice of China Sport Lottery Issuing and Selling Data (中国体育彩票发行销售数据公告).

Genet, Nadine, Wienke Boerma, Madelon Kroneman, Allen Hutchinson, and Richard B. Saltman. 2012. *Home Care across Europe*. Geneva: World Health Organization.

Giles, John, Elena Glinskaya, Xinxin Chen, and Yaohui Zhao. 2016. "What Are the Current and Future Long-Term Care Needs of China's Aging Population." Background Paper, Development Research Group, World Bank.

Giles, John, and Ren Mu. 2007. "Elderly Parent Health and the Migration Decision of Adult Children: Evidence from Rural China." *Demography* 44 (2): 265–88.

Giles, John, Xinxin Chen, and Yaohui Zhao. 2016. "Elder Parent Health, Informal Long-Term Care Arrangements and the Labor Supply of Adult Children: Evidence from China," Background Paper, Development Research Group, World Bank.

Giles, John, Xinxin Chen, Elena Glinskaya, and Yaohui Zhao. 2015. "Elder Parent Health, Informal Long-Term Care Arrangements and the Labor Supply of Adult Children: Evidence from China". Manuscript.

Grabowski, David C., Daryl J. Caudry, Katie M. Dean, and David G. Stevenson. 2015. "Integrated Payment and Delivery Models offer Opportunities and Challenges for Residential Care Facilities." *Health Affairs* 34 (10): 1650–56. http://doi.org/10.1377/hlthaff.2015.0330.

HelpAge International. 2014. *Global Age Watch Report 2014*. http://www.helpage.org/resources/publications/, http://ec.europa.eu/social/main.jsp?catId=1024&langId=en&newsId=2097&furtherNews=yes.

———. 2015. *Care in Old Age in South East Asia and China*. mimeo.

Hu, Hongwei, Cai Xia, and Shi Jing. 2010. "Research on Effective Rural Social Elderly Care Insurance Demands—A Comprehensive Investigation Based on Insurance Willingness and Economic Capacities of Farmers." *Economic Survey* (6).

ICAIA (International China Ageing Industry Association). 2014. "Understanding Nursing Homes in China: A Preliminary Research Presentation." Presentation, International China Ageing Industry Association, Beijing.

Irish Leon, Lester Salamon, and Karla Simon. 2009. *Outsourcing Social Services to CSOs: Lessons from Abroad*. Washington, DC: World Bank.

Jacobs, Josephine C., Audrey Laporte, Courtney H. Van Houtven, and Peter C. Coyte. 2014. "Caregiving Intensity and Retirement Status in Canada." *Social Science in Medicine* 74–82.

Kaiser Family Foundation. 2013. "A Short Look at Long-Term Care for Seniors." *Journal of the American Medicaid Association* 310 (8): 786–87. http://jama.jamanetwork.com/article.aspx?articleid=1733726.

Kasim, Leo. 2013. "Making Ageing Population Lead Active, Healthy Life" (accessed May 19, 2013). http://www.bt.com.bn/news-national/2011/12/20/making-ageing-population-lead-active-healthy-life.

Le Grand J. 2011. "Quasi-Market versus State Provision of Public Services: Some Ethical Considerations." *Public Reason* 3 (2): 80–89.

Leichsenring, Kai, and Andy M. Alaszewski, eds. 2004. *Providing Integrated Health and Social Care for Older Persons: A European Overview of Issues at Stake*. Ashgate: Aldershot.

Leichsenring, Kai, and Andy Alaszewski. 2004. "Providing Integrated Health and Social Care for Older Persons: A European Overview of Issues at Stake in European countries." *International Journal of Integrated Care* 4 (4): 317–19.

Li et al. 2014. *National Population Aging Response Strategy Research Team*. Research on LTC Service System. Hualing Press, 2014.

Liu, Chang, Zhanlian Feng, and Vincent Mor. 2014. "Case-Mix and Quality Indicators in Chinese Elder Care Homes: Are There Differences between Government-Owned and Private-Sector Facilities?" *Journal of American Geriatrics Society* 62 (2): 371–77.

Liu, Lan, Xiaoyuan Dong, and Xiaoying Zheng. 2010. "Parental Care and Married Women's Labor Supply in Urban China." *Feminist Economics* 16 (3): 169–92.

Lorenzini, Luca, David Morgan, and Yuki Murakami. 2015. "Public Expenditure Projections for Health and Long-Term Care for China until 2030." OECD Health Working Papers 84, OECD, Paris. http://www.oecd-ilibrary.org/social-issues-migration-health/public-expenditure-projections-for-health-and-long-term-care-for-china-until-2030_5jrs3c274vq3-en;jsessionid=2ixegr5kmjgkv.x-oecd-live-02.

Maurer-Fazio, Margaret. 2011. "Childcare, Eldercare, and Labor Force Participation of Married Women in Urban China, 1982–2000." *Journal of Human Resources* 46 (2): 261–94.

Meng, Annika. 2011. "Informal Caregiving and the Retirement Decision." *German Economic Review* 13 (3): 307–30.

MOCA (Ministry of Civil Affairs of the PRC). 2013. *China Civil Affairs Statistical Yearbook*. Beijing: China Statistics Press.

———. 2015. *China Civil Affairs Statistical Yearbook 2014*. Beijing: China Statistics Press.

———. 2016. "Statistical Communique on the Development of Social Services." (available at: http://www.mca.gov.cn/article/sj/tjgb/201607/20160700001136.shtml).

———. Various years. "Notice of China Welfare Lottery's Issuing and Selling Data."

National Bureau of Statistics of China. 2006. *One Percent Population Sample Survey in 2005*. Beijing: China Statistics Bureau.

National Population Aging Response Strategy Research Team. 2014. *Research on LTC Service System*. Beijing: Hualing Press.

NBS (National Bureau of Statistics of China). 2011~2015. *China Social Statistics Yearbook (2010–2014)*. Beijing: China Statistics Press.

New Zealand Productivity Commission. 2015. *More Effective Social Services*. www.productivity.govt.nz.

Norton, E. C. 2000. "Long-term Care." In *Handbook of Health Economics*, vol. IB, A.J. Culyer and J.P. Newhouse, eds, 956-94. New York: Elsevier.

OECD LEED (Organisation of Economic Co-operation and Development/Local Economic and Employment Development). 2014. "China's Response to its Ageing Population." In *Fostering Resilient Economies, Demographic Transitions in Local Labour Markets*, Paris: OECD Publishing. http://www.oecd.org/cfe/leed/Fostering-Resilient-Economies_final_opt.pdf.

OECD (Organisation for Economic Co-operation and Development). 2015. *Government at a Glance 2015*. Paris: OECD Publishing. http://dx.doi.org/10.1787/gov_glance-2015-en.

Phillips M., H. Liu, and Y. Zhang. 1999. "Suicide and Social Change in China." *Culture, Medicine and Psychiatry* 23: 25–50.

ROK-ASEAN Cooperation Fund. 2013. *Community-Based Home Care for Older People in South East Asia* (accessed April 26, 2013). http://www.helpage.org/download/4daefd047e0c2/.

Smith, D. B., and Z. Feng. 2010. "The Accumulated Challenges of Long-Term Care." *Health Affairs* 29 (1): 29–34. doi:10.1377/hlthaff.2009.0507.

Song, Y., R. A. Anderson, K. N. Corazzini, and B. Wu. 2014. "Staff Characteristics and Care in Chinese Nursing Homes: A Systematic Literature Review." *International Journal of Nursing Sciences* 1 (4): 423–36.

Stone, Robyn, and Mary F. Harahan. 2010. "Improving the Long-Term Care Workforce Serving Older Adults." *Health Affairs* 29: 109–15.

Teets, Jessica C., and Marta Jagusztyn. 2013. "The Evolution of a Collaborative Governance Model : Public-Nonprofit Partnerships in China." http://umdcipe.org/conferences/GovernmentCollaborationShanghai/Submitted_Papers/Teets_Jagusztyn_Paper.pdf.

UK Department of Health. 2015. *The Adult Social Care Outcomes Framework 2014/15*. https://www.gov.uk/government/uploads/system/uploads/attachment_data/file/263783/adult_social_care_framework.pdf.

UNFPA and HelpAge International. 2011. *Overview of Available Policies and Legislation*. https://www.unfpa.org/sites/default/files/pub-pdf/Older_Persons_Report.pdf.

Van Houtven, Courtney, Norma Coe, and Meghan Skira. 2013. "The Effect of Informal Care on Work and Wages." *Journal of Health Economics* 32: 240–52.

WHO Centre for Health Development. 2004. *A Glossary of Terms for Community Health Care and Services for Older Persons*. Ageing and Health Technical Report, Volume 5.

World Bank. 2010. *The Well-Being of China's Rural Elderly and Old Age Support, Social Protection Group*. Human Development Unit, EASHD, Washington, DC: World Bank.

———. 2016a. *Economic Prospects*. http://www.worldbank.org/en/publication/global-economic-prospects.

———. 2016b. *Live Long and Prosper*. https://openknowledge.worldbank.org/bitstream/handle/10986/23133/9781464804694.pdf.

———. 2016c. *Deepening Health Reform in China: Building High Quality and Value-Based Service Delivery*. Joint Report by the World Bank, World Health Organization, Ministry of Finance, National Health and Family Planning Commission, Ministry of Human Resources and Social Security.

Wu, B., M. W. Carter, R. T. Goins, and C. Cheng. 2005. "Emerging Services for Community-Based Long-Term Care in Urban China: A Systematic Analysis of Shanghai's Community-Based Agencies." *Journal of Aging & Social Policy* 17 (4): 37–60.

Wu, B., Z.-F. Mao, and R. Zhong. 2009. "Long-Term Care Arrangements in Rural China: Review of Recent Developments." *Journal of the American Medical Directors Association* 10 (7): 472–7. http://doi.org/10.1016/j.jamda.2009.07.008.

Xu, Qingwen, and Julian C. Chow. 2011. "Exploring the Community-Based Service Delivery Model: Elderly Care in China." *International Social Work* 54 (3): 374–87. doi:10.1177/0020872810396260.

Yang, H. 2013. "Challenges in the Provision of Community Aged Care in China." *Family Medicine and Community Health* 1 (2): 32–42.

Yin, Shangjing, and Peng Du. 2012. "Research on Current Situation and Tendency of Elderly LTC Demands." *Population Journal* (2).

Yu, Xinxun. 2014. "Study on Marketlized Operation Model of Elderly Service Industry in China and Its Standard" (论我国养老服务业之市场化运营模式及其规范). *Journal of Sichuan University*.

Yue, K. 2005. "People of Chinese Descent." In *Cross-Cultural Caring*, edited by Nancy Waxler-Morrison, Joan M. Anderson, Elizabeth Richardson, and Natalie A. Chambers. 70. Vancouver: UBC Press. http://www.ubcpress.ca/books/pdf/chapters/waxmor.pdf.

Zhan, Heying, Guangya Liu, Xinping Guan, and Hong-guang Bai. 2006. "Recent Developments in Institutional Elder Care in China: Changing Concepts and Attitudes." *Journal of Aging & Social Policy* 18 (2): 85–108. doi:10.1300/J031v18n02_06.

Zheng, Zhenzhen, Ting Feng, and Bao Lin. 2013. *Ageing in China: Potential of Silver Economy of China*. Institute of Population and Labor Economics. Beijing: Chinese Academy of Social Sciences.

CHAPTER 1

Population Aging and Long-Term Care Needs

John Giles, Elena Glinskaya, Yaohui Zhao, Xinxin Chen, and Yuqing Hu

Introduction

The demand for long-term care in China is shaped by demographic trends and affected by a range of socioeconomic and demographic factors. Such factors include the health conditions of the elderly, residency patterns, labor participation of informal care providers, and migration of potential care providers (adult children).

In China, the sheer numbers of elderly and those with functional and cognitive disabilities who require assistance are overwhelming. Already in 2013, nearly one-quarter of elderly over age 60—nearly 46 million people—had a functional or cognitive limited functional ability. Of these, 27.6 percent or 12.7 million people lack assistance.[1] The sheer numbers point to considerable current demand, which is likely to accelerate with sharp increases in the aged share of the population. United Nations (UN) Population projections suggest an over-60 population of 578 million in 2050, out of a total population of 1.3 billion.

To gain a better understanding of future long-term care needs in China, this chapter analyzes some of the main factors affecting the demand for long-term care. It describes patterns of limited functional ability among China's elderly, residency patterns, and the impact of care provision on the labor force participation of adult children in the household. In doing so, it places China's long-term care needs in the context of the significant demographic changes currently underway and examines to what extent (and at what opportunity cost) informal care can respond to these needs. The chapter concludes with discussion of the likely interactions of long-term care arrangements and policies related to rural-urban migration, the appropriate mix of services, and

John Giles is a Lead Economist, Development Research Group, Human Development and Public Services Team, The World Bank. Elena Glinskaya is a Lead Economist and Program Leader for Human Development for China, Mongolia, and the Republic of Korea at the World Bank. Yaohui Zhao is a Professor of economics at the National School of Development, Peking University. Xinxin Chen is an Associate Professor at the Institute of Social Science Survey, Peking University. Yuqing Hu is a World Bank consultant.

Box 1.1 China Health and Retirement Longitudinal Study (CHARLS)

CHARLS is representative of the population over 45 years of age and their co-resident partners irrespective of age. In the survey, both the main respondents and their spouses were asked questions on their education, work history, earnings, and health. They were also asked questions about their families, including information on living children and parents of each respondent and spouse.

In this chapter we use the sample from wave 1 (2011), which consisted of 10,117 households and 17,505 eligible respondents, and the sample from wave 2 (2013), which consisted of 10,822 households and 18,605 individuals (Zhao et al. 2013).

Detailed information about the survey can be found at found at: http://charls.ccer.edu.cn/en.

implications of burgeoning long-term care costs for families. The main data sources for the analysis are UN Population Projections and the China Health and Retirement Longitudinal Study (CHARLS), which is described briefly in box 1.1.

Demographic Trends

China's demographic transition is among the most rapid ever witnessed. The United Kingdom and the United States—which became "aging societies" in 1925 and 1941, respectively—both took 75 years to reach an over-60 dependency ratio of 25. China, by contrast, crossed the "aging society" threshold in 2000 and will take only 30 years before it has an elderly dependency ratio (EDR) of 25 (in 2030) (World Bank 2016).

Both rising life expectancy and the sharp fall in total fertility to approximately 1.5 have driven an increase in the EDR, and UN Population Projections suggest that it will continue to rise at an unprecedented rate in the coming decades. By 2030, 25.3 percent of China's population is projected to be over age 60, which is almost the projected level for the Organisation for Economic Co-operation and Development (OECD) (27.5 percent). Furthermore, the share of China's population over age 80 (the "oldest old") will increase rapidly, from 1.6 percent in 2015 to a projected 11 percent by 2060, even faster than the regional average (which will increase from 1.8 percent in 2015 to a projected 9 percent by 2060). As the "oldest old" are most in need of long-term care, demographic projections suggest that there will be considerable demand for care over the next 40 years.

In terms of the geographic distribution, trends in population aging vary significantly across different areas of China. The number and proportion of the elderly population are higher in the east coast areas than in the central and western areas. In 2000, Shanghai, Jiangsu, and Beijing were the three provinces (metropolitan areas) with the highest proportions of the elderly population in China (15.0 percent, 12.6 percent, and 12.5 percent, respectively) (NBS 2001). However, the distribution pattern changed by 2005, with Chongqing, Sichuan, and Shanghai (metropolitan areas) having the highest proportions of elderly population. The proportion of the elderly population increased most rapidly in Chongqing, Sichuan, Hubei, and Anhui Provinces (metropolitan areas), in large part due to the migration of young and middle-age populations from central and western areas to the east coast areas (NBS 2006).

Overall, China's rural areas are aging more rapidly than its urban areas. From 1982 to 2005, the proportion of population age 60 and over rose from 7.8 percent to 13.7 percent in rural areas and from 7.1 percent to 12.1 percent in urban areas. The disparity between rural and urban areas can be attributed mainly to rural-to-urban migration, as migrants tend to be younger than those remaining in rural areas (Cai et al. 2012). Latest estimates show that the number of rural migrants was approximately 225.4 million in 2008, with 62.4 percent of them outside their home townships (NBS 2009). This outflow of the young rural population is expected to continue to "hollow out" villages, leaving behind older people (Cai et al. 2012).

Elderly Patterns of Limited Functional Ability

Worldwide, the proportion of the population surviving to very old ages (over 80 years) is a major driver of the demand for long-term care, but it is not the only one: among the elderly and adults under age 80, demand for long-term care is greatly influenced by the prevalence of functional and cognitive limitations.[2] A common approach in academic literature to measure these limitations through self-reported responses to questions on the ability to perform activities of daily living (ADLs) and instrumental activities of daily living (IADLs), as described in box 1.2.

Box 1.2 Measuring Limited Functional Ability

For the purposes of this chapter, and as it is common in academic research, patterns of limited functional ability and corresponding long-term care needs are assessed based on a series of questions from the CHARLS survey that specifically identify individuals who have difficulties with physical activities of daily living (ADLs) or cognitive function instrumental activities of daily living (IADLs). The ADLs asked in CHARLS are (1) dressing, including taking clothes out from a closet, putting them on, buttoning up, and fastening a belt; (2) bathing or showering; (3) eating, including cutting up your food; (4) getting into or out of bed; (5) using the toilet, including getting up and down. The IADLs asked are (1) doing household chores; (2) preparing hot meals; (3) shopping for groceries; (4) making phone calls; (5) taking medications.

The response choices are: (1) No, I don't have any difficulty; (2) I have difficulty but I can still perform the activity; (3) Yes, I have difficulty and need help; (4) I cannot perform the activity.

Individuals reporting difficulty and requiring help or having an inability to perform that activity at all are defined as being in potential need of care. CHARLS then asks the identity of the person providing assistance with each ADL and IADL.

Not surprisingly, the prevalence of ADL and IADL disabilities is strongly associated with age. As shown in figure 1.1 below which presents physical functioning limited functional ability rates in China by age cohort in 2011, 9 percent of women ages 65–69 had an ADL limited functional ability, compared to 30 percent for cohorts over age 80.

For each age cohort over 65, the share of men with an ADL limited functional ability is lower than the share of women. The age-related increase in limited functional ability among men and women shows a similar pattern, but for the cohorts over age 80, the gender gap becomes quite significant, with only 24 percent of men exhibiting a limited functional ability.

Figure 1.1 ADL and IADL Disabilities, by Age Group and Gender in China

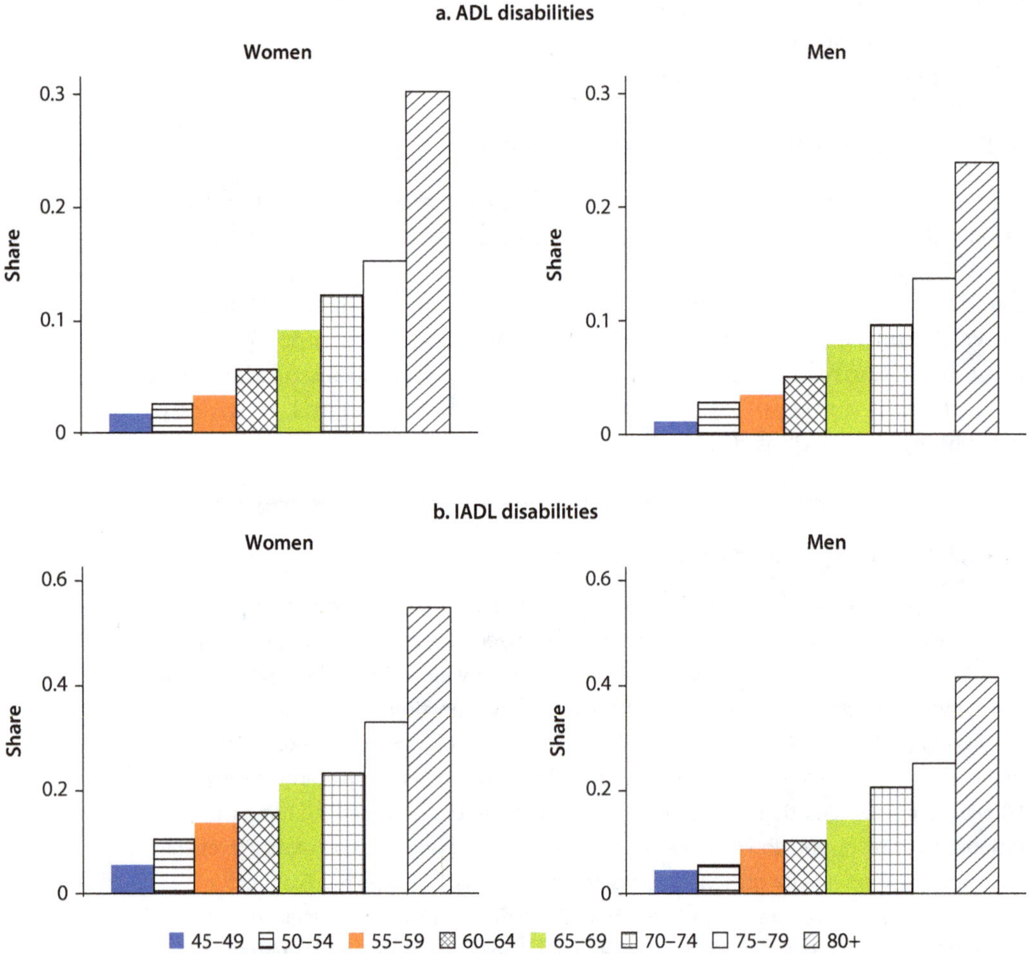

Source: Giles and Glinskaya 2016a using data from CHARLS 2011.
Note: An individual has an ADL difficulty if unable to perform any of the following activities without assistance: (1) dress, (2) bathe, (3) eat, (4) get in or out of bed, or (5) use the toilet. An individual has an IADL difficulty if they are unable to perform any of the following activities without assistance: 1) doing household chores; 2) preparing hot meals; 3) shopping for groceries; 4) managing money, such as paying your bills, keeping track of expenses, or managing assets; or 5) taking medications.

Difficulties performing IADLs are considerably more pronounced than difficulties with ADLs for both men and women in each age cohort, while gender differences in IADLs are similar to those for ADLs and tend to become more pronounced with age. Three factors are likely driving these differences. First, older men have higher mortality rates than women and may not live long enough to develop cognitive disabilities. Second, cognitive function in older age is strongly associated with educational attainment when young, and the gender gap in educational attainment among China's current elderly likely contributes to the gender gap in cognitive function disabilities.[3] The observed convergence in educational attainment between genders for younger cohorts may reduce the gender gap for future elderly. Third, women retire at younger ages than men, which likely contributes significantly to cognitive decline. For many people, retirement leads to a less stimulating daily environment. In addition, the prospect of retirement reduces the incentive to engage in mentally stimulating activities on the job.[4] In urban China, blue-collar women retire at age 50 and white-collar women at age 55, while men retire at age 60. Although agricultural and informal sector workers do not face mandatory retirement, the share of women working at older ages in these sectors is also lower than that of men.

The rate at which China's older adults develop disabilities also increases with age. Using the 2011 and 2013 CHARLS survey data, figure 1.2 shows the share of respondents who developed each of five disabilities over a two-year period. Roughly similar increases can be seen for all groups. Although there are some outliers, it is clear that by age 75, all population subgroups average a 10 percent increase in each of the five physical functioning disabilities over two years (or 5 percent annually).

While women have higher limited functional ability rates than men at a particular point in time, rates of transition to instrumental activity disabilities are more pronounced for men. As these increases are particularly striking for the preparation of hot meals, shopping, and performing household chores, it is quite likely that these large reported increases are a product of gender roles within current elderly cohorts. Men who are not in the practice of cooking and doing chores find that they are unable to perform them when a spouse is unable to do the work. Widowers may face a shock of being unable to care for themselves, but deterioration in physical and instrumental functioning of a spouse may have significant spillover effects, particularly on older men.

According to 40-year projections of future limited functional ability rates of the population over age 45, population aging will drive increases in the share of elderly who have ADL and IADL disabilities. Using the assumption that five-year cohorts will have similar limited functional ability rates through 2050, figure 1.3 shows future limited functional ability rates of the population over age 45, projected based on current ADL and IADL limited functional ability rates. The 40-year projection shows that the share of the elderly having ADL and IADL disabilities will continue to increase, with both the increase and share of individuals with disabilities being higher for women. By 2050, it is projected that 15 percent of women over age 45 will have at least slight ADL disabilities, compared to 8 percent of men.

Figure 1.2 Share of CHARLS Respondents with an Increase in ADL and IADL Disabilities from 2011 to 2013

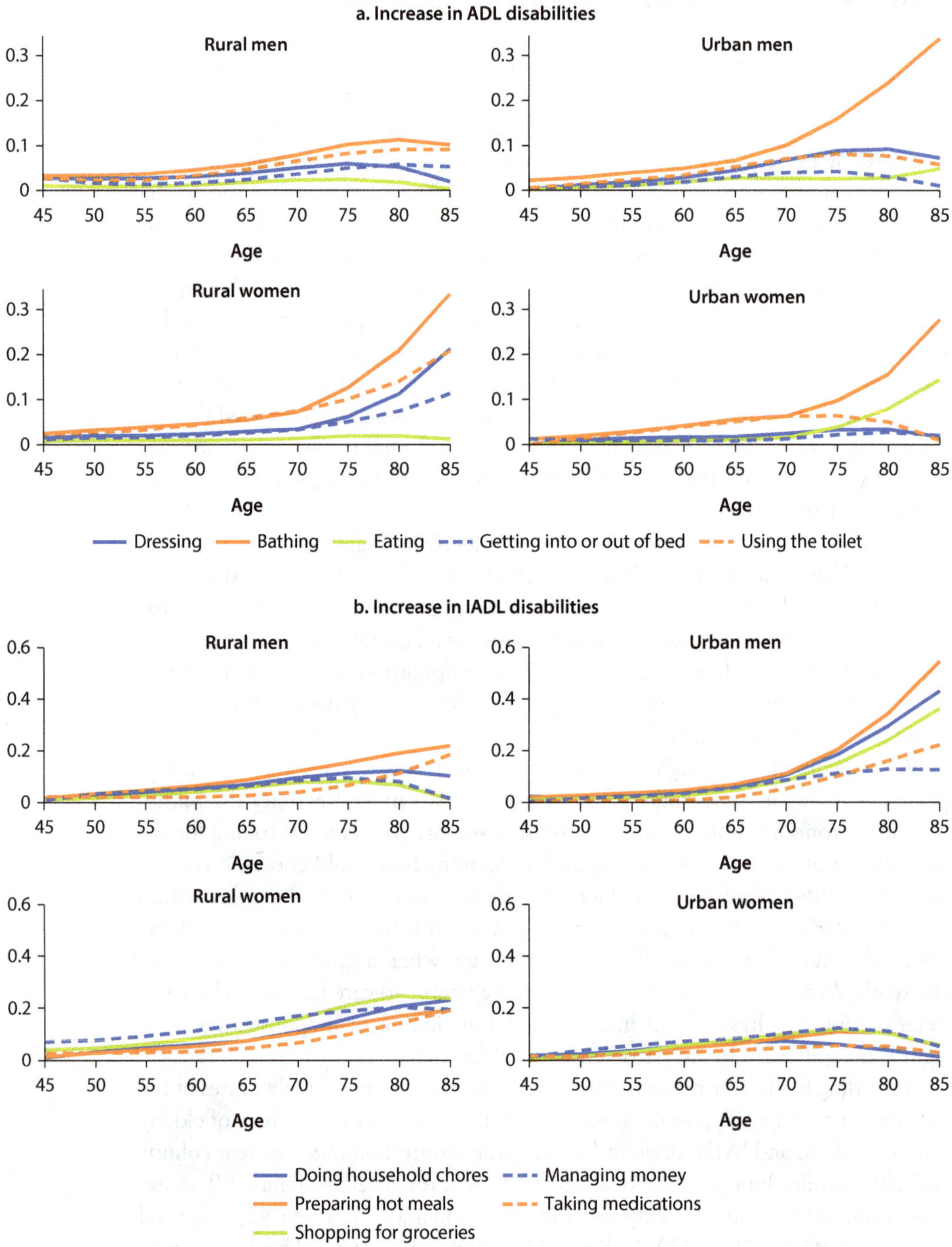

Source: Giles and Glinskaya 2016a using data from CHARLS 2011 and 2013.
Note: An individual has an ADL difficulty if unable to perform any of the following activities without assistance: (1) dress, (2) bathe, (3) eat, (4) get in or out of bed, or (5) use the toilet. An individual has an IADL difficulty if they are unable to perform any of the following activities without assistance: 1) doing household chores; 2) preparing hot meals; 3) shopping for groceries; 4) managing money, such as paying your bills, keeping track of expenses, or managing assets; or 5) taking medications.

Figure 1.3 Projected ADL and IADL Disabilities of the Over-45 Population, by Gender

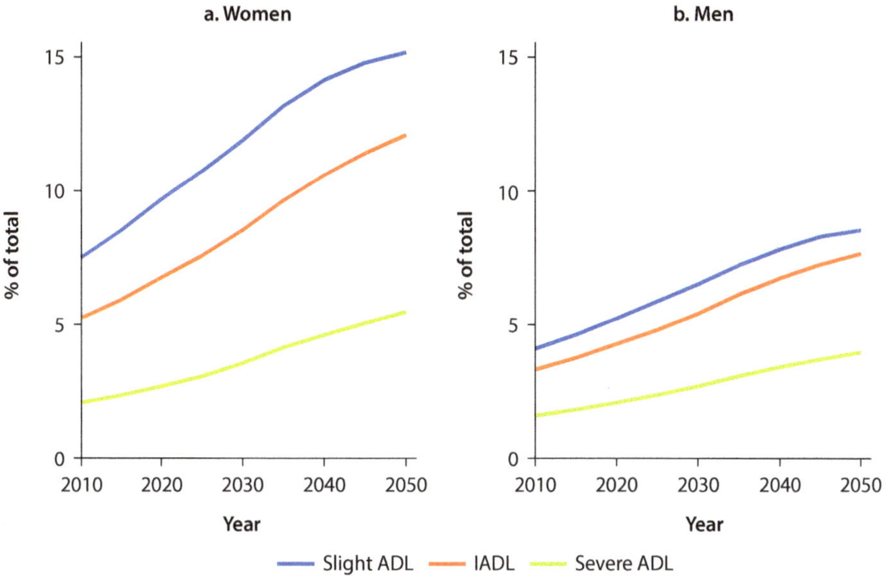

Source: CHARLS 2011; United Nations Population Division, World Population Prospects.

These predictions underscore the likely direction of change and the importance of thinking about future long-term care arrangements, although actual realizations of limited functional ability will likely differ. Both population and limited functional ability predictions face considerable uncertainty in terms of realized fertility and mortality rates. The incidence of ADLs and IADLs could increase or decrease with China's continued development and epidemiological transition.[5]

Older men and women with low levels of education have significantly higher rates of limited functional ability than elderly with a high school education or more. These differences reflect the accumulated effects of differences in nutrition, occupation, and health care utilization over the course of their lives. The relationship between limited functional ability and income quintile shows a similar pattern, which is not surprising given the high correlation between education and pension income and other transfers in old age. With economic development and the transition to the service economy, individuals will have had better nutrition over their lifetimes, and a greater share of the population will be working in less physically demanding jobs. The possibility that these factors will contribute to a decline in limited functional ability is evident when examining socioeconomic gradients for physical functioning.

While several factors such as increased education and better nutrition among younger cohorts could bring a decline in rates of limited functional ability, the greater risk of noncommunicable diseases (NCDs) could have the opposite effect. Age cohorts in their 30s and 40s today completed more school, had better nutrition as children, and are less likely to be working in physically taxing activities, all of which raise the prospect that rates of limited functional ability may decline. However, an epidemiological transition, reflected in the shift in morbidity and mortality from communicable diseases to NCDs, may have the opposite effect on limited functional ability. As a consequence of increased longevity, a higher share of the elderly may suffer from NCDs toward the end of their lives. A higher incidence of diabetes and high blood pressure, in particular, may increase long-term care (LTC) needs. The population cohorts entering their 70s and 80s in the next two decades may have been more exposed to NCD-related risks in middle age than previous cohorts, making them more vulnerable to disabilities in old age.

Projected ADL and IADL limited functional ability rates for rural and urban China show that higher levels of limited functional ability in rural China follow from higher rates of population aging (figure 1.4). By 2050, limited functional ability rates are likely to be highest for rural women at 22 percent of the population over age 45, compared to nearly 15 percent of urban women and only 8 percent of urban men. This is similar to the recent projections of the EDR rate by Cai et al. (2012), pointing to the possibility that EDRs will be much higher in rural areas of China than in urban areas. If current migration and urbanization patterns persist, poorer elderly living in rural areas may face greater long-term care needs.

China has experienced significant increases in mental health problems. There is general consensus that mental health problems are rising in China. The driving forces behind this rise are not well understood, as mental health

Figure 1.4 Projected ADL and IADL Disabilities of the Population over Age 45, by Gender and Urban and Rural Location in China

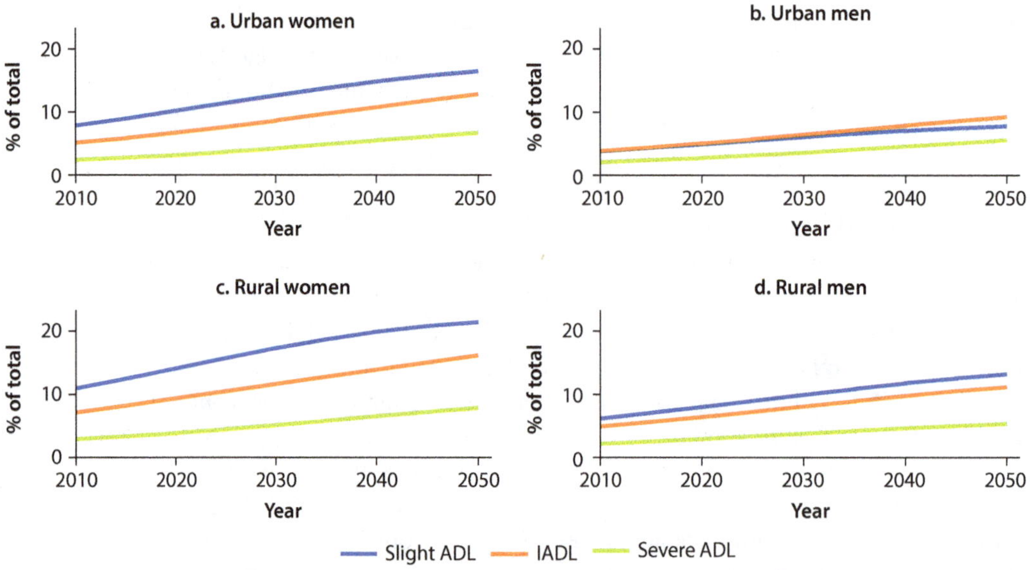

Sources: Giles and Glinskaya 2016a using data from CHARLS 2011; United Nations Population Division, World Population Prospects.
Note: Share of (people having ADL or IADL disabilities) in (each gender and region group)*share of (people in each gender and region group in each year) of (the total population in each year).

remains a closeted topic. The WHO's Global Burden of Disease Study predicts a constant increase in the prominence of mental illness to account for 17.4 percent of all illnesses in China by 2020, an increase of 3 percent relative to 2001 estimates (WHO 2016). This trend has been attributed to several factors, including the dismantling of familial and traditional safety networks, rising numbers of individuals involved in risky economic activities, and increasing work-related pressure and stress (Phillips et al. 1999).

The prevalence of dementia and Alzheimer's disease and the associated cognitive impairment and problems with carrying out ADLs and IADLs are also high in China (Li et al. 2014). Rates of dementia and Alzheimer's disease are similar to those in the European Union (EU) and other OECD countries (Dong et al. 2007). While there are no official data on the prevalence of dementia in China, and estimates often differ due to lack of a common framework for estimation and methodology, estimates from 25 epidemiological studies conclude that prevalence increased from around 2.1 percent during 1985–90 to around 4 percent during 2001–04 (Dong et al. 2007).

Patterns of Informal Care Provision

Around the world, the majority of elderly care is provided by familial caregivers at home. Similarly, the government of China is promoting a "90-7-3 model," which aims for 90 percent of all seniors to receive the care they need in their homes, 7 percent through community-based hospitals and health centers, and 3 percent through nursing homes. As envisaged, 97 percent of elderly who need care will require the assistance of family care providers or informal care providers hired as assistants. Skilled nursing homes are expected to cater to seniors who require long-term specialized nursing care, but even when the elderly are in nursing facilities, many family members will likely continue to be actively engaged in the provision of care.

At present, spouses and/or adult children are the most significant source of care for infirm elderly remaining at home. Estimates based on CHARLS data show that among those receiving assistance with daily living, 90.1 percent in 2011 and 77 percent in 2013 reported that their spouse, adult child, or a combination of the two were the primary source of care. Less than 1 percent of respondents in both the 2011 and 2013 CHARLS waves reported that care was provided by a hired elder care nanny (Giles et al. 2016b).

In urban areas, more women than men report providing care to elderly parents. In rural areas the shares are nearly equal. As shown in table 1.1, in urban areas, women ages 45–49 are more likely than men to report providing care (34 percent versus 28 percent), which is significant as blue-collar women may take early retirement and exit from work at age 45. In rural areas, no statistical differences are observed between genders in the shares providing care to elders for any age cohort. As the majority of co-resident husbands and wives in rural areas work on their own farms or in self-employed activities, provision of care for an elderly parent may be readily shared.[6]

Table 1.1 Incidence and Time Spent Caring for Elderly Parents and Parents-in-Law

	What share of older adults provides care?				*How many hours per week are spent providing care?*			
	Urban		*Rural*		*Urban*		*Rural*	
Age	*Men*	*Women*	*Men*	*Women*	*Men*	*Women*	*Men*	*Women*
Overall	0.14	0.17	0.12	0.12	16.6	17.9	19.4	17.8
45–49	0.28	0.34	0.25	0.26	15.1	17.0	20.4	20.4
50–54	0.27	0.29	0.22	0.21	13.3	17.5	16.0	14.5
55–59	0.18	0.20	0.14	0.14	15.1	16.5	12.6	16.6
60–64	0.10	0.07	0.08	0.06	26.5	20.9	32.2	20.0
65+	0.03	0.02	0.03	0.02	23.8	32.9	24.7	14.9

Source: Giles, Huang, and Hu 2015 using data from CHARLS 2011.
Note: Sample is weighted by individual weights with household nonresponse adjustment.

Elder care responsibilities appear to be shared by spouses. If both husband and wife are contributing to elder care, hours spent providing care by some families are not inconsistent with continuing to work. On average, urban men and women who are caring for elders spend 16.6 and 17.9 hours per week, respectively, on elder care, while rural men and women spend 19.4 and 17.8 hours, respectively. Relative to care for grandchildren, the time cost for elder care is lower as family child care providers typically spend more than 40 hours per week. The difference in hours between elder and grandchild care suggests that the demands of elder care may not be sufficient to drive working-age adults from work. When physical functioning problems become particularly severe, however, elderly family members may require considerably more care during the day than suggested by averages.

In terms of the gender of care recipients, men primarily receive care from spouses, while women—who tend to outlive their spouses—are far more likely to receive care from adult children or other providers. In 2011, 66 percent of infirm urban men and 70 percent of infirm rural men received care from a spouse, but husbands were care providers for 45 percent of infirm urban women and 53 percent of infirm rural women. By 2013, these shares decreased for both men and women and were replaced by either "spouse and children" or other sources of support. Adult children are the other primary source of assistance but are considerably more important for women than for men; 26 percent of women and 14 percent of men received care exclusively from adult children in 2013. While spouses may already be out of their peak earning years, the use of adult children for provision of care may lead to substitution away from employment or other activities.

It appears that the numbers of elderly who need care and who are receiving informal care have been increasing, and the increase reflects provision of care by a combination of sources rather than by one caregiver. Based on two CHARLS data points, the incidence of care receipt rose considerably from 13 percent in 2011 to 18 percent in 2013. The increase is accounted for by receipt of care from three or more sources, indicating the extent to which extended families may be pooling efforts and resources to care for infirm relatives.[7]

Informal care provision is not meeting all care needs of the infirm elderly, with the greatest unmet need being assistance going to the bathroom (figures 1.5 and 1.6).

Figure 1.5 Share of Population with ADL Disabilities Receiving Help in 2013

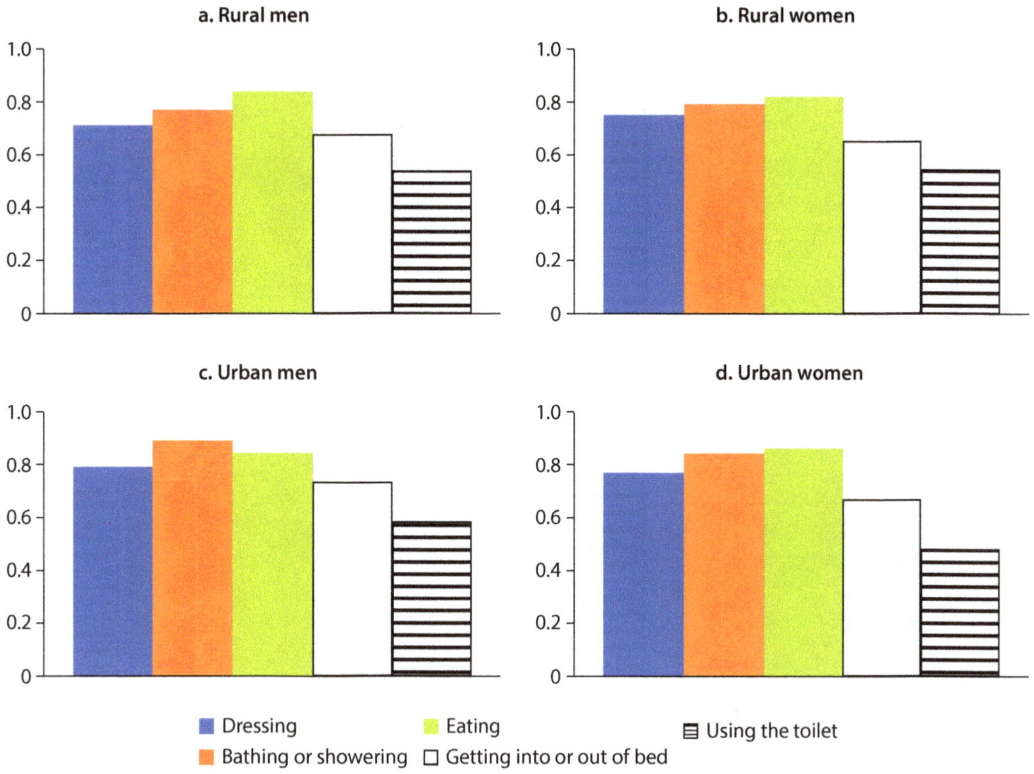

Source: Giles and Glinskaya 2016a using data from CHARLS 2013.

For both genders and in urban and rural areas, unmet needs using the toilet are consistent with patterns of declining co-residence at older ages: only 50 percent of urban women and 56 percent of urban men who require help reported having assistance, and in rural areas, the comparable shares were 58 and 52 percent. The higher frequency of unmet needs using the toilet suggests that those elderly lacking a spouse and relying on non-resident children and others for assistance may not have all needs sufficiently met. Roughly 80 percent of the elderly with each of the other ADL disabilities reported having assistance (with the exception of urban women who require help bathing, at only 60 percent).

In general, elderly with IADLs have lower unmet needs compared to elderly with ADLs (figure 1.6). Lack of assistance taking medications is the most pronounced unmet need among instrumental activities, which may reflect the fact that non-resident family or neighbors are less aware of the need to offer this type of help. As most other activities can be supported with less time-intensive interventions, taking medications also likely proxies for more time-intensive support.

Gender differences in receiving assistance are notable, with greater unmet needs among women. Nearly 90 percent of urban men who need help with

Figure 1.6 Share of the Population with IADL Disabilities Receiving Help in 2013

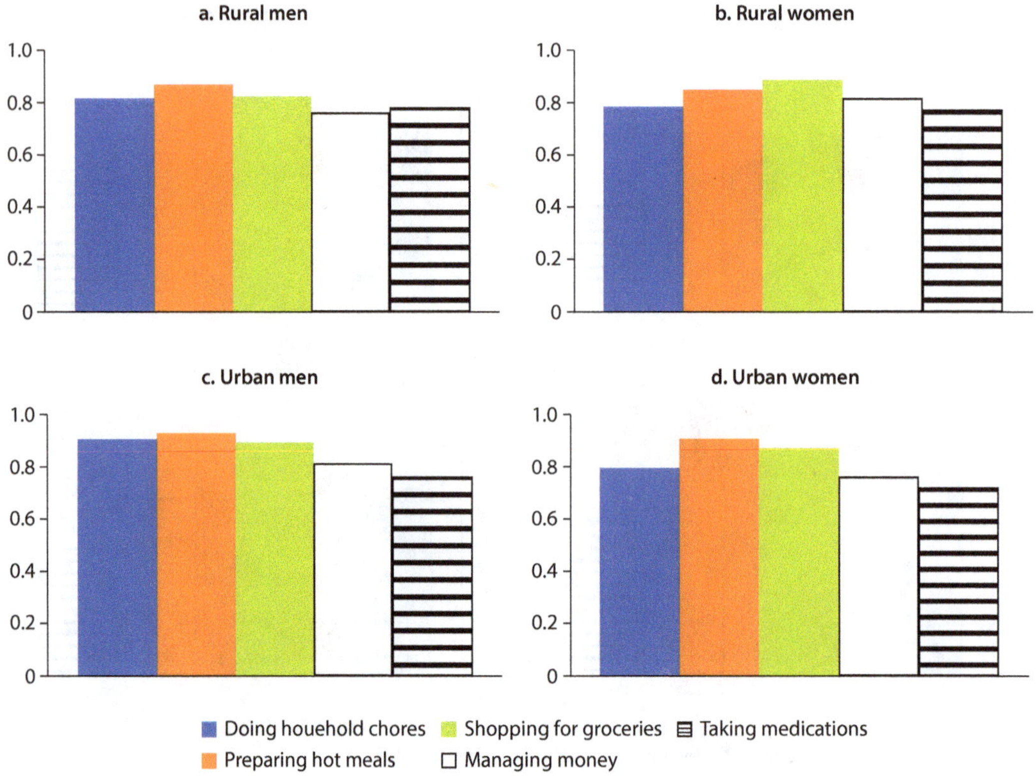

Source: Giles and Glinskaya 2016a using data from CHARLS 2013.

household chores receive assistance, compared to only 80 percent of urban women. Similar to earlier patterns, this highlights the difference in access to support for women who outlive their husbands and the potential benefits of community-based facilities that can provide assistance to the elderly for some of these basic activities.

Development and Demographic Change

Co-Residency Patterns and Migration

The elderly in China have long co-resided with the family of at least one of their adult children, a living arrangement that has often facilitated mutual support. At younger ages, healthy elderly often provide care to grandchildren and assistance with other household chores. The shift toward support of the elderly by younger generations often proceeds gradually and often not before age 80 and beyond. Elderly with relatively minor disabilities and no urgent needs for medical care tend to receive help from co-resident or nearby adult children, and then only move on to more formal arrangements or even residence in assisted living facilities over time.

Changes in family structure and economic development are eroding the easy availability of care from co-resident family members. Two important changes are taking place. First, the likelihood of living with adult children at younger ages of aging parents (between ages 45 and 60) has increased, which reflects an implicit transfer from parents to adult children who face higher housing costs than younger adults of the past. Second, for those aging parents over age 65, the share of elderly living with adult children has fallen from close to two-thirds in the early 1980s to roughly two-fifth by 2011. This decline is likely driven by both increases in migration over the last 30 years and by preferences for privacy among urban children and parents who can afford to live separately.[8] In the absence of co-residence or residence within close proximity, adult children are less likely to be well-informed about the well-being and care needs of their elderly parents. These patterns indicate that informal family-based support for elderly with disabilities is also coming under pressure with changes in living arrangements.

Both continued migration and decreasing family size will reduce the likelihood that adult children live with or in close proximity to the elderly. Evidence from other surveys suggests that many current seniors worry that there will be no one taking care of them. The 2010 Sampling Survey of the Aged Population in Rural/Urban China indicates that 39.8 percent of elderly people worried about having no one to take care of them when required, of whom 23.6 percent were "somewhat worried" and 16.2 percent were "very worried."

Absence of adult children may threaten the ability to provide instrumental care and affect the physical and mental well-being of the elderly. In addition, children who live at a distance from their parents may have less information about both their parents' health and financial needs, contributing to a decline in welfare. In Thailand, migration of adult children is associated with higher incidence of depression among the elderly (Adhikari, Jampaklay, and Chamratrithirong 2011). Antman (2015) shows that Mexican elderly with an adult child in the United States are more likely to report that they are in poor health, suffer from obesity, and exhibit symptoms of depression.

For those who are planning to migrate, the need to provide long-term care to elderly parents carries a high and potentially increasing opportunity cost. Prior research has found evidence that the serious illness of an aged parent influences the decision to work as a migrant. For example, Giles and Mu (2007) used parent mortality in the following two years as a measure of current serious illness, as death in the near future is a proxy for current infirmity, and found a significant negative association between near-term mortality and migration. Many elderly may be disabled for considerably longer periods of time before passing away, so return migration in response to care needs may only occur after an elderly parent has been frail for a considerable period of time. As it becomes more likely that the elderly will live into their 80s, periods of limited functional ability longer than one or two years are likely to become more prevalent.

Urban-born adults may also find it difficult to provide adequate support to aging parents. The observed fall in rates of co-residence with parents in itself does not lead to a decline in the welfare of healthy elderly. However, the burdens associated with care are likely to be significant if a parent becomes infirm. In OECD economies, formal private and public arrangements for provision of long-term care emerged with the transition in living arrangements, and all evidence suggests that this evolution in China is not keeping pace with changes in co-residence patterns.

Market Work of Informal Caregivers

Caring for elderly parents may have two opposing effects on the market work of working-age adults: (1) the time burden of providing care and the high cost of hired care may contribute to reduced labor force participation and a reduction in hours of work, and (2) an "added worker effect"[9] may induce re-entry to work or even longer working hours when provision of care is associated with increased expenditures, particularly health-related expenditures.

Structural estimates of the relationship between the labor supply of adults 45–65 years old and care supply show substantial negative effects on the labor force participation of rural men and women.[10] Specifically:

- Evidence using the CHARLS panel shows that after controlling for retirement status, the presence of a parent or in-law over age 65 in the household is associated with a 5.9 percentage point decline in probability that rural men are working, and the presence in the neighborhood or household is associated with a 4.4 percentage point decline in the probability that rural women are working.
- Conditional on working, the CHARLS panel also shows a negative effect on working hours of women in both urban and rural areas. Urban women work 2.9 fewer hours per week for each elderly parent or in-law living in the community, while employed rural women work 3.4 hours per week less.
- By contrast, employed urban men actually work 5.9 hours more per week when an additional elderly parent or in-law moves into the household.

Notably, some of these effects on labor force participation are not observed if only concentrating on movement into the household. As mentioned earlier, both the elderly and their children may prefer to live separately, and some effects of elderly presence are missed if focusing only on elderly living in the household.

In rural areas, for example, the negative effect of elderly presence on men's labor supply is only evident when elderly move into the household. The simultaneity suggests that care provision decisions and men's labor supply are made jointly, or perhaps, elderly move into the household of sons who are already less active. As work in self-employed activities, particularly agriculture, allows some flexibility in time allocation, the decline in labor force participation of men likely reflects reduced ability to commute outside the township, or even village, for work.

In urban areas, the increase in men's work hours with movement of an elderly person into the household may reflect either an added worker effect associated with the financial burden of providing support, or alternatively, an increase in labor supply may be facilitated by the presence of a healthy elderly parent helping with household chores. Given that change in health status of a co-resident parent has no effect on labor supply, it is more likely that the increase in urban men's hours of work is associated with a retired parent's assistance with chores and child care.

Structural estimates of the relationship between the labor supply of women 45–65 years old and care supply suggest a negative effect on care provision and women's labor supply in rural areas. Giles et al. (2016b) observe an increase in labor force participation among rural women when the health status of a co-resident healthy parent improves. Specifically:

- When an elderly parent's health improves from poor to good, rural women are 11 percent more likely to be working.
- Conditional on working, rural women's labor supply increases by 15.4 hours per week when an elderly parent's health status improves from "poor" to "good."

These findings are consistent with earlier research finding that care provision has negative consequences for female labor supply. A range of studies using household and labor force survey data from the United States and Europe suggests that family-based care provision is associated with fewer working hours and/or increased probability of exit from the workforce (Ettner 1995; Jacobs et al. 2014; Meng 2011; Van Houtven, Coe, and Skira 2013). Although some recent research on China finds a negative association between elder care and women's labor force participation (e.g., Liu, Dong, and Zheng 2010), other work finds the opposite effect, consistent with the added worker effect; Maurer-Fazio (2011) finds that the presence of an elderly parent or in-law over age 75 in the household is associated with an increased likelihood that prime-age women are in the labor force.

In contrast to some earlier work, the magnitudes of the negative effect on labor supply are somewhat reduced, and this is likely because much earlier work may not reflect a causal relationship (e.g., Liu, Dong, and Zheng 2010). Most studies examine the association between care and labor force participation without controlling for retirement status or retirement plans, which could have important implications for determining causality in two respects. First, the relatively young normal retirement age, which may be processed up to five years earlier, may lead women to exit work before elderly parents require care. Second, the studies assume exogenous placement of the elderly person in the household, but a plausible family strategy could be to sort elderly with physical functioning disabilities into households with relatively young retirees. Taken together, these two factors raise the possibility that care provision is not causing exit from work but that incentivized early retirement of women in China facilitates their role as care providers.

While the early retirement of urban women may explain the lack of an effect on labor market participation, this does not mean that they do not face heavy burdens in providing care. The burden on urban women is evident in the effects that unhealthy parents have on the likelihood of depression, and time devoted to leisure activities. Giles et al. (2016b) find a 0.5 standard deviation increase in a standard measure of depression (the Center for Epidemiologic Studies-Depression [CESD]-10 z-score) for urban women when an elderly co-resident parent moves from good to poor health, and decline of 0.36 standard deviation when health of parents improves. Further, the improvement in an elderly parent's health is associated with 23.5 percent and 10 percent increases in the likelihood of participating in a local social club or engaging with social activities with local friends, respectively. Notably, the presence of an ill elderly parent has no impact on either the subjective well-being or time allocation of urban men.

Income of the Elderly

In contrast to countries with well-developed pension systems, the rural and urban elderly populations in China face significantly different retirement systems, with different sources of income in old age. In urban areas, where most long-term residents have formal wage employment before exiting the workforce, older adults retire at a relatively young age and receive substantial support from pensions. Rural residents, by contrast, have lacked pension support and may expect to work in farming or other agriculture-related activities until relatively late in their lives (Giles, Wang, and Cai 2012; Park et al. 2012). Most rural elderly have continued to work as long as their health has allowed them to do so (Benjamin, Brandt and Fan 2003), leading to the familiar characterization that the rural elderly "work until they drop" (Pang, Brauw, and Rozelle 2004). Moreover, rural-to-urban migration of adult children does not necessarily lead to fewer elderly people working; older women, in particular, seem to return to work when their children migrate for work (Mu and van de Walle 2011).

A new pension for rural residents has contributed to increased income for the elderly and lower poverty rates. Zhang, Giles, and Zhao (2014) use the eligibility rules for China's New Rural Pension Program (NRPP) to examine the effects of a modest pension targeting rural residents not recently covered by a pension. From this analysis, it is clear that the NRPP is associated with increases in both earned and total income of the elderly and reductions in the incidence of poverty. For age bandwidth of less than five years, the probability of "retirement" or ceasing productive activity with pension receipt is positive but statistically insignificant. At a bandwidth of five years, the probability that a recipient will stop working increases by 26 percent.

Even with support from the NRPP, elderly with low incomes (including from public transfers) continue to be at risk of falling into poverty even as adult children have employment as migrants. Earlier research using data from the late 1990s and early 2000s suggested that the income-poor elderly with migrant children received enough financial support to raise them out of poverty, although elderly with migrants faced higher variability in income transfers (Cai et al. 2012; Giles, Wang, and Zhao 2010). However, by 2011, data from the CHARLS showed that the income-poor rural elderly were unlikely to receive transfers sufficient enough to live above the poverty line (World Bank 2015).

Implications for Developing Aged Care Policies

The anticipated needs for elder care and patterns of informal care provision require a multi-faceted approach to long-term care provision in China. The discussion in this chapter focuses on the relationship between long-term care arrangements and policies related to rural-urban migration, the appropriate mix of services (home-based, community-based, and institutional), and the implications of burgeoning long-term costs for family budgets. Given private long-term care costs and the likely interactions between long-term care arrangements and retirement decisions, there are clear motivations for public funding to support long-term care provision as China's population ages. Given the cost of formal care, however, an optimal mix of services would harness the intrinsic motivation of young retirees to help provide care for aging members of the family and their community.

Patterns of limited functional ability across rural and urban areas point to a need to develop approaches to long-term care in both settings and to consider the role of migration policies. The needs unmet by informal care are more acute in rural areas, pointing to the need to develop formal care delivery for rural elderly. A complementary approach is to sanction and support the migration of entire families to urban areas. If it is easier for rural cohorts currently in their 40s and 50s to move to urban settings with their adult children, this may facilitate meeting care needs as they age. As there are likely to be economies of scale in the development of assisted living and nursing homes and in the organization of formal mechanisms for elder day care arrangements and support for home care, enabling older adults to move with their migrant children may simplify the provision of elder care to these groups in the future.

In terms of the mix of services, the support needed for the majority of elderly with ADLs and IADLs could be delivered through home- and community-based interventions. Assistance to elders with ADLs and IADLs could come from neighbors or community members lending a hand. For those elderly without family members, neighbors or trusted community-based organizations providing assistance with financial matters like budgeting and shopping for food and household items may provide important and cost-effective support to these seniors.

Evidence on the costs of paid long-term care (both home-based and institutional) suggests that hiring paid care may be viewed as prohibitively expensive for most elderly and their families, so it should be one of many options in the supply of long-term care. Recent case studies detailing the features and costs of indicative long-term care facilities suggest that monthly fees may range from RMB 1,110 in government-run facilities to just over RMB 5,000 for privately developed and operated facilities. While indigent elderly receive publicly subsidized care in government facilities, the costs of formal long-term care are quite high relative to the per capita earnings of China's families. The monthly cost of staying and receiving care in even a modestly priced government facility is equal to the median urban per capita household income of the over-45 population. In terms of home care, a review of internet advertisements for elder care nannies from Zhejiang to Shandong suggests a minimum of RMB 2,000 per month for a live-in nanny and over RMB 4,000 for a more skilled nanny living outside the home. Furthermore, working as an elder care nanny is often less attractive than caring for children, so it may be difficult to retain a nanny in China's tight labor market.

Another policy consideration is the impact of retirement age on long-term care provision. Incentivizing longer working lives may prove difficult if women (and some men) view care for grandchildren and elderly parents to be their responsibility. Focus group interviews and discussions about raising the retirement age are frequently greeted with strong protests, and one often-heard claim is that raising the retirement age for women will complicate the provision of care for grandchildren and elderly parents.[11] However, the actual hours worked providing long-term care (as shown in table 1.1 above), do not seem to preclude work or the sharing of care responsibilities among families within communities.

Mandatory retirement for workers in civil service and formal sector jobs occurs at an early age in urban China, and this age differs by gender and occupation. As noted earlier, blue-collar women retire at age 50, white collar women at age 55, and men at age 60 (as well as women in such occupations as "professor"). While 50 and 55 are quite young, it is possible to retire even earlier. Since the period of economic restructuring in the late 1990s, workers have been able to apply for early-retirement five years before their mandatory retirement age.[12] According to data from the CHARLS survey, retirement before the mandatory age is evident for both men and women. By age 51, nearly 38 percent of urban women are receiving a pension, and only 40 percent are still in the labor force. Nearly 20 percent of urban men are receiving a pension by age 57, while male labor force participation drops from 80 percent at age 45 to 65 percent at age 57.

One way to meet care needs and raise older women's participation in work may be to train highly motivated, young retirees to be care providers for both their own parents and for other elderly living in the community. This may be arranged through community centers or other means of outreach. Folbre (2012), among others, has argued that if women with high intrinsic motivation want to be care providers, the quality of care and well-being of care recipients may decline considerably if providers are incentivized to engage in some other kind of work. To reduce the opportunity cost of providing care, Folbre's work suggests that China might best promote facilities that take advantage of the intrinsic motivations of both volunteers and compensated staff from the community.

Notes

1. Calculated from United Nations (2015).
2. Elderly may be characterized as healthy or unhealthy. Unhealthy elderly may be sick and in need of medical care, or may be frail and in need of LTC. Some elderly who are recovering from illness may require LTC to support their recovery.

3. Lei et al. (2014) use two proxies for adult cognition, episodic memory and intact mental status, and find significant gender differences for older Chinese age cohorts and poorer communities within the CHARLS sample. They further show that this gap is driven primarily by gender differences in the educational attainment of these groups.
4. Using data from the United States, England, and 11 European countries in 2004, Rohwedder and Willis (2010) investigate the effects of retirement on cognition empirically using cross-nationally comparable surveys of older persons. They find that early retirement has a significant negative impact on the cognitive ability of people in their early 60s that is both quantitatively important and causal.
5. World Bank (2015) highlights the differences between long-term projections from the UN's World Population Prospects and subsequent updates.
6. The incidence of caring for elderly is not as high as the incidence of caring for grandchildren. Table A1 in the appendix of Giles et al. (2016b), for example, shows that the overall share of urban women providing care to grandchildren is nearly twice as high as the share providing elder care, with care provision being particularly significant between ages 55 and 65. There is also a larger and more significant gender gap, as women are far more likely to be providing care to grandchildren.
7. CHARLS asked about volunteers and employees of local facilities, but no respondents (or families) reported receiving care from these sources.
8. This is also consistent with global evidence from developing economies (Evans and Palacios 2015), which finds both declining co-residence as economies get richer and lower co-residence among the rich elderly across economies (median co-residence in a sample of 61 developing economies in the mid-2000s was over 83 percent for people age 60+ in the poorest quintile but fell to only 64 percent for the richest quintile).
9. The "added worker effect" generally refers to an increase in spousal labor supply in response to a husband's loss of a job. Coile (2004) highlights an added worker effect associated with health expenditure shocks in the United States. It is also plausible that any shock to the family budget, including a health shock experienced by an elder parent or the costs associated with care of an infirm parent, may lead to an increase in labor supply.
10. This discussion on the impacts of providing care on labor supply summarizes findings from Giles et al. (2016b), which provides greater detail on empirical techniques.
11. In a poll reported in *China Youth Daily*, 94.5 percent of respondents opposed raising the retirement age. Of these, 27 percent opposed it because it will complicate provision of care to grandchildren and elderly (*China Youth Daily*, August 29, 2013). Yang (2014) is a prominent advocate of gradually raising women's retirement age to the retirement age for men, then raising both to 65. She has received considerable publicity for her views but also sharp criticism in social media outlets.
12. Early retirement was initially a means of easing some workers out of jobs in state-owned enterprises during the restructuring efforts of the late 1990s (Giles 2008). As a practice, however, it did not end with the period of restructuring.

References

Adhikari, Ramesh, Aree Jampaklay, and Aphichat Chamratrithirong. 2011. "Impact of Children's Migration on Health and Health Care-Seeking Behavior of Elderly Left Behind." *BMC Public Health* 11: 43.

Antman, Francisca. 2015. "How Does International Migration Affect the Health of Elderly Parents Left Behind? Evidence from Mexico." Department of Economics, University of Colorado.

Benjamin, Dwayne, Loren Brandt, and Jia-Zhueng Fan. 2003. "Ceaseless Toil? Health and Labor Supply of the Elderly in Rural China." Unpublished manuscript, Department of Economics, University of Toronto.

Cai, Fang, John Giles, Philip O'Keefe, and Dewen Wang. 2012. *The Elderly and Old Age Support in Rural China: Challenges and Prospects*. Directions in Development series. Washington, DC: The World Bank.

Coile, Courtney C. 2004. "Health Shocks and Couples' Labor Supply Decisions." NBER Working Paper 10810, National Bureau of Economic Research, Cambridge, MA.

Dong, M. -J., B. Peng, X. -T. Lin, Y. –R. Zhao, and R. -H. Wang. 2007. "The Prevalence of Dementia in the People's Republic of China: A Systematic Analysis of 1980–2004 Studies." *Age and Ageing* 36 (6): 619–24.

Ettner, Susan L. 1995. "The Impact of 'Parent Care' on Female Labor Supply Decisions." *Demography* 32 (1): 63–80.

Evans, Brooks Fox, and Robert J. Palacios. 2015. "An Examination of Elderly Co-residence in the Developing World." Social Protection and Labor Policy Note." No. 17: Pensions. World Bank, Washington, DC.

Folbre, Nancy. 2012. "Should Women Care Less? Intrinsic Motivation and Gender Inequality." *British Journal of Employment Relations* 50 (4): 597–619.

Giles, John, 2008. "Economic Restructuring and Retirement in Urban China." Working Papers, 2008–14 Center for Retirement Research at Boston College, Chestnut HIll, MA.

Giles, John, Dewen Wang, and Changbao Zhao. 2010. "Can China's Rural Elderly Count on Support from Adult Children? Implications of Rural-to-Urban Migration." *Journal of Population Ageing* 3 (3): 183–204.

Giles, John, Dewen Wang, and Wei Cai. 2012. "The Labor Supply and Retirement Behavior of China's Older Workers and Elderly in Comparative Perspective." In *Aging in Asia: Findings from New and Emerging Data Initiatives*, edited by J. P. Smith and M. Majmundar. Washington, DC: National Academies Press.

Giles, John, and Elena Glinskaya. 2016a. "What Are the Current and Future Long-Term Care Needs of China's Aging Population." Background paper, Development Research Group, World Bank.

Giles, John, Elena Glinskaya, Xinxin Chen, and Yaohui Zhao. 2016b. "Elder Parent Health, Family-Based Long-Term Care Arrangements and the Labor Supply of Adult Children: Evidence from China." Background paper, Development Research Group, World Bank.

Giles, John, and Ren Mu. 2007. "Elderly Parent Health and the Migration Decision of Adult Children: Evidence from Rural China." *Demography* 44 (2): 265–88.

Giles, John, Yang Huang, and Yuqing Hu. 2015. "Formal and Informal Retirement in Aging East Asia." Background paper, Development Research Group, World Bank.

Jacobs, Josephine C., Audrey Laporte, Courtney H. Van Houtven, and Peter C. Coyte. 2014. "Caregiving Intensity and Retirement Status in Canada." *Social Science & Medicine* 102: 74–82.

Lei, Xiaoyan, James P. Smith, Xiaoting Sun, and Yaohui Zhao. 2014. "Gender Differences in Cognition in China and Reasons for Change over Time: Evidence from CHARLS." *Journal of the Economics of Ageing* 4: 46-55. https://doi.org/10.1016/j.jeoa.2013.11.001.

Li et al. 2014. "National Population Aging Response Strategy Research Team." Research on LTC Service System, Hualing Press, 2014.

Liu, Lan, Xiaoyuan Dong, and Xiaoying Zheng. 2010. "Parental Care and Married Women's Labor Supply in Urban China." *Feminist Economics* 16 (3): 169–92.

Maurer-Fazio, Margaret. 2011. "Childcare, Eldercare, and Labor Force Participation of Married Women in Urban China, 1982–2000." *Journal of Human Resources* 46 (2): 261–94.

Meng, Annika. 2011. "Informal Caregiving and the Retirement Decision." *German Economic Review* 13 (3): 307–30.

Mu, Ren, and Dominique van de Walle. 2011. "Left Behind to Farm? Women's Labor Reallocation in Rural China." *Labour Economics* 18 (S1): S83–97.

NBS (National Bureau of Statistics). 2001. *Tabulation on the 2000 population census of the People's Republic of China*. Beijing: China Statistical Press.

———. 2006. *Tabulation on the 2005 1% population census of the People's Republic of China*. Beijing: China Statistical Press.

———. 2009. Migrant Workers Monitoring Survey Report 2008.

Pang, Lihua, Alan de Brauw, and Scott Rozelle. 2004. "Working Until You Drop: The Elderly of Rural China." *China Journal* 52: 73–96.

Park, Albert, Yan Shen, John Strauss, and Yaohui Zhao. 2012. "Relying on Whom? Poverty and Consumption Financing of China's Elderly." In *Aging in Asia: Findings from New and Emerging Data Initiatives*, edited by J. P. Smith and M. Majmundar, Washington, DC: The National Academies Press.

Phillips, Michael R., Huaqing Liu, and Yanping Zhang. 1999. "Suicide and Social Change in China." *Culture, Medicine and Psychiatry* 23.1: 25–50.

Rohwedder, Susann, and Robert Willis. 2010. "Mental Retirement." *Journal of Economic Perspectives* 24 (1): 119–38.

United Nations, Department of Economic and Social Affairs, Population Division. 2015. *World Population Prospects: The 2015 Revision*. DVD Edition.

Van Houtven, Courtney, Norma Coe, and Meghan Skira. 2013. "The Effect of Informal Care on Work and Wages." *Journal of Health Economics* 32: 240–252.

WHO (World Health Organization). 2016. *Global Health Estimates*. www.who.int/health info/global_burden_disease/en/.

World Bank. 2015. *Live Long and Prosper: Aging in East Asia and the Pacific*. Washington, DC: World Bank.

———. 2016. *Live Long and Prosper*. https://openknowledge.worldbank.org/bitstream/handle/10986/23133/9781464804694.pdf.

Yu, Xinxun. 2010. "Study on Marketlized Operation Model of Elderly Service Industry in China and Its Standard" (论我国养老服务业之市场化运营模式及其规范). *Journal of Sichuan University* (1): 13–20.

Zhang, Chuanchuan, John Giles, and Yaohui Zhao. 2014. "A Policy Evaluation of China's New Rural Pension Program: Income, Poverty, Expenditure, Subjective Well-Being and Labor Supply" (in Chinese). *China Economic Quarterly* 14 (1): 203–230.

Zhao, Yaohui, John Strauss, Gonghuan Yang, John Giles, Peifeng Perry Hu, Yisong Hu, Xiaoyan Lei, Man Liu, Albert Park, James P. Smith, and Yafeng Wang. 2013. "China Health and Retirement Longitudinal Study: 2011–2012 National Baseline Survey User's Guide."

CHAPTER 2

Policy Framework, Strategy, and Institutional Arrangements

Dewen Wang

Introduction

In response to unprecedented demographic changes, China has accelerated its development of an elderly care system over the past decade.[1] China had long been a young society, but two factors have accelerated the process of its population transition tremendously. The first factor is the family planning policy implemented in the late 1970s, which fundamentally shifted the Chinese family structure toward a 4-2-1 type, most visibly in urban China.[2] The second factor is its rapid economic growth. The reform and opening-up started in the early 1980s brought double-digit growth—"China's economic miracle"—which has greatly improved living standards and health conditions so people can live healthier and longer.

As income grows, the opportunity cost of raising children increases, and fertility declines. With declining fertility and increased life expectancy, China first met the United Nations (UN) definition of an "aging society" in 2000.[3] In 2015, the elderly population 60 years of age and above in China was 222 million, accounting for 16.1 percent of the total population. Looking ahead, the pace of population aging will accelerate further. China will become an "aged society" in 2023 and a "super aged society" in 2034. According to the latest UN population projections, the elderly dependency ratio (EDR), which was 14.2 in 2015, will rise to 25.3 in 2030 and 46.7 in 2050.

Demographic, economic, and social changes have resulted in small family sizes and eroded the role of family support for the elderly. Population census data show that family size has dropped from 4.4 persons per household in 1982 to 3.1 in 2010. China has a tradition of filial piety in which families provide support for older parents, but as the family size becomes increasingly nuclear, it may be difficult for traditional family support to remain the mainstay of care provision. Massive domestic migration has also affected the co-residence

Dewen Wang is a Senior Economist in the Social Protection and Labor Global Practice at the World Bank.

of the elderly living with their adult children in rural areas (Cai et al. 2012), as the latter migrate out for higher earnings.

At present, "empty-nest" elderly families are quite common in both rural and urban areas. Data from the sixth census show that the empty-nest elderly amounted to 62 million in 2010, accounting for one-third of the total elderly population. This proportion rose to up to half of the total elderly population in 2015, according to a report of the National Health and Family Planning Commission (NHFPC 2016). The report also pointed out that the handicapped and disabled elderly totaled about 37.5 million in 2013 and over 40 million in 2015. Representative survey data collected by the Chinese Health and Retirement Longitudinal Study reveal that about 60 to 70 percent of elderly people have chronic diseases (CHARLS Research Team 2013). Therefore, with weakened family support, providing adequate care to meet the needs of the elderly poses tremendous challenges for Chinese society.

In the reform era, China first carried out social security system (social insurance and social assistance) reforms to support and complete the economic transition toward a market economy. As state-owned enterprise (SOE) reform and urban reform started, China introduced a market-compatible social insurance system for urban workers in the late 1990s. With the establishment of the urban worker social insurance schemes, medical and pension insurance schemes were also introduced to rural residents in 2003 and 2007, respectively, and rolled out to cover urban residents not covered by the urban worker social insurance system. In 2015, over 80 percent of the labor force had pension coverage, and over 95 percent of the total population was covered by medical insurance. China also introduced *dibao* and other social assistance programs to provide income and in-kind support to the poor, including the poor elderly.

Compared with the social security system, the establishment of the elderly care system came much later, and its coverage is very limited. Historically, China's social welfare programs had long targeted a small portion of the elderly: the urban "Three No's" and rural *wubao* people. More recently, the Chinese government has accelerated the establishment of a comprehensive elderly care system, with government support that prioritizes the poor, disabled, and partially disabled elderly. In the 12th Five-Year Plan period, China has drafted development plans and amended laws and regulations to promote the establishment of the elderly care system. According to the relevant policy documents, the elderly care system will have three integral components: home-based care as a bedrock, supported by community-based care and supplemented by institution-based care.[4] The government has also introduced numerous policy measures to guide the development of the elderly service industry, leverage the participation of the private sector, and encourage the combination and integration of medical care and social care for the elderly. However, policy interventions largely focus on supply side and are generally pilots and trials, indicating that the elderly care system is still at an early stage with an evolving policy framework.

This chapter documents the current policy framework and institutional arrangements of China's elderly care system and discusses the key issues and challenges. The rest of the chapter is organized as follows: the "Policy Framework and Institutional Arrangements" section presents a short overview of policy evolution and then describes the policy framework and institutional arrangements for the elderly care system in detail. The "Challenges and Recommendations" section discusses key issues and challenges relevant to policy design, institutional arrangements, and policy implementation, and concludes with recommendations.

Policy Framework and Institutional Arrangements

Policy Evolution

China's elderly care policies have evolved through important milestones in the reform era (table 2.1). As discussed below, these include research and awareness in the 1980s, strategic preparation in the 1990s, concept formulation in the 2000s, and framework design and implementation since 2011.

Table 2.1 Policy Evolution of China's Elderly Care System in the Reform Era

Date	*Document no.*	*Topic*	*Government bodies*
12/14/1994	70	China's Seven-Year Development Plan on Aging (1994–2000)	MOH, MOCA, MOL, MOLSS, MOF, MOE, NCA
10/01/1996	73	Law on Protection of the Rights and Interests of the Elderly	NPC
10/20/1999	22	Circular on Establishing the National Working Commission on Aging	State Council
10/08/2000	13	Decisions on Strengthening the Work on Aging	CPC Central Committee and State Council
10/01/2000	97	Circular on the Tax Policy Issues for Elderly Care Institutions	MOF, SAT
07/22/2001	26	10th Five-Year Development Plan of Undertakings on Aging (2001–2005)	State Council
05/31/2001	145	Circular on the Implementation Plan of the Starlight Program of Community Welfare Services for the Elderly	MOCA
11/16/2005	170	Opinions on Supporting Social Forces to Invest in Social Welfare Institutions	MOCA
03/05/2005	48	Circular on Carrying out the Demonstration of Social Service Activities for the Elderly	MOCA
02/09/2006	6	Opinions on Accelerating the Development of Social Services for the Elderly	State Council
08/16/2006	7	11th Five-Year Development Plan of Undertakings on Aging (2006–2010)	NCA
09/25/2006	262	Circular on Establishing Demonstration Units That Have Carried out Social Services for the Elderly	MOCA
01/29/2008	8	Opinions on Comprehensively Promoting the Work of Home-Based Care Services	NCA, NDRC, MOE, MOCA, MOLSS, MOF, MOC, MOH, PFPC, SAT

table coninues next page

Table 2.1 Policy Evolution of China's Elderly Care System in the Reform Era *(continued)*

Date	*Document no.*	*Topic*	*Government bodies*
09/17/2011	28	12th Five-Year Development Plan of Undertakings on Aging (2011–2015)	State Council
12/16/2011	60	Development Plan of the Elderly Service System (2011–2015)	State Council
12/28/2012	72	Law on Protection of the Rights and Interests of the Elderly (Amended)	NPC
12/12/2013	35	Some Opinions on Accelerating the Development of Social Services for the Elderly	State Council
11/18/2015	84	Guidance on Combining Medical Services with Elderly Care Services	State Council
06/24/2016	107	13th Five-Year Development Plan for China's Civil Affairs Sector	MOCA, NDRC

Source: Compilation from MOCA's website.
Note: See annex 2B for a list of acronyms for Chinese Government Agencies shown in this table.

In the 1980s, China started to research and recognize population aging issues. In order to participate in the World Assembly on Ageing, China established the National Committee on Aging (NCA) in 1982, a social organization composed of government bodies, research institutes, and the media, to conduct research, draft strategic plans, and promote coordination and international exchanges. In 1995, the NCA[5] became a public service unit at the vice minister level, supervised by the Ministry of Civil Affairs (MOCA). During this period, rural reform dismantled people's communes by introducing the household responsibility system, and urban reform separated welfare provision from work units. Those reforms weakened the financing basis of the state and the collectives for social welfare institutions. In order to maintain welfare provision of food, medical services, and housing for urban Three Nos and rural *wubao* people, MOCA took measures to encourage the participation of enterprises, public institutions, social organizations, and individuals in opening social welfare institutions[6] and to strengthen the management of rural nursing homes and social welfare institutions.[7] The thinking on social participation in welfare provision was later broadened to encourage the participation of social forces and private capital in the elderly care industry.

In the 1990s, China strategically initiated policy preparation and legislation (annex 2A). Recognizing that China would become an aging society in 2000, ten ministries[8] jointly initiated China's *Seven-Year Development Plan on Aging (1994–2000)* in 1994, calling for preparatory work in the areas of legislation, pensions, and medical insurance, social participation, culture, elderly care services, research, and so on to prepare China for a smooth transition to an aging society. The Plan encouraged the combination of family support with social support as well as greater responsibilities for local governments in financing. In order to strengthen the leadership and government work on aging, the Communist Party of China (CPC) Central Committee and the State Council decided to establish the National Working Commission on

Aging in October 1999, which has shared the same working office at the NCA. In terms of legislation, China promulgated the *Law on Protection of the Rights and Interests of the Elderly* in October 1996. This law had six chapters—general provisions, family support and maintenance, social security, social participation, legal responsibility, and supplementary provisions—which highlighted the social security system (pension, medical insurance and medical services, social assistance) but did not have a single chapter that defined the elderly care system.

In the 2000s, the Chinese government paid increasing attention to the issues of population aging and formulated the concept of the elderly care system. In 2000, the CPC Central Committee and the State Council promulgated the *Decision on Strengthening the Work on Aging*, a leading document that started to frame the concept of China's elderly care system and to define the scope of elderly services such as daily care, health care, fitness, culture, and legal services for the elderly. The Decision introduced the concept that home-based care is the bedrock, supported by community-based care and supplemented by social care. This was the first time China put forward the idea of integrating family, community, and society as an entire mechanism for elderly care.

Following the directives of the CPC Committee and the State Council, China started to subsume aging under the broader Five Year Plans. In 2001, the State Council issued the *10th Five-Year Development Plan of Undertakings on Aging (2001–2005)*, which emphasized increasing inputs to facilities (particularly in rural areas), set targets of 10 beds per 1,000 elderly in cities and 90 percent coverage of rural welfare homes, and highlighted the important role of the community service platform in delivering comprehensive and multi-layer services for the elderly.[9] In 2006, the State Council issued *Opinions on Accelerating the Development of Social Services for the Elderly*, and the NCA released the *11th Five-Year Development Plan of Undertakings on Aging (2006–2010)*, encouraging various social forces to invest in establishing elderly care service institutions at different levels, especially for the provision of care and nursing services for elderly people who cannot or can only partially take care of themselves.

During this period, China increased public investment in building social welfare institutions and launched the "Starlight Program" to strengthen community service facilities. During 2001–04, investment in the "Starlight Program" totaled RMB 13.4 billion and helped set up 32,000 "Starlight Centers for Seniors", which provide family visits, emergency aid, daily care, health and rehabilitation services, and recreational activities, benefiting over 30 million elderly people (Information Office of State Council of the People's Republic of China 2006). With this progress, the concept of home-based care was formally introduced and emphasized. In 2008, ten ministries announced the *Opinions on Comprehensively Promoting the Work of Home Based Care Services*, requiring the establishment of broad coverage of a home care service network in urban communities and promoting the construction of home care services to cover nearly one-third of rural villages. In addition, funding for elderly care services was gradually extended to cover low-income old people or those with economic difficulties and expanded from traditional social assistance to social services and care. A this stage, advocacy of the elderly care service concept helped establish a good foundation for the development of social services for the elderly.

The 12th Five-Year Plan period (2011–2015) was a golden age of design, pilots, and implementation for the elderly care policies. Three leading policy documents outline a vision and policy framework for China's elderly care system. The first one is the *12th Five-Year Plan of Undertakings on Aging*, which provides a blueprint for establishing the social security system and the elderly care system in China. The second one is the *Development Plan of the Elderly Service System*, which defines the objectives and tasks of establishing an elderly service system in five years. The third one is the State Council's *Some Opinions on Accelerating the Elderly Service Industry*, which establishes longer-term targets for development of the elderly care system by 2020. The documents define the scope of elderly care, call for combining social care with medical care, welcome the participation of non-profit organizations and the private sector, and introduce a government purchasing services approach to leverage the development of the elderly care service market.

In 2012, the *1996 Law on Protection of the Rights and Interests of the Elderly* was amended to reflect progress already achieved and the commitments the Government was making for the future regarding the rights and interests of the elderly. The amended law has nine chapters, three of which were newly introduced (social services, social privileges, and livable housing environment), to boost the development of care services for the elderly. It requests that the various levels of government put the aging clause into yearly and five-year socioeconomic development plans, establish a stable financing mechanism through an appropriate fiscal budgeting arrangement, and encourage investment from the whole society. It further describes the roles and responsibilities of families and adult children in caring for their elderly parents: in particular, family members should not neglect the mental needs of their parents and should regularly visit and contact their parents if living apart. It also advocates for gradually developing long-term care programs and establishing and improving the elderly welfare system (such as the subsidy program for the senior elderly) to meet the increasing needs for long-term care. This law had one amendment in 2015, which clearly defines the leading role of the civil affairs agency in guidance, oversight, and management of non-profit and for-profit institutions. Those amendments have expanded the scope of rights, interests, and responsibilities for the elderly; reemphasized the fundamental role of families in the elderly care system; and codified the roles and responsibilities of government and the market in delivering elderly care services.

Policy Framework

As described above, the 12th Five-Year Development Plan and laws and regulations at the national level have formulated a vision and policy framework for developing the elderly care system in China. The *12th Five-Year Development Plan of Undertakings on Aging* is a comprehensive plan covering all areas related to the elderly. It calls for developing a basic strategic framework of medium- and long-term plans to cope with population aging and establishes targets for both the social security system and the elderly care system by 2015. Specifically, those targets include:

- Improve the pension system to cover both urban and rural residents and preliminarily achieve the goal that each elderly person nationwide could receive basic old age support.
- Improve the basic health and medical system, provide health management services, and establish health profiles for people over age 65.
- Establish a three-tiered elderly care system, improve the service network of home-based care and community-based care, and have 30 beds per 1,000 elderly people nationwide.
- Develop technical standards for urban and rural construction for the elderly, upgrade barrier-free facilities, and establish standards for new apartment facilities construction.
- Increase facilities for culture, education, sports, and fitness for the aged and further expand the scale of universities for the aged.
- Strengthen the management of elderly social work and set up committees on aging at different levels, with targets of over 80 percent of retired people for community management, 80 percent coverage of local committees on aging, and more than 10 percent of the elderly population being elderly volunteers.

The *Development Plan for the Elderly Service System (2011–2015)* presents the objective, scope, and structure of the three-tiered elderly care system. It states that the three components of home-based care, community-based care, and institutional-based care are integral parts of China's elderly care system which would meet the actual needs of the elderly and give priority to poor and low-income elderly, the partially and fully disabled, and senior citizens with economic difficulties. The Plan defines the scope of each component as follows:

- *Home care services* cover daily living care, housekeeping services, rehabilitation care, medical care, mental consolation, and family visits. For the independent elderly in healthy physical condition, it will provide housekeeping services, elderly canteens, legal services, and other services. For partially and fully dependent elderly, elderly living alone, and the disabled, it will provide housework, health care, auxiliary equipment, meal delivery, barrier-free upgrades, emergency calls, and security assistance services. Localities with suitable conditions are encouraged to provide special subsidies to the disabled elderly receiving home care and deploy necessary rehabilitation equipment for them to improve daily living and quality of life.
- *Community care services* have two functions: day care and support for home care, mainly for families who have temporary difficulties or fail to provide assisted daily care. Community care services thus back up the provision of

home-based care services. In urban areas, built upon existing community service facilities, new facility sites will be increased to strengthen the capacity and platform of community service delivery. Voluntary activities and elderly mutual assistance services will be mobilized to participate in community care services. In rural areas, township welfare homes will be upgraded with more beds to deliver day care and short-term care and gradually shifted to become regional elderly service centers, providing day care, short-term care support, catering, and other services to the left-behind elderly and other needy elderly. Mutual assistance in rural villages is also encouraged.

- *Institutional care services* largely invests in the facilities of rehabilitation institutions and other elderly institutions, providing skilled nursing services to the partially and fully disabled elderly. The care services include daily living care, rehabilitation care, and sudden illness and emergency rescue help. The rehabilitation institutions are encouraged to equip internal medical departments and provide training to community service stations, staff, and caregivers, which can reach out with services. Other elderly institutions based on their own conditions will provide residential services to meet the various needs of the elderly.

The *Development Plan of the Elderly Service System (2011–2015)* requires that an elderly care system be preliminarily set up by 2015 with a basically sound home care and community care service network. The specific objectives and tasks of this Plan include:

- Increase the number of beds for daily care and institutional care by about 3.4 million and upgrade 30 percent of current beds to reach the construction standard.
- Renovate barrier-free facilities for needy elderly families and develop social service institutions to increase the types and contents of home care services.
- Construct elderly day care centers, nursing homes, elderly clubs, mutual-assistance service centers, and other community facilities to strengthen community service functions and deliver day care services to basically cover all communities in urban areas and more than half of rural communities.
- Construct support, rehabilitation, and medical facilities for the institutions. At least one facility will be constructed in each county to provide care services for the partially and fully disabled elderly. At the provincial and national levels, a number of training facilities for elderly care services will be constructed.
- Encourage the development of professional nursing care equipment and auxiliary equipment and actively promote special vehicles for elderly care services.
- Develop the information system and use modern technology to provide efficient and convenient services and regulate the development of the elderly services industry.

Following the national plans, provinces (cities) have developed sub-national development plans. In particular, a number of provinces (cities) set targets for a 90-7-3 structure—that is, 90 percent of the elderly receive home-based care, 7 percent receive community care, and 3 percent receive institutional care,[10] although the national plans do not explicitly mention such a structure. This structure emphasizes that the family is primarily responsible for elderly care, the community provides support given its advantage of geographical proximity with the elderly, and finally institutional care fills the gap to meet the demands for intensive care.

The State Council's 2013 *Some Opinions on Accelerating the Development of Social Services for the Elderly* proposes longer-term goals and major tasks by 2020 and provides policy directions for developing China's elderly care system. It encourages the establishment of elderly care institutions in both rural and urban areas and the development of home care service networks and urban elderly care facilities, identifies measures for strengthening rural elderly services, and promotes elderly service market development by simplifying administrative and bureaucratic procedures such as licensing, standardization, information disclosure, and registration. By 2020, China will have established the three-tiered elderly care system that covers urban and rural areas with mature functions and appropriate scale. The variety of products for aged care services will become richer, the market mechanisms will be improved continuously, and the aged care service will grow in a sustainable and healthy manner. Specific targets include:

- *Improve the service system.* The services of daily living care, medical care, mental consolation, and emergency help will cover all the elderly staying at home. Day care centers and elderly clubs that meet standards will cover all urban communities, while 90 percent of townships/towns and 60 percent of rural communities will establish comprehensive community service facilities and stations. The number of beds will be 35–40 beds per 1,000 senior citizens.
- *Expand the scale of the industry.* The elderly service industries will achieve all-around development in the areas of daily living care, products, health services, sports and fitness, culture and entertainment, financial services, and tourism. A group of leading enterprises and innovative small and medium-sized enterprises will create over 10 million jobs and more added values that will be a significant portion of the service industry.
- *Create a favorable institutional environment.* Policies and laws for aged care services will be adopted and enhanced, sectoral standards will be introduced, regulation mechanisms will be improved, and service quality will be greatly increased. Social awareness on population aging will be significantly improved, and volunteer services for the aged will be provided in an extensive way, while good traditions of respecting, nursing, and helping the elderly will be promoted further.

The elderly care system will integrate medical care and elderly care. The State Council's 2013 *Opinions* encourage medical institutions to put their resources into elderly care institutions, communities, and homes or create a separate ward for aged patients, conduct home visits by health personnel, sign a medical contract with elderly care institutions, provide health inspection and health consultation, pilot remote medical care, and so on. Hospitals at level 2 and above are required to increase the number of beds for seniors, aiming to prevent chronic diseases of the elderly and provide rehabilitation care. A new medical insurance mechanism will be established to reimburse medical service expenditures for insured workers and rural/urban residents who receive medical treatment from elderly care institutions with an internal medical ward. A medical claim system will be put in place across regions to compensate for medical treatment. Senior citizens are encouraged to buy personal insurance, such as health insurance, long-term care insurance, and accidental injury insurance, while commercial insurance companies are encouraged to provide services.

In 2015, the State Council issued the *Guidance on Combining Medical Services with Elderly Care Services*, further promoting the coordination, harmonization, and integration of medical services and elderly care services. Initially, it aims to set up a coordinated policy, standards, and management system between medical services and elderly care services by 2017, with a number of qualified institutions providing integrated medical services and elderly care services, more than 80 percent of medical institutions offering fast channels of registration and outpatient services for the elderly, and over 50 percent of elderly care institutions providing various medical services for the elderly. By 2020, the objective is to establish an integrated policy and regulations system between medical services and elderly care services and an integrated service network with shared resources. All medical institutions will offer fast channels of registration and outpatient services for the elderly, and all elderly care institutions will be able to provide medical services and health care services to meet the basic needs of the elderly. This policy document calls for establishing and improving a cooperation mechanism between medical institutions and elderly care institutions; encouraging elderly care institutions to run geriatric hospitals, rehabilitation hospitals, nursing homes, Traditional Chinese Medicine (TCM) hospitals, hospice care institutions, and internal clinics or nursing stations; promoting the extension of medical services to communities and families, encouraging social forces to open and run institutions with combined medical services and elderly care services; and encouraging the integration of medical care institutions with elderly care institutions.

In 2016, the *13th Five-Year Development Plan for China's Civil Affairs Sector* was released by MOCA and the National Development and Reform Commission (NDRC), which treats combining medical and social care services as part of the multi-layer elderly care system to be established in China. This plan more emphasis on the development of home- and community-based care services, encourages the development of innovative elderly care investment and financing mechanisms, explores establishing a long-term care system, and piloting the long-term care insurance scheme. These efforts would open up the elderly care service market and expand the supply of elderly care services and products.

Policy Measures

Following the requirements of the State Council's *Opinions*, more than 25 ministries have independently or jointly issued about 30 circulars, notices, guidelines, standards, and administrative measures to push forward the establishment of China's elderly care system in different aspects (see annex 2A), covering almost all the elements of an elderly care system, which includes land provision, financial support and credit, workforce, information system, government subsidy, tax preference, licensing, standards, monitoring and assessment, and management. Public welfare home reform was introduced through various approaches, including a publicly financed private operation, government purchasing services, mixed ownership, and privatization to improve efficiency and service quality. In 2014, MOCA and the NDRC jointly selected 42 cities to carry out national pilots in the areas of elderly care system planning and development, social forces participation, land utilization, taxation, workforce, technology, and service models, aiming to offer experiences for developing the elderly care system nationwide. In 2016, MOCA and the Ministry of Finance (MOF) set up the earmarked central lottery funds to support the national pilots of home-based and community-based elderly care services.

Investment

In 2013, MOF and MOCA decided to arrange earmarked central lottery funds during the 2013–2015 period to upgrade and equip rural happiness homes, including the rural elderly day care centers, nursing homes, elderly canteens, and elderly clubs managed by village committees to provide meals, entertainment, and care services for the rural elderly. Each rural happiness home project receives subsidies of RMB 30,000. In 2014, ten ministries jointly issued a *Circular on Promoting Health and Elderly Care Project*. The scope of project investment covers the health service system, the elderly care system, and sports and fitness facilities.[11] Guidelines on construction planning and technical standards for urban and rural facilities were also developed jointly by the relevant ministries.

Financing

In addition to increased public inputs, financial institutions are requested to develop suitable financial products, expand the scope of collaterals, and offer preferable interest to support development of the elderly care system. In 2013, the liability insurance was introduced for elderly care institutions and insurance funds, and companies were encouraged to invest in the elderly care industry and offer various insurance products. In 2015, local governments were allowed to issue corporate bonds to finance elderly care insurance and leverage social investment.[12] In 2016, policy guidance was taken to provide financial support for accelerating the elderly care industry, which requests to improve the financial service system with various financial products (credit, securities, trust, insurance, collateral, reverse housing mortgage) and broaden financing channels (bond market, security market, and equity market). In addition, MOCA and the China Development Bank signed a Memorandum of Understanding in 2015 to use an RMB 10 billion loan for investing in home care and community care facilities, institutions, training, and industry projects. The loan term is 15 years with a 3-year grace period, and the interest rate will be measured by a loan pricing model (4.2 percent annually).

Private Sector

Private capital and social forces have long been encouraged to invest in the elderly care system.[13] The State Council's 2013 *Opinions* emphasizes that individual investors are encouraged to set up home-based services, while foreign and private capital will be encouraged to set up large-scale old age institutions and provide high-end services. In 2013 and 2014, the Ministry of Commerce and MOCA jointly sent notices to welcome Hong Kong SAR, China and Macao SAR, China service providers and foreign investors to establish for-profit institutions. Those providers and investors will enjoy treatment equal with domestic service providers and investors. In 2015, ten ministries jointly issued a policy initiative[14] with concrete measures that encourage private capital to comprehensively participate in home care and community care services; develop elderly care institutions through shareholding, cooperative, and public-private partnership (PPP) approaches; invest in elderly industries; and promote the integration between medical services and elderly care.

Land

In 2014, the Ministry of Land and Resources (MOLR) issued a guidance that defines the scope, nature, and period of land utilization for elderly facilities. According to this guidance, the occupied land of housing and facilities that provide day care, rehabilitation care, custody, and other services can enjoy favorable policies. Land for building elderly care facilities shall be incorporated in the master plan and annual plan for urban land usage. Non-profit elderly care institutions can use the land allocated by the government or land owned by the collectives. For profit-making elderly care institutions, land leasing is encouraged with favorable rental fees and other policies. Changing the nature of the land or the floor area for the sake of real estate development is strictly forbidden. The land use right is 50 years. The leasing term of elderly homes should not exceed 5 years.

Training and Employment

In 2014, the Ministry of Education (MOE) and eight other ministries jointly initiated policy measures for workforce training. It emphasizes the important role of vocational training in developing the workforce at the current stage and sets a goal for the workforce development system by 2020—namely, to establish vocational education as the mainstay, supported by bachelor's and master's degree education development. It encourages universities and schools to offer majors and training courses in geriatrics, rehabilitation, nutrition, psychiatry, and social work;

develop related teaching materials and curricula; strengthen training for teachers and training bases; introduce dual certificates for academic education and vocational training; and offer opportunities for continuous learning and remote education. Professional training will be subsidized for those who attend training for aged care and occupational skill appraisal. In 2011, the Ministry of Human Resources and Social Security (MOHRSS) introduced the national occupational skills standards for aged care workers. Correspondingly, MOCA has made efforts to provide vocational and technical training for caregivers in recent years.

Government Purchasing of Services

The State Council's 2013 *Opinions* define the role of the government as "purchaser and regulator of elderly care services" rather than direct supplier. In 2014, MOF and other three ministries jointly sent out a notice on government purchasing elderly care services. According to this policy document, the scope of government purchasing of elderly care services can cover home care services, community care services, and institutional care services for the Three No's, low-income elderly, disabled, and semi-disabled elderly with economic difficulties; vocational training and education and continuous education for caregivers; elderly ability and care needs assessment; service performance evaluation; and so on. Funding of purchases comes from government revenue. Over 50 percent of the lottery fund set aside for welfare by MOCA and those of local governments shall be allocated to the development of aged care services, and the share should be increased over time. Subsidies for privately run nursing homes and community centers are provided, usually per bed, both for fixed and operating costs, such as a one-time building subsidy and operation subsidy in Chengdu and Ningxia. Ningxia encourages its local governments to set up a special fund for home-based aged care services, and MOCA funded a vocational school training program to prepare more caregivers with RMB 40 million from a national lottery (Caixin Online 2013).

Government Subsidies

A mechanism for evaluating aged care services will be set up, and a subsidy system for elderly in financial difficulty and those who have lost physical abilities will be established. Based on the needs of aged care services, a government subsidy system, including investment subsidies, credit subsidies, operation subsidies, and service purchases, has been introduced to stimulate and encourage social forces participating in the elderly care system. In 2014, the subsidy system for seniors and the disabled elderly with financial difficulties was proposed to be established nationwide by the end of 2015. The subsidy standards are determined by the provincial governments. The subsidies are funded by local governments and will be used mainly for elderly care services and not for basic living allowances, which will be covered by basic pensions, rural/urban *dibao* programs, and other social assistance programs.

Preferential Taxation

Favorable policies relate to taxes, fees, and charges that are designed to encourage the supply of elderly care services. Non-profit elderly care homes meeting eligibility criteria shall also be exempt from paying corporate income taxes, property taxes, or urban land use taxes for houses and land used for their business activities. Those making donations to them will also be eligible for proportional tax deductions. Construction projects of non-profit elderly care facilities shall be exempt from paying any administrative charges, whereas profit-making elderly care homes will enjoy a 50 percent reduction in administrative charges. Elderly care services provided by elderly care institutions shall not pay administrative fees, and prices for electricity, water, gas, and heat for such institutions shall be the same as those for ordinary citizens but not those for enterprises. Elderly care institutions financed by foreign capital can enjoy the same preferential taxation policies.

Government Stewardship

Following the State Council's 2013 *Opinions*, various measures have been taken at the ministerial level to regulate the elderly care service market and strengthen government management, including:

- *Licensing and management*. In 2013, MOCA issued two policy documents[15] to strengthen management of elderly care institutions, which clearly state that MOCA is in charge of managing all elderly care institutions. For registration, non-profit elderly care institutions will be registered at the civil affairs agencies, while profit-making elderly care institutions will be registered at the industry and commerce departments.
- *Standards*. In 2014, the standardization of the elderly care services was initiated, which calls for the development of a basic common standard system that will cover institutional, community, and home-care service standards, management standards, and operation standards, as well as product standards for the elderly by 2020.
- *Pricing*. In 2015, NDRC and MOCA issued rules to regulate the pricing of elderly care services. The market mechanism will determine the price of elderly care services, in particular for privately financed and operated institutions. For public elderly care institutions, the charges for elderly care services vary among beneficiaries. It is free of charge for Three Nos elderly, while the government guidance price will be charged for those who are widows, disabled, semi-disabled, or who have financial difficulties.
- *Information system*. In 2014, six ministries jointly launched pilot projects, choosing 200 elderly care institutions and 450 communities with a focus on home-based care services to promote integrated information management and service delivery at the community level.
- *Monitoring and evaluation*. In 2013, MOCA provided instructions to introduce the assessment of elderly care services. In 2014, MOCA, the State Administration of Industry and Commerce (SAIC), and the National Bureau of Statistics (NBS) started joint efforts to collect data systematically on elderly care institutions, communities, home care beneficiaries, and related information.

Within these broad guidelines, entitlement to fully or partly subsidized publicly provided elderly care is determined at the local level but is typically restricted to "vulnerable groups." The official implementation plan for accelerating the development of the aged care industry in Anhui, for example, stipulates that the government will fund aged care services for vulnerable elderly who are incapable of working, have no source of income, and have no one to support them. Furthermore, low-income and childless seniors shall have access to aged care services but pay low charges. It also directs public aged care facilities that have enough resources to prioritize government-supported beneficiaries with dementia or those who are disabled, with commensurate increases in subsidies for those with higher degrees of disability.

Institutional Setup

The institutional arrangements for developing China's elderly care system involve the national, ministerial, and subnational levels. The roles of various institutions involved in elderly care policy making and implementation are described briefly below.

National Level

At the national level, the State Council has established the National Working Commission on Aging to plan, coordinate, and guide aging work nationwide, and it drafts medium- and long-term plans and policies to promote and improve the establishment of the elderly care system. The National People's Congress formulates and enacts laws to protect and guarantee the rights and interests of the elderly.

China National Working Commission on Aging: Led by one State Councilor, the Commission comprises 32 state-level departments, with one vice-minister equivalent from each department as its representative. Its responsibilities are to formulate development strategies and major policies for the aged; coordinate the relevant departments and promote the implementation of development plans; and lead, supervise, and check the work at local levels. It is headquartered in MOCA, sharing offices and other resources with the NCA. Each province, prefecture city, and county has offices and aging committees for the daily administration and implementation of policies with special dedicated staff to carry out routine work. This structure ensures a strong network of authority from the central to the local level.

Ministerial Level

At the ministerial level, the line ministries set up sectoral policies and strategic plans; conduct policy advocacy and law enforcement; implement the national and sectoral plans; take measures for manpower development, standards, and quality control; and conduct monitoring and evaluation. Although many ministries are involved in developing the elderly care system, the roles and responsibilities of a few leading ministries are described here.

MOCA: Under the jurisdiction of the State Council, MOCA is responsible for domestic social and administrative affairs in China. It is the central government agency in charge of social welfare and services for the aged, disabled, veterans, and other special populations. More specifically, the national regulatory authority over aged care services rests with the Department of Social Welfare; for rural welfare homes, it is under the Department of Social Assistance. MOCA is one of the line ministries setting national policies for elderly care services and is responsible for issuing regulatory guidelines and standards that are to be followed and implemented by provincial-level Departments (or Bureaus) of Civil Affairs. Apart from overall policy making, it is also involved in the development of national training curricula and accreditation of training programs.

NHFPC: The NHFPC sets national health and family planning policies and is responsible for issuing policy initiatives and standards that guide health reform, public hospital reform, drug administration, health and medical service delivery, and policy implementation at the sub-national level. Under the NHFPC, the Department of Family Planning and Family Development is in charge of healthy aging policies and measures related to disease prevention, health care, medical treatment, rehabilitation, long-term care, hospice, and family support for the elderly. In addition, the Department of Primary Health is responsible for rural health and community health policies, planning, standards, and implementation and for providing guidance on medical treatment, nursing care, health care, and health management at the community level.

NDRC: The NDRC leads the national overall socioeconomic development strategies; drafts the annual, medium-term, and long-term development plans; promotes economic and social reforms; drafts and reviews investment projects and fixed asset investment plans; and monitors macroeconomic trends. Within the NDRC, the Department of Social Development is responsible for development strategies and plans, reforms, and investment projects in the social sectors, including for population aging and elderly care services. For the five-year plan cycle, NDRC drafts a master plan first based on inputs from the line ministries and submits it to the Politburo for approval. With the approved master plan, each ministry drafts a sectoral five-year plan.

MOF: The MOF formulates and implements national fiscal and taxation policies and medium- and long-term plans and strategies; designs and promotes fiscal and taxation reforms; and manages central public revenues, expenditures, budgets, and transfers. Within the MOF, the Department of Social Security is responsible for policies, budgets, expenditures, and social insurance fund management related to human resources and social security, civil affairs, and health, including public spending for social welfare and elderly care services.

MOHRSS: The MOHRSS formulates and implements national employment and social insurance policies and medium- and long-term plans and strategies, and it guides policy implementation at the subnational level. Within the MOHRSS, there are several departments relevant to elderly care services such as the Department of Pension Insurance, the Department of Rural Social Insurance, and the Department of Medical Insurance. The first two are in charge of the urban workers' pension scheme and the rural and urban residents' pension scheme, respectively; at present, the last one is responsible for leading studies on long-term care insurance and has chosen four cities (Shanghai, Nantong, Qingdao, and Jilin) for pilots.

Sub-National Level

At the sub-national level, the provincial government sets implementation plans under the guidelines of the national and sectoral development plans and strategies; promotes policy implementation, workforce training, and data collection for monitoring and evaluation; and strengthens integrated services at the community level and home care service delivery. As shown in figure 2.1, the sub-national level has five layers, from the provincial level to the community/village level. Prefecture cities and counties play big roles in both financing and implementation. Communities and villages are self-governing institutions, not government bodies. Streets, towns, and townships are grassroots government bodies.

Local civil affairs agencies are responsible for implementing and converting the laws and policies enacted by the State Council into on-the-ground realities. They coordinate the work of the different relevant parties; monitor, evaluate, supervise, and analyze the growth and development of the aging industry locally; and promote research to find innovative and best practices. They also set clear rules and regulations for the entry and exit of institutions, quality enforcement, adherence to management norms, and disciplining of wrongdoers. The finance department allocates funds for the speedy development and establishment of aged care institutions. The pricing departments set scientific and reasonable pricing mechanisms. Other departments (e.g., education, food and drugs, commerce, housing, taxation, finance, quality enforcement) are all given duties as per the standards, laws, and regulations established by the State Council.

Community organizations are expected to play a role in the delivery of aged care services. All services and programs that are delivered in the community setting are administrated by and/or in collaboration with the Urban Residents'

Figure 2.1 Stakeholders in Policy Design and Implementation at the Subnational Level

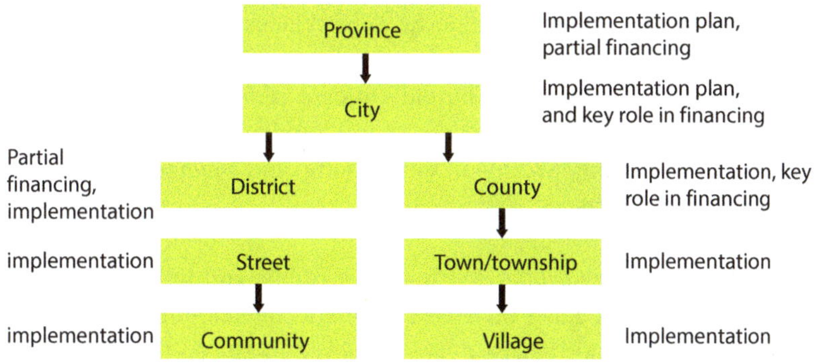

Committee or Rural Villagers' Committee. These Committees are neighborhood-level, quasi-governmental organizations mandated by the central government to take care of older people. Over the past two decades, these Committees have been gradually taking on new responsibilities, pooling community resources, and developing and implementing a wide range of service programs by themselves (Xu and Chow 2011). Non-profit and charity organizations as well as volunteer services are also encouraged to lend support for aged care services.

Challenges and Recommendations

Progress

China's elderly care system has made remarkable progress in the 12th Five-Year Plan period. Achievements include the introduction of a policy framework and legislation, increased public inputs and private capital, enhanced elderly care facilities, expanded coverage and scope of services, and improved capacity and government stewardship as described below.

- *Introduction of policy framework and legislation.* Although the concept of a three-layer elderly care system was formulated in the 2000s, the policy framework was formally defined in the 12th Five-Year Plan period with medium- and long-term goals and policy measures. Realizing that institution-based care was overemphasized, the 12th Five-Year plan redefined the role of institution-based care and envisioned the three-layer elderly care system with home-based care as its bedrock, supported by community-based care and supplemented by institution-based care as mentioned earlier.

- *Increased public inputs and private capital.* Public investment at various government levels for building elderly care facilities amounted to RMB 3.8 billion in 2011 (the first year of the 12th Five-Year Plan) (Tang 2015). Public inputs continued to increase in the following years. From 2012 to 2014, public inputs from the central government reached about RMB 10.2 billion in total. In addition, local governments have increased public inputs to build elderly care facilities. For example, most provinces have listed the establishment of the elderly care system as key provincial projects. In 2013, 18 provinces introduced subsidies for the senior elderly, 22 provinces established a subsidy system for the elderly with financial difficulties, and 3 provinces introduced subsidies for long-term care. The elderly care service market has also been liberalized further to attract domestic and foreign capital. A few provinces (cities) such as Beijing, Shanghai, Guangdong, and Shenzhen have launched foreign capital projects.

- *Enhanced elderly care facilities.* With greater public and private capital inputs, elderly care facilities have increased dramatically, and the goal of reaching 30 beds per 1,000 elderly persons was achieved by the end of 2015. As shown in figure 2.2, the number of total beds doubled from 2.9 million in 2009 to 5.8 million in 2014. The number of beds per 1,000 elderly persons also increased from 17.7 in 2010 to 27.7 in 2014. Table 2.2 shows that the increase in total beds has largely been in urban institutions, rural institutions, and community institutions, although social welfare homes have also had an increase in beds. In 2013, day care centers covered nearly 50 percent of urban communities and 20 percent of rural communities.

- *Expanded coverage and scope of services*. With more beds, urban and rural institutions can now accommodate more needy elderly people. In 2014, 3.2 million elderly persons received institutional care services. The development of home care and community care has also offered various services to millions of elderly people. In 2014, China had 18,927 elderly care facilities and institutions and 40,537 mutual help institutions at the community level. A number of provinces (cities), such as Beijing, Shanghai, Zhejiang, Jiangsu, Anhui, and Hubei, have introduced the government purchasing services approach and offer home-based care services to the elderly. Service coverage has also expanded to cover not only Three Nos and *wubao* people but also the oldest elderly, empty-nest elderly, the disabled and semi-disabled, the poor, and low-income elderly with financial difficulties. In addition, the scope

Figure 2.2 Trends of Total Beds and Care Services Received by the Elderly

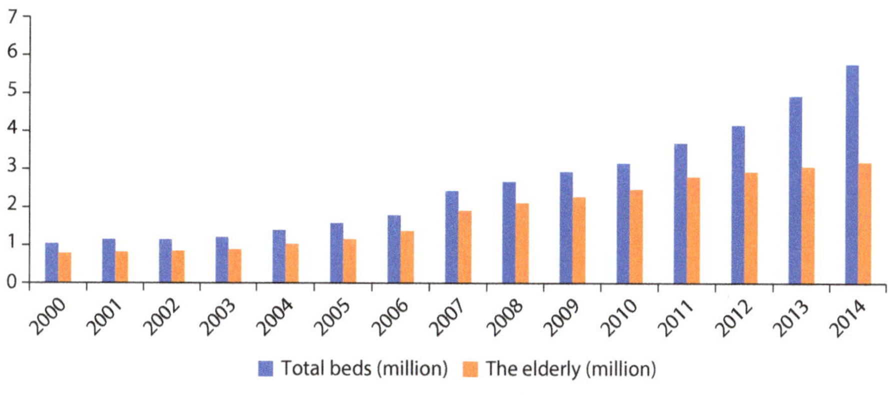

Source: NBS, various years.

Table 2.2 Trends in Total Beds and Their Composition, 2009–13

Year	*2009*	*2010*	*2011*	*2012*	*2013*
Total beds	289.0	307.3	343.2	416.5	493.7
Urban institutions	49.3	56.7	63.0	78.2	97.1
Rural institutions	208.8	224.9	242.1	261.0	272.9
Social welfare homes	22.8	24.5	27.2	30.9	34.6
Community institutions	4.5	1.2	10.9	19.8	64.1

Source: NBS, various years.

of elderly care services has also expanded to include daily living services, rehabilitation care, psychological and mental health care, long-term care, emergency aid, legal assistance, and so on.

- *Improved capacity and government stewardship*. Both the central and local governments have taken a series of policy measures to strengthen management and standardization of institutions and service delivery (e.g., licensing, pricing, standards, information systems), introduced guidelines on the ability and needs assessment for elderly care services, and started to collect data for monitoring and evaluation. Local governments have also started to support coverage of the elderly under accident insurance, comprehensive liability insurance, and/or supplementary commercial health insurance, often by subsidizing their participation. Anhui, for example, established a comprehensive liability insurance system and achieved 100 percent coverage by the end of 2014. The participation expenses are guaranteed by the general fiscal budget and local area welfare lottery fund. In Qingdao (Shandong), all participants in urban workers' health insurance and urban resident basic health insurance are also covered under long-term health care insurance. Zhejiang Province has established general liability insurance in public policy–based aged care agencies. The compensation ranges from RMB 10,000 to RMB 300,000 according to the level of injury of the aged.

Challenges

Although remarkable progress has been made, the development of China's elderly care system still faces many challenges. This section focuses in particular on the challenges in policy design and implementation, including demand-side policy interventions, horizontal and vertical policy coordination, and implementation and management capacity building at the national and local levels.

- *Supply- versus demand-side policy interventions*. Policy design for the elderly care system has long placed much emphasis on the supply side through capital investment and various input subsidies to promote the construction of elderly care facilities. Indeed, institutional beds and facilities have grown very fast, and the targeted number of beds was achieved by the end of 2015. However, the bed utilization rate has declined sharply. As figure 2.3 below shows, the average utilization rate dropped from 78.7 percent in 2009 to 44.9 percent in 2013. During the same period, the utilization rate at urban institutions decreased from 65.5 percent to 38.4 percent; at rural institutions from 82.9 percent to 52.8 percent; at welfare homes from 73.2 percent to 45.7 percent; and at community institutions from 22.2 percent to 5.6 percent. The decline in utilization rates across all types of institutions indicates an oversupply of beds that exceeds the effective demand of the elderly.

Figure 2.3 Utilization Rate of Beds for the Elderly between 2009 and 2013

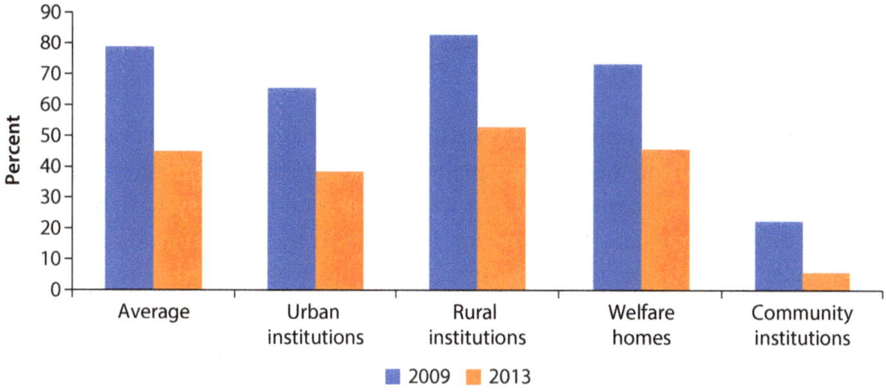

Source: NBS, various years.

- International experiences indicate that China's standard for beds per 1,000 elderly is high for its income level (Development Research Center of the State Council 2014; Tang 2015). Other countries normally choose elderly people 65 years of age and above as a reference for their bed supply standards, while China has chosen elderly people 60 years of age and above. Following international practices of using elderly people 65 years of age and above as the denominator, China's goals are equivalent to 45 beds per 1,000 elderly persons by 2015 and 52–60 per 1,000 elderly persons by 2020. In comparison, the Nordic countries have 60–70 beds per 1,000 elderly persons, while the United States, Australia, the United Kingdom, and France have 40–45 beds, and East Asian and Southern European economies have 20–25 beds.

- On the demand side, some local governments have introduced the elderly needs/ability assessments or elderly voucher programs but have not linked them with needs assessments and income levels. Shanghai has pioneered the ability and needs assessments, and Guangdong also adopted a similar approach at the provincial level in 2015.

- *Horizontal and vertical policy coordination.* Population aging and the elderly care services are cross-cutting issues and involve more than 30 ministries and agencies at the national level. As discussed in "The Policy Framework and Institutional Arrangements" section, following the State Council's 2013 Opinions, a number of ministries have independently or jointly issued many policy initiatives, guidelines, standards, and requirements to accelerate the establishment of China's elderly care system. A major challenge is to make those policy reforms consistent and to coordinate across sectors and agencies. Policy and institutional barriers that constrain the participation of private investors, operators, and service providers as well as workforce development also need to be addressed. At the national level, the China National Working Commission on Aging plays the role of coordinator but does not have the authority to make decisions. Vertically, translating policy design into implementation requires smooth coordination among the six layers of the administrative hierarchy, from the central level down to the community and village level.

- *Implementation and management capacity building at the national and local levels.* The national and local governments have set up targets and taken measures to accelerate the establishment of a three-layer elderly care system, but it will take time to translate those policy measures into implementation. At the national level, stewardship capacity needs to be strengthened to regulate and oversee the development of the elderly care service market. At the same time, capacity building for implementation also needs to be strengthened at the local level (Yeung, Fung, and Lee 2015).

Recommendations

While China has made remarkable progress in the 12th Five-Year Plan period, the development of its elderly care system remains at an early stage. It faces challenges as described above. Continuous reforms need to put more effort into strengthening community-based care and home-based care, expanding elderly care in rural areas, incorporating the ability assessment with needs assessments, and strengthening standards, information systems, and monitoring and evaluation. The following chapters will discuss policy suggestions in detail.

Annex 2A Policies for Developing the Elderly Care System in the 12th Five-Year Plan Period

Areas	*Date*	*Document no*	*Topics*	*Government bodies*
Public Institutions Reform	12/13/2013	369	Circular on the Pilot Work of Carrying out the Public Elderly Care Institution Reform	MOCA
National Pilots	12/27/2013	23	Notice on Carrying out Comprehensive Reform Pilots for the Elderly Care Service Industry	MOCA, NDRC
National Pilots	07/13/2016	200	Circular on Reform Pilots of Home- and Community-based Elderly Care Services with the Central Finance Support	MOCA, NDRC
Investment and Financing	04/28/2013	56	Management Measures on the Central Special Lottery Funds to Support the Rural Happiness Home Project	MOF, MOCA
Investment and Financing	09/12/2014	2091	Circular on Promoting Health and Elderly Care Project Construction	NDRC, MOCA, MOF, MOLR, MOHRUD, NHFPC, PBC, SAT, GASC, CBRC
Investment and Financing	05/28/2014	116	Circular on Promoting the Construction Work of Urban Facilities for the Elderly Care Services	MOCA, MOLR, MOF, MOHRUD

table coninues next page

Areas	*Date*	*Document no*	*Topics*	*Government bodies*
Investment and Financing	01/28/2014	23	Circular on Strengthening the Construction Work of the Elderly Care Service Facility Planning	MOHURD,MOLR, MOCA, NCA
Investment and Financing	02/28/2014	47	Instructions on Promoting Liability Insurance of Elderly Care Institutions	MOCA, CIRC, NCA
Investment and Financing	04/14/2015	78	Opinions on Development Finance to Support the Construction of the Elderly Care Service System	MOCA, CDB
Investment and Financing	03/03/2016	65	Guidance on Financial Support to Accelerate the Development of the Elderly Care Service Industry	PBC, MOCA, CBRC, CSRC, CIRC
Investment and Financing	04/07/2015	817	Guidelines on Issuing Special Bonds for the Elderly Care Industry	NDRC
Investment and Financing	10/09/2016		Notice on Supporting the Integration and Deployment of Idle Social Resources to Develop the Elderly Care Services	MOCA, NDRC, MOE, MOF, MOLR, MOEP, MOHURD, NHFPC, SASAC, SAT, SAB
Private Sector	07/24/2012	129	Opinions on Encouraging and Guiding Private Capitals into the Elderly Care Sector	MOCA
Private Sector	02/17/2013	67	Notice on Hong Kong SAR, China and Macao SAR, China Service Providers Opening Profit Elderly Nursing Homes and Institutions for the Disabled in the Mainland	MOFCOM, MOCA
Private Sector	11/24/2014	81	Announcement on Encouraging Foreign Investors to Establish for-Profit Institutions Engaged in the Elderly Care Services in China	MOFCOM, MOCA
Private Sector	02/03/2015	33	Opinions on Encouraging Private Capitals to Participate in the Development of Service Industry for the Elderly Care	MOCA, NDRC, MOE, MOF, MOHRSS, MOLR, MOHRUD, NHFPC, CBRC, CIRC
Land	04/17/2014	11	Guidance on Land Utilization for the Elderly Care Facilities	MOLR
Workforce	06/10/2014	5	Opinions on Accelerating the Cultivation of Workforce for the Elderly Care Service Industry	MOE, MOCA, NDRC, MOF, MOHRSS, NHFPC, CCO, CCYL, NCA
Workforce	11/14/2011	104	National Occupational Skills Standards for Aged Care Workers	MOHRSS
Workforce	05/12/2014	13	Opinions on Making Efforts to Carry out Vocational and Technical Training for Caregivers in Civil Affairs Sector	MOCA
Government Purchasing Services	08/26/2014	105	Notice on the Work of the Government Purchasing the Elderly Care Services	MOF, NDRC, MOCA, NCA
Senior Elderly Subsidies	09/10/2014	113	Notification on Establishing and Improving a Subsidy System for the Senior and Disabled Elderly with Economic Difficulties	MOF, MOCA, NCA

table coninues next page

Areas	Date	Document no	Topics	Government bodies
Fee Exemption	11/01/2014	77	Circular on Reducing and Exempting Administrative Charges for the Elderly Care and Medical Institutions	MOF, NDRC
Licensing	06/28/2013	49	Licensing Measures on Establishment of Elderly Care Institutions	MOCA
Management	06/28/2013	48	Management Measures on Elderly Care Institutions	MOCA
Standards	02/10/2014	17	Instructions on Strengthening Standardization of the Elderly Care Services	MOCA, CSAC, MOFCOM, GAQSIQ, NCA
Pricing	01/19/2015	129	Instructions on Regulating Service Charges of Elderly Care Institutions to Promote a Healthy Development of the Elderly Care Service Industry	NDRC, MOCA
Information System	12/16/2014		Notification on Pilot Projects of the Information System Development for the Elderly Care and Community Services	MOCA, NDRC, MOF, MPC, MIIT, NHFPC
Assessment	10/05/2013	127	Instructions on Promoting the Assessment Work of the Elderly Care Services	MOCA
Statistics	12/08/2014	251	Circular on Carrying out the Statistical Work of the Elderly Care Service Industry	MOCA, SAIC, NBS

Source: Compilation from MOCA's website.

Annex 2B Acronyms of Chinese Government Agencies

Abbreviations	Full name
CCO	Central Civilization Office
CCYL	China Communist Youth League
CDB	China Development Bank
CBRC	China Banking Regulatory Commission
CIRC	China Insurance Regulation Commission
GAQSIQ	General Administration of Quality Supervision, Inspection and Quarantine
GASC	General Administration of Sport of China
MIIT	Ministry of Industry and Information Technology
MOC	Ministry of Construction (now merged with MOHRUD)
MOCA	Ministry of Civil Affairs
MOE	Ministry of Education
MOEP	Ministry of Environmental Protection
MOF	Ministry of Finance
MOFCOM	Ministry of Commerce (MOFCOM, formerly Ministry of Foreign Trade and Economic Co-operation)
MOHRSS	Ministry of Human Resources and Social Security
MOHRUD	Ministry of Housing, Rural and Urban Development
MOP	Ministry of Personnel (now merged to MOHRSS)
MOLSS	Ministry of Labor and Social Security (now merged with MOHRSS)

table continues next page

Abbreviations	*Full name*
MOLR	Ministry of Land and Resources
NBS	National Bureau of Statistics
NCA	National Committee on Aging
NDRC	National Development and Reform Commission
NHFPC	National Health and Family Planning Commission
NPC	National People's Congress
NSAC	National Standardization Administration of China
PBC	People's Bank of China
PFPC	Population and Family Planning Commission (now merged with NHFPC)
SASAC	State Owned Assets Supervision and Administration Commission
SAB	State Administration Bureau
SAIC	State Administration of Industry and Commerce
SAT	State Administration of Taxation

Source: Compilation from MOCA's website.

Notes

1. In the Chinese context, policy documents advocate for the establishment of a socialized elderly service system. It is important to distinguish between three terms: "elderly support," "elderly care," and "elderly services." The traditional "elderly support" concept covers both income support and care services. The term "elderly care" refers to health care and social care. The scope of "elderly services" is much broader and has a meaning in the service industry. This chapter focuses on the elderly care system.
2. This refers to a typical family with 4 grandparents, 2 parents, and one child.
3. The United Nations classifies a country as an aging society, an aged society, or a super aged society if the proportion of the elderly population 60 years of age and above is over 7 percent, 14 percent, or 21 percent of the total population, respectively.
4. On May 27, 2016, President Xi made a speech on China's Aging, and advocated that China's elderly care system will be home-based care as a bedrock, supported by community-based care, supplemented by institution-based care, and combining medical and social care services.
5. This was renamed the China Aging Association, but the original English name remains unchanged for consistency.
6. See the 1994 policy document *Deepening the Reform of Welfare Institutions to Speed up the Socialization of Social Welfare*, issued by MOCA.
7. In 1997, MOCA promulgated the *Interim Procedures for Management of Rural Nursing Homes*, requiring the provision of food, medical services, and funeral services for the elderly. In 1999, MOCA launched the *Interim Procedures for Management of Social Welfare Institutions*, providing guidance on construction sites, sanitary standards, caregivers, and so on.
8. The 10 ministries included the National Planning Commission, Ministry of Civil Affairs, Ministry of Labor, Ministry of Personal, Ministry of Health, Ministry of Finance, National Education Commission, All-China Federation of Trade Unions, All-China Women's Federation, and National Committee on Ageing.

9. MOCA also issued a series of policy documents such as *Opinions on Promoting Urban Community Construction Nationwide* and *Opinions on Strengthening and Improving Community Services* and took active measures to strengthen community construction and service delivery. By the end of 2005, there were 195,000 urban community service amenities and 8,479 comprehensive social service centers in China.
10. Shanghai first introduced a 90-7-3 structure, and other cities borrowed this concept afterward. When preparing for the 13th Five-Year Development Plan, a number of cities such as Beijing, Chengdu, and Shijiazhuang proposed a 90-6-4 structure.
11. For the health service system, the project investment includes general hospitals, TCM hospitals, specialty hospitals, rehabilitation hospitals and nursing homes, hospice, health services, and primary health care facilities. For the elderly care system, the project investment goes to community elderly day care centers, nursing homes, nursing homes with medical services, and rural elderly service facilities. For sports and fitness facilities, the project investment covers sports venues and facilities, public health centers, outdoor fitness venues, schools, sports facilities, and fitness rooms.
12. See NDRC's *Guidelines on Issuing Special Bonds for the Elderly Care Industry* (2016).
13. In 2012, following the State Council's *Some Opinions on Encouraging and Guiding Private Capitals into Health Development*, MOCA issued *Opinions on Encouraging and Guiding Private Capital into the Elderly Care Sector.*
14. The *Opinions on Encouraging Private Capitals to Participate in the Development of Elderly Care Service Industry (2015).*
15. They are the *Licensing Measures on the Establishment of the Elderly Care Institutions* and the *Management Measures on the Elderly Care Institutions.*

References

Cai, Fang, John Giles, Philip O'Keefe, and Dewen Wang. 2012. *The Elderly and Old Age Support in Rural China: Challenges and Prospects*. Directions in Development. Washington, DC: World Bank.

Caixin Online. 2013. "Blues for Gray Hair: What's Wrong with China's Elder Care Section." March 6. http://english.caixin.com/2013-06-03/100536498.html.

Development Research Center of the State Council. 2014. "China's Elder Care System—Progress, Existing Problems and Reform Ideas. Research Department of Social Development." World Bank TCC5 Project.

Information Office of the State Council of the People's Republic of China. 2006. "The Development of China's Undertakings for the Aged." Beijing.

NHFPC (National Health and Family Planning Commission). 2016. *2015 China Family Development Report*. Beijing: China Population Press.

NBS (National Bureau of Statistics). Various years. *China Social Statistics Yearbook (2010–2014)*. Beijing: China Statistics Press.

CHARLS (China Health and Retirement Longitudinal Study) Research Team. 2013. *Challenges of Population Aging in China: Evidence from the National Baseline Survey of the China Health and Retirement Longitudinal Study (CHARLS)*. http://online.wsj.com/public/resources/documents/charls0530.pdf.

Tang, Jun. 2015. "The Status, Problems and Prospects of China's Elderly Care Services." *Journal of Chinese Academy of Governance* (3): 75–81.

Xi, Jinping. 2016. "Promoting the Comprehensive, Coordinated and Sustainable Development of Undertakings on Aging." http://news.xinhuanet.com/politics/2016-05/28/c_1118948763.htm.

Xu, Qingwen, and Julian C. Chow. 2011. "Exploring the Community-Based Service Delivery Model: Elderly Care in China." *International Social Work* 54 (3): 374–87. doi:10.1177/0020872810396260.

Yeung, Agnas K. C., Kwok Kin Fung, and Kim Ming Lee. 2015. "Implementation Problems in the Development of Urban Community Services in the People's Republic of China: The Case of Beijing." *The Journal of Sociology & Social Welfare* 26 (3), article 10.

CHAPTER 3

Building a Long-Term Care Delivery System with a Balanced Mix of Services

Zhanlian Feng, Qinghua Li, Elena Glinskaya, Nan Tracy Zheng, and Joshua M. Wiener

Introduction

Current policy initiatives in China have focused on increasing the overall supply of aged care services of all types, as they are still at an early stage of development. The central government's *Twelfth Five-Year Plan (2011–15) for Socioeconomic Development* lays out a policy framework for developing a three-tiered system of social services and supports for older people. At the core of this planned system is in-home care, to be supplemented by community-based services and supported by institutional care. Among many other goals, the Plan aims to add more than 3.4 million new residential care beds (more than twice the number of licensed nursing home beds in the United States in 2013) in five years to increase total capacity to 6.6 million beds, or 30 beds per 1,000 elders aged 60 and over, by 2015 (all these targets were met, according to recent government statistics). In 2013, the State Council released a policy document that calls for accelerating the development of the senior care services industry, with the government looking to the private sector for market-driven solutions to help fill the supply-need gap quickly. A follow-up policy directive, jointly issued in 2015 by 10 ministery-level government agencies led by the Ministry of Civil Affairs, urges local authorities to implement measures to encourage and facilitate the entry of private-sector capital into the senior care sector.

For policy makers, it is important to plan and develop an optimal mix of services that meet consumer needs and preferences and that are delivered in the least restrictive settings where independence, autonomy, dignity, and quality of life are

---

Zhanlian Feng is a Senior Research Analyst at RTI International. Qinghua Li is a Research Analyst at RTI International. Elena Glinskaya is a Lead Economist and Program Leader for Human Development for China, Mongolia, and the Republic of Korea at the World Bank. Nan Tracy Zheng is a Senior Research Analyst at RTI International. Joshua M. Wiener was a Distinguished Fellow at RTI International and the former director of RTI's Aging, Disability, and Long-Term Care Program.

valued and maximized. Increasingly, these are desirable policy goals targeted across economies, at least in principle. However, in reality, a myriad of practical and programmatic hurdles can make it challenging to achieve those goals.

This chapter presents a review of international experiences in long-term care provision, drawing primarily on research literature and observations from the United States and other Organisation for Economic Co-operation and Development (OECD) countries. These international experiences provide historical precedents and lessons that Chinese policy makers can use to guide the development of a viable long-term care system that fits the socioeconomic, cultural, and political contexts as well as the market environment in China. This review is followed by an up-to-date analysis of China's evolving senior care landscape, focusing on recent policy initiatives and emerging models of service provision in selected provinces and municipalities across the economy. The chapter concludes with a discussion of key policy issues and challenges for China in further developing aged care services in the years ahead. Where appropriate, policy suggestions are made.

International Experiences in Long-Term Care Provision

Internationally, the provision of long-term care varies in terms of the mix of services available and the delivery of those services, shaped by each economy's unique policy context and social and political circumstances (Wiener 2011). This notwithstanding, a universal preference for home- and community-based services (HCBS) rather than institutional care is observed, which is consistent with the broad trend across many countries of shifting long-term care services from institutional settings to home- and community-based settings. Yet, what constitutes an optimal and balanced mix of services and how to get there remain elusive to policy makers in many economies.

Universal Preference for Home- and Community-Based Care

Understanding consumer preferences and providing flexible options for services and supports are critical for person-centered care, which is increasingly recognized as an essential component of the effective delivery and quality of long-term care. Preferences for long-term care options include both settings (where care is rendered) and providers of care (individuals or organizations that provide care). Long-term care is provided in three broadly defined settings: home, community, and institutions. In home- and community-based settings, care is provided mostly by family members and other informal (i.e., unpaid) caregivers, supplemented by formal (i.e., paid) services and supports where they are available and affordable. In institutions, care is provided by formal caregivers. The discussion in this chapter focuses on formal long-term care services and supports, particularly those that are publicly financed, given their policy relevance.

Across OECD economies and elsewhere, research and public opinion polls invariably show that the majority of older people with long-term care needs prefer receiving services in their homes or in community-based settings rather than in institutions (Colombo et al. 2011; Eckert, Morgan, and Swamy 2004; Kane and Kane 2001; Keenan 2010; Wolff, Kasper, and Shore 2008). This preference appears to be universal, regardless of cultural differences across economies. In the United States and other OECD economies, the predominant long-term care providers are family members and other informal caregivers (Fujisawa and Colombo 2009; Gibson and Houser 2007; Kaye, Harrington, and LaPlante 2010). This reflects the general preference of older people to be cared for at home or in the community (Eckert, Morgan, and Swamy 2004) but also the limited availability or affordability of formal services and supports in these preferred settings.

Older people, especially those with lesser physical and cognitive impairments, live healthier and happier lives when they are able to remain in their own homes and in the local community (Keenan 2010). This is congruent with the fact that most older people value independence and autonomy (Welford et al. 2010; Wolff, Kasper, and Shore 2008), which are more likely to be achieved in home- and community-based settings. In contrast, research shows that large institutions tend to create dependency rather than autonomy (Barkay and Tabak 2002; Welford et al. 2010). In institutions, residents have limited or little involvement in decision making concerning their daily lives and care. Providing personalized (i.e., individualized) care to older people is difficult in an institutional setting. Moreover, an institution epitomizes the model of agency-directed care, where the arrangements of care and services are more for the convenience of the facility than for the client. Research has shown that compared to agency-directed care, people receiving consumer-directed long-term care have a higher quality of life and are more satisfied with the care they receive (Foster et al. 2003).

The majority of older people with long-term care needs actually live in their own home or in the home of a family member and wish to continue to do so. Across OECD countries, about 70 percent of long-term care users receive care in their homes or local communities (Colombo et al. 2011). In the United States, an estimated 12 million people are in need of long-term services and supports, and among them, over 10 million are receiving care in their homes or community-based settings (Kaye and Harrington 2015). With appropriate support, older people would be able to remain where they most want to be for as long as possible, a concept known as "aging in place."

In most circumstances, institutionalization is used as the last resort only after all other meaningful options have been exhausted and more professional care is needed. As physical and cognitive impairments progress, the care needs may become so complex and increase to such a level that professional care provided in institutional settings is more appropriate. Research suggests that the preference for home- and community-based long-term care weakens as the care needs increase (Guo et al. 2015; Wolff, Kasper, and Shore 2008). Despite the shift in preferences toward institutional long-term care associated with advancing physical disabilities and cognitive impairments, aversion to institutional care is generally strong and common among the elderly.

Balancing the Mix of Services across Settings and Providers

To account for all circumstances, the best practice approach would be a long-term care continuum with a balanced mix of services across settings that meet older people's needs and preferences. If the care system is focused primarily on institutional care, it neglects the home- and community-based care that most people prefer and actually need.

In OECD economies, the mix of services has shifted increasingly toward HCBS, reflecting both the preferences of older people and the direction of long-term care policies in these countries. Across OECD economies, the historical root of formal long-term care was almost always in institutions operated by local governments, religious organizations, or charities (Mor, Leone, and Maresso 2014; Smith and Feng 2010). The demand for and development of HCBS have typically come about much later, and not surprisingly, the long-term care landscape tends to be dominated by institutional services and providers in many of these economies. However, over the past two or three decades, long-term care provision in almost all OECD economies has shifted away from institutions toward home- and community-based settings.

An important driver of this policy shift is the desire to contain long-term care costs while meeting increased needs. Institutional care is substantially more costly than home- and community-based alternatives (Kaye, Harrington, and LaPlante 2010). In 2008, institutional care accounted for 62 percent of total long-term care costs across OECD countries, while on average only a third of long-term care users received care in institutions (Colombo et al. 2011). In the United States, the per-recipient cost of nursing home care is five times higher than that of community-based care (Kaye, Harrington, and LaPlante 2010). With the projected increase in the elderly population and their long-term care needs, policies to allocate resources across long-term care settings need to be financially sustainable, particularly when governments are hard-pressed with budgetary constraints in times of economic downturn.

In response to older people's predominant preference for home-based care and to contain long-term care expenditures, OECD countries employ a range of policies to encourage home care, using a mix of demand- and supply-side interventions. These include direct expansion of home care supply (e.g., Canada, Ireland, New Zealand, Sweden, and Poland), regulatory measures, and financial incentives. Finland and the Czech Republic, for example, have developed guidelines to promote home care and enforce admission of those with high care needs only. Similarly, Hungary has restricted budgets and imposes stricter criteria for admission to nursing homes. In Sweden, the Act on Support and Service for Persons with Certain Functional Impairments (1995) moved a large number of people with functional impairments from hospitals into their own apartments in the municipalities. In some countries, financial incentives (e.g., cash benefits in Austria, the Netherlands, Sweden, the United States, and the United Kingdom) are directed either at users or providers to enhance user choice and stimulate a rebalancing of services and resources toward home- and community-based care.

In the United States, publicly financed long-term care (mainly through Medicaid, a federal-state jointly funded health insurance program for the needy) has been shifting away from nursing home care toward HCBS over the past two decades (Feng et al. 2011a; Wiener, Anderson, and Brown 2009). Health reforms established by the Affordable Care Act of 2010 aim to further expand HCBS and to accelerate the pace of rebalancing. The HCBS Plan Option gives states the flexibility to expand HCBS benefits. Under the "Community First Choice Option," states providing supports and services for home caregivers can receive higher federal funding. States also receive additional funding for each Medicaid beneficiary transitioned from an institution to the community under the "Money Follows the Person" initiative. Started in 2005, these programs have increased federal funding for states to assist programs that stimulate service provision at the place where people needing care want it delivered, for instance in their own homes. In addition, through increased federal financial aid, the "State Balancing Incentive Program" incentivizes states to increase the proportion of Medicaid spending on home- and community care (Colombo et al. 2011). These efforts are congruent with older people's preferences and are intended to redress the "institutional bias" that has long characterized the traditional approaches to long-term care in the United States (Smith and Feng 2010). While progress has been made, the bulk of total long-term care spending still goes to institutional care.

Other countries have also adopted policies to help stimulate rebalancing. Both Ireland and France, the latter in the context of the 2007–10 Old Age Solidarity Strategy and the 2008–12 National Alzheimer Plan, have set targets for increasing services in the community. Finland aims to reduce residential care use from 6.5 percent to 3 percent of the elderly population by 2012, encourage community care, and improve care provision at home. Other countries like Australia, Austria, Finland, and Luxembourg have improved benefit packages for home (and palliative) care. In 2004, Canada developed a ten-year plan to strengthen health care which provides some short-term home care services free of charge (Colombo et al. 2011).

Similar policies that support the provision of care in a home or community setting have also been adopted in Asia, starting in the early 2000s. In 2006, the Japanese government passed a reform that emphasizes comprehensive community support for the elderly, with Musashino City being a prime example of successful adoption of holistic community care. The payment for long-term care services in Japan differs according to the care recipient's limitations in activities of daily living, but the difference in payments from the most severe to least severe cases was initially less than 20 percent, so providers had an incentive to admit patients with mild limited functional ability (Ikegami, Yamauchi, and Yamada 2003). To correct for this perverse incentive, the payment for those with the lowest level of care needs—accounting for more than half of all patients in long-term care beds—has been set below the care production cost since 2006. Additional payments are offered to institutions that have been successful in enabling a certain percentage of recipients to return home.

Singapore promotes home care through a national grant for caregivers who want to undertake training. In Thailand, policies to prolong the time older persons can remain in their own homes (e.g., through financial grants of B 15,000 for home modifications) are part of the National Plan on Long-Term Care implemented in 2011 (Colombo et al. 2011; HelpAge International 2014).

Progress in developing home care is reflected in the rising share of long-term care users receiving care in their homes. Over the past decade, the share of home care users increased across most of the OECD countries for which data are available (except in Finland and Spain, where there has been a downward trend). Figure 3.1 shows recent trends in the proportion of long-term care users aged 65 years and older who received formal care at home in selected OECD countries. In France, for example, the share of home care users increased from 41.8 percent in 2002 to 61.3 percent in 2010. From 2009 to 2013, the share of home care users in Portugal more than doubled from 14.9 percent to 34.0 percent (not shown). In Hungary, Israel, Japan, Norway, Sweden, and New Zealand, over 70 percent of current elderly long-term care users received care in their homes, with the highest share in Israel (over 90 percent).

The distribution of long-term care expenditures on home care relative to institutional care has shifted as well. Across OECD countries, the annual growth rate of public spending on home care from 2005 to 2011 was 5 percent, compared to 4 percent for institutional care (OECD/European Union 2013). In the United States, expenditures on home- and community-based care have expanded considerably over the past two decades. As shown in figure 3.2, the proportion of total Medicaid long-term care spending for HCBS (including those for

Figure 3.1 Proportion of Long-Term Care Recipients Aged 65 Years and Older Receiving Care at Home in Selected OECD Countries, 2000–13

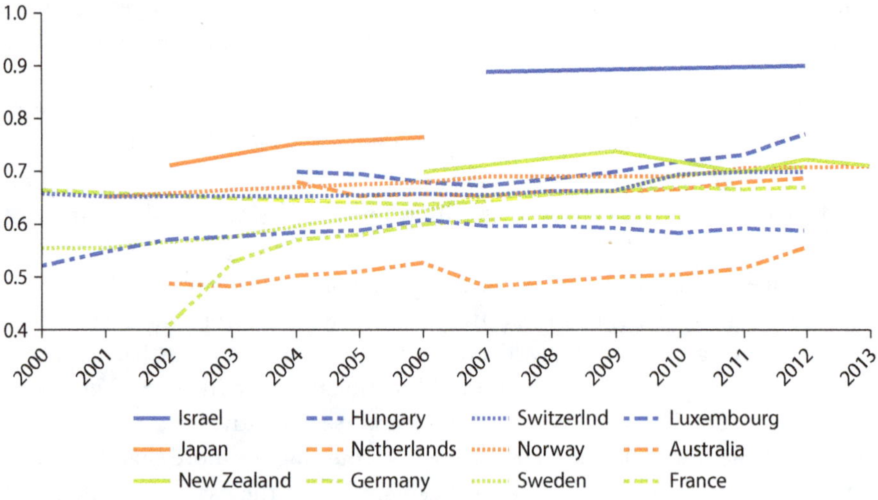

Source: Authors' analysis of data from OECD Health Statistics, 2014.
Note: Long-term care recipients include people who received formal (paid) long-term care in institutions or at home.

Figure 3.2 Proportion of Total Medicaid Long-Term Care Expenditures for Institutional Care versus Home- and Community-Based Services in the United States, 1995–2012

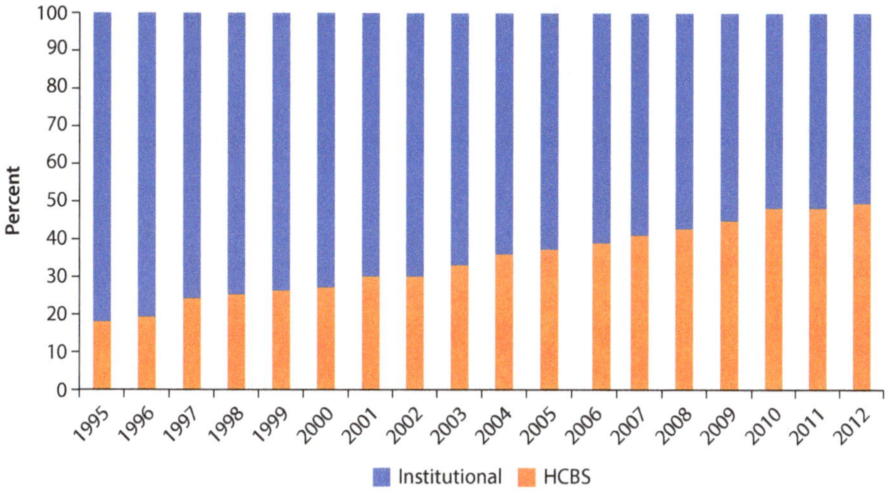

Source: Eiken et al. 2014.

non-elderly people with intellectual and developmental disabilities) increased from 18 percent in 1995 to nearly 50 percent in 2012. In contrast, the proportion of institutional care spending has been shrinking.[1]

Nonetheless, although home- and community-based care has expanded in most OECD countries, a high proportion of long-term care expenditures is still allocated for institutional care. This is partially due to the greater need for care for institutionalized people and the higher costs of professional caregivers in institutions.

The rebalancing of long-term care toward home- and community-based settings is projected to continue. The optimal and sustainable allocation of resources in homes and communities versus institutions will depend on the need mix of service users, their preferences for care, and the availability of informal caregivers.

Challenges in Home- and Community-Based Long-Term Care

Rebalancing the long-term care system and reallocating resources accordingly require an understanding of population and societal preferences as well as the benefits and challenges of home- and community-based care. A key assumption driving the expansion of home- and community-based long-term care is that such care is more cost effective than institutional care and will help contain long-term care expenditures. However, solid empirical evidence supporting this assumption is lacking.

Regarding cost effectiveness, the current evidence is at best inconclusive, and the strength of previous studies on this topic is low or insufficient (Grabowski 2006; Konetzka 2014; Weissert, Cready, and Pawelak 1988; Wysocki et al. 2012). Concerns have been raised about the possibility that home and community-based care may not necessarily be cost-saving and may ultimately increase long-term care expenditures (Konetzka 2014). Two factors may contribute to higher-than-expected costs: the "woodwork" effect (the availability of home- and community-based care may prompt utilization by people who would otherwise not use institutional care) (Eiken, Burwell, and Sredl 2013; Kane et al. 2013) and the costs of informal care provided by unpaid family caregivers that are usually not accounted for in the estimation (Konetzka 2014).

There is also a dearth of evidence on the quality of home- and community-based care, partly due to difficulties in quality monitoring and enforcement in home- and community-based settings. The heterogeneity in service users, care providers, and funding sources adds to the challenges not only in service delivery (U.S. Government Accountability Office 2015) but also in measuring and monitoring the quality of home- and community-based care (U.S. Centers for Medicare and Medicaid Services 2014). It is reasonable to expect that quality in certain domains may be lower in homes and communities than in institutions. For example, institutions may be safer and more appropriately designed to meet the needs of disabled and frail older people, and institutional staff can provide more professional and higher-quality care than informal family caregivers. Another quality concern is the psychosocial well-being of the elderly. While staying in homes and communities allows older adults to maintain autonomy and privacy (which they prefer and value), isolation, loneliness, and depression are potential "side effects" that are detrimental to health and quality of life. This is of particular concern for people with limited mobility and inadequate assistance and those living in remote rural areas. In contrast, people with similar functional and cognitive status residing in institutions may have more opportunities to interact with other residents and enjoy a more social life.

Another potential hurdle for providing high-quality home- and community-based care is the readiness of communities to meet the increasing needs of the aging population, especially those with disabilities or cognitive impairment. In the United States, for example, recent research conducted by the Harvard Joint Center for Housing Studies reveals that the current housing stock is not well-prepared to meet the community-based long-term care needs for the aging population (Joint Center for Housing Studies of Harvard University 2014). First, high housing costs may limit the affordability of basic life necessities and health care for older people. Second, most houses may not have basic accessibility features to accommodate the needs of older people—as a result, they are not safe and suitable for people with functional or cognitive impairments. Moreover, insufficient transit options may limit the mobility of community-dwelling older people, especially those in suburban and rural communities, resulting in isolation and social disconnection.

Public versus Private Sector Roles in Service Provision

Aged care service providers include a mix of government-run, nonprofit, and for-profit organizations. In most of today's developed economies, long-term care services are typically provided by private sector entities rather than directly by the government (notable exceptions are the Nordic countries, where local municipalities provide a substantial share of services directly, but even they are moving somewhat toward private provision of care). This pattern is consistent with a market-oriented economy in which private sector providers are generally believed to be able to produce and deliver services in a more efficient manner than their public sector counterparts. In addition, private sector long-term care providers are more often proprietary (i.e., for-profit) than non-proprietary (i.e., not-for-profit), despite variations in the ownership mix across countries.

In the United States, the nursing home industry has historically shifted away from government-owned and voluntary homes to proprietary facilities, with an increasing concentration of ownership in multi-facility chains (Hawes and Phillips 1986). Currently, for-profit nursing homes constitute 69 percent of all U.S. nursing homes and 71 percent of all nursing home beds, whereas non-profit nursing homes account for roughly 25 percent of all facilities and nearly 24 percent of all beds. Government-owned nursing homes remain the smallest sector, accounting for approximately 6 percent of all facilities and 6 percent of all beds (Centers for Medicare and Medicaid Services 2013). From 2003 to 2012, the number of for-profit nursing homes increased slightly (from 10,717 to 10,825 facilities), while the number of non-profit facilities decreased nearly 16 percent (from 4,633 to 3,912 facilities) and government-owned homes decreased 11 percent (from 1,030 to 915 facilities) (Centers for Medicare and Medicaid Services 2013).

The process of privatizing the few remaining public nursing homes in the United States continues today as local governments, increasingly under budgetary pressures, try to minimize their roles as direct service providers (Amirkhanyan 2008). Among residential care facilities serving relatively less disabled elders than nursing homes (such as assisted living facilities and board-and-care homes), approximately 82 percent are private, for-profit facilities, while the remaining 18 percent are private, nonprofit facilities or are owned by state, city, or local government (Park-Lee et al. 2011). Other types of long-term care providers such as homemaker services, home health agencies, and adult day service providers are also dominated by private, for-profit ownership.

In England in the early 1980s, the majority of care home providers were publicly owned and community-based services were limited, but today, the overwhelming majority of adult social care service providers are in the private sector (Malley et al. 2014). Local authorities traditionally ran care homes, but the number of private, for-profit facilities exploded during the 1980s and 1990s, leaving government facilities with less than 10 percent of all care homes (United Kingdom Commission for Social Care Inspection 2009). The theory behind this privatization is that competing organizations will provide more choices to consumers at lower cost, with more flexibility, and with greater consumer orientation. In the Republic of Korea, almost all long-term care providers (residential care facilities and home care providers) are private (Jung et al. 2014). Private, nonprofit providers play a larger role in some countries, such as Germany and Australia.

An exception worldwide is the so-called Scandinavian model such as in Sweden, where most providers are government agencies and institutions, although there has been movement toward privatization (Swedish Ministry of Health and Social Affairs 2007). The goal of government ownership is to provide care without consideration of whether an activity is profitable. However, government-managed and provided services are often fraught with bureaucracy, waste, and inefficiency. This is the main reason why in most of the market-oriented economies, the governments choose to play the role of service purchasers by partnering with the private sector rather than become direct service providers.

Current Long-Term Care Landscape in China

Traditionally, elder care in China has been confined to the familial sphere, long enshrined by the Confucian norm of filial piety. Under this cultural mandate, which is also codified in current Chinese law, adult children are required to care for elderly parents physically, financially, and emotionally. Over the past several decades, however, rapid demographic and socioeconomic changes have eroded the family care system for the aged, escalating concerns that families alone may not continue to be able to shoulder the responsibilities for and burdens of elder care. These concerns are compounded by China's one-child family policy that has been in effect for more than 30 years (which officially ended in 2015), further straining the capacities of family caregivers.

Against this backdrop, a new sector of formal long-term care services—alternative forms of care outside the traditional informal support network—has recently emerged to meet the needs of disabled and frail elders who can no longer be cared for adequately by family caregivers. This nascent sector is evolving rapidly across China, catalyzed by government policies and private sector initiatives. Due to lack of data, obtaining a clear picture of this fast-growing sector is difficult. The scant evidence revealed by recent published studies portrays a rather lopsided landscape characterized by a booming sector of residential care facilities (Feng et al. 2014; Feng et al. 2011b; Zhan et al. 2006) and, in contrast, the limited development of services in home- and community-based settings (Wu et al. 2005; Xu and Chow 2011). A description of recent developments in both settings is provided below, drawing on current information where available.

A Booming Residential/Institutional Care Sector

As signaled in a series of recent policy directives, the central and local governments in China have actively encouraged the development of elder care facilities by the private sector through increased financial inducements such as lump-sum subsidies for new construction and ongoing operating subsidies for each occupied bed. Public sector investment in residential care facilities has increased, as well.

This has helped fuel the rapid growth of institutional elder care in recent years (Feng et al. 2014; Feng et al. 2011b).

According to government statistics, the total number of beds in aged care facilities nationwide increased from nearly 3.15 million in 2010 to 5.78 million in 2014, a net increase of more than 2.63 million or 83 percent over this short five-year period alone. In relative terms, the number of aged care facility beds per 1,000 people age 60 and over rose from 17.7 in 2010 to 27.2 in 2014, a nearly 54 percent increase (table 3.1).[2] While the total bed supply grew steadily over this period, the total number of aged care facilities fluctuated from year to year and actually decreased from 39,904 in 2010 to 33,043 in 2014, suggesting that much of the growth in bed supply resulted from expansion or consolidation of existing facilities during this period. The majority (roughly three-quarters) of these facilities are rural homes for the aged (*jing lao yuan*), which are financed and managed by local governments.

Despite this growth, China still has far fewer long-term care beds on a per capita basis than most developed economies. An estimated 1.5 to 2 percent of older Chinese (age 65 and over) live in residential care facilities, compared to rates of 5 to 8 percent in Western countries (Chu and Chi 2008; Gu, Dupre, and Liu 2007).

Historically, institutional elder care in China was rare and limited to a small number of publicly supported welfare recipients. In urban areas, they are referred to as "Three No's" (*san wu*)—people who have lost the ability to work, have no source of income, and have no legal guardians to support them or have guardians who do not have the ability to support them (State Council Information Office 2006).[3] In rural areas, a different term is used for people who also qualify as "Three No's–Five Guarantees" (*wubao*), elders who are guaranteed food, clothing, housing, medical care, and burial expenses by the local government. In the past, institutionalized elders were stigmatized, and few families could imagine placing a loved one in an institution to be cared for by strangers. Most residential care homes were run by the state, municipalities, local governments, or collectives.

Catering to growing consumer demand, residential aged care facilities have expanded significantly in both the public and private sectors, although in urban areas, the private sector has dominated recent growth.[4] For example, Tianjin had only 4 facilities in 1980 (all government-run), rising to 13 by 1990, 68 by 2000, and 157 (20 government-run and 137 private facilities) by 2010 (Feng et al. 2012a).

Table 3.1 Residential Aged Care Facilities and Beds in China

	2010	*2011*	*2012*	*2013*	*2014*
Aged care facilities	39,904	40,868	44,304	42,475	33,043
Beds in aged care facilities (million)	3.149	3.532	4.165	4.937	5.778
Beds in aged care facilities per 1,000 people age 60+	17.7	19.1	21.5	24.4	27.2

Source: Statistical Communique on the Development of Social Services, Ministry of Civil Affairs (retrieved from: http://cws.mca.gov.cn/article/tjbg/).

In Nanjing, government ownership dominated facilities built before 1990 (96 percent) but became more rare in the 1990s (60 percent) and diminished significantly in the 2000s (23 percent).

In the mid-1990s, China implemented reforms to decentralize the operation and financing of state welfare institutions. Since then, these institutions have shifted their financial base from reliance on public funding to more diversified revenue sources, including privately paying individuals. In private sector facilities, daily operating revenues come almost exclusively from private-payer residents. Even in government-run facilities, the majority of current residents are paying privately for their care. In Nanjing, a typical government-run facility currently draws close to 60 percent of its operating revenues from private payment sources; in Tianjin, it is nearly 70 percent (Feng et al. 2012a).

Broadly, China has three main types of institutional care facilities today, differentiated by target clientele, source of revenues, and levels of care provided: public social welfare facilities, nursing homes, and retirement/community homes. Public social welfare facilities have been around for decades and used to exclusively serve welfare recipients such as childless elders, orphans, the mentally ill, and developmentally disabled adults without families. Many such facilities, mostly in urban areas, have recently expanded to also take in non-welfare individuals who pay for their care privately and constitute the majority of current residents. The services and amenities available in a public social welfare facility depend to a large extent on which level of government owns and runs the facility. Municipal government-run facilities, many of which are known to keep a long waitlist for interested clients, typically are better equipped and offer a more attractive array of services and amenities than facilities run by lower-level (e.g., district or county) governments. Nursing homes are facilities that have professional staff (e.g., nurses, therapists, physicians) available to provide skilled nursing, rehabilitation, or medical services. Retirement homes or community-based facilities may include senior apartments or assisted living facilities that provide various levels of personal care assistance but less professional services.

In terms of ownership, facilities could be broadly characterized as government-built and government-operated, government-built and privately operated, and privately built and privately operated facilities (see examples in box 3.1 below). The latter two are among the various *modi operandi* the government has been promoting to encourage private sector engagement in the development of institutional aged care services. In particular, the government-built and privately operated mode is viewed as a public-private partnership (PPP) model in which the government contracts with a competent private sector entity that delivers the desired services and manages daily operations of the facility while enjoying generous public subsidies (e.g., free or below market value rental, discounted utility rates, tax exemption).

Private sector senior care facilities that primarily target affluent and high-income elders are also emerging in China.[5] They are relatively few in number, vary in quality, and are often too expensive for most elderly people (Zhan et al. 2006).

Box 3.1 Examples of Institutional Care in China

Examples of *government-built and government-operated* facilities include Xiyanghong Senior Care Home in Anyang City, Henan Province. It started in 2005 and currently has a capacity of 260 beds. Monthly charges include RMB 2,600 per bed and RMB 480–850 for meals. It provides health care and social and recreational activities. Another example is Dezhou Senior Care Center in Dezhou City, Shandong Province. It started in 1998, with a current capacity of 300 beds. Monthly charges include RMB 550–650 per bed and RMB 300–600 for meals, with additional charges of RMB 260–960 for services that vary according to different care plans suited to individual care needs (independent living, semi-dependent, or fully dependent). It also provides rehabilitation and medical services.

One example of a *government-built and privately operated* facility is Zhengzhou Heyou Care Home in Zhengzhou City, Henan Province. Started in 2010, it has a current capacity of 298 beds and allegedly meets international/American industry standards. Monthly fees include RMB 800–1,200 per bed, RMB 260–800 for meals, and service charges of RMB 150–5,000 depending on type of care plan. It provides personal care, rehabilitation, and skilled nursing care.

One example of a *privately built and privately run* facility is Zhineng Yibai Senior Care Home in Xuzhu City, Jiangsu Province. Started in 2011, it currently has 316 beds (only 158 occupied as of ICAIA [2014]). Monthly fees include RMB 400 for meals, and RMB 400–1,500 for different nursing care plans. Services are provided by the physicians and nurses of Xuzhou Geriatrics Hospital.

One example of a *privately developed and privately operated* facility is Shuxin Gangwan Zhongqi Senior Care Home in Jinan City, Shandong Province. It started in 2011 and has a current capacity of 362 beds (only 200 occupied according to ICAIA [2014]). Monthly charges include RMB 1,480 per bed, RMB 600 for meals, and RMB 200–1,500 for different nursing care plans varying by dependency level. All health care workers have received professional training from the local Bureau of Civil Affairs. The facility provides recreational and medical services. Another example is Yifa Hongri Senior Nursing Home in Nanjing City, Jiangsu Province. Started in 2012, it has a current capacity of 352 beds (only 203 occupied according to ICAIA [2014]). Monthly fees include RMB 2,040–3,330 per bed, RMB 600 for meals, and RMB 300–1,200 for different nursing care plans varying by dependency level. It also provides recreational services in addition to medical care.

Source: ICAIA 2014.

The Gonghe Garden facility in Beijing is one such example. The 269-unit complex provides a full range of care and services with a price tag ranging from RMB 7,000 to RMB 16,800 per month, unaffordable for most.[6] The company operating Gonghe Garden believes such facilities cater to the top 0.1 percent of the market (Caixin Online 2013). Many such high-end facilities currently operate far below full capacity, due in large part to the lack of effective demand.

Indeed, existing facilities in both the public and private sectors have many empty beds, although in general, government facilities have higher occupancy rates than private facilities in urban areas. In Nanjing, for instance, the average occupancy rate (share of occupied beds out of total available beds in a facility) was 69 percent in private sector facilities as of 2009, compared to an average of 83 percent in government facilities. In Tianjin, the averages as of 2010 were 76 percent and 91 percent in private and government facilities, respectively (Liu, Feng, and Mor 2014). The lower occupancy rate in private sector facilities could be a result of high pricing (beyond the means of many elders and their families) and/or poor quality. Nevertheless, the limited evidence available suggests that there is no clear difference in quality between public and private sector facilities, although when the staffing-to-resident ratio is gauged relative to the level of functional impairments of residents, private sector facilities are more likely to be understaffed than government facilities (Liu, Feng, and Mor 2014). In rural homes for the aged (*jing lao yuan*), anecdotal reports reveal woefully low occupancy rates in many parts of China, often with more than half of available beds empty.[7] A combination of poor conditions, few services and amenities, bad reputations, and the persistent stigma associated with living in such facilities contributes to underutilization even among *wubao* elders (the target clientele), let alone others who seek quality care and pay for that care out of their own pockets.

Lack of adequately trained staff—among many other factors such as weak regulatory oversight—is a major barrier to improving the quality of institutional elder care in China (Feng et al. 2012a). A recent review points out that staff in Chinese nursing homes are older and have lower education levels compared to their counterparts in Western countries, and few facilities use established qualification standards to prepare staff for their roles in the facility (Song et al. 2014). In urban facilities, most direct-care staff are migrant workers from nearby rural areas or locals who were laid off from state-run enterprises in the process of public sector reform and restructuring (Feng et al. 2011b; Song et al. 2014).

Home- and Community-Based Services Falling Short of Demand

Since the 1990s, the Chinese government has launched several initiatives to promote community-based social service programs. Most of these initiatives have been health-related, such as house calls, emergency aid, adult day care programs, health and wellness clinics, and recreational activities (Xu and Chow 2011). Home- and community-based elder care programs have also emerged and expanded in recent years, but they are largely concentrated in major metropolitan areas (Wu et al. 2005), and even there, existing services remain spotty. Few, if any, such programs are found in rural areas, despite a strong policy stance in favor of their development.

In urban areas, community-based social services are typically managed and organized by quasi-governmental community organizations and delivered primarily by private small business service providers and volunteers (Xu and Chow 2011). These new social programs are premised on increasing the role of local government and community responsibility in the provision and delivery of services for older people. Xu and Chow (2011) distinguish between services that are funded by public welfare assistance funds and therefore targeted to low-income beneficiaries of the *dibao* (government-provided minimum living guarantee for the needy) system and other welfare programs and community-oriented initiatives funded from various sources. The first type of services are funded directly by the government and are usually delivered free or at minimal charge.[8] The second type of services—encompassing adult day care centers, in-home care, community-sponsored meals programs, community kitchens, recreational centers, and mutual aid networks—are funded by community and governmental sources, which include individuals, corporations, schools, hospitals, and other organizations. These services require payment and therefore are affordable only to elders who have the ability to pay. The subsidy amount for provision of these services depends greatly on local funding, availability of good-quality staff, and the enthusiastic participation of the community.

An earlier example of community-based services was the Starlight Program, under which the government invested a total of RMB 13.4 billion (roughly US$2.1 billion) to build urban community-based senior service centers from 2001 to 2004. By 2005, the program had established 32,000 Starlight Senior Centers nationwide. However, these centers apparently did not serve their intended purpose. After 2005, the Starlight Program lost momentum due in part to dwindling financial support from the government, raising questions about the viability of similar initiatives (Feng et al. 2014).

In Beijing, the local government created a model called "four nearby solutions" which offers older people resources for study, social activities, caregiving support, and opportunities to participate in community affairs. However, recent evaluations suggest that the caregiving support functions in the community and at home are often ill-defined, suffer from weak coordination across different agencies and service providers, and have proven expensive to sustain in the absence of unit cost appraisals and standards.

More recently, a new type of home-based elder care model, dubbed Virtual Elder Care Home or Elder Care Home without Walls, has gained popularity in China. It features home care agencies providing a wide range of personal care and homemaker services in elders' homes. Services are initiated by phone calls to a local government-sponsored information and service center, which then directs a qualified service provider to the elder person's home. Participating providers contract with the local government and are reimbursed for services purchased by the government on behalf of eligible care recipients, the majority of whom are Three No's or otherwise vulnerable. Since its inception in 2007 in the city of Suzhou in Jiangsu Province, the Virtual Elder Care Home model has spread to many parts of China, including Gansu Province, in northwest China (Feng et al. 2012a).

Chengdu city in Sichuan Province aims to accelerate the development of community-based aged care. The district-level government has set up community stations that provide day care and temporary services. These publicly built, privately run community stations are quite in demand, but they operate with marginal profit. In Chongqing municipality (one of four provincial-level municipalities in China), initial observations of home- and community-based aged care services revealed low quality of services, with affordability limited to those elders in the high-income bracket.

In Tianjin municipality, four districts have set up Virtual Elder Care Homes since 2011, where the elderly can order a variety of services (e.g., shopping, medical care, homemaking, and catering services) through equipment with access to the Internet. It seems that the services are mainly provided to elders who are *dibao* beneficiaries, extremely poor, disabled, or in the oldest age group (age 80 or older). One such Virtual Elder Care Home has 15 workers and serves a pool of about 5,000 seniors. In Gansu Province, since 2009, Virtual Elder Care Homes have attracted 95 enterprises to provide the services, with 90,000 elders registered in the system, of whom 25,000 people are frequent users of the service.

In Hangzhou city of Zhejiang Province, the Xihu district developed respite care since 2011 as an attempt to provide temporary relief to family caregivers. Based on application, free elder care services could be provided for 5 to 30 days, 8 hours per day. Family members who have taken care of an elder for more than a year could get temporary respite services. About 60 households apply for the service each year. The government allocated RMB 2 million to finance the service, which is being piloted in only one district of Hangzhou. A more practical approach currently under discussion is to let private aged care providers give short-term care.

Tianjin has established day care centers which can provide temporary nursing services. Adult children who need to travel for a couple of days could send an elderly relative there. The government aims to establish more than two adult day care centers in each district of Tianjin. In Guangzhou city of Guangdong Province, community elder care resources are integrated in a network of home-based comprehensive service centers, supported by an investment of RMB 139 million in 132 residential areas of the city in 2012. Special funds have been provided for the purchasing of maid and other personal services.

In terms of aged care services in rural China, a few notable achievements have been made in several provinces. For instance, Hebei Province launched the "Five in One" Program in rural areas which integrates five types of care institutions (for demobilized servicemen, *wubao* elders, retired military cadres, welfare homes, and other social welfare institutions) into one. The province already has 215 institutions of this kind now, which collectively support 60 percent of *wubao* elders. It has also built rural cooperatives, called Happiness Homes (*xing fu yuan*), where groups of rural elders live together in village housing. No service staff are employed; instead, the elders support each other. The villages provide housing and utilities for free. Living expenses for *wubao* elders are covered by the government, while others must pay for their expenses privately (themselves or by family members).

Similarly, Gansu Province has set up urban community-based adult day care centers and rural Happiness Homes for the elderly, both supported by welfare lottery funds collected by the central and provincial-level governments. In Heilongjiang Province, five villages/towns were selected in 2010 as pilot areas for the rural aged care service system. The pilot aimed to expand the target group of aged care services in rural areas.

Nationally, community-based adult day care centers covered nearly 32 percent of urban communities in 2014, and the target set by the central government was to cover 60 percent by 2015. In 2014, Rural Happiness Homes (first established in 2012) covered about 12 percent of villages. The high-income segment of the community and home care market has also been developing. For example, Right at Home, an American company specializing in home care, has been in China since 2011 and offers 24-hour nursing care in Beijing for RMB 15,000 per month (Caixin Online 2013). A number of high-end providers are in the market in Shanghai and Guangzhou.

Despite the progress made, home- and community-based long-term care services remain underdeveloped and face many challenges in both urban and rural China (Yang 2013). Their scant visibility and availability pale in comparison to the explosive growth of institutional-based services that have thus far dominated China's evolving aged care landscape.

Public versus Private Sector Roles in Service Provision: Current Practices and Issues

The shift away from public provision of aged care services that can be seen across the world is also emerging in China. This coincides with the overall growth in the number of residential care facilities. While social welfare institutions (which exclusively served welfare recipients and were financed and run by the state) once dominated the landscape, private sector facilities have been the main driver of recent growth (Feng et al. 2014; Feng et al. 2011b). The current system has two types of institutional elder care: one is directly invested, owned, and managed by the government, and the other is market-driven and developed, owned, and run by the private sector (Feng et al. 2012a).

A strategic shift in policy direction has recently occurred in China, with the government's role being repositioned from being the direct supplier and provider to being a purchaser and regulator of services, since it is no longer able to respond to pressing needs without enlisting the private sector. Accordingly, the government has issued a series of national policy directives over the last decade to speed up private sector development of social services for the aged. These directives urge local government authorities to offer preferential policy treatments such as tax exemptions, government subsidies for new and existing beds, land appropriation or leasing for new construction, and reduced rates for utilities to encourage private sector investment in the senior care industry. A 2013 State Council policy document (Document No. 35) also clearly signaled that major reforms are underway to privatize the operation and management of publicly built aged care facilities further. Various approaches are encouraged, ranging from state-built and privately run facilities to privately operated facilities with government support and subsidies for construction and operations.

In Anhui Province, the official implementation plan for accelerating the development of aged care services has several provisions aimed at encouraging private sector investment in aged care facilities. Measures include allowing operations in multiple sites with one business license, operating with a business license and getting a permit later on, eliminating the minimum capital threshold required for registration, streamlining the permit process and procedures, relaxing filing requirements for community-based organizations, and providing a three-year exemption from paying rents for non-profit operators that rent public aged care facilities to provide aged care services. Furthermore, as far as government budgetary subsidies are concerned, private service providers enjoy the same level of subsidies as their public sector counterparts, and foreign-invested service facilities enjoy the same preferential policies and subsidies as domestic ones.

Many provincial governments set targets for private sector provision of elder care. In Jiangsu Province, one policy target for 2010–15 is to increase the share of beds in private sector elder care facilities to at least 50 percent of the total bed stock. An example of a publicly built, privately operated model is the home-based Aged Care Service Center in Anhui, with support of RMB 10 million from the local government. The Center provides services for more than 1,000 elders per week. Another example is a privately run, publicly supported nursing home in Longnan city of Gansu Province, a rural facility which was established with the support of local resources. Each *wubao* elder receives an allowance of RMB 1,200 each year from the government and is provided with about 1.5 *mu* (roughly 0.25 acre) of farmland which could be rented out to generate income of about RMB 1,800 per year. The combined total of RMB 3,000 is used to cover the elder's living expenses. Medical expenses will be covered by the local New Cooperative Medical Scheme (NCMS) for rural residents.

The co-existence of public and private sector residential aged care facilities raises concerns about unfair competition between providers in the two sectors. Government-owned and operated facilities enjoy a multitude of advantages over their private sector counterparts, such as: public financing; generous subsidies on rents, utilities, and operating costs; and greater integration with local communities and professionals.

The co-existence of public and private sector residential aged care facilities also raises concerns about potential inequalities in consumer choice and access to services. Research shows that in major cities like Tianjin and Nanjing, government-owned and operated elder care facilities have significantly higher occupancy rates than private sector facilities; however, their residents tend to be healthier and have fewer functional impairments on average than those in private sector facilities (Feng et al. 2012b; Liu, Feng, and Mor 2014). These case-mix differences are likely the result of selective or discriminatory admission policies that favor relatively healthy residents, more so in government facilities than in private sector homes. One study reported that government-owned care homes are more likely to be reserved for upper-class or wealthy families and retired government cadres, whereas poorer, sicker elders have fewer options and choices (Zhan et al. 2006). The higher occupancy rate in government-run facilities is also indicative of the popular demand for publicly subsidized institutional care and the challenges that many private sector facilities face in filling their empty beds.

As China's public sector reforms unfold, government-run aged care facilities should reconsider their admission policies and target services to disabled, frail, and otherwise vulnerable elders who are most in need of publicly supported institutional care.[9] Another concern is that the shift of service provision to the private sector might compromise the quality of senior care in the absence of effective regulatory oversight (Feng et al. 2014; Liu, Feng, and Mor 2014).

Looking Ahead: Issues for China's Development of an Aged Care Continuum

The government's overarching policy framework for a three-tiered long-term care system aptly emphasizes HCBS. In China as elsewhere, older people generally prefer receiving long-term care in their homes or communities (*China Daily* 2014; *Shanghai Daily* 2013).

In actuality, however, current policies and resource allocations incentivize institutional care more than HCBS (Feng et al. 2012a). This is partly because building facilities and beds (physical plant) is easier than providing and managing services in the home and community settings. Because residential care facilities and the kinds of services they provide are more tangible and visible than HCBS, local authorities have a tendency to emphasize the former more than the latter.

Moreover, because of the current government policy of setting targets for the number of beds (and sometimes the number of staff), there is a danger that the emerging aged care system in China may become biased toward institutional care rather than giving the highest priority to home care. A central function of the care system should be to prevent older people from unnecessary hospitalizations and to avoid or delay institutionalization. Setting global targets for the number of beds runs the risk of defeating this priority and neglecting the preferences of many older people and their families. This may be a factor behind the large number of empty beds in existing and newly built facilities, a waste of resources that could be better used to support older people at home or in the community where they prefer to be.

Self-sustaining home- and community-based long-term care services barely exist except in a few major urban centers (like Shanghai), but the few services that do exist at the neighborhood and village levels show the importance of, and the potential for, further outreach to older people living in their homes and enabling them to "age in place." This might include a visiting service and home delivery of meals. Community senior activity centers might be incorporated into programs to facilitate support at the local level. Achieving the full development of this model would require close cooperation and coordination among municipal, district, and street/neighborhood authorities. The overarching goal of this model should be to enable older people to remain independent in their own homes for as long as possible, with increasing levels of support as their needs rise. If successful, this model would be superior to most care systems in the West.

The need for more facilities and residential care beds may be justified, but Chinese policy makers should be careful to avoid an institutional bias in the country's fledgling long-term care system. Instead, they should use available policy instruments (e.g., tax exemptions, subsidies, and other financial incentives) to help build a balanced mix of services that reflect older people's preferences and best meet their needs. Application of these instruments should also be consistent with the broad policy goal of establishing a three-tiered system of aged care services with home-based care as its bedrock, supported by community-based care and underpinned by institutional care. To the extent possible, long-term care should be provided in the least restrictive settings.

The current senior care landscape in China is being shaped by providers of various ownership types and structures. It also provides a testing ground for a range of operational models for service development and delivery, such as state-built and operated, state-built and privately run, privately operated with government support, government subsidies for construction and operating costs, and government purchasing of services from the private sector. Which model produces the best results remains to be seen.

As mentioned above, as the provision of aged care services increasingly shifts toward the private sector, concerns over the quality of care will soon emerge. In the United States and other OECD countries, a large body of research has documented a negative association between for-profit ownership and the quality of care in nursing homes (Comondore et al. 2009; Grabowski and Stevenson 2008; Harrington et al. 2001). Currently, virtually all of the private-sector residential care facilities in China are registered as non-profit, non-enterprise entities, a status required to receive tax exemptions and other favorable policy treatments. In actual operations, however, they tend to behave more like for-profit facilities, and this situation is complicated by a lack of legal clarity in the definition of ownership and property rights. Evidence from limited research in China suggests that there is little difference between government-run and private sector facilities in selected process and outcome aspects of quality (Liu, Feng, and Mor 2014). Nevertheless, private sector homes are more likely to be understaffed despite having residents who are sicker and more disabled than those in government facilities. Many private sector facilities will therefore find it more difficult to meet their residents' needs, raising potential quality of care concerns.

Quality assurance may be difficult without a robust public financing system to enforce sanctions for poor quality. Financing aid to providers, such as subsidies for new construction and operating costs and discounted charges for utilities, are not appropriate instruments for enforcing quality standards. Furthermore, there are concerns that government-run facilities, which are heavily subsidized with public resources, may impede fair competition with private sector service providers (Feng et al. 2012b). Therefore, developing a reimbursement (or pricing) strategy is essential. International experiences in this area point to using a "prime contractor" approach in which providers are paid a capitated amount for a pre-defined package of services or receive payments that are linked to key performance metrics (pay-for-performance). However, these approaches hinge upon a substantial and systematic public long-term care financing system, which does not exist currently in China.

Notes

1. These shifts have been fueled in part by the U.S. Supreme Court's 1999 ruling (in *Olmstead v. L.C.*) which stipulates that unjustified segregation of people with disabilities is a form of unlawful discrimination under the Americans with Disabilities Act (signed into law in 1990) and that it is a violation of civil rights law to separate people with disabilities into institutions when they could live in the community with some limited support. This landmark decision requires states to ensure that people with disabilities can receive services in the most integrated setting appropriate to their needs.
2. It is important to note that there is a lack of differentiation of the different types of aged care facilities in China. Although policy makers have an interest in classifying facilities into meaningful categories according to the kinds of residents served and services provided in each facility, which can aid in regulatory efforts, not much progress has been made thus far. As a result, government statistics and data from published studies tend to lump together various types of facilities covering a wide spectrum, ranging from small board-and-care homes and senior apartments that provide little professional care to large, modern nursing homes that are equipped with nursing services, rehabilitation, and even medical care (Feng et al. 2014; Song et al. 2014). In addition, some private facilities (most likely small board-and-care homes) that are in operation may not be officially registered, but the number of such facilities is unknown.
3. Historically, the term Three No's was phrased simply as "no children, no income, and no relatives." Despite an updated definition, the population to which the term applies remains essentially the same.
4. Private elder care facilities are rare in rural areas, primarily because few rural elders and their families can afford to pay for the care even though the price may be significantly lower than in urban areas. Another factor is cultural: traditional beliefs and the cultural norm of filial piety have a stronger hold in rural areas than in urban areas. In short, rural China is not yet where the market is for the emerging sector of formal aged care services.
5. China also has senior living real estate complexes or retirement communities that have so far focused on remote suburbs, far from city centers and mature urban clusters, which many experts consider a bad bet. As elsewhere, most Chinese elders prefer a location of residence that is close to where their adult children live and convenient for family visitors. Indeed, location is among the top considerations for older people and their family members when choosing an aged care facility.
6. In comparison, the average monthly wage for employees in Beijing in 2013 was RMB 5,793 (http://www.ecovis.com/focus-china/chinas-social-security-system/). Average monthly pensions for retirees are substantially lower. For state enterprise retirees

in Beijing, for example, the current average monthly pension is RMB 3,355, which reflects the most recent upward adjustment for 2015 (http://www.chinanews.com/sh/2015/03-13/7128422.shtml).

7. "Low Occupancy in Rural Homes for the Aged: Ill Equipped Facilities and Poor Management to Blame" (*ChinaNews* 2013).
8. Xu and Chow (2011) characterize China's community-based service model as consisting of "vertical and horizontal" structures of service delivery. It is financed vertically by the government and financed horizontally through the government as well as community and individual sources.
9. It is encouraging that in some localities progress is being made in the right direction. In Beijing, for example, a high-profile nursing home run by the municipal government is changing its admission policy to exclusively serve seniors who have outlived their children. In the future, this facility will only accept people who have lost their only child. The plight of individuals caught in this heart-breaking situation has received increasing attention in recent years as the first generation of couples subjected to China's one-child policy is approaching retirement age (Xinhua 2015).

References

Amirkhanyan, A. 2008. "Privatizing Public Nursing Homes: Examining the Effect on Quality and Access." *Public Administration Review* 68 (4): 665–80.

Barkay, A., and N. Tabak. 2002. "Elderly Residents' Participation and Autonomy within a Geriatric Ward in a Public Institution." *International Journal of Nursing Practice* 8 (4): 198–209.

Caixin Online. 2013. "Blues for Gray Hair: What's Wrong with China's Elder Care Section." March 6. http://english.caixin.com/2013-06-03/100536498.html.

Centers for Medicare and Medicaid Services. 2013. *Nursing Home Data Compendium 2013 Edition*. http://www.cms.gov/Medicare/Provider-Enrollment-and-Certification/CertificationandComplianc/downloads/nursinghomedatacompendium_508.pdf.

China Daily. 2014. "In-Home Nursing Gains Popularity in Aging China." March 13. http://www.chinadaily.com.cn/business/2014-03/14/content_17346869.htm.

ChinaNews. 2013. "Low Occupancy in Rural Homes for the Aged: Ill Equipped Facilities and Poor Management to Blame." January 21. http://www.chinanews.com/sh/2013/01-21/4505572.shtml.

Chu, L. W., and I. Chi. 2008. "Nursing Homes in China." *Journal of the American Medical Directors Association* 9 (4): 237–43.

Colombo, F., A. Llena-Nozal, J. Mercier, and F. Tjadens. 2011. *Help Wanted? Providing and Paying for Long-Term Care*. Paris: OECD Publishing.

Comondore, V. R., P. J. Devereaux, Q. Zhou, S. B. Stone, J. W. Busse, N. C. Ravindran, K. E. Burns, T. Haines, B. Stringer, D. J. Cook, S. D. Walter, T. Sullivan, O. Berwanger, M. Bhandari, S. Banglawala, J. N. Lavis, B. Petrisor, H. Schunemann, K. Walsh, N. Bhatnagar, and G. H. Guyatt. 2009. "Quality of Care in for-Profit and Not-for-Profit Nursing Homes: Systematic Review and Meta-Analysis." *BMJ* 339: b2732.

Eckert, J. K., L. A. Morgan, and N. Swamy. 2004. "Preferences for Receipt of Care among Community Dwelling Adults." *Journal of Aging & Social Policy* 16 (2): 49–65. doi:10.1300/J031v16n02_04.

Eiken, S., B. Burwell, and K. Sredl. 2013. "An Examination of the Woodwork Effect Using National Medicaid Long-Term Services and Supports Data." *Journal of Aging & Social Policy* 25 (2): 134–45.

Eiken, Steve, Kate Sredl, Lisa Gold, Jessica Kasten, Brian Burwell, and Paul Saucier. 2014. *Medicaid Expenditures for Long-Term Services and Supports in FFY 2012*. https://www.medicaid.gov/medicaid-chip-program-information/by-topics/long-term-services-and-supports/downloads/ltss-expenditures-2012.pdf.

Feng, Z., M. L. Fennell, D. A. Tyler, M. Clark, and V. Mor. 2011a. "Growth of Racial and Ethnic Minorities in US Nursing Homes Driven by Demographics and Possible Disparities in Options." *Health Affairs* 30 (7): 1358–65.

Feng, Z., X. Guan, X. Feng, C. Liu, H. Zhan, and V. Mor. 2014. "Long-Term Care in China: Reining in Market Forces through Regulatory Oversight." In *Regulating Long Term Care Quality: An International Comparison*, edited by V. Mor, T. Leone, and A. Maresso, 409–43. Cambridge, U.K.: Cambridge University Press.

Feng, Z., C. Liu, X. Guan, and V. Mor. 2012a. "China's Rapidly Aging Population Creates Policy Challenges in Shaping a Viable Long-Term Care System." [Research Support, N.I.H., Extramural]. *Health Aff (Millwood)* 31 (12): 2764–73. doi:10.1377/hlthaff.2012.0535.

Feng, Z., H. J. Zhan, X. Feng, C. Liu, M. Sun, and V. Mor. 2011b. "An Industry in the Making: The Emergence of Institutional Elder Care in Urban China." *Journal of American Geriatrics Society* 59 (4): 738–44.

Feng, Z., H. J. Zhan, X. Guan, X. Feng, C. Liu, and V. Mor. 2012b. "The Rise of Long-Term Care Facilities in Urban China: Emerging Issues of Access Disparities" (in Chinese). *Population and Development* 18 (6): 16–23.

Foster, L., R. Brown, B. Phillips, J. Schore, and B. L. Carlson. 2003. "Improving the Quality of Medicaid Personal Assistance through Consumer Direction." *Health Affairs-Millwood* 22 (3SUPP): W3–162.

Fujisawa, R., and F. Colombo. 2009. "The Long-Term Care Workforce: Overview and Strategies to Adapt Supply to a Growing Demand." OECD Health Working Papers 44, OECD Publishing, Paris.

Gibson, M. J., and A. Houser. 2007. "Valuing the Invaluable: A New Look at the Economic Value of Family Caregiving." *Issue Brief (Public Policy Institute [American Association of Retired Persons])* (IB82) 1–12.

Grabowski, D. C. 2006. "The Cost-Effectiveness of Noninstitutional Long-Term Care Services: Review and Synthesis of the Most Recent Evidence." *Medical Care Research Review* 63 (1): 3–28.

Grabowski, D. C., and D. G. Stevenson. 2008. "Ownership Conversions and Nursing Home Performance." [Research Support, Non-U.S. Gov't]. *Health Services Research* 43 (4): 1184–203. doi:10.1111/j.1475-6773.2008.00841.x.

Gu, D., M. E. Dupre, and G. Liu. 2007. "Characteristics of the Institutionalized and Community-Residing Oldest-Old in China." *Social Science & Medicine* 64 (4): 871–83.

Guo, J., R. T. Konetzka, E. Magett, and W. Dale. 2015. "Quantifying Long-Term Care Preferences." *Medical Decision Making* 35 (1): 106–13.

Harrington, C., S. Woolhandler, J. Mullan, H. Carrillo, and D. U. Himmelstein. 2001. "Does Investor Ownership of Nursing Homes Compromise the Quality of Care?" *American Journal of Public Health* 91 (9): 1452–55.

Hawes, C., and C. D. Phillips. 1986. "The Changing Structure of the Nursing Home Industry and the Impact of Ownership on Quality, Cost, and Access." In *For-Profit Enterprise in Health Care*, edited by National Research Council, 492–542. Washington, DC: The National Academies Press.

HelpAge International. 2014. *Home Care for Older People: The Experience of ASEAN Countries*. HelpAge International.

ICAIA (International China Ageing Industry Association). 2014. *Understanding Nursing Homes in China: A Preliminary Research Presentation*. ICAIA.

Ikegami, N., K. Yamauchi, and Y. Yamada. 2003. The Long Term Care Insurance Law in Japan: Impact on Institutional Care Facilities." *International Journal of Geriatric Psychiatry* 18 (3): 217–21. doi:10.1002/gps.818.

Joint Center for Housing Studies of Harvard University. 2014. *Housing America's Older Adults: Meeting the Needs of an Aging Population*. Joint Center for Housing Studies of Harvard University.

Jung, H. Y., S. N. Jang, J. E. Seok, and S. Kwon. 2014. "Quality Monitoring of Long-Term Care in the Republic of Korea." In *Regulating Long Term Care Quality: An International Comparison*, edited by V. Mor, T. Leone, and A. Maresso, 385–408. Cambridge, UK: Cambridge University Press.

Kane, R. L., and R. A. Kane. 2001. "What Older People Want from Long-Term Care, and How They Can Get It." *Health Affairs* 20 (6): 114–27.

Kane, R. L., T. Y. Lum, R. A. Kane, P. Homyak, S. Parashuram, and A. Wysocki. 2013. "Does Home- and Community-Based Care Affect Nursing Home Use?" *Journal of Aging & Social Policy* 25 (2): 146–60.

Kaye, H. S., and C. Harrington. 2015. "Long-Term Services and Supports in the Community: Toward a Research Agenda." *Disability and Health Journal* 8 (1): 3–8.

Kaye, H. S., C. Harrington, and M. P. LaPlante. 2010. "Long-Term Care: Who Gets it, Who Provides It, Who Pays, and How Much?" *Health Affairs* 29 (1): 11–21.

Keenan, T. A. 2010. "Home and Community Preferences of the 45+ Population: AARP." http://assets.aarp.org/rgcenter/general/home-community-services-10.pdf.

Konetzka, R. T. 2014. "The Hidden Costs of Rebalancing Long Term Care." *Health Services Research* 49 (3): 771–77.

Liu, C., Z. Feng, and V. Mor. 2014. "Case-Mix and Quality Indicators in Chinese Elder Care Homes: Are there Differences between Government-Owned and Private-Sector Facilities?" *Journal of American Geriatrics Society* 62 (2): 371–77. doi:10.1111/jgs.12647.

Malley, J., J. Holder, R. Dodgson, and S. Booth. 2014. "Regulating the Quality and Safety of Long-Term Care in England." In *Regulating Long Term Care Quality: An International Comparison*, edited by V. Mor, T. Leone, and A. Maresso, 180–210. Cambridge, UK: Cambridge University Press.

Mor, V., T. Leone, and A. Maresso, eds. 2014. *Regulating Long Term Care Quality: An International Comparison*. Cambridge, UK: Cambridge University Press.

OECD/European Union. 2013. *A Good Life in Old Age? Monitoring and Improving Quality in Long-term Care*. OECD Health Policy Studies. Paris, France: OECD.

Park-Lee, E., C. Caffrey, M. Sengupta, A. J. Moss, E. Rosenoff, and L. D. Harris-Kojetin. 2011. "Residential Care Facilities: A Key Sector in the Spectrum of Long-Term Care Providers in the United States." *NCHS Data Brief* (78), 1–8.

Shanghai Daily. 2013. "Elderly Prefer to be Cared for at Home." http://english.eastday.com/e/130923/u1a7675125.html.

Smith, D. B., and Z. Feng. 2010. "The Accumulated Challenges of Long-Term Care." *Health Affairs (Millwood)* 29 (1): 29–34.

Song, Y., R. A. Anderson, K. N. Corazzini, and B. Wu. 2014. "Staff Characteristics and Care in Chinese Nursing Homes: A Systematic Literature Review." *International Journal of Nursing Sciences* 1 (4): 423–36.

State Council Information Office. 2006. *China Publishes a White Paper on Its Undertakings for the Aged*. December 12 (accessed October 10, 2012), http://www.china.org.cn/english/China/191990.htm.

Swedish Ministry of Health and Social Affairs. 2007. *Care of the Elderly in Sweden*. http://www.sweden.gov.se/content/1/c6/08/76/73/a43fc24d.pdf.

United Kingdom Commission for Social Care Inspection. 2009. *The State of Social Care in England*. United Kingdom Commission for Social Care Inspection, London, UK. http://www.dhcarenetworks.org.uk/_library/Resources/Housing/Support_materials/Other_reports_and_guidance/The_state_of_social_care_in_England_2007-08.pdf

U.S. Centers for Medicare and Medicaid Services. 2014. "Medicaid Program; State Plan Home and Community-Based Services, 5-Year Period for Waivers, Provider Payment Reassignment, and Home and Community-Based Setting Requirements for Community First Choice and Home and Community Based Services (HCBS)." Waivers. *Federal Register* 79 (11). http://www.gpo.gov/fdsys/pkg/FR-2014-01-16/pdf/2014-00487.pdf.

U.S. Government Accountability Office. 2015. *Older Adults: Federal Strategy Needed to Help Ensure Efficient and Effective Delivery of Home and Community-Based Services and Supports (GAO-15-190)*. Washington, DC.

Weissert, W. G., C. M. Cready, and J. E. Pawelak. 1988. "The Past and Future of Home- and Community-Based Long-Term Care." *The Milbank Quarterly* 66 (2): 309–88.

Welford, C., K. Murphy, M. Wallace, and D. Casey. 2010. "A Concept Analysis of Autonomy for Older People in Residential Care." *Journal of Clinical Nursing* 19 (9–10): 1226–35.

Wiener, J. M. 2011. "Long-Term Care Financing, Service Delivery and Quality Assurance: The International Experience." In *Handbook of Aging and the Social Sciences*, edited by R. Binstock and L. George, 309–22. 7th ed. London: Elsevier.

Wiener, J. M., W. L. Anderson, and D. Brown. 2009. *Why Are Nursing Home Utilization Rates Declining?* Report prepared for the Centers for Medicare and Medicaid Services. Washington, DC: RTI International.

Wolff, J. L., J. D. Kasper, and A. D. Shore. 2008. "Long-Term Care Preferences among Older Adults: A Moving Target?" *Journal of Aging & Social Policy* 20 (2): 182–200.

Wu, B., M. W. Carter, R. T. Goins, and C. Cheng. 2005. "Emerging Services for Community-Based Long-Term Care in Urban China: A Systematic Analysis of Shanghai's Community-Based Agencies." *Journal of Aging & Social Policy* 17 (4): 37–60.

Wysocki, A., M. Butler, R. L. Kane, R. A. Kane, T. Shippee, and F. Sainfort. 2012. *Long-Term Care for Older Adults: A Review of Home and Community-Based Services versus Institutional Care*. AHRQ Comparative Effectiveness Reviews, Agency for Healthcare Research and Quality (US), Rockville, MD.

Xinhua. 2015. "Beijing Nursing Home to Offer Exclusive Service for Childless Seniors." June 23. http://www.shanghaidaily.com/article/article_xinhua.aspx?id=289057.

Xu, Q., and J. C. Chow. 2011. "Exploring the Community-Based Service Delivery Model: Elderly Care in China." *International Social Work* 54 (2): 374–87.

Yang, H. 2013. "Challenges in the Provision of Community Aged Care in China." *Family Medicine and Community Health* 1 (2): 32–42.

Zhan, H. J., G. Liu, X. Guan, and H. G. Bai. 2006. "Recent Developments in Institutional Elder Care in China: Changing Concepts and Attitudes." *Journal of Aging & Social Policy* 18 (2): 85–108.

CHAPTER 4

The Role of the Private Sector in China's Senior Care Industry

Yvonne Li, Charlie Wang, and Heather Wong

Introduction

Although China's senior care market has been fast growing in recent years, the industry remains largely underdeveloped. The emerging long-term care options for China's over 200 million seniors are characterized by a "home- and community-care based, and institutional care supported" model following the national government's "90-7-3" (adopted in Shanghai and most cities in China) or "90-6-4" (in Beijing) policy guidelines. The policy guidelines suggest that 90 percent of elderly people be cared for at home, 7 percent (6 percent in Beijing) in communities, and the remaining 3 percent (4 percent in Beijing) in institutions.

In order to meet the needs of China's growing population of senior citizens, it is imperative that the government adequately encourages and supports private sector provision of senior care services and products while reforming the service delivery system in the public sector. In the last several years, the government has made significant strides in revising policies to incentivize private sector growth and has thrown open the doors to all investors, including foreign investors and firms. The private sector can provide senior care service at all levels of the market, from low- to middle- to high-end. With clear policy and guidelines as well as proper incentives from the government, the private sector (both domestic and foreign companies) can respond quickly by increasing the scope and improving the quality of services for Chinese seniors.

China's private sector broadly consists of two types of organizations: for-profit and non-profit organizations (NPOs). These organizations differ in their goals, source of financial capital, and how they charge for services and products, as summarized in table 4.1. Domestic or foreign for-profit commercial organizations tend to provide senior care services in the mid- to high-end price range of

Yvonne Li is a Founder and Chairperson of the International China Ageing Industry Association (ICAIA). Charlie Wang and Heather Wong are, respectively, a Research Associate and a Consulting Associate at ICAIA.

Table 4.1 Types of Senior Care Organizations in the Private Sector

Type	*Primary goal*	*Financing/capital*	*Charge for services/ products*
Commercial for-profit organization	Generate a healthy return on investment	Private or public funding	Market rates are charged to seniors (mid to high end)
Non-profit organization (NPO)	Provide affordable services with little or some financial return	Donations and grants, or procurement of services	Seniors make minimal payments (low to lower mid end)

the market. Their primary goal is to maintain a healthy and sustained profit margin while providing high-quality services. NPOs may include domestic civil society, faith-based organizations, and community-based organizations. Their primary goal is to provide affordable services with little or limited expectation of financial returns.

This chapter examines the current role of the private sector in community-, home-, and institutional-based senior care in China as well as its potential for growth. It discusses actions needed to enhance private sector participation in these three settings of care delivery and highlights examples of successful business models through case studies in China, with comparisons made to noteworthy overseas models.

Community and In-home Senior Care Services

The majority of Chinese seniors receive basic care at home from their families, although some receive care at home or in the community from non-government organizations (NGOs), government welfare agencies, or private firms. The goal of home- and community-based care is to allow seniors to live independently and age in place, reduce hospital admissions, and delay their need for moving into senior care facilities. Care provided directly at home may take the form of non-medical services such as assistance with activities of daily living (e.g., bathing, feeding, household chores) and medical care services (e.g., nursing, rehabilitation).

China's in-home service market is expected to grow almost fourfold from RMB 130 billion in 2010 to RMB 500 billion by 2020 (China Research Centre on Ageing 2013). This is one of the most promising market segments in China's senior care industry in terms of not only its market size but also its potential to serve 34 percent of all seniors.[1]

The government has recognized that liberalizing the market is essential to grow China's senior care industry and the private sector needs to play an increasing role. While local governments have set up and managed community centers for the elderly in recent years, these efforts have not been very successful partly because the government's use of resources is not as efficient as the private sectors. In 2012, the Ministry of Civil Affairs issued regulations to support private capital to invest in elderly home- and community-based care through subsidies. The government would purchase services at the community level, provide coordination assistance, and develop national standards.

Community Care in China

Services at the community level are usually of two types, one of which is the physical community center. Physical community centers can include provision of cooked meals, organization of social activities, basic diagnostic health checks, rehabilitation equipment and rehabilitation through basic exercise, assistance with personal tasks, companionship, and service referrals. These services are provided during the day, and some centers may also set up beds for seniors to stay overnight. Seniors are encouraged to get out of their homes to meet at the community centers to socialize with their peers and receive non-medical services. Most services are provided free-of-charge, while some services may be offered at below-market prices. Different systems are in place for payment, depending on local circumstances. Beijing has citywide pricing structures for community centers—currently, seniors are charged RMB 12 for dinner and RMB 5 for a man's shave. Shanghai has developed a coupon system in which seniors are categorized by their level of care needs, and the monthly set of coupons can be redeemed for services at local community centers.

The second type of community services offered in China is the information network that links community services to seniors. Many local communities host a hotline specifically for seniors, which is either set up and staffed by the local Department of Civil Affairs or outsourced to a private vendor. In addition to community centers, some private companies and NGOs have trained elderly care workers and coordinate their services for disabled seniors who cannot leave their homes.

Types of Community Centers for the Elderly

Community day care centers can enrich the lives of seniors by drawing them out into the community and increasing their social interactions with others. Centers that have been successful in attracting seniors, such as Fuzhou Jin Tai Yang (福州金太阳) which is described below, encourage seniors to come out by organizing monthly birthday parties for the seniors. Other centers provide specific complimentary rehabilitation services like those of Pinetree, also described below. Seniors are also drawn out when complimentary goods such as staple food are handed out or when health equipment is made available for them to utilize freely, as in the case of Xing Fu Jiu Hao (幸福9号), a successful e-commerce platform especially for seniors.

In the last few years, the community care market has witnessed the proliferation of different types of community day centers that offer various non-medical services. However, since most community centers lack a self-sustaining business model, the development of community elderly care services is limited to the district level as they rely on the local government for reimbursements. Below are some examples of the different types of community centers.

- Community day care center with an elderly university or interest club. Opening up elderly universities or interest classes for seniors is a good way to expand the community care model. A large number of community day care centers are partnering with elderly universities to offer activities. The elderly university of Shenzhen Hualing Lianhua North Elderly Day Care Center (深圳华龄莲花北老年日间照料中心) (in Guangdong Province) has more than 3,000 elderly students each year, and according to its manager, 30 percent of customers who purchase services from the center come from its elderly university. Thus, elderly universities can help attract potential day care customers, as the seniors who come to elderly universities or interest clubs may have needs for day care services. Meanwhile, seniors in day care centers can enjoy classes from elderly universities or interest clubs, which can enhance customer retention for day care centers. As such, it is a win-win strategy.
- Community day care center with a small number of beds. Having beds available at the community centers is an additional service for partially or fully dependent seniors who need respite care or short-term stays, such as when family members are out of town. These community centers do not provide nursing, and the overnight stays might only involve a caregiver. Community centers are encouraged by the government to set up beds, since they receive a bed construction subsidy which is more than what they pay for the space and cots. Organizations that have set up beds in community centers include Jin Tai Yang in Fuzhou (in Fujian Province) and Infinitus in Beijing. However, the take-up of community beds for overnight stays is not high, because seniors who have some degree of mobility limitations prefer to stay at home overnight and avoid the expense altogether.
- Community day care center with a call center e-platform. The central government has urged local governments to set up call center e-platforms to link up service providers in the community with seniors who live at home. The call center e-platform functions as a social service and emergency network for seniors who are lonely and for those who need assistance with activities of daily living, care services delivered at home, or emergency dispatch services. The local government must purchase such services, pay for the set up, and provide free rental for the elderly community centers.

In 2007, Fuzhou Jin Tai Yang established its call center e-platform with a 24-hour hotline for seniors in the Gulou district. For over 25,000 seniors within its community network, the local district government pays Jin Tai Yang a low monthly fee of RMB 20 per person for maintenance of the call center service and the community center. Jin Tai Yang staff are available around the clock to assist seniors in the community centers or at home. A highlight of this model is the service promise that staff can visit seniors at home within 15 minutes after taking a call request. Jin Tai Yang also cooperated with a national telecommunications company to give away mobile phones to seniors in an effort to promote its call center e-platform and community or at-home care services. The organization, which launched 80 community centers in 2012–13, dubbed their community and at-home care services a "nursing home without walls" in China and became a leading model for other cities and provinces.

Government Procurement of Community Services

The majority of service providers catering to Chinese seniors at the community level are subsidized by the local government. Generally, they are offered free rent and setup of day care community centers, while in other cases, their services are procured by the local government. Most of these providers are NGOs rather than for-profit companies, as NGOs are perceived to be socially oriented and are able to maintain low prices thanks to the government subsidies and their not-for-profit status. However, Chinese NGOs lack training or management skills, which is a key impediment to their expansion.

Table 4.2 summarizes some of the public-private partnerships (PPP) that exist in China for community care services.

Table 4.2 Types of Community Care Services Procured by the Government

Stakeholders	*Area*	*Characteristics*	*Strengths*	*Weaknesses*
Government leads and manages	Central and western areas	Government is the project leader and manager; three-tier administrative agencies are set up at the district and street levels and in residential communities	Suits local economic and social development, convenient and fast to execute	Over-involvement of the government hinders market development, limited service items and low professional level
Government leads, private sector delivers service	Developed areas in eastern China and large and middle coastal cities	Model One: Build-Own (Government), Operate and Transfer (Private Sector); Model Two: Government provides assistance and subsidies to private sector	Government saves financial and fiscal resources; builds capacity of nonprofit social organizations to improve service quality; introduces market mechanism to create greater efficiency	Under-development of NGOs and private sector may hinder service delivery; Insufficient government supervision hampers the development of the private sector
Government supports, private sector expands services through franchise model	Areas with relatively mature care providers and high professional levels	Government or community-funded program to contract or aid professional care operators to set up and manage community care facilities and service access points	Government involvement to lower burden and costs for care operators; professional operators to focus on service quality and long-term care development	Care operators are hard to sustain without government support; insufficient professional equipment

table continues next page

Table 4.2 Types of Community Care Services Procured by the Government *(continued)*

Stakeholders	*Area*	*Characteristics*	*Strengths*	*Weaknesses*
Government procures services from private sector	Areas with a developed market economy and mature market concepts	Fully or partially funded government procurement programs to purchase basic services for eligible elderly; service providers set up facilities and access points in communities, employ and train care workers	Market is the driving force; Government provides investments and support; increased service efficiency and quality	Insufficient government support; a big gap between the elderly's purchasing power and their care needs; low-pay or low-profit services driven out of market

Source: ICAIA Analysis.

For-Profit Organizations

Most for-profit companies focus on community care services as part of the retirement real estate developments that target mid- to high-income seniors or their families. Property management firms are inclined to establish community centers and deliver home care services within the residential real estate projects they manage. Since these property management companies already own the retail network, it is far easier for them to set up community centers and deliver home care services. An example is Changcheng Property, which partners with U.S. Home Instead Senior Care to introduce a U.S.-Shenzhen franchise model to build its community-based and in-home elderly services.

Community Care Case Studies

China Case Study: Fuzhou Jin Tai Yang Community Centers + Dispatch Home Services

Fuzhou Jin Tai Yang (in Fujian Province) has a successful PPP with the local government. Jin Tai Yang's not-for-profit status has made it easy for the local government to procure their community and call center services. Its operations almost lose money due to high operating costs from maintaining many staff at the community centers and sharing revenue with the telecommunications company, but this is offset by low marketing costs because the strong government support brings many customers to the organization. Its future revenue lies in partnering with other service or product providers that wish to reach the organization's wide network of elderly customers in Fuzhou. Some of Jin Tai Yang's key operational features, including services offered, charges, business model, and staffing characteristics, are summarized in box 4.1.

Overseas Case Study: United States On Lok Lifeways Community Centers + PACE

On Lok, started in the city of San Francisco as a not-for-profit in the early 1970s, was one of the first senior community day care centers in the United States.

Box 4.1 Fuzhou Jin Tai Yang

Highlights

- Founded in 2008 by Xiaorong Huang
- Received angel investment of RMB 5 million in 2013
- Chosen as case study for Social Enterprise Programme and participation in Social Investment Platform by British Embassy
- Chosen as national case study for integrated community care model for other cities by Ministry of Civil Affairs
- Partnership with local insurance companies, banks, and telecommunications companies to promote elderly products and services such as mobile phones, financial services, and service platform
- Crowd funding to sell service coupons

Own Services and Features

- 24-hour call centre: for daily use or emergency use. Seniors can call via their landline or through the mobile phone donated by China Unicom.
- 24-hour dispatch home service: service promise of sending Jin Tai Yang staff to the senior's home within 15 minutes of a call.
- Community centers: established more than 100 centres in Gulou District in Fuzhou and now expanded to over 155 branches. These community centers contain a small library, a small canteen, massage chairs, basic blood pressure monitoring equipment, beds for short overnight stays, and other recreational amenities suitable for seniors.
- Aged care facilities: purchased a nursing home in 2011, and along with their community centers, they now have over 607 beds.

Charges

- In-home care: basic fee of RMB 120 / month; companion for RMB 20 / hour; assisting service amount depends on service content.
- Nursing home: RMB 2,000 / month for independent living; RMB 4,000 / month for nursing
- Community day care centers: estimated RMB 2,000 / month

Third-Party Services and Features

- Dispatch of home care services: home, health care, and non-medical care services are dispatched by Jin Tai Yang's local vendors and coordinated by Jin Tai Yang.
- Time bank: volunteers deposit their service time to seniors into personal accounts so they or their relatives can later enjoy equivalent volunteer services in return. Jin Tai Yang is the promoter and organizer of the time bank. This service has incentivized young retirees and family members to volunteer their time for older seniors in the community.

Business Model and Staffing

- Public-private partnership model: government procurement is a key source of Jin Tai Yang's revenues. The Fuzhou city government purchased annual services of RMB 1 million from Jin

box continues next page

Box 4.1 Fuzhou Jin Tai Yang *(continued)*

Tai Yang in 2012. According to Xiaorong Huang, each district currently spends around RMB 2 million a year to purchase services.

- Gross revenue: over RMB 7 million in 2012, has exceeded RMB 10 million since 2013 and is expected to increase steadily.
- Profit: No profit until now but expected to make money in a few years, according to Ms. Huang.
- Staffing:
  - *Full-time employees:* 632 (2013)
  - *Community centers:* Jin Tai Yang has over 155 service branches covering Fuzhou city. Each center has 1 to 3 staff, and at least one of them stays overnight in the center.
  - *Mobilized volunteers:* 1,739 volunteers between the ages of 20 to 70 have provided pro-bono services to their seniors.

Source: Expert interview, ICAIA analysis.

Frail elderly persons in these community centers received hot meals, health and social services, and supervision during the daytime, and returned to their homes in the evening. The health and social services, which were pioneering at the time, included primary care health services as well as case management of acute and chronic health problems. With the support of the city government, On Lok piloted a comprehensive model of community health care and in-home care services through an interdisciplinary team (physicians, nurses, physical and occupational therapists, social workers, dietitians, health workers, and drivers) in 1979. The inter-disciplinary team formulated and managed care plans for their seniors that covered both medical care and non-medical services provided in communities and at home (if necessary).

Today, On Lok manages several organizations that deliver a variety of services, including On Lok Lifeways, a Community Center, On Lok Intergenerational Program, and 3 Affordable Housing developments. Box 4.2 provides information on Lifeway Services, which is a comprehensive health and long-term care plan that acts like an insurance policy.

Given the success of On Lok's Lifeways program in reducing seniors' hospitalization or need for senior care facilities, the program received the backing of the government and was named the Program of All-inclusive Care for the Elderly (PACE) in 1986. PACE has been rolled out across the country, with over 100 service operators in more than 30 states. Under the PACE program, the state government reimburses local operators for maintaining the health of seniors. PACE service providers enjoy a high degree of autonomy despite the government's procurement of services, and their services and care plans are designed uniquely and tailored to the types of residents residing in the community. The PACE model emphasizes seniors' self-help and encourages volunteer service from young retirees.

Box 4.2 On Lok Lifeways (PACE Program) in the United States

Targeted Customers

- People who are 55 years old or older
- Live in the service area of a PACE organization
- Users of the PACE program are certified by the state's nurses as needing a fairly high level of care, but not quite needing senior care facilities just yet
- Able to live safely in the community with the help of PACE services at the time of enrollment

Service Providers

- Qualified seniors are cared for by an inter-disciplinary group of primary care and specialists from a panel of in-house On Lok staff and other third-party service providers
- On Lok's own staff consists of doctors, nurses, nutritionists, social workers, physical and occupational therapists, and recreational therapists, while other services such as dental and x-rays are outsourced

Services

- Medical services: physicians, specialists, and nurses; prescription medicine and durable medical equipment; dental, eye, and foot care; physical therapy, occupational therapy, and speech therapy; labs and x-rays; hospital, emergency, and skilled nursing facility care
- Non-medical services: day centers; recreational therapy; meals and nutritional counselling; social services; home care; transportation
- Other services as determined necessary by the team of health care professionals to improve and maintain elderly people's overall health

Pricing

On average, it costs the state US$ 4,656 per person a month for the integration of all services managed by the PACE program

Venue

- On Lok community centers: PACE centers, which meet state and federal safety requirements and include adult day programs, medical clinics, activities, and occupational and physical therapy facilities
- Senior's home
- Other specialists and other medical care as needed by the senior

Financing

- PACE provides all normally covered Medicaid and Medicare services
- At On Lok, 95 percent reimbursement by the government through:
  - Medicare (national health insurance for seniors and disabled young adults)
  - Medicaid (national health insurance for the poor)
- At On Lok, 5 percent revenue resulting from consulting services of other PACE partners

box continues next page

Box 4.2 On Lok Lifeways (PACE Program) in the United States *(continued)*

Characteristics

- The PACE program helps seniors with chronic diseases age in their home and community.
- One-stop service for the senior. Once they enroll in PACE, On Lok will manage their overall health and well-being. On Lok's inter-disciplinary professionals work together to assess and continually manage the health of the senior.
- Reimbursements direct to PACE provider through Medicare and Medicaid programs.
- Other health services and centers are involved in the PACE program to offer various medical and other specialist services to members.
- The responsibility of the state governments is merely assessment of seniors' needs and supervision of PACE program providers.

Source: ICAIA analysis.

China–United States–Hong Kong SAR, China Case Study: China Changcheng Property + US Home Instead + Hong Kong Society for Rehabilitation

Changcheng Property Management Group Co. Ltd. (长城物业集团股份有限公司), a large property management company with an extensive residential real estate portfolio in China, aims to build an ecosystem of senior care services within the residential communities it manages by partnering with a reputable international organization. This partnership benefits Changcheng since it had little expertise in senior care in the past.

The organization set up a subsidiary in 2012 called Shenzhen Sharing Community Senior Caring Co. Ltd. (深圳市共享之家护理服务有限公司) as a mini-elderly institution (微小护理机构) and created a strategic partnership with the Hong Kong Society for Rehabilitation (香港复康会) to develop their senior health and rehabilitation assessments and training. Sharing Community has developed two community services, which are offered through their community centers established in the residential complexes they manage, namely: 24-hour continuous care via the 40-bed community center that they manage, and day care community services.

Changcheng also became a master franchisee for Shenzhen of U.S. Home Instead Senior Care in December 2013. Home Instead is the largest at-home care organization in the United States, with more than 1,000 independently owned and operated offices worldwide, and specializes in providing non-medical in-home services for the elderly. Home Instead U.S. will provide their brand, operating manual, systems, and training to Shenzhen Home Instead personnel, as described in box 4.3.

Box 4.3 Community Sharing and Home Instead, Shenzhen

Operator

- Changcheng Property Management Company and its subsidiary Sharing Community and Home Instead Shenzhen
- These firms are for-profit companies

Targeted Group

- Seniors with middle to high incomes who prefer to age at home, supported by services in the community
- Targeted at the elderly and people with special care needs such as chronic diseases, Parkinson's, or dementia
- Main customers are from private residential communities managed by Changcheng Property Management Group

Level of Care and Services Provided

- Community Care Center: 9-hour day care or 24-hour overnight care
  - Day care: meals, companionship, assistance with daily activities, rehabilitation
  - services, entertainment and exercise
  - activities, care for the disabled
  - Overnight stay: respite care, hospice care through the 3H Senior Care and Rehabilitation Center
  - 3 levels of care available: general care, attention care, nursing care
  - 3 types of dormitories, 2 types of single suites, and double bed suite
  - Total 42 beds, more than 20 people living there; current occupancy rate is about 60 percent
- Home Care:
  - Non-nursing services including companionship, meals, transportation, household duties, respite care, hospice care, 24-hour and live-in care support
  - Nursing care: to support those with dementia, Parkinson's, diabetes, arthritis, care after stroke
  - 3 levels of care available: companionship, personal care, and specialized care

Contract Type

- Master franchisor: Changcheng is the Shenzhen Master franchisee of U.S. Home Instead; expansion through direct operation or joint venture with Property Management Company
- Strategic partnership: Community Sharing is in partnership with the Hong Kong Society for Rehabilitation, which provides its senior assessment standards and training

box continues next page

Box 4.3 Community Sharing and Home Instead, Shenzhen *(continued)*

Charge

- Community center (3H Senior Care and Rehabilitation):
  - 24-hour care with overnight at community center: RMB 12,460 to RMB 17,360 per month depending on the type of dormitory and care needed. Price includes all care (general, rehabilitation to nursing), overnight nurse, all meals and day activities at the centers.
  - 9-hour day care: RMB 2,199 per month including lunch and dinner provided at their community center
- At-home care (provided by Home Instead Shenzhen):
  - Hourly services: RMB 50 to RMB 80 per hour
  - 12-hour service: RMB 3,500 to RMB 9,500 per month
  - 24-hour service: RMB 5,800 to RMB 10,800 per month

Personnel Management and Training

- Community care:
  - 30 professional nurses currently
  - Regular training; operational guidance from the Hong Kong Society for Rehabilitation
- Home Instead:
  - Weekly training in theory plus three-week practical operations
  - Mainly part-time workers

Source: ICAIA Analysis.

Challenges and Options for Developing Community Care Market

Challenges Facing Community Care Service Providers

- Weak and inefficient NPOs. At present, the quality and effectiveness of NPOs' delivery of services to seniors are weak. NPOs are rarely sustainable and rely primarily on the government for funding and market access. Chinese NGOs are in great need of capacity building to improve their ability to manage, better understand elderly needs, deliver quality services, and monitor their own performance.
- Funding from government and not market-driven. The government is the most significant and powerful investor of community services for the elderly. Since the government pays for minimal services from local NGOs, seniors are not encouraged to purchase services from the best service providers in town.
- Lack of quality standards for services and staff training. The standards set by the government are limited in scope, and due to the quality of caregivers who have low educational backgrounds, community care organizations seldom conduct training for their staff.
- Community centers are not age-friendly in design. A robust community center should have common areas for the seniors to interact, a canteen, some basic health care diagnostic equipment, a library, and computers. Few community centers are designed with age-friendly facilities or are equipped with barrier-free transportation vehicles.

Challenges Facing the Government

- Not encouraging greater efficiency. The government seemingly is encouraging the private sector to play a greater role in delivering community care services, but so far, the government has only offered assistance to NPOs. Much greater efficiency and better services resulting from healthy competition could be achieved if the government were to open up to procuring services from social enterprises as well as for-profit firms. Procurement of services based on merit rather than lowest bidding price should help to foster a healthy market.
- Lack of supervision and evaluation. The government has yet to set up a management and evaluation system for community care organizations. There are instances of NPOs double-counting their staff in order to meet the government's eligibility requirement for funding.

Way Forward for Developing the Market and Private Providers of Community Care

To strengthen the private sector's role in delivering in-home and community services, the following suggestions are made for the government and the industry to consider.

- Broadening reach with information network. A robust elderly information system is needed that connects the community with seniors and their families. The integrated information system should collect seniors' personal and health information through a smart health management system and link up health care service, at-home care, and community service providers. Properly used, the information would also benefit seniors and their families by monitoring care quality, regulating the assessment of service providers as well as providing counseling and support services to seniors.
- Strengthening capacity building of caregivers. Strengthening the training of community caregivers and other service providers on the needs of seniors will help improve the professionalism of the industry. The government could establish regular training for community care organizations to ensure that every caregiver has adequate skills to serve seniors.
- Supporting a cohesive and business-friendly environment. Formulating and implementing preferential policies are essential to cultivate an integrated in-home and community senior care market. The government needs to implement these favorable policies by making it easy for the private sector to take advantage of free rentals and reduced water and electricity costs, providing stimulation funds, lowering taxes, reducing red tapes for obtaining permits and licenses, and procuring services from community organizations.
- Supervision of the community care industry. It is recommended that the government step back from providing community services directly and instead focus on developing policies and standards, funding the services, and supervising the providers.
- Renovation of community day care centers. In order to meet the future needs of seniors, all community centers should be built or reconstructed with age-friendly and barrier-free designs so they can serve all seniors with various needs.

In-Home Care Services

For seniors who prefer or need care at home, in-home care can help with their personal care, housekeeping, basic nursing care, rehabilitation exercises, health education, companionship, and counseling services. A comparison of China's in-home care services market and selected overseas models is provided in table 4.3 below.

Table 4.3 Assessment and Scope of In-home Care in Selected Economies

	United States	*United Kingdom*	*China*	*Hong Kong SAR, China*	*Taiwan, China*
Care needs assessment	Functional eligibility requirement for frail Medicaid users; varies across states	Local government adopts own criteria in assessing service needs based on guidelines from the Department of Health	No unified assessment mechanism	Standardized Care Needs Assessment Mechanism	Each service agency has its own criteria for care assessment
Day/respite Care	Yes	Yes	Yes	Yes	Yes
Domestic Assistance	Yes	Yes	Yes	Yes	Yes
Transport	Yes	Yes	Yes, few private sector providers	Yes	Yes
Emergency Response	Yes	Yes	Yes	Yes	Yes
Case management	Yes	Yes	Yes, few private sector providers	Yes	N/A
Meal delivery/ preparation	Yes	Yes	Yes	Yes	Yes
Nursing/personal care	Yes	Yes	Yes	Yes	Yes
Special needs care	Yes	Yes	Yes, few private sector providers	N/A	N/A
Financing model	Private insurance for some elderly; Medicare for eligible home health services; Medicaid for low-income elderly	Local governments as the main bodies providing funding for in-home care, with grants from central government; local governments are free to put up co-payment or means-test arrangement	Local governments are tasked to devise, implement, and fund local initiatives of in-home care; a mixed funding model of "majority of out-of-pocket payment, minority of public subsidy" is still the norm	Government subsidy with means-test	Government subsidy with means-test

table continues next page

Table 4.3 Assessment and Scope of In-Home Care in Selected Economies *(continued)*

	United States	*United Kingdom*	*China*	*Hong Kong SAR, China*	*Taiwan, China*
Public-private shares	In-home care providers mostly are private the majority are for-profits	In-home care providers mostly are private or non-profit	In-home care providers mostly are public and non-profit	In-home care providers mostly are private or non-profit	In-home care providers mostly are private or non-profit
Informal caregiver assistance	N/A	The government provides cash support to informal caregivers of qualified elderly through a Caregiver's Allowance Scheme	Pilot reform in some cities	N/A	N/A

Sources: Hong Kong Elderly Commission 2011; ICAIA Analysis.

Government Purchasing of Basic Home Care Services

In some cities, including Beijing, Wenzhou (in Zhejiang Province) and Hangzhou (capital of Zhejiang Province), local governments purchase basic home care services such as cleaning and companionship from independent service providers for seniors living at home who are welfare recipients.[2] The government may pay for the full costs of the services, while in some cases the government is only partially subsidizing the costs. When the government is only partially subsidizing the costs, the in-home care providers will pass the remaining costs to service users.

Private Firms Targeting Mid- to High-End Market

Other than the government contract models, private in-home service providers aim for seniors with middle to high incomes. As these firms are market and profit driven, they seek distribution channels through hospital and social work networks, rather than relying on the government for purchases or subsidies that may cap the fees they charge.

All foreign-funded senior care companies entering China are targeting seniors with middle to high incomes, with a focus on major cities. Thanks to healthy competition, these firms are differentiating themselves in a variety of ways. For example, Singapore Active Global Ageing is providing only trained nurses, U.S. Right At Home (RAH) delivers caregiving and housekeeping services through university-graduate caregivers, and Pinetree offers at-home skilled care to seniors who are semi- or fully dependent.

In-Home Care Case Studies

Case Study: Pinetree, Beijing

Founded in 2004 by Wang Ninie, Pinetree (青松老年看护服务北京有限公司) began as one of the earliest professional in-home care service providers for semi- and fully dependent older persons. Pinetree focuses on providing services to seniors with chronic illnesses, those in need of skilled nursing, and those with diabetes, dementia, or other rehabilitation needs. Pinetree also accepts service coupons from seniors that are provided by the government. It has so far set up more than 40 day care centers in Beijing and Shanghai that often offer rehabilitation and other specialized care to residents at their community centers with support of the local Civil Affairs Bureau (box 4.4).

Box 4.4 Pinetree in Beijing

Organization Profile

- Established as a for-profit firm since 2007
- Has operations in Beijing and Shanghai

Targeted Group

- Seniors with low to middle incomes who prefer to age at home supported by services in the community
- "Three-without" seniors supported by the government, since Pinetree customers can use the government's coupons at their community centers
- Targeted at the elderly, people with special care needs such as chronic illness, Parkinson's, dementia, and other rehabilitation needs such as recovering from falls or stroke

Features

- In-home care only targets skilled nursing and professional rehabilitation services, leaving out domestic services, companionship, assisted living services, and so on.
- Will provide training to family members to help them gain essential caregiving knowledge. Pinetree's goal is to let family members be the main caregivers, instead of depending on nurses from Pinetree.
- Set up service stations or day care centers within communities in Beijing and Shanghai as bases for staff to provide in-home or community-based skilled nursing and professional non-medical or rehabilitation care services to residents within or near those communities.

Service Scope and Features

- Service process includes 1) online application, 2) in-home evaluation, 3) making personal care plan, and 4) providing in-home personal care by skilled caregivers

box continues next page

Box 4.4 Pinetree in Beijing *(continued)*

- Individual care plan based on needs assessment and consultation with individual families
- Provision of skilled nursing and professional non-medical services at home: care for dementia, Parkinson's patients, rehabilitation care for stroke patients, other nursing services for diabetes and other special needs
- Provision of rehabilitation services and other assistance with daily living services at community centers in Beijing and Shanghai
- Membership card structure with several tiers for customers to choose corresponding services items and membership discounts
- O2O shop launched in 2012 on China's most popular e-commerce website: Online shop—(Pinetree Home Rehab Care Taobao Shop)

Charge and Service Frequency

- Per visit charge:
  - In-home care
    - Changing or maintaining nursing equipment (such as breathing tube): RMB 280 per visit
    - Rehabilitation/skilled nursing services: RMB 260 per visit
    - Actual expenditures will vary based on different care needs and plans evaluated by Pinetree
  - Community day care center/service station
    - In-home care: same as above
    - Community day care service: RMB 820 per month[a]
- Service frequency: maximum 6 times per week, at least 1 hour per visit

Source: Expert interview, ICAIA analysis.
a. Data from Pinetree Zuo Jia Zhuang community day care center in 2011.

Case Study: Right at Home In-Home Care, Beijing

RAH, a leading American provider of in-home elderly care, was introduced to China in 2011 through Yao Li. As one of the 250 global franchisees of RAH U.S., RAH China provides comprehensive in-home care services from daily care such as companionship, meal assistance, and bathing assistance to medical services such as specialized rehabilitation, medical care, and end-of-life care services. RAH tailors a care package specifically for each customer based on individual needs and assessment by its professional team. It targets middle-income seniors who have the ability to pay privately. RAH consolidates the demands of a large number of families, efficiently manages the company's human resources, develops suitable service packages and caregiver training based on the psychological and physical needs of Chinese seniors, and introduced advanced mobile medical and communication equipment.

However, RAH no longer targets only the elderly and has expanded its customer group to high-income families. Its services have expanded to include specialized nursing care, domestic services, and high-end private household management services for all members of the family. RAH China has set up service centers in local communities where its customers live and work. Since 2011, RAH has set up 4 shops in Beijing and recruited and trained nearly 300 caregivers. Currently, RAH has 15 shops in 10 cities, covering the eastern, central, and western regions of China and forming an integrated network (box 4.5).

Box 4.5 Right at Home In-Home Care and Assistance, Beijing

Targeted Group

- Originally targeting seniors, RAH now also targets disabled persons, people with chronic diseases, and discharged patients who need care at home
- Middle- to high-income seniors and their families

Process

- Caregiving consultation to determine the level of care required for the customer
- Identify the best specialized caregiver for the customer and personalize the service plan
- Ongoing quality control and support for seniors and their family members

Level of Care

- Comprehensive care from semi- to fully dependent care
- Assistance with daily activities: 24-hour care, post-discharge care, and specialized care
- General care: companionship, household chores, cooking

HR Management

- Recruit university graduates and provide thorough training to new employees
- Continuous training provided to staff through the U.S. company: 3-week training in theory plus practical operations
- Mainly full-time employees

Charge

- Professional nurse: RMB 500 for 2 hours, twice per week; about RMB 4,000 per month
- Personal care: personal cleaning for RMB 100 per hour, maximum RMB 15,000 per month
- Family care service such as cleaning and accompanying: RMB 60 per hour

Type and profit making

- Right At Home operates through a master franchiser in China; RAH China will expand to other cities and provinces through direct operation or major ownership in a local joint venture
- RAH China accepts management by headquarters including business model, management, training, supervision, and the headquarters charges franchise fee from RAH China.
- Intellectual property rights belong to the USA Inc., so in addition to the franchise fee, the company will charge push money from each franchisee.
- Agreed-on standard service process; all networks including internal computer network, network between caregivers and customers, and financial network are all connected with American headquarters.

Source: Expert interview, ICAIA analysis.

The following steps should be considered in order to further develop China's in-home senior care market:

- Establishing a robust legal and regulation framework. The government should provide clear guidelines for the private sector to obtain government procurement orders, clarify the service standards that are required, and make the bidding process transparent.
- Developing service standards and supervising the in-home care market. The government is the overall steward of the industry and should be responsible for setting service standards and providing or supervising training for in-home care organizations.
- Integrating national insurance policies and stimulating commercial insurance to cover in-home care services. Efforts are needed to enhance the social welfare system and foster the development of commercial insurance to cover in-home care services, even including high-end services.

Institutional Care Industry

The institutional senior care industry in China is still underdeveloped. According to the "Report on Development of the Silver Industry in China" (referred to as "the Report" below) published by the Ministry of Civil Affairs in 2013, China had only 3.9 million residential care beds by 2012, but it needs at least 5.5 million beds. Of all existing beds in China, 72 percent are in public residential care facilities and 28 percent are in privately run facilities.

The institutional senior care market in China can be divided into five categories according to the level of care and the income level of seniors (figure 4.1). Institutional care services in China are mainly provided by public senior care facilities and social welfare homes that are operated by the local government. Many private senior care facilities, senior apartments, and retirement communities such as continuing care retirement communities (CCRCs) cater to seniors or their families with high incomes and are more of a senior housing proposition.

Current Supply of Institutional Care by the Public and Private Sectors

Public Senior Care Facilities and Social Welfare Homes

Local governments invest in and operate public senior care facilities, the majority of which are located in rural areas (known as *jing lao yuan* in Chinese). Social welfare homes are located in urban areas and mainly target people who qualify as "Three No's" and low-income seniors. Although both public senior care facilities and social welfare homes claim that they provide services for disabled or dependent elders, the majority of residents are healthy individuals because the managers of these facilities are inclined to accept independent and healthy seniors as opposed to semi-dependent or dependent seniors.

Since public senior care facilities are operated by the government, they enjoy various free public resources such as land, buildings, and equipment and therefore have the ability to charge lower fees. According to a 2009 survey

Figure 4.1 Types of Institutional Care in China

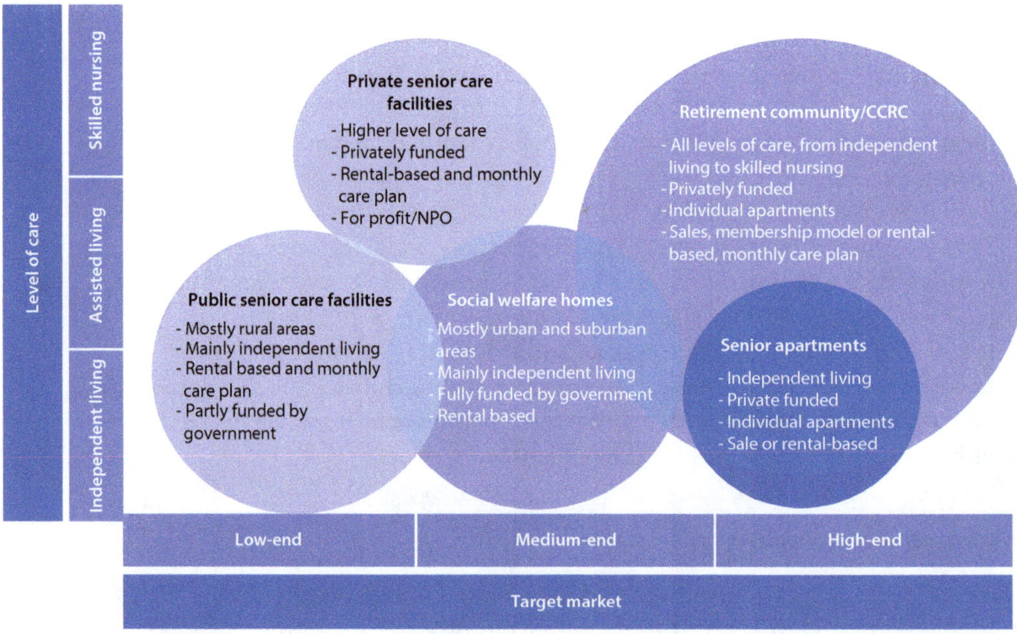

Sources: ICAIA Analysis.

Table 4.4 Sources of Funding for Elderly Care Facilities, 2009

Source of funding	*Public institutions (%)*	*Private institutions (%)*	*All institutions (%)*
Government	42.2	2.4	19.5
Private funding	56.9	96.2	79.3
Other sources	0.8	1.5	1.2
Government bed subsidies	50.8	84.8	70

Source: Feng et al. 2011.

conducted in several Chinese cities, public institutions receive 42.2 percent of their operating budget through the government, while the remainder largely comes from the fees they receive from residents (table 4.4). Their low prices make public institutions popular among seniors, and the best institutions usually have an average waiting list of 5–10 years.

Private Sector Facilities

The number of private senior care facilities varies from province to province depending on the local regulatory policy, income levels of seniors, and elderly demographics. In Beijing, private senior facilities accounted for 49 percent of all available beds in 2014.[3] In contrast, private facilities accounted for only 28 percent of total beds in Hebei Province in 2013.[4] In Jilin Province, the private sector accounted for 60 percent of facilities and 47 percent of all beds in 2014.[5]

Overall, the private sector is constrained to become a major provider of institutional senior care in China due to its inability to compete with public institutions on prices. International China Ageing Industry Association (ICAIA) estimates show that in 2014 nearly 40 percent of private senior care facilities in China are operating in deficit, and only 9 percent of them make a profit (China Voice 2016). High capital investment, long pay-back periods, and low returns continue to deter growth of the private sector in the institutional senior care market.

Since 2012, the national and local governments have stepped up efforts to encourage the private sector to set up senior care facilities. Starting from 2013, local Civil Affairs Bureaus uploaded data including the number of private senior care facilities on their website, suggesting the increasing importance of private sector engagement in the senior care industry.

Comparison of Institutional Care Development in Selected Economies

China's elderly care industry is nascent compared with other Organisation for Economic Co-operation and Development (OECD) countries. Industry watchers often refer to China's institutional care market as not having a full continuum of care services available to seniors. Table 4.5 outlines major differences between China's institutional care sector and those in several other countries or regions.

Role of the Private Sector in Institutional Care

Chinese Real Estate and Insurance Companies in the Senior Housing Market

With government-run facilities focused on the low- to mid-end of the market, private senior care facilities in China are targeting customers in the mid- to high-end market. Senior housing projects have sprouted up in China since 2009. Some notable ones such as Cherish Yearn (亲和苑) in Shanghai and Langdent and Sun City (太阳城) in Beijing have used a membership model as well as a monthly rental and care service model.

From 2012 to 2014, many of China's real estate companies and insurance companies announced and made efforts to enter the senior housing market. Vanke, one of China's largest real estate developers, has launched senior housing projects in Hangzhou and is now developing a 10-year senior care expansion strategy. Greentown launched its senior housing project combined with the elderly university in 2013. Union Life (合众保险) launched the first genuine U.S.-based CCRC, a 3,000 bed facility in Wuhan (in Hubei Province) in 2014. Taikang Life's (泰康保险) CCRC project opened its 258-unit senior retirement facility in Changping in 2015.

Foreign and Local Collaboration in the Institutional Care Market

Since 2011, many foreign companies have entered the Chinese institutional senior care market through partnerships (table 4.6). For example, Japan's Long Life Group opened its first high-end nursing home in Qingdao in 2011, with the expectation of expanding to 100 facilities in 10 years. RIEI Co. (リエイ) from Japan set up a wholly owned subsidiary in Beijing

Table 4.5 Institutional Care: China versus Selected Economies

	United States	*United Kingdom*	*China*	*Hong Kong SAR, China*	*Taiwan, China*
Introduction	Institutional care has been well developed. Scope of services depends on individual needs for care. It ranges from minimum level of living assistance for independent elderly to assistance with daily living to nursing care for fully dependent elderly.	Institutional care has been well developed. Scope of services depends on individual needs for care. It ranges from minimum level of living assistance for independent elderly to assistance with daily living to nursing care for fully dependent elderly.	Institutional care is under-developed. The ratio of nursing home beds to elderly is 1.59%, much lower than that of developed countries (7%) and developing countries (3%).	Hong Kong SAR, China has over-relied on institutional care, with a ratio of residential beds to elderly of 6.8%, higher than the international range of 1–5%.	Institutional care is relatively well developed compared to neighboring regions. Rate of institutionalization and ratio of residential beds to elderly are comparable to those in the United States.
Financing model	Seniors enjoy Medicare and Medicaid insurance. Medicare is for all seniors but does not cover long-term care, while Medicaid is means-tested and only covers the poor. However, private insurance can help seniors pay for mid- to high-end care services.	Majority of seniors' needs for long-term care and medical care are addressed by the public sector through the National Health Service (NHS) and local government budgets.	Majority of elderly depends on a mixed funding model of out-of-pocket payment and pension, as the pension is not sufficient to cover long-term care expenses. There is also public support for welfare recipients even though it is very limited in scope of coverage.	Government provided majority of financing through direct subsidies to non-profit private elderly homes or service purchasing from non-profit and for-profit private elderly homes.	Majority of elderly depend on a mixed funding model of out-of-pocket payment and insurance, as the national health care insurance is not sufficient to cover long-term care.
Services and levels of care	Assistance with daily living includes: bathing, dressing, shaving, toilet and incontinent care, around-the-clock monitoring, and transportation and companionship when necessary. Specialized care: administering medication, rehabilitation therapy, skilled nursing, respite care, hospice care.	Assistance with daily living includes: bathing, dressing, shaving, toilet and incontinent care, around-the-clock monitoring, and transportation and companionship when necessary. Specialized care: administering medication, rehabilitation therapy, skilled nursing, respite care, hospice care.	Institutional care in China typically includes accommodation and assistance with daily living. Specialized care is limited. Few institutions accept seniors with memory loss, and few are able to provide the full range of nursing care or rehabilitation.	Assistance with daily living includes: bathing, dressing, shaving, toilet and incontinent care, around-the-clock monitoring, and transportation and companionship when necessary. Specialized care: administering medication, rehabilitation therapy, skilled nursing, respite care, hospice care.	Assistance with daily living includes: bathing, dressing, shaving, toilet and incontinent care, around-the-clock monitoring, and transportation and companionship when necessary. Specialized care: administering medication, rehabilitation therapy, skilled nursing, respite care, hospice care.

table continues next page

Table 4.5 Institutional Care: China versus Selected Economies *(continued)*

	United States	*United Kingdom*	*China*	*Hong Kong SAR, China*	*Taiwan, China*
Basic nursing or skilled nursing when required	The full range of nursing care is provided.	The full range of nursing care is provided.	Most elderly homes can only provide basic services (such as domestic services, accompanying, and other non-medical services), while very few can provide specialist nursing care.	Yes, the full range of nursing care is only provided at a number of skilled nursing facilities.	Yes, the full range of nursing care is only provided at a number of skilled nursing facilities.
Special needs care (e.g., memory care)	Relatively commonly provided.	Relatively commonly provided.	Few institutions have the capacity or interest to take in residents with memory problems.	Only large established elderly homes have the capacity.	Only large established elderly homes have the capacity.
Planned social and recreational events	Widely provided.	Widely provided.	Still developing to provide social and recreational events.	Still developing to provide social and recreational events.	Still developing to provide social and recreational events.

Source: ICAIA Analysis.

Table 4.6 Cooperation between Foreign and Domestic Companies in Institutional Senior Care Projects

Foreign company	*Country*	*Chinese partners*	*Chinese company type*	*Institutional facility*	*Region*
Colisee	France	China Merchants Group Ltd	State-owned enterprise	Memory care, day care center, senior apartment to be opened in 2016	Guangzhou
Orpea	France	Gulou Hospital, Xianlin District, Nanjing	Local government hospital	Rehabilitation hospital with dementia research center opened in 2015	Nanjing
Domus Vi	France	Hanfor Holdings Co., Ltd	Assessment management company	N/A	N/A
日本长乐控股株式会社 (ロングライフホールディング, Long Life Group)	Japan	Hiking Group Ltd	Large local company	Nursing home opened in 2011	Qingdao
日本RIEI株式会社 (RIEI, 株式会社リエイ)	Japan	Sieton Group	Large local company	Opened in 2011 in Beijing, 2013 in Shanghai	Beijing, Shanghai
日本木下集团 (株式会社 木下ホールディングス, Kinoshita)	Japan	Beijing CHJ-Care Investment Co., Ltd.	State-owned enterprise	Opened in 2014	Beijing
Emeritus Senior Living, Columbia Pacific Management Co.,	United States	Sino-Ocean	State-owned enterprise	Rehabilitation nursing home Cascade opened in 2012	Shanghai, Beijing
Meridian Senior Living	United States	Sino-Ocean	State-owned enterprise	Took over Cascade management in 2014	Shanghai, Beijing
Fortress Investments	United States	Fosun International Limited	Large local conglomerate	CCRC opened in 2013	Shanghai
Cornerstone Affiliates/ ABHOW	United States	Taikang Insurance	Large insurance company	CCRC opened in 2015	Beijing
Merrill Gardens	United States	Related Company	Large local company	Facilities opened in 2015	Shanghai, Wuxi

Source: ICAIA Analysis.

(理爱 (北京) 企业管理咨询有限公司) in 2011 and cooperated with Shanghai Sieton Group to open a for-profit nursing home in Shanghai in 2013. Sino Ocean Land initially partnered with Emeritus Senior Living, a large U.S. senior living company, in its Beijing Yizhuang Project and has now collaborated with Meridian Senior Living, another U.S. senior living operating firm, in its Shanghai Cascade Project. Chinese conglomerate Fosun (复星集团) partnered with US Fortress (保峰投资, a senior housing investment specialist fund, to develop the Starcastle brand (星保养生) and senior retirement projects in Shanghai.

In 2014, several French care providers (including Colisee, Orpea, and Domus Vi) also entered China's senior care market but did not choose Beijing and Shanghai as their original destinations, unlike the aforementioned U.S. and Japanese companies. Colisee will be opening a nursing home that provides skilled nursing care and memory care in Nanjing. Orpea signed a contract with Nanjing Drum Tower Hospital to reconstruct a rehabilitation nursing home with 180 beds. The other three Orpea projects will be located in Shenzhen, Chengdu, and Kunming. Usually, Chinese companies provide funds, land, and facilities, while foreign companies are responsible for operation, management, and training.

Breadth of Private Sector Service Offerings

In many large cities, private firms are operating specialized facilities that mainly serve middle- and upper-class seniors, and they must offer a higher level of services to attract and retain a demanding and educated clientele. Data shows that 10 percent of private senior care facilities provide rehabilitation services, and 3 percent provide hospice care. According to statistics from the Ministry of Health in 2012, 155 out of 301 rehabilitation hospitals in China are private facilities, 38 out of 60 skilled nursing facilities are private facilities, and almost all 58 nursing stations are privately owned (Health and Population Commission 2014). Private senior care facilities generally provide a wider and higher level of care that might not be available in public senior care facilities.

Private Sector Growth through Government Reform and PPP

In the last few years, local and foreign real estate firms, operators, and Chinese institutional investors targeted wealthy Chinese seniors with assisted living facilities, senior care facilities, and CCRCs. Only a few indicate that they will enter the medium-income market in the future.

The central government has well noted the gap in middle-income skilled senior care facilities and since 2013 has the encouraged private sector's engagement in the middle range of the market through PPP and reform of public institutions. At the end of 2013, the Ministry of Civil Affairs started the pilot reform of public senior care facilities, requiring at least one public facility to be reformed in each province. By September 2014, 124 public senior care facilities from 28 provinces were selected to participate in the reform, which allows some private operators to be engaged in the management of public senior care facilities through a government bidding system.

The government's encouragement of the private sector extends all the way down to the local level. In each province, city, and district, the government is encouraging private sector participation by offering free or cheap land, infrastructure support, bed construction subsidies, equipment, free operating costs for water and gas, and in some cases subsidies for some care costs. In return for these subsidies, the government will request that a portion of beds be made available to seniors on welfare at a price equal to the actual cost of care, thus alleviating the government's need to develop and manage new public senior care facilities.

These favorable policies greatly reduce the investments and facility operating costs for the private sector. Whether NPOs or for-profit firms, they are encouraged to manage or develop and manage skilled nursing facilities. Local operating firms such as Life Care in Shanghai and the Golden Sun in Qingdao have greatly benefited from this policy, managing a number of senior care facilities the government has built. Yet, the private sector is reluctant to get involved in skilled nursing due to the price distortion of public facilities and high operational risk.

Institutional Care Case Studies

The private sector has developed many different business strategies for China's challenging business environment. Private sector participation in institutional care services varies widely by region in China. This section describes in detail a few relatively successful business models that may have an impact on the industry.

High-End Assisted Living

High-end senior care facilities serve wealthy seniors in cities across China. Many of them provide assisted living and charge high rental and care fees. There are numerous examples of high-end for-profit senior care facilities in China, such as Golden Heights. Most developers of high-end senior care facilities or retirement communities are overseas companies and large Chinese real estate or insurance companies. Box 4.6 presents the example of Shuangjin Golden Heights, part of the Landgent Group, which was chosen by the Beijing government as a pilot

---

Box 4.6 Shuangjin Golden Heights in Beijing

Description

Opened in 2012.

239 rooms, 439 beds in total.

Residents: healthy, semi-independent, and fully dependent seniors; dementia patients accepted.

Land was purchased.

Service

Personal care, health care, medical services, rehabilitation service, memory care, meal service, respite service.

Highlights

Located in Shuangjing district of Beijing, very convenient location and traffic.

Collaborates with Memory 360 to provide quality memory care.

Combines senior services and medical services through close cooperation with hospital and Beijing Emergency Center, with two ambulances in facility.

box continues next page

Box 4.6 Shuangjin Golden Heights in Beijing *(continued)*

Rapid Expansion

- Long-term care (meals included and nursing expenses excluded): RMB 9,800–RMB 15,600 per month, varying by room type. The fee should be paid in one go, and the customers may enjoy a 5 percent discount if they pay for one year or more. The elderly should live here for at least one month.
- Nursing expenses:
  - Group nursing: RMB 80-220 per day, varying by nursing level
  - Personal nursing: at least RMB 6,000 per month
- Charge deposit of RMB 50,000 as medical guarantee, refundable
- Medical insurance can be used for medical care in its own hospital since May 2015.
- Two other facilities built in two years, Hainan Province and Zhejiang Province
- Plan to establish one more facility in Beijing and three in Zhejiang Province
- Golden Heights faces competition from other overseas senior care providers in the high-end market
- Sustainable growth requires developing an independently profitable model

Source: Expert interview, ICAIA analysis.

project for combining medical services with senior care. Golden Heights targets the high-end market and provides professional medical services, personal nursing, and life support devices.

Private High-End Skilled Nursing Home

Hong Tai Friendship House, part of Vcanland Senior Living Investment Group, is a high-end nursing home (box 4.7). Friendship House provides international-standard, comprehensive, and customized professional care services, including nutritional catering, daily care, professional medical services, health care management, and community activities.

Public-Private Partnership for a Mid-Range Nursing Home

Tianjin Wuqing District Second Nursing Home was developed by the local government but is run by a private operator. As described earlier, China's government has long been fostering PPP through leasing and management contracts. However, many cases fail as the bidding price is too high for most private senior care facilities targeting the mid-range market. As described in box 4.8, Tian Yihe Senior Nursing Home has been successful at adapting to a PPP.

Constraints and Recommendations

The private sector has a positive role to play in China's senior care market by improving efficiency and quality as well as expanding services to low-income and middle-class seniors. However, numerous obstacles must be addressed. Below, five broad recommendations are proposed which are imperative for

Box 4.7 Hong Tai Friendship House, Tianjin

Description

- Opened in 2012
- An English-style villa residence: 21 rooms consisting of 16 single-bed rooms and 5 double-bed rooms (26 beds total)
- Residents: people age 50 or older without a mental or infectious disease, and symptoms that are not suitable for collective activity

Highlights

- The service standard is based on an international standard but also considers special Chinese characteristics and culture.
- Food is customized according to the residents' physical conditions, such as meals for diabetes, dyslipidaemia, and hypertension.
- Cooperated with a professional hospital that is only hundreds of meters away from Friendship House
- Integrated recovery service into daily entertainment activities so that seniors can undertake training happily.

Service

- Personal care, customized catering service, nursing service, recovery service, customized health care service, medical service, social activity, dementia care

Charge

- Long-term care: RMB 9,000–RMB 12,000 per month (including bed fees, nursing expenses, meals)
- The price level is divided into self-care, primary nursing, secondary nursing, and advanced nursing according to the senior's physical condition
- Each level charges corresponding nursing fees, meal fees, and accommodation fees based on the orientation and type of the room.
- Charges RMB 99,000 emergency medical deposit

Challenges

The number of rooms is relatively small, so only a few seniors can enjoy the service

Source: Expert interview, ICAIA analysis.

policy makers, regulators, nursing home operators, and other stakeholders to improve institutional care for the elderly in China.

Broaden Financing Channels for Long-Term Care

Financing channels for long-term care, such as a national social security system and commercial insurance, are critical to sustain the senior care market in China. Although China has established a three-pillar pension system (table 4.7), the wage replacement rate in the national pension system is low, and the role of

Box 4.8 Tianjin Wuqing District Second Nursing Home

Government Built

Wuqing District Civil Affairs Bureau and Xuguantun Subdistrict Office

Facility profile

- Opened in 2013
- 600+ beds
- 2 blocks of traditional Chinese medicine physiotherapy and 1 block of medical service with 10 departments

Government support

- 28,666 m^2 land and investment of nearly RMB 80 million on construction
- No rental and little management fees
- Helps reduce expenses charged by different local government departments (e.g., water, gas, electricity)
- Plans to build a supermarket and hotel to attract more residents
- Price guidance by government
- National health insurance available
- Age-friendly design

Private Operator

Tian Yihe Senior Nursing Home

- Provides better-quality services
- Established a new hospital with 10+ medical professionals specializing in Traditional Chinese Medecine physiotherapy
- Residents: currently more than 100, mainly low-income elderly who receive government subsidies
- Expected mix of residents: 30% independent living, 20% assisted living, 50% memory care/ dependent seniors
- Price: RMB 200-300 cheaper than other private nursing homes in that area
- Independent living: RMB 1580 per month
- Assisted living: RMB 2,000 per month
- Nursing care: RMB 2,600 per month

Source: Expert interview, ICAIA analysis.

corporate annuity and private commercial insurance is limited. Moreover, given the low pensions for most people, it is unlikely that many people can afford formal long-term care. In other words, it is difficult to expand the long-term care market if access to services for most people depends on the ability to pay.

By fostering inclusion in risk-pooling arrangements, the government can broaden the financial channels for long-term care. Risk-pooling arrangements such as Japan's long-term care insurance are widely regarded as a better way to finance long-term care compared to out-of-pocket payments. The government

Table 4.7 China's Three-Pillar Pension System

Type	*Key Characteristics*	*National Average Level of Pension*
National pension system	Classically non-profit, financed primarily by government-mandated payroll contribution Low replacement rate Financial burden on government	RMB 1,793
Corporate annuity	Typically non-profit, a supplementary retirement insurance system contributed to by both enterprises and employees Plays a limited role in China	RMB 1,200
Private commercial insurance	For-profit Individual can purchase coverage from private insurers	RMB 991

Sources: China Health and Retirement Longitudinal Study 2011; ICAIA analysis.

can develop a sound and coherent national pension system, such as enhancing the implementation of recent pension reform that targets public sector privileges as well as providing greater incentives for people to enroll in corporate annuity and private commercial insurances through tax breaks for companies and individuals as is the case in Australia.

Develop Mechanisms for Unified Standards and Assessments

The quality of care varies greatly across residential facilities, causing distrust by seniors and their families. These issues could be addressed by having a legal system that protects both the residents and the operators and a system of assessment and quality standards that are transparent and enforceable. In order to encourage the involvement of private senior care facilities, the government could further provide support by:

- Setting minimal standards and establishing demonstration projects. Many local government agencies rush to set standards and collaborate with local parties that are not professional enough to give advice. Central government agencies can work with overseas parties that are well known for best practices and with local partners to adapt service standards and assessment tools to the local context. In addition, it is important for the central government to raise professional standards step by step and be flexible in continuing to raise standards, rather than immediately setting the bar too high. Local governments can establish demonstration projects first and then organize forums to share best practices or learn from failures.
- Strengthening the enforcement of existing regulations and assessments. Both the Ministry of Civil Affairs and local Civil Affairs Bureaus have issued many regulations regarding elderly physical and cognitive assessments and nursing home operations in recent years. However, there has been a lack of effort to vigorously monitor and enforce these regulations. A government agency or

ideally a third-party inspection system could be established to meet this need. This can be aided by regular training, proper incentives, engagement of professional associations, and public reporting mechanisms.

Streamline the Registration Process and Encourage Private Sector Involvement

In China, local governments often impede the development of private senior care facilities through cumbersome regulatory processes and inadequate human resource policies. Interviews with several private nursing home operators highlighted issues related to administrative approvals and the implementation of preferential policies. Compared with NPOs/NGOs, it is more complicated for for-profit companies to open senior care businesses since qualifications and administrative approvals are much more difficult to obtain (table 4.8).

The complicated regulatory process limits the involvement of private senior care facilities. On the one hand, NPOs cannot enjoy ownership of property even it is purchased with their own funds. Under Chinese law and the banking system, it is not possible to seek bank financing for the land and building construction, and they would need to raise the whole amount of capital investment and operating funds themselves. On the other hand, obtaining land through auction is quite expensive for for-profit private firms. For-profit senior care facilities theoretically are able to receive the same subsidies, such as cheaper land, reduced taxes and utilities, as not-for-profit facilities. However, most of them are not able to receive the benefits due to inconsistent and opaque local government systems. Moreover, setting up a nursing home in China requires more than 15 registration certificates, some of which are extremely difficult to obtain. One nursing home took one year to obtain the certificate from the Fire Department for one facility in Guangdong Province.

Table 4.8 Differences between Public-Run Facilities and For-Profit Private Senior Care Facilities

Item	*Public-run facilities*	*For-profit firms*
Registration for business license	Bureau of Civil Affairs	Bureau of Commerce
Profit distribution/tax payment	No dividend, privatization prohibited, and establishment of subsidies forbidden (for only government-run facilities), no income tax	No limitations; income tax
Insurance	Elderly Comprehensive Liability Insurance and Employee Liability Insurance; 80 percent of coverage provided by government	
Price	Follow government's guidance	No limitations
Rating	Bureau of Civil Affairs	Not applicable
Nature of land	Land for educational, scientific and technological, cultural, health care, or sports purposes (50 years of grant) Little or no land transferring fee	Land for residential, commercial, tourism, or recreational purposes (40–70 years of grant) Obtained from land administration department by auction
Financial support	Difficult to get loan from banks	No limitations

Source: ICAIA analysis.

To address these regulatory issues, the government should seek opportunities to:

- Unify the application process for operational licenses of all types of private senior care facilities. The operational licenses to set up a nursing home can be unified through the Civil Affairs Bureau or through a newly set up Elderly Commission to help accelerate facility construction and development. It is also convenient for a unified regulatory body to supervise the development and operations of all private senior care facilities, whether for-profit or not-for-profit.
- Liberalize regulations on profit distribution and ownership of nursing facilities. Non-profit senior care facilities should be allowed to use their property as collateral for obtaining financing from financial institutions.

Stimulate Development of Human Resources for Institutional Care

Senior care facilities have long suffered from a shortage of trained staff, posing a significant impediment to the development of the senior care industry in China. According to national research, the senior care industry needs 10 million workers, of which a great majority would provide caregiving in institutional care facilities. However, by 2015, China had only 600,000 elder care workers (Xinhua News 2016). The shortage of care workers is not a surprise, as elder care is regarded as a low-end, low-paying job with few prospects for career advancement. Even if they could choose, care workers would prefer to go to public institutions since the benefits are guaranteed.

To stimulate the development of human resources for the senior care sector, the government and the industry should:

- Re-examine staffing policies related to medical professionals. The availability of medical services is one of the most important factors for seniors when selecting a care facility. The government could promulgate policies that allow public sector doctors to provide services privately, including those in nursing homes and residential care facilities. Recently, the Beijing municipal government made substantial progress by implementing new policies that make specialized drugs for chronic diseases available at community pharmacies and allow doctors to run community clinics.
- Encourage private senior care facilities to provide training for health care professionals and senior management. Private senior care facilities can incentivize staff through better pay, training, and benefits and, most importantly, by linking salary and promotion with professional qualifications obtained.

Channel Public Funds through the Private Institutional Sector

The government is increasingly looking to leverage the private sector to meet the needs of the mid-range institutional care market, which accounts for the majority of the total market. The public and private sectors can collaborate in various ways, as described below and in table 4.9. At present, management contracts and leasing are the two most common types of PPP.

In 2014, the Ministry of Civil Affairs began a pilot reform of public senior care facilities to channel government funds through the private sector and

Table 4.9 Types of Public-Private Partnerships in Institutional Care

Type	*Description*
Procurement	Local municipality purchases beds from private senior care facilities
Management contracts	Private nursing home operators assume management responsibilities (e.g., staffing, supplies, training) for public senior care facilities
Leasing	Temporary operation and management of public senior care facilities by private nursing home operators; private senior care facilities bear all risks and retain profits but do not have ownership of the facilities
Service contract	Public senior care facilities outsource a set of services such as housekeeping, catering, and laundry to the private sector
Shareholdings	The ownership structure of public senior care facilities is diversified by engaging the private sector in operations and as shareholders.

Sources: Yu 2014; ICAIA analysis.

hence provide a base level of stable income for private nursing home operators. The private sector, however, is reluctant to bid on public nursing home management contracts for two reasons: the bidding system of local government is not transparent and fair, and bidding prices are too high to secure sufficient financial interest as there are too many competitors. Although the regulatory system is undergoing reform, China's local bidding system is well known for corruption. The government needs to improve the transparency of the bidding system and should not choose a private operator based solely on the lowest bidding price.

Conclusion

While the government should continue to support the public provision of senior care, particularly at the lower end of the market, the best approach going forward seems to be to leverage complementary capabilities and resources from the public and private sectors. As the role of the private sector is still taking shape, the government needs to structure industry regulations and continue to provide stewardship to the industry while encouraging greater participation of the private sector.

As the overall steward of the senior care industry, the Chinese government has a critical role in formulating and reforming industry policies as well as integrating the various services and products provided by industry stakeholders. Several recommendations are proposed below for government policy makers.

- Establishing national and local regulations and guidelines. As with most industries in China, the government should develop policies and guidelines for various needs of the market. These policies and guidelines will also highlight where future development and growth might take place.
- Enforcing regulations and monitoring industry standards. Upholding regulations and monitoring industry standards will be challenging, especially at the local level.

- Financing elderly care infrastructure. The national and local governments have the primary responsibility for funding the health care and elderly care infrastructure. However, according to provincial-level government budgets, only 8 provinces established special funds for the development of senior care services. What the government should pay for and how much it should pay are still under discussion. Policies or guidelines about how to pay for care for the majority of elders with limited income and ability to pay are also needed.
- Providing services to the most vulnerable. The government should focus on providing suitable and low-cost care for the most vulnerable—seniors who are unable to take care of themselves and have limited means of paying for needed care and services.

As described in this chapter, China still faces many significant impediments to further the development of a sustainable and vibrant private senior care sector. To overcome these barriers, the government should:

- Pay attention to industry standards and assessments by setting minimal standards, establishing demonstration projects, and strengthening the enforcement of existing regulations and assessments;
- Broaden financing channels for long-term care by developing a sound and coherent national pension system, creating incentives for people to enroll in corporate annuities to enhance their ability to pay, and developing private commercial insurance;
- Improve the implementation of local policies that foster the role of the private sector by streamlining bureaucratic process and lifting restrictions on public sector health professionals so they can also practice in the private sector; and
- Channel public funds through the private institutional sector by encouraging public-private partnerships (PPPs) and improving transparency in the bidding process.

In addition, it is valuable to identify and disseminate best practices in both the public and private sectors, including policies, laws and regulations, training, business models, operations and so on. Furthermore, the private sector needs to be encouraged and incentivized to expand or innovate in new areas and at all levels of the care continuum, thereby contributing to improving China's senior care market.

About the International China Ageing Industry Association (ICAIA)

ICAIA is a premier business-to-business (B2B) industry association servicing Chinese and overseas stakeholders committed to building a vibrant elderly care industry ecosystem in China. ICAIA promotes a knowledge-based industry and fosters business opportunities among its members and the elderly care industry in China.

The ICAIA Community consists of members and experts that make up a dynamic network of investors, operators, product providers, expert intermediaries, and researchers with a strong track record of investments, services and operational experience, product and technology innovation, successful market development, specialized advisory services, and cutting-edge research.

The association convenes global leaders, transforms research and ideas into actionable agendas, and fosters collaboration through strategic PPPs and business and investment opportunities.

Notes

1. The estimate is derived by multiplying the 97 percent of all seniors who receive in-home care by 35 percent of seniors who live in urban areas. In-home care here only refers to that in urban areas. Senior care in rural areas is different and not discussed in this chapter.
2. In China, elderly welfare recipients are known as "Three No's" (san wu), referring to people who have lost the ability to work, have no source of income, and have no legal guardians to support them or have guardians who do not have the ability to support them.
3. Beijing Statistical Information Net.
4. Hebei BCA.
5. Jilin BCA.

References

China Health and Retirement Longitudinal Study. 2011.

China Voice. 2016. "Media Investigation: 40 Percent Private Aged Care Institutions in China Suffer from Long Time Deficit" (媒体调查：我国民办养老机构40%长年亏损). http://china.cnr.cn/news/20160103/t20160103_521005916.shtml.

China's Research Centre on Ageing. 2013. *China Report of the Development on Silver Industry*.

Feng, Z., H. J. Zhan, X. Feng, C. Liu, M. Sun, and V. Mor. 2011. "An Industry in the Making: The Emergency of Institutional Elder Care in Urban China." *Journal of the American Geriatrics Society* 59 (4): 738–44.

Health and Population Commission. 2014. *Report of the Development on China's Silver Industry*. Beijing: Social Science Literature Press.

Hong Kong Elderly Commission. 2011. *Consultancy Study on Community Care Service for the Elderly*. http://www.elderlycommission.gov.hk/en/download/library/Community%20Care%20Services%20Report%202011_eng.pdf.

Xinhua News. 2016. "Elderly Care Providers: Large Gap in Quantity and Quality Needs to be Improved" (养老护理员：数量缺口大 素质待提高). http://news.xinhuanet.com/gongyi/yanglao/2016-01/19/c_128643799.htm.

Yu, Xinxun. 2014. "Study on Marketlized Operation Model of Elderly Service Industry in China and Its Standard" (论我国养老服务业之市场化运营模式及其规范). *Journal of Sichuan University* (1): 13–20.

CHAPTER 5

Long-Term Care Financing: Issues, Options, and Implications for China

Joshua M. Wiener, Zhanlian Feng, Nan Tracy Zheng, and Jin Song

Introduction

The affordability and financing of formal long-term care have critical implications for the sustainability of such services. In China as in many other countries around the world, population aging and the weakening of traditional family care for older people are increasing the need for formal long-term care services. To address this growing demand, the Chinese government has launched a series of policy initiatives aimed at developing a system of long-term care services and has increasingly called on the private sector to assist in this development. Although current policies focus on boosting supply and building an infrastructure for service provision, financing the recurrent cost of those services and making them widely affordable is a key challenge. Long-term care services are expensive and will not be sustainable (in terms of attracting private service providers) unless there is some dependable way of paying for them on an ongoing basis.

This chapter reviews existing long-term care financing systems in developed economies, mostly those in the Organisation for Economic Co-operation and Development (OECD) and the European Union, with a focus on key issues and design options for policy makers in those countries. Drawing on insights gained from this review as well as research and observations for this study in China, the chapter then discusses the implications of international experiences for China's long-term care financing.

Joshua M. Wiener was a Distinguished Fellow at RTI International and the former director of RTI's Aging, Disability, and Long-Term Care Program. Zhanlian Feng is a Senior Research Analyst at RTI International. Nan Tracy Zheng is a Senior Research Analyst at RTI International. Jin Song is an Associate Professor at the Institute of World Economics and Politics, CASS.

Background and Why Financing Is Important

Long-term care financing is important to the access to and provision of services as well as to government budgets. As discussed below, it has an impact on access to services, the balance among institutional and home- and community-based services, and quality of care. It also has implications for government spending and revenues.

In terms of access, long-term care services are expensive and unaffordable without some third-party coverage for most people throughout the developed world, especially for older people with disabilities. For example, in the United States, the average cost of a semi-private room in a nursing home was US$80,300 per year as of 2015, and the cost of four hours a day of home care, five days a week, was US$20,800 per year (Genworth Financial 2015). In contrast, the median income of households headed by people age 85 and older was only US$20,000 in 2011 (Wu 2013).

Largely because services are not affordable for the vast majority of people with disabilities, long-term care is financed primarily through government or quasi-government programs (such as sickness funds) in developed economies (Colombo et al. 2011). For example, over 75 percent of nursing home residents in the United States have their care paid for by government programs (Kaiser Family Foundation 2013b). The type of financing helps determine the level of spending and its distributional consequences. No economies with well-developed long-term care systems have services mostly paid out-of-pocket.

Despite the high cost of services, public long-term care expenditures are a relatively small proportion of the economy and of the health care system in almost all countries, generally accounting for about 1–2 percent of gross domestic product (GDP) in OECD countries in 2006–10 (de la Maisonneuve and Martin 2013). In general, the Nordic countries are outliers, with Denmark and the Netherlands spending 2.2 and 2.3 percent of GDP, respectively, on public long-term care expenditures. Within the OECD, lower-income countries such as Portugal, the Czech Republic, and Hungary spent less than 0.5 percent of GDP on long-term care services.

With the aging of the population in virtually all countries (including China), expenditures for long-term care services are likely to increase dramatically over the next 40 years. For example, researchers at the European Commission project that the proportion of GDP spent on public long-term care expenditures in the European Union will double from 1.8 percent in 2010 to 3.6 percent in 2060 (Lipszyc, Sail, and Xavier 2012). Based primarily on demographic and other non-financing changes, one projection estimated that public long-term care expenditures in China will increase from 0.2 percent of GDP in 2012 to 0.5–0.6 percent of GDP in 2030, a much larger percentage increase than public spending for health care (Lorenzoni et al. 2015).

However, three caveats should be taken into account in considering these projections:

- The projected need for formal long-term care services is a function of longevity, limited functional ability rates, availability of unpaid family care,

availability of paid care, consumer preferences, the price of services, and the financing available to pay for them. In practice, it is impossible to project all of these factors with any degree of accuracy significantly into the future. For example, in the United States, despite large increases in the number of people age 85 and older over the last 20 years, the number of nursing home residents has not increased (Wiener et al. 2013).
- Without adequate financing, the need may not be translated into effective demand. That is, people may go without paid services (or may rely on informal services) because they have no way to pay for them. To some extent, this is already happening in China, with substantial vacancies in some high-end residential care facilities.
- There are many possible substitutes for individual long-term care services, and the combination of services may affect expenditure levels substantially. Thus, it is commonly argued that part of what may be occurring in the United States is the substitution of assisted living facilities and other home- and community-based services for nursing home care, although the empirical evidence for this is not very strong (Wiener, Anderson, and Brown 2009).

Nonetheless, for almost all countries, the aging of the population means that long-term care spending will be a larger proportion of GDP than it is at present, although the amount of increase will likely be as much a function of the financing choices as it is of population structure. An analysis by the OECD found that there is only a modest statistical relationship between the proportion of the population age 80 and older and the percentage of GDP spent on long-term care for older people (Colombo et al. 2011).

Beyond its effect on public and private expenditures, the structure of public long-term care financing has large impacts on the balance among institutional and home- and community-based services, the quality of care, and the supply of services. In the United States, the availability of financing through Medicaid was critical to creating a more balanced system of long-term care funding in which home- and community-based services now plays a major role (Eiken et al. 2014). In addition, for both publicly and privately provided services, the financing system in the United States largely establishes the level of resources available to provide care, which sets a floor on the acceptable level of quality of care. Because private nursing homes in the United States are so dependent on public financing, they have an incentive to meet the minimum quality requirements for participation in Medicare and Medicaid, the two major sources of financing for nursing home care and home- and community-based services. Thus, threatening to terminate participation in the government financing program is the principal enforcement mechanism for addressing poor quality of care (Wiener et al. 2007).

Like most other government programs, public long-term care financing systems are also potentially redistributive. The redistribution is a function of the method of raising the funds and a function of the eligibility for financing, the services used, and the reimbursement. At the very least, long-term care financing systems redistribute money from people without disabilities to people with disabilities. Most public systems also redistribute resources from younger (less likely to be disabled), working people to older, retired people. Depending on the system, resources can also be redistributed from higher-income to lower-income people. Although limited functional ability affects people of all ages and income/wealth levels, people with disabilities are disproportionately lower-income and have less wealth than people without disabilities. For example, in 2001, the median income of older people in the United States with no disabilities was about twice that of older people with severe disabilities, while the median total household net worth for people with no disabilities was four times that of people with severe disabilities (Johnson and Wiener 2006). As a result, even universal coverage financing systems in which all people are potentially eligible for services regardless of income and assets serve a disproportionately low-income and low-asset population (Wiener, Illston, and Hanley 1994).

Financing Design Choices

In designing their long-term care systems, countries make choices about the roles of the public and private sectors in meeting the needs of people with disabilities and how each sector should be structured, funded, and regulated.

Public Financing

Countries face several critical choices in designing their public long-term care financing systems, including whether to means-test eligibility or provide for universal coverage, whether to provide services directly or act as a third-party payer or insurer, the degree to which the financing is the same throughout the country, and the relationship of long-term care to the medical care system.

Means-Tested versus Universal Coverage

Within public sector programs, some countries have means-tested approaches while other countries have universal coverage programs, and some countries have features that combine both of these types of systems. Countries operating primarily means-tested programs limit public benefits to people who are poor (usually a definition that takes into account both income and assets) or who become poor due to the high costs of medical and long-term care. The philosophical premise behind means-tested programs is that the primary responsibility for care of older people and younger persons with disabilities rests with individuals and their families and that the government should act only as a payer of last resort for those unable to provide for themselves. The long-term care financing systems of England, New Zealand, and the United States largely reflect this view (Colombo et al. 2011).

An alternative philosophical approach is that the government should take the lead in ensuring that all people with disabilities should be eligible for the long-term care services they need, regardless of financial status. In this type of system, social solidarity is highly valued, and the right to long-term care is viewed similarly to the right to medical care. The long-term care financing systems of Germany, Japan, France, the Netherlands, and Sweden reflect this view (Colombo et al. 2011; Wiener 2011). For example:

- In Germany, the primary source of financing is through a universal social insurance program for long-term care (*Soziale Pfgeversicherung*) that provides nursing home and home care benefits for people of all ages with disabilities (Campbell et al. 2010; Cuellar and Wiener 2000; Gibson and Redfoot 2007). The social insurance program is administered by sickness funds for roughly 70 million Germans, and private health insurers cover an additional 10 million, mostly upper-income individuals.
- The Republic of Korea introduced national long-term care insurance in 2008, which mainly covers individuals age 65 and older regardless of income. The program is financed jointly through mandatory premium contributions from participants (which account for 60–65 percent of total funds), government subsidies (20 percent) and out-of-pocket payments by service users (15–20 percent) (Jung et al. 2014; Kwon 2009). Taiwan, China is also developing public long-term care insurance programs.
- In Japan, the primary source of financing is the government-operated long-term care insurance, *Kaigo Hoken* (Campbell and Ikegami 2000, 2003; Campbell, Ikegami, and Gibson 2010). The program pays for benefits for people who have disabilities and who are age 65 or older, as well as for persons who are age 40 or older and have an "aging-related" condition (such as early-onset Alzheimer's disease), a group added partly to justify charging premiums to the younger, working population. Younger people with disabilities, such as people with spinal cord injuries due to a car accident, are not covered by the insurance program. As a result of these restrictions, only about 3 percent of beneficiaries are under age 65 (Campbell, Ikegami, and Gibson 2010). The insurance program is administered by the municipalities, with funding split between the national government, insurance premiums paid by enrollees, and the national government.

Direct Provision of Services versus Third-Party Payment Systems

Although long-term care financing is overwhelmingly supplied by public resources in developed countries, actual services can be provided by government-run organizations or non-government-run organizations. In the Scandinavian model such as in Sweden, most providers are government agencies and institutions, although there has been movement toward privatization (Swedish Ministry of Health and Social Affairs 2007). The goal of government ownership is to provide care without consideration of whether an activity is profitable. However, where government agencies provide the services, there is no arms-length relationship between the provider and the payer leading to lower efficiency of spending.

Non-governmental organizations (NGOs) include both non-profit organizations and for-profit companies. The theory motivating privatization is that competing organizations will provide more choice to consumers at a lower cost, with more flexibility, and with greater orientation to the needs of consumers. In England, local authorities historically ran care homes, but the number of private for-profit facilities exploded during the 1980s and 1990s, with government facilities comprising less than 10 percent of all care homes (United Kingdom Commission for Social Care Inspection 2009). In the United States, about 70 percent of nursing homes are for-profit companies, about one-quarter are non-profit organizations, and only about one-sixteenth are government-owned facilities (Centers for Medicare and Medicaid Services 2015). Although controversial, for-profit nursing homes in the United States have a lower quality of care than non-profit facilities, which critics argue is the result of a focus on profit-making rather than the needs of residents (Commodore et al. 2009; Harrington et al. 2012).

In systems such as the United States, Germany, and Japan where government-owned providers are not the principal types of providers, the government functions as a third-party payer, reimbursing providers for covered services. These systems typically have the functions of insurers, although the people receiving the benefits may not technically be insured, in that they may qualify for benefits because they meet a means test rather than that they have paid premiums for their insurance coverage. Financing systems that operate as third-party payers must develop systems of enrolling eligible providers; determining eligible beneficiaries; setting reimbursement rates; monitoring compliance with quality, administrative, and fiscal standards; and paying providers for services. Some public programs operate on a grant or block payment system in which private providers receive a fixed amount of money for services which is not directly tied to providing services to particular individuals, but these types of funding arrangements are less commonly used.

National versus Sub-National

One of the key issues in the design of long-term care systems is the level of government responsible for financing and delivery. Many developed countries, including the United States, the United Kingdom, Sweden, the Netherlands, and Canada, rely heavily on subnational governments to design and administer their long-term care systems, albeit often with substantial policy guidance from the national government. For example, Sweden devolves virtually all responsibility for the financing, organization, and administration of long-term care to municipalities, even though it is a small country with less than 10 million people (Swedish Ministry of Health and Social Affairs 2007).

Advocates for devolution make three arguments in favor of assigning responsibility for long-term care to smaller geographic governmental units (Wiener 1996). First, states, provinces, and municipalities are heavily involved with a variety of social services in many countries. Thus, a local approach can establish needed linkages between long-term care and other services often needed by people with disabilities. Second, long-term care is an intensely personal service involving decisions about how consumers want to live their lives. Thus, the planning and delivery of services can be influenced by local circumstances, norms, and values as well as by the local preferences of the disabled population, their caregivers, and providers. Finally, because subnational governments are less driven to routinize their decision making process and because individual cases loom larger in the policy process, locally administered programs are arguably less rigid and bureaucratic than centrally run programs.

At the other end of the continuum are countries such as Germany and Japan which have a more nationalized and centralized approach to long-term care, although subnational governmental entities are often still involved. For example, under the long-term care insurance program in Japan, 2,895 municipal governments or alliances of municipalities are the insurers and have a general responsibility to provide adequate services (Campbell and Ikegami 2000, 2003). However, because almost all aspects of the program—eligibility, most benefits, and reimbursement rates—are fixed at the national level, the ability of the municipalities to shape the program is strictly limited. Thus, although premiums are set at the municipal level, almost all parameters of the financing are set at the national level.

Two main arguments favor consolidation at the national level (Wiener and Tilly 2003). First, a uniform national program helps guarantee horizontal equity across geographic areas. In other words, national rules help ensure that similarly situated individuals in different geographic areas of the country are treated basically the same way, especially in terms of benefits. In England, for example, which relies on subnational governmental units for the design and administration of most long-term care services, beneficiaries often complain of a "postcode lottery" in which persons with similar needs and financial status are treated very differently because they live in different local authorities (Wiener and Cuellar 1999). In those financing arrangements, the services received by an individual depend on where that individual lives. In the United States, Medicaid coverage of home- and community-based services varies enormously by state (Ng et al. 2015). In countries with insurance approaches such as Germany, regional variations are thought to be unfair, and efforts are made to eliminate them (Cuellar and Wiener 2000). Second, developing a single national program may involve less administrative expense because program rules and systems need to be developed only once, and each subnational governmental unit need not reinvent procedures and systems.

Relationship between Medical Care and Long-Term Care Financing

In almost all countries, individuals with disabilities must cope with fragmented financing and delivery systems that separate medical and long-term care services. In the United States, for example, acute care for older people and younger persons with disabilities is primarily the responsibility of the national government through the Medicare program, whereas long-term care is primarily the domain of states and the Medicaid program for the poor (Wiener and Tilly 2003). The Medicare program covers short-term, post-hospital care geared toward rehabilitation, while the Medicaid program covers long-stay nursing home residents such as people with Alzheimer's disease. This fragmentation creates difficulties because people with disabilities typically have a combination of medical and long-term care needs. For example, a substantial body of research in the United States shows that nursing home and home care users have high hospitalization rates, a substantial portion of which is potentially avoidable (Feng et al. 2014a; Konetzka, Karon, and Potter 2012; Walsh et al. 2012). On the one hand, fragmentation makes integrating acute and long-term care difficult; on the other hand, a separate long-term care program helps protect funding for these services and militates against the unnecessary medicalization of long-term care.

The degree of separation between medical and long-term care services differs across countries. In the United States, the Netherlands, Japan, Germany, Sweden, and the United Kingdom, long-term care is financed and organized apart from acute care. In many countries such as Belgium, France, Italy, Portugal, Spain, and the United Kingdom, the skilled nursing or "medical" component of home care and sometimes nursing home care is part of the health care system, while the "social" component is part of the social service system (Genet et al. 2012).

In the United Kingdom, for example, medical care services are provided through the National Health Service, a tax-financed system of private physicians and public hospitals. The National Health Service is also responsible for paying for skilled nursing services in nursing homes. Long-term care is financed and managed through local authorities, which are subnational governmental units, often roughly equivalent to counties in size. While services are available from the National Health Service free at the point of use, long-term care services are means-tested. Without the administrative and financing structures of managed care organizations through which a single entity can receive funds for both health and long-term care services for an enrolled individual, initiatives for service integration in England have focused on joint commissioning between the National Health Service and local authorities' social services departments (Goodwin 2007).

Japan also separates its long-term care insurance from its acute care insurance, but it provides some medical care in its long-term care benefits and continues to provide a substantial amount of institutional long-term care through its medical insurance (Campbell, Ikegami, and Gibson 2010). Several medical services are included in the list of covered services under long-term care insurance, including visiting nurses and rehabilitation. The long-term care insurance program also covers physician supervision, but the benefit is not used very widely, in part because no natural relationships exist between family doctors and care managers. Before the introduction of the long-term care insurance program, hospitals were major providers of institutional care, partly because older people paid little in out-of-pocket costs for these services. A major goal of the insurance program is to convert hospitals that functioned primarily as nursing homes to long-term care beds. This conversion has been slower than expected, partially because it is more prestigious to be a hospital than a nursing home.

Sweden places responsibility for acute care at the county level and responsibility for long-term care at the municipal level (Swedish Ministry of Health and Social Affairs 2007). Reducing the discharge backlogs in hospitals was the major impetus for the Adel reforms of 1992 (*Ädelreformen*), which consolidated responsibilities for long-term care at the municipal level for older people in hospitals who no longer needed hospital-level care. Backlogged hospital patients waiting for discharge were primarily people waiting for nursing home care, home care, or rehabilitation services. The reforms reduced the backlog by providing a strong financial incentive for municipalities to use their long-term care resources to find lower-cost placements for patients waiting unnecessarily in hospitals.

Private Sector Financing: Out-of-Pocket Spending and Private Long-Term Care Insurance

Out-of-Pocket Spending

Out-of-pocket spending is a substantial part of long-term care financing, although it is not the principal source of financing in any country with a developed long-term care service system. In countries with public long-term care insurance, consumers typically must pay a coinsurance for services or supplement the amount paid by the insurance plan (Colombo et al. 2011). In Japan, there is a 10 percent coinsurance for services, except for the low-income population (Campbell, Ikegami, and Gibson 2010). The coinsurance has two purposes: (1) for home- and community-based services, a coinsurance serves to limit demand for services that may be inherently desirable even to people who are not disabled, such as homemaker services, and (2) for institutional services, the copayment amount is conceptually designed to be equivalent to the normal living costs of room and board that individuals would incur even if they were not disabled and living in a nursing home. In countries with public long-term care insurance such as Germany and Japan, means-tested public assistance programs provide help with the coinsurance for people who cannot afford it.

In countries with means-tested programs, people who do not meet the income and asset requirements must pay out-of-pocket for all of their care. Given the high cost of care, this is a substantial financial burden for most service users, many of whom deplete their savings and impoverish themselves until they qualify for the means-tested coverage. In a study that examined people age 50 and older in the United States over a 10-year period, two-thirds to three-quarters of nursing home residents who were eligible for Medicaid (the means-tested program) spent down to the program threshold and were not originally eligible for the program prior to admission (Wiener et al. 2013). In the United Kingdom, the impoverishment of middle-class older people who entered care homes was the primary motivation for enacting limits on out-of-pocket spending for social care (United Kingdom Department of Health 2013). The implementation of these limits, however, has been postponed until 2020. In the United Kingdom, an individual's house is counted as an asset in determining eligibility for means-tested programs, so most people must sell their houses when they enter a care home in order to cover the costs; in the United States, the home is an excluded asset in determining eligibility for services.

Means-tested programs typically require that people in institutions contribute all of their income toward the cost of their care, except for a small to modest personal needs allowance. This contribution helps further limit the cost of the program, since the government will only pay the difference between the government-set payment rate and the contribution toward the cost of care. In the United States, Medicaid programs are legally required to recover the cost of long-term care from the estates of deceased Medicaid beneficiaries (typically the house), but enforcement of that requirement is not widespread (Karp, Sabatino, and Wood 2005).

Private Long-Term Care Insurance

It has long been the hope of many observers, especially private-market-oriented conservatives and those who worry about the future societal financial burden of long-term care, that private long-term care insurance could play a major role in financing long-term care, especially for middle- and upper-middle-income people. Particularly in countries with means-tested financing systems, expansion of private long-term care insurance is seen as a potential strategy for reducing catastrophic out-of-pocket costs for individuals and lowering public spending (Rivlin and Wiener 1988; Wiener, Illston, and Hanley 1994). Particularly with the aging of the population and the large projected increase in demand, some countries are examining this option as a way to reduce the need for public spending.

Despite these hopes, private long-term care insurance does not play a major role in financing long-term care in any country (Colombo et al. 2011). In France, which has significant market penetration, long-term care insurance is integrated with health insurance, but the benefits are limited, and private insurance accounts for less than 1 percent of long-term care expenditures (Doty, Nadash, and Racco 2015). In Germany, private insurance is primarily offered as an alternative for upper-income people and government officials to the mandatory statutory sickness funds.

In the United States, which has had an active market in private long-term care insurance since the mid-1980s, only about 12 percent of the 65-and-older population has any long-term care insurance (almost all of which has substantial restrictions on coverage), and it accounts for only about 7 percent of total expenditures (Frank, Cohen, and Mahoney 2013; Kaiser Family Foundation 2013a). Despite the aging of the population, the market has deteriorated greatly over the last 15 years, with most companies leaving the market and sales plummeting. In 2000, 125 companies competed in the private long-term care insurance market; by 2012, fewer than 15 companies were actively selling standalone policies (Cohen, Kaur, and Darnell 2013). The employer group market—which accounts for about one-quarter of sales and is key to making coverage affordable to large numbers of people—has been hit especially hard by insurance company exits.

Moreover, new sales in the individual market, which account for the bulk of sales, fell by 83 percent, from 754,000 new policies in 2002 to only 129,000 new policies in 2014 (National Association of Insurance Commissioners 2015). Part of the reason is that many insurers have imposed large price increases, raising premiums by 25–90 percent even for existing policy holders. Insurers have also tightened medical underwriting, with many companies now requiring applicants to take blood tests and excluding people with mental illnesses (Forte 2015).

The factors behind these trends are straightforward. In the past, most of the premiums were calculated assuming that there would be fairly high rates of return on the funds that insurers held in reserve and that people would allow their policies to lapse at a predicted rate. However, with the collapse of the stock market in 2008, low interest rates, and the recession and slow economic growth that followed, insurers are now receiving much lower rates of return on their reserves, which drives up premiums. At the same time, insurers have seen fewer policy holders than anticipated allowing their coverage to lapse—meaning that more people are still holding policies when they need care, resulting in insurers having to pay benefits that they had not planned on paying. The combined effect is that most insurers find it too risky to try to predict expenditures for long-term care over a period of 20–40 years, and the bad publicity from skyrocketing premiums is not worth the trouble. Although the probability that private long-term care insurance would cover large portions of the population was never high, recent developments have made it even worse.

In countries with long-term care insurance such as Germany, private long-term care insurance may play a role in supplementing the public plan. In countries with means-tested financing systems, the insurance is meant to substitute for the government programs.

Reasons for the low market demand for private long-term care insurance include:

- *The cost of private long-term care insurance is high.* In the United States, a policy with three years of coverage and US$150 a day in benefits with 5 percent inflation protection costs US$2,853 a year if purchased at age 65 (Federal Long-Term Care Insurance Program 2015). Numerous studies have found that private long-term care insurance in the United States is unaffordable for most people (Feder, Komisar, and Friedland 2007; Wiener, Illston, and Hanley 1994), and recent dramatic price increases make the policies less affordable. Moreover, at least 40 percent of the premiums is for profit, commissions for sales agents, marketing costs, and other overhead expenses. While premiums are lower at younger ages and when purchased through employers, younger individuals typically have competing demands on their income, including home mortgages, child care, education expenses for their children, and saving for retirement. Moreover, even when employers in the United States offer policies, they do not help pay for them. Almost all employer-based policies are on an employee-pays-all basis. Thus, take-up of voluntary private long-term care insurance in employer-based settings is typically very low (generally around 7 percent of eligible individuals).

Most options to jumpstart the market for private long-term care insurance are geared toward reducing the price of insurance policies. One option is to provide tax deductions or credits for the purchase of private long-term care insurance. A related option would be to allow people to use funds from their tax-sheltered income retirement plans to pay for long-term care insurance. Current U.S. federal law allows qualifying long-term care insurance premiums to be deducted from income as part of medical expenses, but only if total out-of-pocket medical expenses exceed 10 percent of adjusted gross income (7.5 percent for taxpayers age 65 and older) and only for the expenses that exceed the expenditure threshold. However, given the high threshold, few people qualify for these deductions. In addition, at least 36 states and the District of Columbia provide some tax incentive for the purchase of private long-term care insurance (Baer and O'Brien 2010), but several studies suggest that tax incentives are unlikely to affect the purchase of private long-term care insurance unless the subsidy is very large (Feder, Komisar, and Friedland 2007; Goda 2010; Nixon 2008; Wiener, Illston, and Hanley 1994).

An alternative approach to expanding the market would be for the government to pay for long-term care costs beyond what is covered in an approved private long-term care insurance policy. This strategy provides lifetime coverage without requiring people to buy a costly private long-term care insurance policy that provides lifetime benefits, a type of policy that has largely disappeared from the marketplace. A version of this approach, the Long-Term Care Partnership, is currently being implemented in many states in the United States, with Medicaid providing the government backup. Under this approach, people can keep more financial assets than would normally be allowed and still qualify for Medicaid. Although a favorite among policy analysts, this approach has not generated a large increase in sales (Hawaii Long-Term Care Commission 2012). Studies differ as to whether the Long-Term Care Partnership will save or cost money for Medicaid (Bergquist, Font, and Swartz 2015; Sun and Webb 2013; Wiener, Illston, and Hanley 1994).

- *Medical underwriting excludes substantial numbers of people from purchasing policies.* Since private long-term care insurance is always purchased voluntarily, there is the risk of adverse selection—that is, people with a higher risk of using long-term care services will disproportionately want to purchase policies because the cost of the premium (even if high) will be less than the cost of services they want to use. To protect against adverse selection, insurers typically medically underwrite policies, preventing people with various types of chronic diseases or disabilities from purchasing policies. Although data on underwriting methods are considered proprietary information, in 2009, insurers in the United States declined individual coverage for 14 percent of people ages 50–59 and 23 percent of people ages 60–69 who applied, even after preliminary screening by sales agents (American Association for Long-Term Care Insurance 2010). As noted earlier, the medical underwriting standards in the United States have tightened in recent years.

- *People do not expect to need long-term care insurance.* While virtually everyone expects to need physician and hospital services and prescription drugs eventually, few people expect to become severely disabled and to need help with basic activities like eating, bathing, and dressing. However, using microsimulation modeling, Favreault and Dey (2015) estimate that about half (52 percent) of Americans turning age 65 today will develop severe disabilities. Most will need assistance for less than two years, although about one in seven adults will have a limited functional ability for more than five years. In a recent study in the United States, most people expected to live a long time but not to use nursing home care (Khatutsky et al. 2015). In some countries such as the United States where some short-term post-acute nursing home and home health services are covered by the government health insurance program (i.e., Medicare), many people mistakenly believe that the existing health insurance programs will cover extended long-term care services and that there is no need to buy long-term care insurance.

Current Long-Term Care Financing in China

In China, much of the government funding for aged care comes from the Public Welfare Lottery Fund. The Ministry of Civil Affairs of the PRC (MOCA) reports that between the mid-1980s and 2010 about three-fifths of national elderly welfare-related expenditures were funded from the Public Welfare Lottery Fund (PWLF), while local governments contributed about one-quarter of spending, and other sources accounted for about 15 percent (Song and Glinskaya 2016). Money for the PWLF is derived from the proceeds of the Welfare Lottery and the Sport Lottery. Total revenues from these two lotteries more than doubled in nominal terms between 2010 and 2014 and in 2014, the Welfare Lottery received RMB 206 billion and Sports Lottery about RMB 175 million (figure 5.1).

The allocation of lottery funds is complex. After deducting lottery prices (about half of all revenues) and administrative costs (around 15 percent of revenues), the remaining 35 percent is placed in the PWLF. Accordingly, the estimated amount retained in the PWLF in 2014 was approximately RMB 133 billion. The funds in the PWLF are shared equally between the National and provincial authorities. Funds retained at the provincial level are required to be spent on public welfare, and about half of Welfare Lottery proceeds (but not the Sports Lottery proceeds) are directed toward various elderly welfare projects and activities. In 2014 an estimated RMB 18 billion nationwide was appropriated from the PWLF for elderly welfare by the provincial authorities. From the proceeds retained at the national level, elderly-welfare-related expenditures were estimated at 1–1.5 percent of the PWLF or RMB 0.9 billion in 2014.

Figure 5.1 Lottery Sales Volume, 2010–15

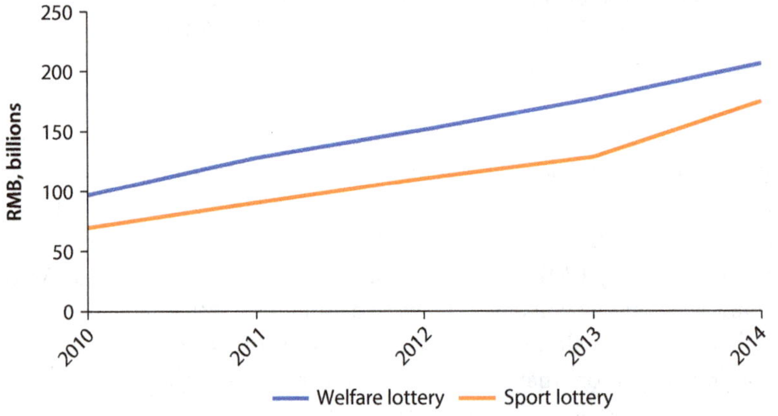

Sources: MOCA, various years; General Administration of Sport, various years.

These calculations place the amount of public expenditures on elderly care in China at 0.02–0.04 percent of GDP. In addition to that, some forms of care for frail elderly (health care, rehabilitation, nursing care) are covered by the health insurance system and the health budget, but there are no reliable estimates of these expenditures attributed to long-team care for the elderly.

Between the mid-1980s and 2010, PWLF funds appropriated for elderly welfare by the provincial authorities, were spent at the provincial level (about 40 percent of total, on average), prefecture level (about 40 percent of total, on average), and at the district/county level (about 20 percent). There is a trend in recent years to increase the proportion in total PWLF spending executed at the prefecture and county level, (with a relative decline of the provincial-level share).

Overall, about 90 percent of all PWLF funds are spent on infrastructure, with share of non-infrastructure being higher at the provincial and prefecture level and lower at the district/county level. Non-infrastructure expenditures include various subsides to the elderly and other activities. By the end of 2014, 18 provinces had used PWLF resources to launch the subsidy policies for elderly aged 80 and above, 22 provinces launched subsidies for elderly in economic difficulties, and 4 provinces launched subsidies for nursing care, targeting elderly with mental impairments and economic difficulties (MOCA 2014). There is a trend in recent years of an increase in the share of non-infrastructure spending at all levels. Still, PWLF expenditures are mostly for financing various types of infrastructure, including new construction, reconstruction, or expansion of existing facilities, such as nursing homes, rural old people's homes, honor homes (for veterans), as well as cultural, recreational, and activity centers for the elderly.

Overall, public funding is mostly limited to: (1) some support to welfare recipients, commonly known as the "Three No's" as described below, by serving them in government welfare homes as well as direct purchasing of aged care services; (2) help with land acquisition for constructing residential care facilities, nursing homes, and community centers for the elderly; (3) subsidies to privately run nursing homes and community centers (usually per bed, both for fixed and operating costs) but not directly to individual residents; (4) training for aged care workers; and (5) subsidies for medical insurance coverage (which covers some skilled services).

Financial Support to the "Three No's." The government pays the full costs of living (including long-term care) for a small number of strictly defined welfare recipients commonly known as the "Three No's"—people who have lost the ability to work, have no source of income, and have no relatives or legal guardians to support them or have guardians who do not have the ability to support them—who either live in the community or in government-run social welfare institutions. Known as *wubao* (literally, "five guarantees"), local governments have a responsibility to provide food, clothing, housing, medical care, and burial expenses. This role for the public sector is long-standing, but not many people receive services through this financing mechanism. According to government statistics, China had 76,000 Three No's in urban areas and 5.29 million *wubao* recipients in rural areas nationwide in 2014 (MOCA 2015). Altogether, these welfare recipients accounted for less than 2.5 percent of the total population age 60 and over in China in 2014.

Supply-side subsidies: Government subsidies to service providers for construction and operation. The government provides financial inducements for the development of new long-term care facilities by the private sector in the form of subsidies for new construction and ongoing operating subsidies for beds. These subsidies—in conjunction with other preferential policy treatments such as tax exemptions, land allotment or leasing for new construction, and reduced utility rates—are intended to encourage private sector investment in the development of senior care services. Importantly, the operating subsidies are linked not to the individuals using the services but to the facility providing the services. The operating and capital subsidies vary by a number of complicated categories, creating a system that varies greatly across service characteristics and geographic areas.

These subsidies are geared toward new institutional construction and vary across provinces but are typically fairly low, especially for facility operation. These types of subsidies are available on an opportunistic basis, generally when there is new construction, and exist in Beijing, Anhui Province, Ningxia, Nanjing (Jiangsu Province), Chengdu (Sichuan Province), Jinan (Shandong Province), and elsewhere. Most of these subsidies are linked to residential settings, but some subsidies are available for new construction in some community-care settings (e.g., Chongqing, one of the four province-level municipalities in China). In general, these subsidies are not linked explicitly to quality of care or other performance standards.

In Beijing, for example, the municipal government provides a construction subsidy of RMB 8,000–16,000 per new bed and an operating subsidy of RMB 100–200 per month per occupied bed. In Anhui Province, private service providers receive a one-off subsidy for their construction cost, regular operation subsidy, loan interest, and a service subsidy. In terms of the operation subsidy, prefecture and county governments provide a subsidy of no less than RMB 200 per person per month. For aged care facilities or social organizations that receive service subsidies from the government, the subsidy level is based on the types and standards of service provided. Facilities serving older people with disabilities or dementia receive a subsidy based on the limited functional ability level of the residents. The operation and service subsidy depends on whether the residents are categorized as having mild, moderate, or severe impairments, with the amounts varying by 50 percent, 100 percent, and over 200 percent, respectively, of the standard amount.

In Ningxia, non-profit organizations that build their own facilities receive a one-time building subsidy of RMB 8,000 per bed, RMB 3,000 from the general provincial-level fiscal budget, RMB 3,000 from provincial-level lottery revenues, RMB 2,000 from the county-level budget if the facility is located in a county, and an additional RMB 1,000 from the prefecture and district-level budget if it is located in a district. In Nanjing, the municipal government provides financial inducements for new construction in the amount of RMB 2,000–4,000 per new bed and an ongoing operating subsidy of RMB 80 per occupied bed each month.

Demand-side subsidies (vouchers) to service users. Local governments across China are experimenting with providing limited allowances—either in cash or vouchers redeemable for eligible services—to targeted segments of the elderly population, such as persons age 80 or older or frail elders who do not have children living with them. While the funds are rarely enough to purchase significant amounts of long-term care, they do improve the financial position of people with a high risk of needing long-term care. If focused on characteristics such as age or receipt of cash welfare assistance, this approach can have low administrative costs because individuals do not need to undergo complicated assessments for their functional capacities and needs.

As an example of this approach, Beijing provides service vouchers to older people for the purchase of community-based care. As of 2010, Beijing provided people over the age of 60 with a monthly RMB 100 service voucher to be used to pay for items such as household chores, rehabilitation assistance, and other home-based services. The beneficiaries accounted for approximately 15.2 percent of the registered permanent residents age 60 or older in Beijing. The Beijing municipal government had about RMB 500 million worth of senior care vouchers in circulation in 2013. Reportedly, a large majority of the funds were spent on basic items such as food rather than on services (Caixin Online 2013).

Similarly, in Anhui Province, various categories of people who qualify as "Three No's" receive vouchers worth RMB 40 to RMB 600 which must be used within a month. Services that can be purchased with the vouchers include help with daily living, medical rehabilitation, and housekeeping.

Prefecture-level and district-level governments share the expenses equally. Baohe district (of Hefei city) government provides two types of vouchers to the very poor: a RMB 20 information service subsidy and a RMB 100 care service subsidy.

Relationship with the Health Care Financing System. Over the last 40 years, China has extended basic health insurance to its population, now covering over 95 percent of its population (Blumenthal and Hsiao 2015; Yip and Hsiao 2015; and Yip et al. 2012). Although enormous progress has been made in health care, the system is still hindered by waste, inefficiency, poor quality, and scarcity and misdistribution of the workforce (Yip et al. 2012).

In general, the health and long-term care systems are separate and distinct, although some nursing homes are located next to or are affiliated with public hospitals, and some long-term care facilities have medical (as opposed to nursing) staff (International China Aging Industry Association, undated). Despite the separation, several cities and provinces—including Qingdao (Shandong Province), Weifang (Shandong Province), and Nanjing (Jiangsu Province)—are experimenting with using health insurance to provide long-term care insurance. In Qingdao, for example, small amounts of funds from medical insurance (0.2 percent) and money from the Public Welfare Lottery Fund are transferred into a long-term care insurance account. Covered services include home-based care, hospital care, and services in certain long-term care institutions. Weifang and Nanjing have similar pilot projects.

Although it does not appear to be linked to health insurance, in the Haidian District of Beijing, the government is subsidizing premiums for long-term care insurance that covers home care. The subsidies vary by age.

Implications for China

China is often described as a country that is "getting old before getting rich," which means that older people in need of long-term care services (which are expensive in China as elsewhere) and their families will not have enough resources to pay for such services. Therefore, although the needs for long-term care are real and rising rapidly, substantial portions of these needs may not translate into effective demand. According to a recent survey of Chinese seniors in 10 cities conducted by the China Research Center on Aging in 2013 (Dang 2014), the average monthly pension among the respondents was RMB 2,532, which was the primary source of income for 89 percent of all respondents in the survey. In comparison, the average cost for a live-in paid caregiver is RMB 2,220 per month; the average price for adult day services is almost RMB 50 per day or about RMB 1,500 per month; and the average cost of homemaker services is RMB 19 per visit. The costs are even higher for institutional care, which partly explains the high vacancy rates in many private sector senior care facilities, especially the more luxurious ones (Feng et al. 2011).

Without substantially increasing public support to more older people who need long-term care services but lack the means to pay for them, the government will find it challenging to expand and sustain the senior care industry. Although it has recently begun to provide supply-side financial inducements to the private sector in the form of subsidies for new bed construction and some operating subsidies for existing residential care beds as described earlier, these inducements will not allow for ongoing oversight and enforcement of quality of care standards and will not allow the government to shape the desired balance of institutional-, home-, and community-based services.

The difficulties and failures many countries have experienced in promoting private long-term care insurance do not bode well for China. Although there is an emerging interest in private long-term care insurance (mostly in the commercial insurance sector) in China as a way to enable people to pay for services, it most likely will not work. In no country is private long-term care insurance a major source of long-term care financing, except where it is offered as an alternative to a mandatory public system. Experience in other countries shows that private long-term care insurance is simply too expensive and that insurers cannot price policies accurately.

A key issue in the development of a more robust public financing system will be the division of responsibilities between the central and provincial/local governments. As discussed earlier, a centralized system is best for ensuring horizontal equity but can be bureaucratic and unresponsive to local conditions, needs, and traditions. A more decentralized approach runs the risk of creating or institutionalizing disparities across regions and individuals and may result in inefficiencies as each geographic unit must decide how to design and manage its system.

China may wish to start with a broader means-tested public long-term care financing system that is less restrictive than the current system that primarily supports the Three No's and *wubao*. A logical next step would be for the government to widen the safety net to cover a greater number of elders most in need of long-term care (those with disabilities), but without adequate financial resources to pay for needed care. However, as evidenced by the experiences of other countries (e.g., the United States and England), a means-tested public financing system has inherent flaws and many undesirable features, such as a sense of stigma (rather than entitlement) felt by care recipients and high administrative burdens associated with "gatekeeping" for eligibility and benefits. Moreover, a means-tested approach cannot prevent catastrophic out-of-pocket costs, and the resulting impoverishment is incongruous with a situation in which the vast majority of people with functional needs would qualify financially.

In the medium to long run, China should consider developing a universal public long-term care financing system similar to the universal social insurance models adopted in the Netherlands, Germany, Japan, and more recently in Korea. As with health care and income support for older people, this approach recognizes that needing long-term care is a normal life risk that the vast majority of people cannot address on their own.

References

American Association for Long-Term Care Insurance. 2010. *The 2010 Sourcebook for Long-Term Care Insurance Information*. Westlake, CA: American Association for Long-Term Care Insurance.

Baer, D., and E. O'Brien. 2010. *Federal and State Income Tax Incentives for Private Long-Term Care Insurance*. Washington, DC: AARP. http://assets.aarp.org/rgcenter/ppi/econ-sec/2009-19-tax-incentives.pdf.

Bergquist, S., J. C. Font, and K. Swartz. 2015. "Long Term Care Partnerships: Are They 'Fit for Purpose'?" Munich: Ludwig-Maximilians University's Center for Economic Studies and the Ifo Institute. http://papers.ssrn.com/sol3/papers.cfm?abstract_id=2555540##.

Blumenthal, D., and W. Hsiao. 2015. "Lessons from the East—China's Rapidly Evolving Health Care System." *New England Journal of Medicine* 372 (14): 1281–85.

Caixin Online. 2013. "Blues for Gray Hair: What's Wrong with China's Elder Care Section." March 6. http://english.caixin.com/2013-06-03/100536498.html.

Campbell, J. C., N. Ikegami, and M. J. Gibson. 2010. "Lessons from Public Long-Term Care Insurance in Germany and Japan." *Health Affairs* 29: 87–95.

Campbell, John Creighton, and Naoki Ikegami. 2000. "Long-Term Care Insurance Comes to Japan." *Health Affairs* 19: 26–39.

———. 2003. "Japan's Radical Reform of Long-Term Care." *Social Policy and Administration* 37: 21–34.

Centers for Medicare and Medicaid Services. 2015. *Nursing Home Data Compendium, 2015 Edition*. Baltimore: Centers for Medicare and Medicaid Services. https://www.cms.gov/Medicare/Provider-Enrollment-and-Certification/CertificationandComplianc/Downloads/nursinghomedatacompendium_508-2015.pdf.

Cohen, M. A., R. Kaur, and B. Darnell. 2013. *Exiting the Market: Understanding the Factors behind Carriers' Decision to Leave the Long-Term Care Insurance Market*. Assistant Secretary for Planning and Evaluation, Washington, DC. http://aspe.hhs.gov/daltcp/reports/2013/MrktExit.pdf.

Colombo, F, A. Llena-Nozal, J. Mercier, and F. Tjadens. 2011. *Help Wanted? Providing and Paying for Long-Term Care*. Paris: Organization for Economic Co-operation and Development.

Commodore, V. R., P. J. Devereaux, Q. Zhou, S. B. Stone, J. W. Busse, N.C. Ravindran, K. E. Burns, T. Haines, B. Stringer, D. J. Cook, S. D. Walter, T. Sullivan, O. Berwanger, M. Bhandari, S. Banglawala, J. N. Lavis, B. Petrisor, H. Schünemann, K. Walsh, N. Bhatnagar, and G. H. Guyatt. 2009. "Quality of Care in For-Profit and Not-for-Profit Nursing Homes: Systematic Review and Meta-Analysis." *BMJ* 339: b2732. doi:10.1136/bmj.b2732.

Cuellar, Alison Evans, and Joshua M. Wiener. 2000. "Can Social Insurance for Long-Term Care Work? The Case of Germany." *Health Affairs* 19 (3): 8–25.

Dang, J. 2014. "Survey of 10,000 Seniors in 10 Cities on the Current Situation of In-Home Care" (in Chinese). News release, China Research Center on Aging. http://www.cncaprc.gov.cn/jianghua/43280.jhtml.

de la Maisonneuve, C., and J. O. Martin., 2013. "Public Spending on Health and Long-Term Care: A New Set of Projections." Organization for Economic Co-operation and Development, Paris. http://www.oecd.org/eco/growth/Health%20FINAL.pdf.

Doty, P., P. Nadash, and N. Racco. 2015. "Long-Term Care Financing: Lessons from France." *Milbank Quarterly* 93 (2): 359–91.

Eiken, Steve, Kate Sredl, Lisa Gold, Jessica Kasten, Brian Burwell, and Paul Saucier. 2014. *Medicaid Expenditures for Long-Term Services and Supports in FFY 2012*. https://www.medicaid.gov/medicaid-chip-program-information/by-topics/long-term-services-and-supports/downloads/ltss-expenditures-2012.pdf.

Favreault, M., and J. Dey. 2015. *Long-Term Services and Supports for Older Americans: Risks and Financing*. Office of the Assistant Secretary for Planning and Evaluation/U.S. Department of Health and Human Services, Washington, DC. https://aspe.hhs.gov/sites/default/files/pdf/106211/ElderLTCrb-rev.pdf.

Feder, J., H. L. Komisar, and R. B. Friedland. 2007. *Long-Term Care Financing: Policy Options for the Future*. Georgetown University, Washington, DC. http://ltc.georgetown.edu/forum/ltcfinalpaper061107.pdf.

Federal Long-Term Care Insurance Program. 2015. *Premium Calculator*. Office of Personnel Management, Washington, DC. https://www.ltcfeds.com/ltcWeb/do/assessing_your_needs/RCPrePack?event=calculate.

Feng, Z., L. A. Coots, Y. Kaganova, and J. M. Wiener. 2014a. "Hospital and ED Use among Medicare Beneficiaries with Dementia Varies by Setting and Proximity to Death." *Health Affairs* 33 (4): 683–90.

Feng, Z., X. Guan, X. Feng, C. Liu, H. Zhan, and V. Mor. 2014b. "Long-Term Care in China: Reining in Market Forces through Regulatory Oversight." In *Regulating Long Term Care Quality: An International Comparison*, edited by V. Mor, T. Leone, and A. Maresso, 409–443. Cambridge, U.K.: Cambridge University Press.

Feng, Z., H. Zhan, X. Feng, C. Liu, M. Sun, and V. Mor. 2011. "An Industry in the Making: The Emergence of Institutional Elder Care in Urban China." *Journal of the American Geriatrics Society* 59 (4): 738–44.

Forte, P. E. 2015. "Long-Term Care Insurance: Past, Present, Future." *Contingencies*. May/June: 19–26. http://www.contingenciesonline.com/contingenciesonline/may_june_2015?pg=21#pg28.

Frank, R.G., M. Cohen, and N. Mahoney. 2013. "Making Progress: Expanding Risk Protection for Long-Term Services and Supports through Private Long-Term Care Insurance." The SCAN Foundation, Long Beach, CA. http://www.thescanfoundation.org/sites/thescanfoundation.org/files/tsf_ltc-financing_private-options_frank_3-20-13.pdf.

General Administration of Sport. Various years. "Notice of China Sport Lottery Issuing and Selling Data" (中国体育彩票发行销售数据公告).

Genet, N., W. Boerma, M. Koneman, A. Hutchinson, and R. Saltman. 2012. *Home Care across Europe*. Geneva: World Health Organization. http://www.euro.who.int/__data/assets/pdf_file/0008/181799/e96757.pdf.

Genworth Financial. 2015. *Genworth 2015 Cost of Care Survey: Home Care Providers, Adult Day Health Care Facilities, Assisted Living Facilities and Nursing Homes*. Richmond, VA: Genworth Financial. https://www.genworth.com/corporate/about-genworth/industry-expertise/cost-of-care.html.

Gibson, Mary Jo, and Donald L. Redfoot. 2007. *Comparing Long-Term Care in Germany and the United States: What Can We Learn From Each Other?* Report No. 2007–19. Washington, DC: AARP Public Policy Institute. http://assets.aarp.org/rgcenter/il/2007_19_usgerman_ltc.pdf.

Goda, G. S. 2010. "The Impact of State Tax Subsidies for Private Long-Term Care Insurance on Coverage and Medicaid Expenditures." NBER Working Paper 16406. National Bureau of Economic Research, Cambridge, MA.

Goodwin, N. 2007. "Developing Effective Joint Commissioning between Health and Social Care: Prospects for the Future Based on Lessons from the Past." *Journal of Care Services Management* 1: 279–93.

Harrington, C., B. Olney, H. Carillo, and T. Kang. 2012. "Nurse Staffing and Deficiencies in the Largest For-Profit Nursing Home Chains and Chains Owned by Private Equity Companies." *Health Services Research* 47 (1 Pt 1): 106–28.

Hawaii Long-Term Care Commission. 2012. *Long-Term Care Reform in Hawaii: Report of the Hawaii Long-Term Care Commission*. Honolulu: University of Hawaii at Manoa.

ICAIA (International China Ageing Industry Association). Undated. *Cross-Region Elderly Care—Hankou Golden Heights*. http://www.icaia.net/en/EnRESEARCH/SilverCoverage22/1051.html.

Johnson, R.J., and J. M. Wiener. 2006. *A Profile of Frail Older Americans and Their Caregivers*. Washington, DC: The Urban Institute. http://www.urban.org/publications/311284.html.

Jung, E. H. Y., S. N. Jang, J. Seok, and S. Kwon. 2014. "Quality Monitoring of Long-Term Care in the Republic of Korea." In *Regulating Long-Term Care: An International Comparison*, edited by V. Mor, T. Leone, and A. Maresso, 385–408. Cambridge, UK: Cambridge University Press.

Kaiser Family Foundation. 2013a. *Overview of Nursing Facility Capacity, Financing, and Ownership in the United States in 2011*. Washington, DC: Kaiser Family Foundation. http://kff.org/medicaid/fact-sheet/overview-of-nursing-facility-capacity-financing-and-ownership-in-the-united-states-in-2011/.

———. 2013b. "A Short Look at Long-Term Care for Seniors." *Journal of the American Medicaid Association* 310 (8): 786–87. http://jama.jamanetwork.com/article.aspx?articleid=1733726.

Karp, N., C. P. Sabatino, and E. F. Wood. 2005. *Medicaid Estate Recovery: A 2004 Survey of State Programs and Practices*. Washington, DC: AARP. http://assets.aarp.org/rgcenter/il/2005_06_recovery.pdf.

Khatutsky, G., J. M. Wiener, N. T. Thach, and A. M. Greene. 2015. *What Do People Know about Long-Term Services and Supports?* Research Triangle Park, NC.

Konetzka, R. T., S. L. Karon, and D. Potter. 2012. "Users of Medicaid Home and Community-Based Services Are Especially Vulnerable to Costly Avoidable Hospital Admissions." *Health Affairs* 31 (6): 1167–75.

Kwon, Soonman. 2009. "The Introduction of Long-Term Care Insurance in South Korea." *Eurohealth* 15 (1): 28–29.

Lipszyc, B., E. Sail, and A. Xavier. 2012. "Long-Term Care: Need, Use and Expenditure in the EU-27." European Commission, Brussels. http://ec.europa.eu/economy_finance/publications/economic_paper/2012/pdf/ecp469_en.pdf.

Lorenzoni, L., D. Morgan, Y. Murakami, and C. James. 2015. "Public Expenditure Projections for Health and Long-Term Care for China until 2030." OECD Health Working Papers 84. OECD Publishing, Paris. http://www.oecd-ilibrary.org/docserver/download/5jrs3c274vq3.pdf?expires=1459215900andid=idandaccname=guestandchecksum=9C6B39B738B0B008661 5BAA54D99140E.

MOCA (Ministry of Civil Affairs of the PRC). 2014. *China Civil Affairs Statistical Yearbook 2013*. Beijing: China Statistics Press.

———. 2015. *Statistical Communique on the Development of Social Services: 2014*. http://cws.mca.gov.cn/article/tjbg/201506/20150600832439.shtml.

———. Various years. *Notice of China Welfare Lottery's Issuing and Selling Data*. MOCA.

NAIC (National Association of Insurance Commissioners). 2015. *NAIC Long-Term Care Insurance Experience Exhibit Report for 2014*. Kansas City: NAIC.

Ng, T., C. Harrington, M. B. Musemeci, and E. L. Reaves. 2015. *Medicaid Home and Community-Based Services Programs: A 2012 Update*. Washington, DC: Kaiser Family Foundation. http://files.kff.org/attachment/report-medicaid-home-and-community-based-services-programs-2012-data-update.

Nixon, D. 2008. *Tax Incentives for Family Caregiving: A Cost-Benefit Analysis*. Honolulu: University of Hawaii at Manoa. http://www.publicpolicycenter.hawaii.edu/documents/paper003.pdf.

Rivlin, Alice M., and Joshua M. Wiener. 1988. *Caring for the Disabled Elderly: Who Will Pay?* Washington, DC: Brookings Institution.

Song, J., and E. Glinskaya. 2016. *Technical Note on the Public Financing of Elderly Care Services in China*. Beijing, China: World Bank (unpublished).

Sun, W., and A. Webb. 2013. "Can Long-Term Care Insurance Partnership Program Increase Coverage and Reduce Medicaid Costs?" Center for Retirement Research at Boston College, Chestnut Hill, MA. http://crr.bc.edu/wp-content/uploads/2013/03/wp_2013-8-508.pdf.

Swedish Ministry of Health and Social Affairs. 2007. *Care of the Elderly in Sweden. Stockholm: Swedish Ministry of Health and Social Affairs*. http://www.sweden.gov.se/content/1/c6/08/76/73/a43fc24d.pdf.

United Kingdom Commission for Social Care Inspection. 2009. *The State of Social Care in England*. United Kingdom Commission for Social Care Inspection, London. http://www.dhcarenetworks.org.uk/_library/Resources/Housing/Support_materials/Other_reports_and_guidance/The_state_of_social_care_in_England_2007-08.pdf.

United Kingdom Department of Health. 2013. "Landmark Reform to Help Elderly with Care Costs." London. https://www.gov.uk/government/news/landmark-reform-to-help-elderly-with-care-costs.

Walsh, E. G., J. M. Wiener, S. Haber, A. Bragg, M. Freiman, and J. G. Ouslander. 2012. "Potentially Avoidable Hospitalizations of Dually Eligible Medicare/Medicaid Beneficiaries from Nursing Facility and Home and Community-Based Services Waiver Programs." *Journal of the American Geriatric Society* 60 (5): 821–29.

Wiener, Joshua M. 1996. "Long-Term Care Reform: An International Perspective." In *Health Care Reform: The Will to Change*, 67–79. Health Policy Studies No. 8. Paris: Organisation for Economic Co-operation and Development.

———. 2011. "Long-Term Care Financing, Service Delivery and Quality Assurance: The International Experience." In *Handbook of Aging and the Social Sciences*, edited by R. Bitstock and L. George, 309–22. 7th ed. London: Elsevier.

———. 2013. "What the Long-Term Care Commission Needs to Know." Presented at a Workshop on Long-Term Care Financing, Institute of Medicine, National Academy of Sciences, Washington, DC.

Wiener, J.M., W. L. Anderson, and D. Brown. 2009. *Why Are Nursing Home Utilization Rates Declining?* Report prepared for the Centers for Medicare and Medicaid Services, RTI International, Washington, DC.

Wiener, J. M., W. L. Anderson, G. Khatutsky, Y. Kaganova, and J. O'Keeffe. 2013. *Medicaid Spend Down: New Estimates and Implications for Long-Term Services and Supports Financing Reform*. The SCAN Foundation, Long Beach, CA. http://www.thescanfoundation.org/sites/default/files/rti_medicaid-spend-down_3-20-13.pdf.

Wiener, Joshua M., and Alison Evans Cuellar. 1999. "Public and Private Responsibilities: Home and Community-Based Services in the United Kingdom and Germany." *Journal of Aging and Health* 11 (3): 417–44.

Wiener, J.M., L. H. Illston, and R. J. Hanley. 1994. *Sharing the Burden: Strategies for Public and Private Long-Term Care Insurance*. Washington, DC: Brookings Institution.

Wiener, J. M., and J. Tilly. 2003. "Long-Term Care and American Federalism: Can States Be the Engine of Reform?" In *Federalism and Health Policy*, edited by J. Holahan, A. Weil, and J. M. Wiener, 249–92. Washington, DC: Urban Institute Press.

Wiener, J. M., J. Tilly, A. E. Cuellar, A. Howe, C. Doyle, J. Campbell, and N. Ikegami. 2007. *Quality Assurance for Long-Term Care: The Experiences of England, Australia, Germany, and Japan*. Washington, DC: AARP. http://assets.aarp.org/rgcenter/il/2007_05_ltc.pdf.

World Bank. 2016. *Live Long and Prosper: Aging in East Asia and Pacific*. Washington, DC: World Bank. doi:10.1596/978-1-4648-0469-4.

Wu, K. B. 2013. *Income and Poverty of Older Americans, 2011*. Washington, DC: AARP. http://www.aarp.org/content/dam/aarp/research/public_policy_institute/econ_sec/2013/income-and-poverty-of-older-americans-AARP-ppi-econ-sec.pdf.

Yip, W., and W. C. Hsiao. 2015. "What Drove the Cycles of Chinese Health Systems Reforms?" *Health Systems & Reform* 1 (1): 52–61.

Yip, W. C-M., W. C. Hsiao, W. Chen, S. Hu, J. Ma, and A. Maynard. 2012. "Early Appraisal of China's Huge and Complex Health-Care Reforms." *Lancet* 379: 833–42.

CHAPTER 6

Commissioner-Provider Relations: International Experience and Implications for China's Policy

Jan M. Bauer, Lizzy Feller, and Elena Glinskaya

Introduction: Why Separate the Roles of Commissioner and Provider?

Rising demand for elderly care compelled governments to search for efficiency improvements. The longest experience with publicly supported long-term care services has been in Europe, where particularly the northern countries (i.e., England, Germany, the Netherlands, and Scandinavia) were the first to act on the growing demand for elderly care. Starting in the late 1960s, European long-term care schemes were mostly built on public provision with little emphasis on competition. Rising expenditures and growing demand led to a number of reforms in those countries during the 1990s. Over the last 20 years, elderly care also became an important public issue in parts of Asia. With their fast demographic transitions of low fertility rates coupled with longer life expectancies, Japan, Hong Kong SAR, China, and the Republic of Korea are in a similar situation as most Western countries.

While an increasing number of governments around the world have acknowledged that support for elderly people is a necessity, many have moved away from providing care services directly and opted for the introduction of a private market into the long-term care system. This decision is mostly guided by the New Public Management (NPM) idea. Most governments have shifted their efforts away from public provision and fostered market-based solutions, including private companies. Splitting the responsibility for long-term care coverage and the delivery of those services has been one of the major changes,

---

Jan M. Bauer is an Assistant Professor in the Department of Management, Society and Communication, Copenhagen Business School, Denmark. Lizzy Feller is a freelance consultant, having retired (in 2013) from European Commission services (ETF). Elena Glinskaya is a Lead Economist and Program Leader for Human Development for China, Mongolia, and the Republic of Korea at the World Bank.

which is now compulsory in some European countries (Robinson, Figueras, and Jakubowski 2005; Rodrigues, Leichsenring, and Winkelmann 2014).

Arguments in favor of NPM state that the government should focus on the role of a steward and contract the delivery of social services out to the private market. Overall, this separation between tasks ought to improve the provision of public services in several ways by: (1) strengthening the responsiveness and innovative potential of the sector, (2) increasing the cost effectiveness of service provision, and (3) improving service quality through clear accountability and greater transparency of formal contracts (Blöchliger 2008).

This NPM approach combines the advantages of competition with the mandate for securing public health and overcomes market inefficiencies. The example of Europe has shown that elderly and disabled people demand influence over the types of services and benefits they receive. Particularly in the home care setting, where care arrangements are highly variable and require a complex interplay between informal and formal care, individual choice can help to produce the best outcome. Additionally, the growing market for long-term care technology is most likely to influence service provision in the future. Therefore, lean and specialized private companies are needed as innovators to provide tailor-made services and promote the efficient application of new technology (Irish, Salamon, and Simon 2009).

Closely linked to this innovative advantage and in line with the view, the most cost-efficient way to provide long-term care services should be the result of competition in a free market. Consumers will only choose the best providers, leading to high service quality and lower costs overall. To survive in the market, private companies have the incentive to provide the best outcomes for the elderly. This core idea of NPM stands in contrast to public monopolies that lack motivation for cutting costs. A long-term care sector in which governments exclusively "contract" with their own providers lacks management incentives that come from competition.

While the expansion of private provision in the long-term care sector offers great potential, it may also bring risks at the expense of the most vulnerable. The design of the provider structure has important implications not only for quality and the cost of services but also for the diversity of consumer choices. Therefore, successful implementation of a long-term care sector is complex and requires intelligent design and a strong government involvement to ensure the reliability of market mechanisms.

Advantages of NPM rely on the existence of a functioning market mechanisms that may not be directly present in the long-term care sector, which means that outsourcing services could also pose potential risks for governments and the people needing those services. The major concern in outsourcing services arises from a principal-agent problem. The principal (governmental entity) contracts with the agent (private sector) to deliver a range of services (Tynkkynen, Keskimäki, and Lehto 2013). If the principal cannot easily observe the agent's action, the latter might act in its own interest, which is detrimental to the principal. When the market is highly competitive, the risk that such "shirking" behavior leads to large efficiency losses is small, as providers who follow their own interests at the expense of the principal will lose their contracts to more efficient and less shirking competitors. However, the formal care market is not always competitive, so contracts with shirking providers often continue. The two main reasons for the lack of competition in the providers' market are low contestable markets and difficulties in assessing output; therefore, governments need instruments to overcome the lack of self-regulating market competition (Rodrigues, Leichsenring, and Winkelmann 2014). Notably, the theoretical assumption about conflicting interests differs from the classical stewardship model, in which both parties have common goals and the relationship is based on trust. In reality, however, both seemingly conflicting approaches often coexist (Jing and Chen 2012).

Instruments to address these issues include monitoring, licensing, and contractual regulations that are used to assess provider performance. The use of formal contracts is a very important part of the commissioner-provider split as the contracts define the relationship between both parties. Formal contracts provide the opportunity to set certain quality standards for the provider and allow the commissioner to hold the provider legally accountable for delivering the contracted services. Formal contracts also increase transparency, which can additionally help to uphold a high level of service quality, as the government and consumers have better knowledge and control over the services that the private sector must deliver. However, proper contracting creates certain transaction costs, as both parties need to gather information for the bargaining of contracts, and the commissioner must undertake monitoring to ensure that the provider works in the commissioner's best interest. At the same time, regulations that are too strong can potentially reduce the productivity of the private sector and lower the innovative potential (Irish, Salamon, and Simon 2009).

As the advantages of private markets in social service provision are still disputed, the implementation of NPM differs among the countries. Governments in Scandinavia still rely on predominantly public models, while the majority of countries use mixed markets that allow for private providers in long-term care. Those markets differ by the degree of competition (e.g., the corporatist model of Germany vs. competition in the Anglo-American systems) (Irish, Salamon, and Simon 2009).

This chapter summarizes the theoretical and empirical aspects to be considered for successful promotion of private participation in the long-term care sector in China. As the Chinese experience with formal care services is limited, the chapter provides an overview of experiences in several European and Asian economies that expanded participation of private providers in social services in the past. It then describes the current situation in China and highlights the most important elements that contribute to a successful market in long-term care. The chapter finishes with recommendations for the implementation of a long-term care sector in China.

Developments in the Long-Term Care Sector

International Experience

The design of long-term care markets, which have often been developed in the context of national health care systems, varies substantially across countries. The discussion of international experience here mainly draws on England and Germany but also uses examples from Asia, namely Japan, Hong Kong SAR, China, and Korea. All of these economies rely predominantly on private provision, and governmental entities act as regulators and purchasers. A general distinction can be made in the approach to financing long-term care services: while Germany, Japan, and Korea opted for the implementation of national insurance, England and Hong Kong SAR, China use tax money to finance the long-term care sector.

Germany was the first country to establish mandatory long-term care insurance (LTCI) in 1994. The system is based on a consumer choice model, and people entitled to benefits can decide between home (in cash or in kind) or residential care support. Generally, home care is prioritized (and preferred by consumers) over residential care. Benefits are capped for all options, making co-payments for residential care up to 50 percent common (Rodrigues, Leichsenring, and Winkelmann 2014).

The Japanese insurance usually covers 90 percent of the costs, but benefits are also capped based on an assessed limited functional ability level. Notably, for home care, most people use around 40–60 percent of their maximum budget, which suggests that moral hazard remains a minor issue (Tamiya et al. 2011). Short supply and rising demand preceded the Korean implementation of LTCI in 2008. Except for the poor, people entitled to benefits must co-pay 20 percent for residential care and 15 percent for home care (Won 2013). From 2008 to 2011, the number of entitled people nearly doubled. Like Japan, the implementation of LTCI went along with opening of the markets to for-profit providers. However, there are still areas without sufficient supply, where people receive substitutive cash benefits.

With the Community Care Act in 1993, the commissioner-provider split for care provision became compulsory for local authorities in England. Until the introduction of the Personal Budget, care managers were responsible for assessing needs (as entitlement is means tested) and purchasing services on behalf of the consumer. Now, consumers can manage their budgets themselves and receive cash in the form of so-called direct payments. As in the case of Germany, the Community Care Act was advocated as an advancement in user choices but was also intended to contain costs and foster the private market (Gash et al. 2013).

A mixed market of non-profit and for-profit companies provide Hong Kong SAR China's elder care capacity. While non-profits receive direct transfers, the for-profit private sector receives funding indirectly, as many of their customers receive public assistance (Wing-tak et al. 2009). While the latter financial support is means-tested, the highly subsidized residential homes (up to 80–90 percent of the costs) are available to everyone, which contributes to an extremely high share of institutionalized elderly. In 2011, nearly 7 percent of people above age 65 were institutionalized (Chui 2011).

Despite different institutional and cultural settings, most national long-term care systems are facing similar problems. They struggle to balance rising budgetary pressures with a broad supply of affordable and high quality care. Even though some economies like Korea and Hong Kong SAR, China are still trying to fully develop the supply of services, most recent reforms aim to cut costs (Gash et al. 2013; Rodrigues, Leichsenring, and Winkelmann 2014). However, such efforts are often criticized for reducing the quality of care and causing further deterioration in the already unfavorable working conditions in the sector (Sunwoo 2012). Against this backdrop, many governments have been following the common trend of trying to foster preventive actions, home care arrangements, and private sector service provision.

The Landscape in China

The long-term care sector in China has undergone a major transition in recent decades. As in Western countries, the elderly in China generally prefer to remain in their own homes rather than move into a nursing home. Following the Confucian norms of filial piety, families have traditionally been at the core of Chinese elder care (Feng et al. 2011). However, due to the erosion of these traditions and social changes, family arrangements no longer provide sufficient protection against increasing morbidity and care needs in old age. First, low fertility rates, precipitated by China's One-Child Policy, reduce the informal care potential of children. Second, employment opportunities and rising wages associated with China's growth have increased the opportunity cost of providing informal work; in particular, high labor force participation among women reduces informal care arrangements (e.g., Carmichael, Charles, and Hulme 2010). Third, increased labor mobility has led to a movement toward China's more industrialized urban areas, leaving rural areas and their elderly behind (Giles, Wang, and Zhao 2010).

In light of these changes, China has fostered the expansion of formal care services for the elderly. In the mid-1990s, reforms decentralized care provision, and social welfare institutions shifted from pure public funding to a mix of income sources, including charging user fees (Feng et al. 2012). Public provision of care was mostly restricted to welfare institutions that provided food and shelter to poor elderly but that were not able to care for people with severe physical and mental disabilities (Wu, Mao, and Zhong 2009). With increased decentralization, the share of the private sector increased steadily over time, and the market for residential care gained momentum particularly in urban areas. According to a White Paper by the Chinese government, by the end of 2005, China had nearly 40,000 social institutions which provided a broad range of services to the elderly (State Council Information Office 2005). In 2012, China had 3.9 million beds in residential care facilities, with 20.5 beds per 1,000 senior citizens, which is still less than half the international average (Yanzhang 2013).

Recently, the provision of social security through insurance coverage seems to have regained momentum. In 2014, the State Council released the *Opinion on Accelerating the Development of Modern Insurance Industry,* which further highlighted the need for extended insurance coverage for the elderly, especially when they cannot rely on familial support. According to the State Council's opinion, a market-oriented insurance industry should provide comprehensive protection and develop adequate long-term care products by 2020. In addition, the national government recently announced that China's long-term strategy aims to combine medical services and services for the elderly as part of the *13th Five-Year Plan.*

Key Elements of the Commissioner-Provider Relationship

The specific features of the long-term care sector vary among countries, as they have adopted the ideas of NPM in different ways. Some experts argue that the commissioner-provider split goes beyond contracting, payment schemes, or provider competition and requires a broad system approach to reach its full potential (Busse et al. 2007). Therefore, policy makers need to account for a complex set of components which are often interdependent and difficult to separate clearly. The most important aspects are summarized below.

The Government

Regardless of the actual design of the long-term care sector (i.e., how tasks and responsibilities are distributed), the government remains accountable for the overall performance of the system. This governmental role as a steward is considered the most important function and should therefore be a top government priority (Figueras, Robinson, and Jakubowski 2005; Travis et al. 2002). Stewardship can be defined as "the careful and responsible management of the well-being of the population" (WHO 2000, xiv). In this function, the government formulates policy directives and develops an adequate framework for implementation. To ensure a functioning long-term care sector, governments can rely on the following mechanisms (Figueras, Robinson and Jakubowski 2005):

- The government can define basic services that should be available to the people deemed to be in need. This allows for incorporating efficiency criteria and restricts purchasers to contracting only services that are proven to be efficient. For example, Germany and Hong Kong SAR, China both explicitly prioritize home care over residential care. Such regulation should also set standards for the quality and costs of these services. In addition, national health plans can include strategic planning to ensure that local governments or other commissioning entities provide a sufficient supply of services. Setting standards for a minimum number of nursing home beds in a certain area also helps ensure a minimum level of equity within the economy.

- Given the design of the long-term care system, the government should ensure the efficient use of purchasing. This can be achieved through a regulatory framework that provides rules and oversight or by direct involvement in the commissioning process. For example, if purchasing is done by insurance funds, the government can be represented on their boards. Even in the case of commissioning at the national level, experts recommend that the commissioning institution be separate from the steward function of the government (Ovretveit 1995).

- The government can establish regulations to increase transparency and public information. To empower consumers and facilitate the market dynamics, information must be publicly available in a systematic and easy-to-understand fashion. Regulations on reporting do not need to be limited to providers but can also be extended to the commissioning entity. Such efforts toward a more transparent system prevent misconduct and increase accountability.

- Equity is an essential issue and is directly linked to the access of the less affluent and the consumer costs of care services. In a competitive environment, efficient access to services is usually regulated by their prices, which reflect the production costs in some way, and utilization follows consumers' willingness to pay. In the case of long-term care services, however, the determination of prices by the market and the willingness to pay—closely related to the ability to pay—is often considered to be a socially undesirable mechanism for access. Therefore, governments can address the distributional effects through regulation (Figueras, Robinson, and Jakubowski 2005). Providing access for the less affluent can be achieved through vouchers, reduced fees, or direct income support.

The core governmental functions vary among international systems, but generally, some governmental entity is entrusted to ensure an adequate supply of long-term care services. The German government, for example, opted for a universal and compulsory LTCI that provides equal support for every citizen. The German Social Code strongly regulates the relationship between all stakeholders. The law mandates cooperation between the sickness funds (see section on the Commissioner for more details), states, municipalities, and providers, and it entrusts all with ensuring the provision of an adequate supply of high-quality care. Therefore, sickness funds are only allowed to contract with providers that comply with national quality standards. Such standards not only regulate the facilities' outfit, staff training, and enumeration but also require the implementation of quality management systems. To ensure sufficient provision of long-term care services, states and municipalities must develop a plan for local care demand and subsidize certified institutions when more service is needed. Further regulation assigns monitoring to the *Medical Service of the Health Funds*, a joint entity of the sickness funds that assesses individual care needs and evaluates residential and home care. This complex set of regulations at the federal and national level ought to ensure the adequate provision of high-quality care and also access to those services as guided by legislation.

As the insurance benefits are capped, the government makes close relatives of service users financially accountable but also pays the coverage gap through social security for people who could not afford the services otherwise. Generally, the market for long-term care services is predominantly shaped by cooperation instead of competition. The rising importance of elderly care led to several laws that further regulate the labor market and promote informal caregiving to reduce expensive formal services.

In England, the *Department of Health* works with key bodies that represent the local government adult social care sector, the *Local Government Association* and the *Association of Directors of Adult Social Services,* to develop and implement policy. The Care Act gives local authorities the responsibility for promoting "individual well-being" among the elderly. The law defines well-being as a holistic concept that includes personal dignity, emotional well-being, and protection against abuse and neglect.[1] The Care Act also highlights the importance of integration, prevention, and information. Furthermore, local authorities have the duty to ensure "the efficient and effective operation of a market in services for meeting care and support needs."[2] The national legislation therefore sees local authorities as market makers who have to cooperate with all relevant stakeholders. The law provides a narrow framework that guides most actions of the local authorities and thereby ensures broad access to long-term care services.

In China, the regulatory framework is still at an early stage, and no overall national health program currently exists to regulate formal long-term care coverage and ensure the access of the less affluent. There are broad regulations that govern the system—i.e., in 1996, the government passed a *Law of the People's Republic of China on Protection of the Rights and Interests of the Elderly*, which was revised in 2012. The elderly (people above the age of 60) have "the right to obtain material assistance from the State" and "it is the duty of the entire society to protect…the interests of the elderly."

With the beginning of the new millennium, the Chinese central government published *The Opinions on Accelerating the Socialization of Social Welfare Institutions* to promote private investment in the long-term care sector further. To regulate the procurement of public services, the 2002 *Law of Government Procurement of the PRC* sets the framework for provision through nongovernmental institutions. The law outlines a number of minimum requirements for providers and allows the use of commercial procuring intermediaries who perform the procurement activity on behalf of the government. In line with the ideas of NPM, the process of procurement shall comply with the "fundamental principles of openness and transparency, fair competition, impartiality and integrity." Regardless of the method of procurement, the law requires monitoring of provider performance, which must be outsourced to professional certified institutions when procured projects are highly complex. The results of these assessment mechanisms for the quality and quantity of the commissioned services should be publicly available and influence budget decisions (NDRC 2015).

To address the challenges of elder care, the central government's 2006 *Opinions on Accelerating Developing Services of Caring the Aged Industry* introduced various measures to promote the life of the elderly within China. To expand the supply of long-term care services, the government supports the non-profit and private sector through purchasing services, providing funding, and cooperation. In addition, the central government released the *12th Five-Year Plan for the Development of China's Undertakings for the Aged* in 2011. It acknowledged the need for action given the still insufficient supply of care services for the elderly and lack of proper care management, leading to suboptimal living conditions for the Chinese elderly. The central government announced the establishment of a framework of strategies to respond to the needs of the elderly and implement a long- and mid-term plan that supports the elderly in health and financial issues. In terms of long-term care, the government made a strong commitment to improve the situation of the elderly by providing home- and community-based care services and extending the service network nationwide to 30 beds per 1,000 elderly people. The Five-Year Plan also promoted the expansion of a regulatory framework, stronger supervision of the sector, and nongovernmental provision.

The Commissioner

As the government is responsible for ensuring the availability of social services but does not provide services itself, it entrusts commissioning entities that contract with the private sector to provide sufficient supply. If elderly care services are part of the social security system, the commissioner often acts as a purchaser and directly buys services for people in need. As individual needs are diverse, local purchasing can benefit from regional considerations to better meet the demands of the population. However, there is a lower bound to local purchasing: if the purchaser agency becomes too small, it cannot reach sufficient economies of scale and lacks specialization. If the range of coverage of a purchaser is limited, the competition for services with higher fixed costs (i.e., residential care facilities) will be limited. Local management may also lack the ability to negotiate beneficial contracts with professional private providers (Blöchliger 2008). In Finland's health care system, for example, purchasing on the municipality level led to agencies that were responsible for less than 1,000 inhabitants, a problem later addressed by state incentives for mergers between small municipalities (Tynkkynen, Keskimäki, and Lehto 2013).

In the tax-based system of England, local authorities receive a finite amount of funding and are free to determine how the budget is used. However, there are national guidelines on charging for residential and home care, as well as minimum standards for qualifications of the long-term care workforce. As eligibility is means-tested, more than 50 percent of people receiving residential care still pay out of pocket (Rodrigues, Leichsenring, and Winkelmann 2014). Despite the introduction of cash benefits to promote user choice, local authorities are still the dominant purchasers. Their practice of choosing preferred providers in a local area allows for economies of scale and lower transportation costs and leads to more security for providers, but at the same time, it limits market entry for new providers (Baxter, Glendinning, and Greener 2011; Rodrigues, Leichsenring, and Winkelmann 2014).

As in the case of England, the rise of user choice models leads to care systems in which commissioners decreasingly purchase the services themselves but ensure access of the population to high-quality care services for affordable fees. Regulation of the supply side of the care market often takes place at the local level and therefore varies not only between nations but also within one country. A more complex user choice model was implemented in Germany, which includes demand-side competition between commissioning sickness funds. People can freely choose their compulsory LTCI among more than 100 funds, which is usually linked to the choice of general health care insurance. However, real differences only exist in health care plans and motivate people to change the insurer. The insurance funds act in a highly regulated environment, where *de facto* competition is low. Legislation not only sets the premium amounts but also regulates the entitlements and payouts for LTCI. As Germany is based on a consumer choice model, the actual commissioning of funds is mostly restricted to collective price negotiations with providers. Therefore, the lack of demand-side competition does not necessarily lower purchaser performance (Busse et al. 2007). In addition, the municipalities provide subsidies to providers if there is a need for services according to a local care plan.

Country systems can vary even if there is only one purchasing institution, as the responsible entity can function on different vertical levels (local, regional, national). Generally, purchasing on the national level is associated with more equity, while local decision making tends to increase responsiveness and flexibility (Figueras, Robinson, and Jakubowski 2005). In Japan's LTCI system, the municipality insures people, and therefore the system has competition only on the provider side. Premiums, however, differ greatly between those municipalities. As the insurer also assesses eligibility, some empirical studies raise the concern that municipalities with financial difficulties grant less access to long-term care benefits (Shimizutani 2013).

Commissioning of public services is growing in China and has been applied by different levels of government. Starting with large cities in urban areas, the ideas of NPM have been adopted increasingly by rural areas and small local governments. The *Procurement Law of the People's Republic of China* provides the main guidelines for commissioning entities. The law regulates any type of public procurement by state organs on various levels, public institutions, and social organizations. The *Opinions of the State Council on Implementing Government Procurement of Service from Social Forces* define the commissioning entities as "administrative organs at various levels and public institutions administrated by the public servant law and with administrative functions." Those entities should commission service when actually needed and are supported by the central government. In Anhui, for example, government commissioning takes place on several levels, from the provincial down to the city level (NDRC 2015). Shanghai commissions at three levels of government, including the municipality, 18 districts, and streets (townships) in local (rural) areas (Jing and Chen 2012).

Home-based long-term care and community public health commissioned by local governments are now growing, albeit from a very low base. The governments typically entrust social organizations with service provision to ensure sufficient capacity. Even though local governments are mostly responsible for funding long-term care, they can set up non-profit procuring intermediaries or entrust certified commercial procuring intermediaries to do the purchasing on their behalf (Standing Committee 2002).

With local governments being responsible for a growing number of social services, proper funding for commissioning remains an issue. As there is insufficient legal and institutional support, the funding for social services remains uncertain and is often decided case by case. The generally low budget gives local government little leeway to expand social service provision (NDRC 2015).

Local governments also have little experience with commissioning social services. They often lack proper training and have insufficient staff to ensure provider competition (Jing and Chen 2012; Teets and Jagusztyn 2013). Provider performance and compliance with the contract require monitoring and the use of adequate indicators. In the field of social services, standardized purchasing procedures are still lacking, and performance assessment remains limited (NDRC 2015).

Contracts and Competition

Through contracts, commissioning entities ensure that the governmental agenda comes into practice and that providers act, at least to some extent, in the public interest. Two main types of contracts can be found in the health care sector: contracts can regulate how providers can enter the market, and contracts can regulate how financial resources are used to manage long-term care provision (Figueras, Robinson, and Jakubowski 2005). Market entry contracts are prevalent in health care sectors in the majority of countries and include licensing, accreditation, quality standards, and planning procedures. Particularly with a user choice model, providers need to meet certain quality standards and offer information that allows users to make educated choices. Additionally, consumer choice might be restricted from the provider side, especially when demand exceeds supply. The provider's right and ability to reject certain consumers can lead to "cream-skimming" by giving preference to financially attractive applicants. This practice is incompatible with the public's mandate to provide for the elderly population and, therefore, often prohibited via contracts.

Contracts are required where market mechanisms fail to incentivize optimal provider behavior. Because market characteristics differ among the types of service, it is useful to discuss them separately. The importance of efficient contractual frameworks can differ between home and residential care markets as well as between rural and urban areas. Generally, setting up a home care service requires little investment, and consumers can change providers relatively easily, which makes these markets often more contestable. In many countries, only minimum standards are required to qualify for market entry, so home care markets are usually more competitive and require less regulation. In contrast, residential homes require large investments in infrastructure, and the commissioner often limits access to the market by combining market entry contracts with process contracts (Meagher and Szebehely 2013). Such planning by the commissioner can help avoid overcapacities, reduce risks, and exploit economies of scale. In those cases, competition among providers may only take place during the bidding procedure and not in the market for customers. Based on defined criteria (e.g., price), companies compete by bidding for the market of, for instance, residential care in a certain area for a certain time. If provider performance is unsatisfactory (e.g., due to insufficient quality), a competitor will be awarded the contract in the next round (Blöchliger 2008). Regarding regional variation, in urban areas with high population density, the market for new providers is more contestable than in sparsely populated rural areas. In larger cities with good transportation infrastructure, consumers can easily switch from an unsatisfying local provider, as additional transportation costs to a competitor are relatively low. This is less likely to be the case in rural areas, as the second-next provider might be too far away (Busse et al. 2007).

In Germany, the insurance funds offer tiered benefits in cash or in kind, and while recipients can spend the cash benefits without any regulation, the types of in-kind services and their prices are a result of negotiation. Within every federal state, these negotiations by the associations of the long-term care service providers, the sickness funds, and the Medical Service of the Health Funds lead to so-called framework contracts. Eligible people in need can freely choose from providers that were represented in these negotiations and therefore have a contract with the insurance funds. Home care services are only available in regulated standard packages which provide certain services at a given price. For example, people in need of personal care can use their budget to purchase a "small morning service" (which includes dressing, washing, and brushing of teeth), but cooking or shopping packages are also available. This contractual framework prohibits excessive pricing and motivates provider competition over quality. In addition, a broad choice of packages allows for adjusting the services to individual demand and provides clear information about what services to expect. However, this purchasing scheme leaves little room for innovative service ideas, as they must go through a long bureaucratic process to be included as a standard package. For residential homes, market entry contracts set minimum standards that make providers contractually obliged to ensure the quality of services. These contracts not only regulate the outfit of the facility but also staff training. However, the municipality determines the need for nursing homes based on local demand. New residential care facilities will only receive public subsidies if more beds are required to ensure sufficient coverage of the local population—a regulation intended to avoid public funding for unnecessary care supply. In addition, providers who do not come to an agreement during the negotiation of a framework contract and who therefore charge their customers directly and outside of LTCI generally cannot receive subsidies from the government.

In England, the local authorities provide a Personal Budget that is determined by individual care needs and their personal means and that varies among local authorities. This budget can be used (either by a case manager or users through direct payments) to purchase services that are related to eligible needs. Determining the kinds of services that are offered by providers and covered by the personal budget is part of a bargaining process between local authorities and local providers (Comas-Herrera et al. 2010). Commissioning is based on multiple objectives including reducing costs, improving quality, integrating with health care, empowering users, ensuring national standards, and promoting local experimentation. It involves collaboration not only between local authority commissioners and independent providers but also among different public agencies to ensure the integration of health services and social care. Local authorities are often the most important customer for a service provider and therefore have considerable market power, which leads to lower fees. Local authorities abandoned spot contracts (buying individual care service on demand) in favor of block contracts (buying service coverage for a certain population for a given period) (Lewis and West 2013). Block contracts provide more security to providers and therefore foster investments and staff training (Baxter, Glendinning, and Greener 2011), as well as create some leeway that provides incentives for innovation within the elderly care services market. However, the transition toward block contracts primarily reflects the increasing budgetary pressure on local authorities as these contracts often allow for lower unit prices. This practice has been criticized as it is associated with a reduction in user choices and lower care quality (Gash et al. 2013; Rodrigues, Leichsenring, and Winkelmann 2014). A notion supported by a recent study, which found that highly competitive markets can lead to reduced care quality within English nursing homes (Forder and Allan 2014).

In Hong Kong SAR, China, the government heavily funds long-term care provision by private companies through several channels. The services include residential as well as home care services, which are closely monitored by the Social Welfare Department. In the residential care market, nongovernmental organizations (NGOs) receive the most support, as the government provides them with premises at low rates, covers capital costs for construction and outfit, and operating costs for staff. To reduce waiting lists of people in need, the government also purchases capacity from the private sector, which reduces user fees. These additional efforts to increase capacity and high-quality services led to competitive bidding for the operation of subsidized residential homes (Wing-tak et al. 2009).

The governmental bodies in China must commission or procure goods, projects, or services through methods regulated by the *Law of Government Procurement of the PRC*. The procurement should rely on the method of public bidding if the item exceeds a certain volume, unless special circumstances do not allow for that process (e.g., in cases with too little private competition for the service contract or in emergencies that require urgent services). In those cases, governments can contract services by using invitations for bidding, competitive negotiation, single-source procurement, requests for quotations, and other methods that must be authorized by the State Council. In Hubei Province, for example, commissioning bodies must announce publicly the bidding content, requirements for providers, and performance assessment methods. This way of purchasing should ensure competition and an effective use of public money (NDRC 2015).

In practice, however, the law has not been commonly applied in the field of social services, and public commissioning often still lacks provider competition. One issue is the incomplete catalogue of detailed service items that fall under the procurement law. In 2010, *The Enforcement Regulation of the Law of Government Purchase of the PRC* emphasized that the procurement law refers to all kinds of services within the centralized procurement directory. However, the directory was particularly vague in the context of social services, and the lack of normative procedures led to weak application of the procurement law. Therefore, service contracts with a long duration, such as in long-term care, often receive public funding in a non-competitive way. Some social organizations receive a budget from the public to provide services to the local population. Such arrangements have no fixed duration and continue if no major service problems occur (NDRC 2015). In addition to this direct commissioning, local governments use subsidies as an indirect way to expand social service provision by the market. The subsidies predominantly enter the market through the supply side, and providers receive a fixed amount of money for offering a service unit. The use of public funds to incentivize the private sector through tax breaks and subsidies has been a prevalent way to increase capacity in the long-term care sector. In Nanjing, for instance, the local government supports the construction of every new bed with RMB 2,000–4,000 and provides around RMB 80 per bed per month in operating subsidies. However, the capacity building efforts take place with little regulatory oversight, raising questions about the efficiency of public funding and the quality of services (Feng et al. 2011). On the demand side, in some cases consumers receive vouchers that can be used to buy social services. Both indirect ways alone do not ensure adequate coverage with high-quality care services, but they do reduce the effective market price and thereby foster utilization.

Additional problems arise when market mechanisms and promotion of for-profit providers conflict with local inherent practices or political interests. For example, if local authorities allocate large funds to public welfare institutes to improve the quality of care services, they can create uneven competition with private providers. Private providers cannot grow in a market environment when they are unable to provide similar care quality or have to charge higher prices than their publicly subsidized competitor (Wu, Mao, and Zhong 2009). In other cases, non-profits work in close relationship with local governments and the separation between public and private is not always clear-cut (for more information on this, see the section on providers). This can commonly lead to a situation in which local governments create a monopoly for their affiliated institutions and thereby inhibit provider competition (Jing and Chen 2012). In addition, many private companies choose to be non-profit to receive tax breaks. Local governments would be the beneficiaries of these taxes and are also responsible for approving these companies' land for construction. Hence, some private sector companies were unable to build facilities since local authorities preferred to "wait" for a for-profit company (Feng et al. 2012).

One case study on competitive contracting in Shanghai found that local practices diverged from the national agenda of creating a competitive environment (Jing and Chen 2012). In 2009, the Shanghai Municipal Bureau of Civil Affairs officially adopted a competitive bidding procedure including formal procurement requirements such as: approval of the bidding offer, the receipt of at least three proposals, external evaluation, and random monitoring of implementation. The selection criteria further include organizational capacity, implementation plan, project management capacity, and bidding price. In practice, however, the formal competitive procedure did not lead to the intended outcomes for several reasons. First, local authorities urged disinterested providers to submit proposals to meet the minimum requirement of three bids. Second, government and non-profit agencies did not have the capacity or knowledge to maintain competitive bidding. For example, non-profit managers were unable to write a proposal given the unclear description of the offer or did not know how to plan projects properly. Third, non-profits that were affiliated with the commissioning local government had clear advantages and received funding and information to win the official bid. Therefore, competition remained limited, and incumbent local non-profits won the contracts in most cases. Overall, the average rate of cost reduction was found to be 6 percent. This difference between the highest possible funding in the public offer and the one actually contracted varied between 36 percent and 0 percent. Nearly 40 percent of the projects showed a cost reduction of less than 1 percent (Jing and Chen 2012).

The Provider

Competition among providers is one key element of the NPM as a mechanism for improving efficiency. Separated from the task of commissioning (purchasing), providers are contracted to deliver the demanded long-term care services. In many countries, opening the market has attracted more for-profit private companies, which compete (depending on the country) over the price or quality of services. Generally, some studies suggest that private companies are more efficient than public ones, as they have more flexible labor relations and less rigid organizational rules and tend to find more innovative services that adapt to consumer demand (Farsi and Filippini 2004). However, the effects appear to be stronger in the short run than in the long run.

In addition, larger shares of the efficiency gains should be attributed to the competitive environment rather than the genuinely higher efficiency of private provision (Blöchliger 2008).

The market composition is determined by regulation and varies among countries as well as between home and residential services. While the public sector still directly provides services in some countries, other markets rely solely on private provision. Many countries have prohibited the provision of long-term care services by private for-profit companies until recently, and some still do. These governments fear that profit-seeking and asymmetric information about quality might mitigate possible efficiency gains and disadvantage the consumers (Blöchliger 2008).

In the case of Germany, provider competition mostly takes place on the quality level since prices are the outcome of a joint negotiation process with little difference between providers. Traditionally, large non-profit organizations are key players in the market for long-term care services and still receive some benefits compared to for-profit organizations. Non-profit care providers can accept donations, receive tax breaks, and are granted higher public subsidies (Rodrigues, Leichsenring, and Winkelmann 2014). However, the marketization of LTCI led to a dramatic shift in the provider structure over the last 20 years. Private for-profit organizations gained large market shares from the incumbent non-profit welfare organizations (Theobald 2012). In 2013, 64 percent of home care service companies were for-profit, while the for-profit share among residential homes was 42 percent (Statistisches Bundesamt 2013). Notably, increased competition with for-profit providers also forces non-profit providers to become more cost-conscious (Augurzky and Mennicken 2011).

In England, the market for long-term care also changed substantially. Currently, about three-quarters of home and residential care providers are private for-profit companies, compared to 2 percent of home care in 1992 (Baxter et al. 2011). Both markets, however, differ in the extent of market concentration because in contrast to the diverse home care sector, residential care became dominated by a few large companies (some owned by private equity firms) (Knapp et al. 2001).

In Hong Kong SAR, China, the intense public funding by the Social Welfare Department shapes the market for long-term care services. While NGOs receive direct subsidies from the government, private for-profit providers benefit from the public assistance to consumers. While the low capacity in non-profit residential homes led to an over 50 percent market share among for-profits, home care remains dominated by the non-profit sector (Chui 2011).

Providers in Japan are public and private for-profit or non-profit companies as well as semi-public welfare organizations (Shimizutani 2013). All providers are licensed and supervised by the municipality, and prices are fixed by regulation. However, for-profits are not allowed to run residential care facilities. The government has barely expanded residential care capacity, and there are usually long waiting lists for a bed in such facilities. In contrast, home care has expanded with the market entry of for-profit organizations, and the private sector has played an increasingly important role in ensuring broad access to long-term care services. Therefore, opening the residential care market to for-profit companies is currently being debated, but the outcome depends on the effectiveness of performance measures that ensure high quality residential care services (Shimizutani 2013).

Korea already allows the provision of residential care by for-profit companies to avoid having "insurance without service" (Seok 2010). As a result, the number of care facilities increased substantially: within a few years after the introduction of LTCI, the private sector provided around two-thirds of total capacity. Over this period, the number of health care employees increased about eight-fold (Sunwoo 2012). However, the large increase in supply cannot be solely attributed to market forces, as the government set a preparation phase to train staff and provided funds for capacity building prior to the actual implementation in 2008 (Rhee, Done, and Anderson 2015).

Even though the government is still involved in direct service provision, China started with commissioning in the late 1970s (Jing and Chen 2012). Between 2002 and 2004, the government already used outsourcing for one-third of total service expenditures (Jing 2008). In practice, social services are mostly purchased from non-profit organizations, which are required to meet certain standards. To qualify to provide services in Guangdong Province, organizations must comply with a series of "Catalogues of Social Organizations Qualified for Undertaking Government Function, Transfer Functions, and Procurement of Services," which include lawful registration, professional management and financial structure, high-quality staff and equipment, and compliance with monitoring. If social organizations can not comply with the regulation, they can receive subsidies to develop their organizational structure (NDRC 2015).

The provider structure in China is complex, and a clear separation between public and private companies is sometimes difficult. The procurement law does not specify any organizational type of provider, so all companies are allowed to provide social services. Generally, long-term care providers can be categorized into four sectors: the state, for-profits, non-profits, and the informal sector (Johnson 1999). In China, the classification is not that simple as there are many hybrid organizations, and the official legal status may vary from actual operations. For example, a study in Nanjing found that all nongovernmental residential care facilities were registered as non-profits, but the lack of transparency and regulation makes it difficult to monitor the flow of capital within or outside those companies, and their real financial status remains unclear (Feng et al. 2011). According to the Ministry of Civil Affairs of the PRC, more than 350,000 non-profits were registered in 2007, but many of those non-profit institutions are at least partly state-controlled and operate only semi-autonomously.[3] To maintain governmental control, non-profit organizations are highly regulated in China. Institutions must register with the local government and are required to allow public officials to be involved in management and oversee daily activities (Jing and Chen 2012; Wong and Jun 2006). Despite this regulation, a large number of non-licensed NGOs still provide services to seniors (He 2013).

A study of Chinese elder care homes in Guangzhou, Shanghai, and Tianjin identified five different types of formal providers: individual-run, shareholder-run, community-run, enterprise-run, and joint venture units. Individual-run and shareholder-run facilities are private organizations that differ in their ownership structures. In the survey, one-third of the facilities were run by a single entrepreneur or investor (individual-run). While community homes are funded by the government and are often run by local authorities, enterprise-run homes are managed and funded by state-owned enterprises. The joint ventures are mixed organizations, which could be a collaboration between individual investors and local authorities (Wong and Jun 2006).

The Consumer

In recent years, most countries have gradually increased consumer choice in long-term care. In contrast to the purchasing of services by public authorities for the consumer (usually based on geographical proximity or predetermined contracts with certain providers), allowing consumer choice of providers and services is associated with several advantages. First, consumers know best which services would be most beneficial to the person in need. The individual situation of care receivers is determined by multiple factors such as activities of daily living (ADL) limitations, housing environment, informal care resources, and individual preferences, so the standard care package purchased by a care manager might be inadequate. Second, providing choices to people in need has an intrinsic value, as self-determination and autonomy are associated with higher user satisfaction (Rodrigues, Leichsenring, and Winkelmann 2014). Third, if consumers have choices, they can express dissatisfaction by switching to a new provider. This market mechanism gives providers the incentive to deliver high-quality services and promotes competition. In addition, the market becomes responsive to consumers' needs and increases the innovative potential. The introduction of new technology (e.g., advancements in telecare) can improve the utility of consumers and thereby allow providers to capitalize on their advantage over their competitors.

However, not all elderly people prefer or are able to make their own choices. As shown in the case of England, the majority of consumers let their budgets be managed by a third person, a phenomenon that might be related to the fact that the right to choose is also associated with certain risks. As long-term care decisions are likely to be made under emotional stress or social pressure or for the distant future, they can be prone to irrationality and non-optimal judgment (e.g., Kahneman, Knetsch, and Thaler 1991). In addition, too many options are known to cause disutility among consumers (Schwartz 2014), and making an educated choice requires time and information that can create high transaction costs. This can lead to a possible advantage for people with higher education, income, and social status as they tend to make better choices, which raises concerns about equity (Glendinning 2008; Greve 2009).

In Germany, consumers can select among all formal service providers that fulfill minimum standards and have a framework contract with sickness funds.

To support informed consumer choice for home and residential care providers, the funds provide quality assessments and user recommendations through a joint website. The website provides a search engine for home and residential care and displays previous consumer ratings.

To improve consumer choice in England, the Personal Budget is available to all new eligible people in need. People have three options for spending their budgets: (1) manage the money themselves as a direct payment to purchase services, (2) let the Local Authority purchase the care services, or (3) let a third party purchase services on behalf of the elderly. With the direct payments, consumers can officially hire informal caregivers (excluding the closest relatives) or purchase services from service providers themselves (Baxter, Glendinning, and Greener 2011). Residential care, currently excluded for direct payments, is being discussed for inclusion in the future (AgeUK 2015). Only a small share (8 percent) of elderly opted for direct payments in 2013, meaning that few people prefer to manage their personal budget autonomously, this share, however, doubled from 2008 to 2014 (Health and Social Care Information Centre 2014; Rodrigues, Leichsenring, and Winkelmann 2014). Given the infrequent use of direct payments and the general concerns regarding equity issues, the introduction of more consumer flexibility and open markets was criticized early as having brought little benefit to the elderly (Glendinning 2008).

In Japan, the elderly in need receive only benefits in kind, with no cash alternatives. In theory, consumers can freely choose from institutional and home-based services, but in reality, the care plans are often made by care managers. Those certified professionals design a care arrangement that accounts for level of limited functional ability, individual living environment, and family background. The care manager is entrusted with the entire planning for an individual and monitors the care process to make any necessary adjustments. The main purpose of the care managers is to arrange an optimal combination of care services among different providers to extend independent living as long as possible (Matsuda and Yamamoto 2001; Tsutsui and Muramatsu 2007).

Currently, formal long-term care services in China remain limited and are mainly available for out-of-pocket payments. Therefore, the lack of general access to elderly care services is still an important issue in many parts of China. Until recently, however, informal care was the main source of support for impaired elderly, and care facilities slowly emerged over the last 30 years. For example, Nanjing had only three care facilities in 1980. Although coverage varies substantially by region, access to home-care services generally remains difficult and access is mostly limited to the more affluent families.

Formal care support remains particularly limited in rural areas: according to a 2012 survey in Zhejiang Province, less the 6 percent of the rural elderly in need utilize formal care, while the share in urban areas is more than six times larger (37 percent) (Li et al. 2013). Urban areas have experienced a boom in the residential care sector, with governmental efforts for capacity building leading to a doubling of facility beds in Nanjing from 2000 to 2009 (Feng et al. 2011).

However, the focus was mostly on capacity building and due to the lack of a national regulatory framework and oversight, quality of care often remains low, as minimum standards are not enforced properly. This lack of a variety of services was addressed in the *12th Five-Year Plan*, which outlines a new care system that structures the supply of services in a three-tiered system. Elderly care should be primarily based on home care, which is more in line with the cultural norms and der elderly's preference to remain in their own homes. This home-based care should be backed by community-based services and by institutional care as the last tier of support (Feng et al. 2012).

Even though the government does not provide direct funding to most people in need of care, subsidies on the supply side are used to expand access and reduce user fees. Direct transfers are only available to the poor elderly without family, assets, and the ability to work. These so-called "Three Nos" represent around 3.5 percent of the population over age 60 and receive special protection from the government which provides them with "five guarantees" covering the costs of food, clothing, housing, medical care, and burial (State Council Information Office 2005). These government efforts sustain elderly care homes for the Three Nos in rural areas, with about 50 percent of them being institutionalized in 2004. Access for poor elderly outside the Three Nos group remains very limited, even though acceptance by welfare institutions became more open over the last years. However, elderly suffering from dementia or functional dependencies are not accepted in these facilities or will be discharged if they develop such a severe condition (Wu, Mao, and Zhong 2009). This practice is partly due to the limited funding, but also related to the lack of a qualified and professional workforce (Feng et al. 2012).

Implications for China

Given the rising number of people in need, China's long-term care sector is facing great challenges and will require joint efforts and cooperation among the national government, local authorities, providers, and families. The design of a comprehensive national long-term care system in China will help improve conditions for a large number of impaired elderly. A successful approach will provide quality care to a large number of elderly, ensure access for the less affluent, and keep costs at an acceptable level.

China can benefit from advancements in the service commissioning literature and the experience of other countries while adapting the approach to China's unique culture and social context. Following international trends and the NPM approach, efficient care provision will depend on the successful implementation of a transparent and flexible care market. The market design must reward good providers and allow them to grow, while bad providers must be held accountable for poor performance and ultimately exit the market. However, in the context of long-term care, these important market mechanisms must act within a regulatory framework and require government oversight and sufficient funding to ensure an adequate supply of high-quality care for the population.

As described in the section on government, the national strategy requires government involvement at all levels of the system to promote private sector engagement and ensure consumers' well-being, rather than to exercise control. The available data suggest that there are still many cases in which current state actions hinder the expansion of private sector service provision or fail in regulatory oversight and quality assurance (Feng et al. 2012; Jing and Chen 2012; Wu, Mao, and Zhong 2009). The national government should expand its role as a steward, set up a comprehensive long-term care system, and implement measures for efficient operation. The development of a functioning market requires several stages, as outlined in figure 6.1.

Market Structure

The design of the market structure is a core government task and requires a debate on the overall policy goals of the long-term care market and the general market structure needed to achieve those goals. As highlighted in the 2011 *12th Five-Year Plan for the Development of China's Undertakings for the Aged*, the government aims at "establishing a basic strategic framework to deal with ageing; formulating and implementing medium and long-term plans for the development" that provides "universal coverage of basic old-age security" in urban and rural areas. More specifically, long-term care should be focused on home-based services and promote family and voluntary involvement. The government also plans to increase beds in residential care facilities by 3.42 million over the five years. To reach those goals, the private sector may be incentivized by preferential policies. In addition, the government will "formulate policies with regard to the purchase of services for elderly people with special needs by the government." While these regulations provide a broad framework for a long-term care industry

Figure 6.1 Commissioning Structure, Based on Gash et al. 2013

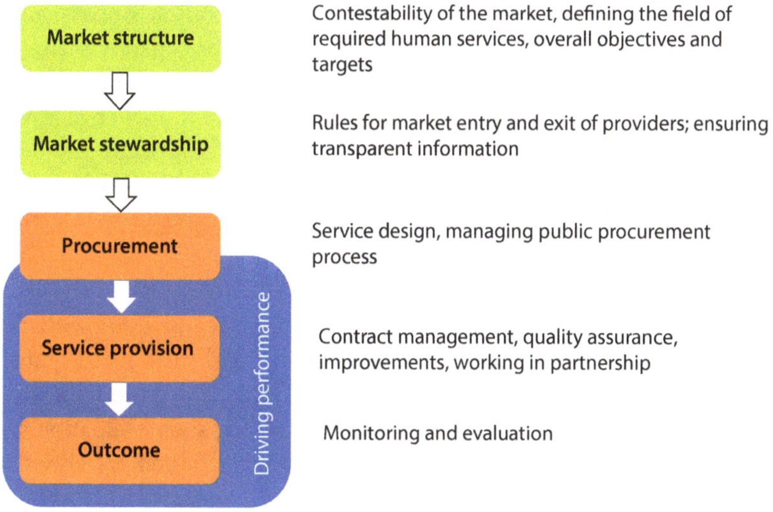

and generally follow the direction of international developments, there is little emphasis on user choices, and public funding is mostly provided to the supply side of the market.

Market Stewardship

Against this backdrop, the national government needs to execute market stewardship to ensure that these goals are reached. To date, reality still lags behind many of the aspirations. For example, despite the emphasis on home care, most financial resources have been used to increase residential care capacity (Feng et al. 2012). In addition, the way public funding is allocated to providers often lacks competition, and many private providers face uneven competition with well-funded state providers (Wu, Mao, and Zhong 2009). Such issues are related to a lack of sufficient government oversight and unclear responsibilities that hinder the performance of the sector.

Good stewardship is challenging and requires a specific set of capabilities, which include an understanding of the policy environment and market dynamics and knowledge of finance and business. Efficient oversight also requires a high level of professionalism in the government to manage the complex interplay among all stakeholders. A successful long-term care market in which the public sector commissions non-state providers to offer a broad range of services to the elderly relies on professional government activity at every stage of the process, from the national to the local levels. The government needs to acknowledge this challenge and promote the change in responsibilities and tasks in all participating public entities. Commissioning bodies should be professional, and the responsible individuals require adequate training (Gash et al. 2013). For example, England has established a Commissioning Academy that aims to train public employees who work on defining policy, shaping public service provision, or allocating resources for services to citizens.

Because regulatory oversight requires a clear understanding of the market and all parties involved, the government should implement an information system to gather statistics on care demand and ensure consistent data collection across all regions. For the allocation of funds and proper capacity planning, the government not only needs to understand current demand but should also anticipate future developments. The government should also engage with all stakeholders such as users, various types of providers, and local authorities to improve the understanding of the market and incorporate different perspectives into decision making, as oversight requires knowledge of both the demand and the supply sides of care (Gash et al. 2013).

The government should also enable consumer choice by providing them with sufficient information about service quality and prices to help with rational decision making. Countries like Germany, England, and the United States have set up rating websites that support the elderly and their family members in finding the right provider. If different choices are available, such evaluation systems enable consumers to execute an important market function by choosing the best providers. Particularly in home care markets, experience has shown that consumers who are "voting with their feet" can positively affect service quality. Ultimately, the goal of social service provision is to increase consumer well-being, so consumers themselves should be viewed as an important part of the successful market.

Failure in social service provision and public oversight is often related to a lack of accountability and unclear responsibilities among different players, so the national government needs to assign clear roles and structure the public entities. A well-designed accountability system also includes monitoring and enforcement. The Community Care Act in England entrusts local authorities to ensure a working care market. This decentralization of responsibility provides some leeway for innovation, with local governments having the opportunity to cooperate with providers to create new solutions which can be scaled up if successful.

Sufficient funding should be provided to the commissioning entities based on local demand. Excessive budget pressure on commissioners or providers usually leads to a deterioration in service performance and can reduce user choices (Gash et al. 2013). One way to reduce budget pressure is to implement some sort of means testing, which allows for less public funds for people who are better able to pay. As shown in the case of Hong Kong SAR, China, if public subsidies are given to providers (rather than to consumers) this might be more difficult to achieve (Chui 2011).

Even though market mechanisms should ultimately crowd out bad service providers, control mechanisms are needed to ensure the health and dignity of service users. Virtually all of the care systems reviewed here rely on some sort of accreditation or licensing to ensure a minimum level of quality. To ensure long-term compliance, a neutral entity should monitor providers and report misconduct to the government. However, monitoring efforts should be suitable and not too costly for small providers (Irish, Salamon, and Simon 2009).

Procurement

To ensure equal opportunities, procurement practices should be specified at the national level to guide local procurement activities (NDRC 2015). Although procurement of long-term care services is regulated under the *Law of Government Purchase of the PRC*, the available legislation is vague and provides an insufficient framework which is not properly enforced. Successful public procurement requires an appropriate legal framework in order to be sustainable, with rules that are transparent and properly enforced to ensure that the best candidate is able to make the best offer. Commissioning entities need to provide sufficient information and increase communication with providers to remove information asymmetries. A clear understanding on both sides about the procurement item is needed to improve the efficiency of the process and ensure the service performance of successful providers. In addition, service contracts should include incentive arrangements to encourage cost savings, efficiency, and effectiveness (Irish, Salamon, and Simon 2009).

If the Chinese government wants to increase service quality, procurement should go beyond the common practice of construction and operation subsidies based on beds provided (NDRC 2015). In addition, public procurement is often too focused on price rather than quality. Particularly in the case of long-term care, measuring the quality of the service is difficult. However, if contracts are only awarded to the lowest bidder, this is often associated with a race to the bottom in quality. Good commissioning drives innovation by influencing providers to achieve better overall outcomes (Gash et al. 2013). The review of long-term care systems shows that commissioners use multiple instruments to transfer public funding to providers. Particularly in light of China's continued efforts to expand health insurance among the population, commissioners can, for example, create incentives that foster integrated services and prevention within residential homes. An example from the United States shows that such services are often underdeveloped in a free market but can lead to better health for the elderly and lower costs for the health sector (Grabowski et al., 2015).

Service Provision

Commissioning non-state companies for service provision bears a certain risk to the government as it separates the responsibility for high-quality services from the actual provision, making it important to ensure that the companies have the necessary capabilities. This inherent principal-agent problem is usually addressed with contracts and competition, although some countries like Germany engage in a cooperative partnership with private providers and build a relationship of trust. Non-profits, in particular, share common goals with the local government as they usually have no desire for rent seeking. However, strong government involvement in the daily management of many non-profit companies hampers competition in the public bidding process. As the history of private non-profits is comparably short in China, those institutions often lack professionalism and sufficient financial means to invest. Shortage of skills is still a common issue for providers of long-term care in Western countries, which can lead to low service quality and high staff turnover. The government should invest in such institutions to develop their innovative potential and help them grow to become independent and capable partners in the provision of long-term care services (NDRC 2015; Teets and Jagusztyn 2013). In many European countries, regulation fosters government collaboration with non-state institutions and requires incorporating welfare corporations into large parts of the planning and design of service provision (Irish, Salamon, and Simon 2009).

To ensure a broad range of services, the government needs to give adequate incentives to the market and provide sufficient and transparent funding to providers. Providers must be able to at least recover their full costs, and low government funding is linked to higher user fees. If the government wants to expand access to long-term care services to the less affluent who can only afford low user fees, sufficient funding must be provided. Only large financial incentives provide the government with enough leverage to influence user fees.

Outcomes

To achieve the desired outcomes, it will be important to ensure careful monitoring of the progress and performance of the long-term care system. The long-term care market is prone to market failures, and despite substantial efforts, no country has found a best practice solution. All care systems reviewed suffer from dangerously escalating costs and require regular adjustments. The development of a service market with non-state provision requires much "learning by doing" and constant adaptation and improvement. However, measuring long-term care performance is a difficult endeavor. Internationally, performance measures have shifted from outputs (e.g., beds available) to outcomes. In England, for instance, measures include users' quality of life, independence, and experience of care. A systematic, continuous, and independent evaluation of outcomes allows the government to assess provider performance, helps ensure comparable service quality between local governments, and allows the objective evaluation of local innovation. Easily accessible information that is available in a timely manner helps ensure service supply and allows for quick action if needed.

Notes

1. §1 Care Act 2014: http://www.legislation.gov.uk/ukpga/2014/23/pdfs/ukpga_20140023_en.pdf.
2. §5 (1) Care Act 2014.
3. http://www.chinabusinessreview.com/setting-up-international-nonprofit-organizations-in-china/.

References

AgeUK. 2015. *Factsheet: Personal Budgets and Direct Payments in Adult Social Care.* London: AgeUK.

Augurzky, B., and R. Mennicken. 2011. Projektbericht Faktenbuch Pfl ege—Die Bedeutung privater Anbieter im Pflegemarkt.

Baxter, K., C. Glendinning, and I. Greener. 2011. "The Implications of Personal Budgets for the Home Care Market." 37–41. http://doi.org/10.1080/09540962.2011.560702.

Blöchliger, H. 2008. "Market Mechanisms in Public Service Provision." 626. http://www.oecd-ilibrary.org/economics/market-mechanisms-in-public-service-provision_241001625762.

Busse, R., J. Figueras, R. Robinson, and E. Jakubowski. 2007. "Strategic Purchasing to Improve Health System Performance: Key Issues and International Trends." *HealthcarePapers* 8 (Spec No): 62–76.

Carmichael, F., S. Charles, and C. Hulme. 2010. "Who Will Care? Employment Participation and Willingness to Supply Informal Care." *Journal of Health Economics* 29 (1): 182–90. http://doi.org/10.1016/j.jhealeco.2009.11.003.

Chui, E. W.-T. 2011. "Long-Term Care Policy in Hong Kong: Challenges and Future Directions." *Home Health Care Services Quarterly* 30 (3): 119–32. http://doi.org/10.1080/01621424.2011.592413.

Comas-Herrera, A., L. Pickard, R. Wittenberg, J. Malley, and D. King. 2010. *The Long-Term Care System for the Elderly in England*. London: ANCIEN.

Farsi, M., and M. Filippini. 2004. "An Empirical Analysis of Cost Efficiency in Non-Profit and Public Nursing Homes." *Annals of Public and Cooperative Economics* 75 (3): 339–65. http://doi.org/10.1111/j.1467-8292.2004.00255.x.

Feng, Z., C. Liu, X. Guan, and V. Mor. 2012. "China's Rapidly Aging Population Creates Policy Challenges in Shaping a Viable Long-Term Care System." *Health Affairs* 31 (12): 2764–73. http://doi.org/10.1377/hlthaff.2012.0535.

Feng, Z., H. J. Zhan, X. Feng, C. Liu, M. Sun, and V. Mor. 2011. "An Industry in the Making: The Emergence of Institutional Elder Care in Urban China." *Journal of the American Geriatrics Society* 59 (4): 738–44. http://doi.org/10.1111/j.1532-5415.2011.03330.x.

Figueras, J., R. Robinson, and E. Jakubowski. 2005. *Purchasing to Improve Health Systems Performance*. Open University Press.

Forder, J., and S. Allan. 2014. "The Impact of Competition on Quality and Prices in the English Care Homes Market." *Journal of Health Economics* 34 (1): 73–83. http://doi.org/10.1016/j.jhealeco.2013.11.010.

Gash, T., N. Panchamia, S. Sims, and L. Hotson. 2013. *Making Public Service Markets Work*. http://www.instituteforgovernment.org.uk/sites/default/files/publications/Making_public_service_markets_work_final_0.pdf.

Giles, J., D. Wang, and C. Zhao. 2010. "Can China's Rural Elderly Count on Support from Adult Children? Implications of Rural-to-Urban Migration." *Journal of Population Ageing* 3 (3–4): 183–204. http://doi.org/10.1007/s12062-011-9036-6.

Glendinning, C. 2008. "Increasing Choice and Control for Older and Disabled People: A Critical Review of New Developments in England." *Social Policy and Administration* 42 (5): 451–69. http://doi.org/10.1111/j.1467-9515.2008.00617.x.

Grabowski, D. C., D. J. Caudry, K. M. Dean, and D. G. Stevenson. 2015. "Integrated Payment and Delivery Models Offer Opportunities and Challenges for Residential Care Facilities." *Health Affairs* 34 (10): 1650–56. http://doi.org/10.1377/hlthaff.2015.0330.

Greve, B. 2009. "Can Choice in Welfare States be Equitable?" *Social Policy and Administration* 43 (6): 543–56. http://doi.org/10.1111/j.1467-9515.2009.00679.x.

He, D. 2013. "New Rules for NGOs to Improve Operations." http://www.chinadaily.com.cn/china/2013-04/17/content_16413055.htm.

Health and Social Care Information Centre. 2014. *Personal Social Services Expenditure and Unit Costs*.

Irish, L. E., L. M. Salamon, and K. W. Simon. 2009. *Outsourcing Social Services to CSOs: Lessons from Abroad*. Washington, DC: World Bank.

Jing, Y. 2008. "Outsourcing in China: An Exploratory Assessment." *Public Administration and Development* 28 (2): 119–28. http://doi.org/10.1002/pad.488.

Jing, Y., and B. Chen. 2012. "Is Competitive Contracting Really Competitive? A Case Study of Restructuring Government-Nonprofit Relations in Shanghai." Center for Nonprofit Strategy and Management Working Paper Series.

Johnson, N. 1999. *Mixed Economics of Welfare: A Comparative Perspective*. London: Prentice Hall, Europe.

Kahneman, D., J. L. Knetsch, and R. H. Thaler. 1991. "Anomalies: The Endowment Effect, Loss Aversion, and Status Quo Bias." *Journal of Economic Perspectives* 5 (1): 193–206. http://doi.org/10.1257/jep.5.1.193.

Knapp, M., B. Hardy, and J. Forder. 2001. "Commissioning for Quality: Ten Years of Social Care Markets in England." *Journal of Social Policy* 30 (2): 283–306. http://doi.org/10.1017/S0047279401006225.

Lewis, J., and A. West. 2013. "Re-Shaping Social Care Services for Older People in England: Policy Development and the Problem of Achieving 'Good Care'." *Journal of Social Policy* 43 (1): 1–18. http://doi.org/10.1017/S0047279413000561.

Li, M., Y. Zhang, Z. Zhang, Y. Zhang, L. Zhou, and K. Chen. 2013. "Rural-Urban Differences in the Long-Term Care of the Disabled Elderly in China." *PLoS ONE* 8 (11): 1–7. http://doi.org/10.1371/journal.pone.0079955.

Matsuda, S., and M. Yamamoto. 2001. "Long-Term Care Insurance and Integrated Care for the Aged in Japan." *International Journal of Integrated Care* 1 (September): e28.

Meagher, G., and M. Szebehely. 2013. *Marketisation in Nordic Eldercare: A Research Report on Legislation, Oversight, Extent and Consequences*. Stockholm University.

NDRC (National Development and Reform Committee). 2015. *Research on Government Procurement of Services from Social Organizations*. NDRC.

Ovretveit, J. 1995. *Purchasing for Health: A Multidisciplinary Introduction to the Theory and Practice of Health Purchasing*. Buckingham: Open University Press.

Rhee, J. C., N. Done, and G. F. Anderson. 2015. "Considering Long-Term Care Insurance for Middle-Income Countries: Comparing South Korea with Japan and Germany." *Health Policy* 119 (10): 1319–29. http://doi.org/10.1016/j.healthpol.2015.06.001.

Robinson, R., J. Figueras, and E. Jakubowski. 2005. *Purchasing to Improve Health Systems Performance*. Open University Press. http://www.mcgraw-hill.co.uk/html/0335213677.html. London: McGraw-Hill.

Rodrigues, R., K. Leichsenring, and J. Winkelmann. 2014. *The "Make or Buy" Decision in Long-term Care: Lessons for Policy*.

Schwartz, B. 2014. *The Paradox of Choice—Why More Is Less*. Harper Perennial.

Seok, J. E. 2010. "Public Long-Term Care Insurance for the Elderly in Korea: Design, Characteristics, and Tasks." *Social Work in Public Health* 25 (2): 185–209. http://doi.org/10.1080/19371910903547033.

Shimizutani, S. 2013. "The Future of Long-Term Care in Japan." RIETI Discussion Paper Series, 13-E-064, Research Institute of Economy, Trade, and Industry, Tokyo.

Standing Committee. 2002. *The Government Procurement Law of the People's Republic of China*. http://www.gov.cn/english/laws/2005-10/08/content_75023.htm.

State Council Information Office. 2005. *The Development of China's Undertakings for the Aged*. Beijing: State Council Information Office.

Statistisches Bundesamt. 2013. "Pflegestatistik 2013." Pflege im Rahmen der Pflegeversicherung Deutschlandergebnisse. https://www-ec.destatis.de/csp/shop/sfg/bpm.html.cms.cBroker.cls?cmspath=struktur,vollanzeige.csp&ID=1019863.

Sunwoo, D. 2012. "The Present Situation and Problems of the Long-Term Care Insurance in South Korea: From Comparative Perspectives between South Korea and Japan." *Japanese Journal of Social Security Policy* 9(1). http://www.ipss.go.jp/webj-ad/WebJournal.files/SocialSecurity/2011/spring/Web%20Journal_Dr%20Sunwo.pdf.

Tamiya, N., H. Noguchi, A. Nishi, M. R. Reich, N. Ikegami, H. Hashimoto, J. C. Campbell. 2011. "Population Ageing and Wellbeing: Lessons from Japan's Long-Term Care Insurance Policy." *The Lancet* 378 (9797): 1183–92. http://doi.org/10.1016/S0140-6736(11)61176-8.

Teets, J. C., and M. Jagusztyn. 2013. "The Evolution of a Collaborative Governance Model: Public-Nonprofit Partnerships in China." http://www.umdcipe.org/conferences/GovernmentCollaborationShanghai/Presentations/Teets_Jagusztyn_Presentation.pdf.

Theobald, H. 2012. "Combining Welfare Mix and New Public Management: The Case of Long-Term Care Insurance in Germany." *International Journal of Social Welfare* 21 (SUPPL.1): 61–74. http://doi.org/10.1111/j.1468-2397.2011.00865.x.

Travis, P., D. Egger, P. Davies, and A. Mechbal. 2002. *Towards Better Stewardship: Concepts and Critical Issues*, 1–21. Geneva: World Health Organization. http://www.who.int/healthinfo/paper48.pdf.

Tsutsui, T., and N. Muramatsu. 2007. "Japan's Universal Long-Term Care System Reform of 2005: Containing Costs and Realizing a Vision." *Journal of the American Geriatrics Society* 55 (9): 1458–63. http://doi.org/10.1111/j.1532-5415.2007.01281.x.

Tynkkynen, L. K., I. Keskimäki, and J. Lehto. 2013. "Purchaser-Provider Splits in Health Care-The Case of Finland." *Health Policy* 111 (3): 221–25. http://doi.org/10.1016/j.healthpol.2013.05.012.

WHO (World Health Organization). 2000. *The World Health Report 2000*. Vol. 78. Geneva: WHO. http://www.who.int/whr/2000/en/whr00_en.pdf.

Wing-tak, C., C. Kin-sun, C. Ming-lin, K. Suk-fan, and L. Chi-kin. 2009. *Elderly Commission's Study on Residential Care Services for the Elderly*. The University of Hong Kong. http://www.elderlycommission.gov.hk/en/download/library/Residential%20Care%20Services%20-%20Final%20Report(eng).pdf.

Won, C. W. 2013. "Elderly Long-Term Care in Korea." *Journal of Clinical Gerontology and Geriatrics* 4 (1): 4–6. http://doi.org/10.1016/j.jcgg.2012.11.001.S

Wong, L., and T. Jun, T. 2006. "Non-State Care Homes for Older People as Third Sector Organisations in China's Transitional Welfare Economy." *Journal of Social Policy* 35 (2): 229–46. http://doi.org/10.1017/S0047279405009505.

Wu, B., Z.-F. Mao, and R. Zhong. 2009. "Long-Term Care Arrangements in Rural China: Review of Recent Developments." *Journal of the American Medical Directors Association* 10 (7): 472–77. http://doi.org/10.1016/j.jamda.2009.07.008.

Yanzhang, D. 2013. *Examining the Development Situation of China Aged Industry in the First Year of the Industry*. http://english.wcsdf.org/recently-news/examining-the-development-situation-of-china-aged-industry-in-the-first-year-of- the-industry/.

CHAPTER 7

Strengthening Regulations, Standards, and Quality Assurance for Long-Term Care

Nan Tracy Zheng, Joshua M. Wiener, and Zhanlian Feng

Introduction

The aged care sector in China is still at an early stage of development. To date, the Chinese government and other stakeholders have focused on the shortage of long-term care services, with government and private initiatives aiming to increase supply quickly to meet escalating needs. The government is now changing its role from a direct supplier and provider to a purchaser and regulator and is encouraging private sources to enter the service delivery system.

To ensure that Chinese seniors receive care that meets their health and functional needs and improves their quality of life, developing an effective regulatory framework and quality assurance system is critical. Currently, regulatory oversight and other strategies to ensure adequate quality are lacking and are a relatively low priority on the policy agenda. While media stories about poor quality of care and safety concerns in the senior care sector occasionally surface (Xinhua Net 2013), there are few data on which to assess the quality of existing and new services.

This chapter focuses on the challenge of strengthening regulations, standards, and quality assurance for China's long-term care sector. It begins with a review of international experiences in long-term care quality assurance. These experiences offer lessons for Chinese policy makers in developing a quality assurance system that fits China's political and market environment. Recent developments in long-term care quality assurance in China, both nationally and in selected provinces and municipalities, are then described and analyzed. Finally, the chapter concludes by highlighting key policy challenges in this area and suggesting future directions and potential strategies to meet those challenges.

Nan Tracy Zheng is a Senior Research Analyst at RTI International. Joshua M. Wiener was a Distinguished Fellow at RTI International and the former director of RTI's Aging, Disability, and Long-Term Care Program. Zhanlian Feng is a Senior Research Analyst at RTI International.

Long-Term Care Quality Assurance Systems: An International Overview

This section provides an overview of the long-term care quality assurance systems in selected countries, drawing primarily on experience in the United States and observations from England, Australia, Germany, and Japan. Quality assurance for long-term care is on the political agenda in all of these countries, in part because of the substantial public funds allocated to these services and the heavy reliance of long-term care providers on public funding (Wiener 2011).

These countries all rely heavily on inspection and regulation of long-term care providers to assure quality. Although subnational government entities play a role in all of the countries, quality assurance, particularly for institutional care providers, is predominantly a national government responsibility. All countries emphasize inspection more than enforcement. Sanctions such as fines and revoking certificates are seldom used in these countries, partially because these measures inevitably have negative consequences for the service users, and the ultimate goal of regulation is to improve quality rather than penalize providers.

Although long-term care consumers are increasingly clinically complex (e.g., multiple chronic diseases and dementia), training requirements for long-term care workers are generally low, with substantial variation across countries. The training requirement for an entry-level certified care worker in Japan is a minimum of 130 hours, compared to 75 hours in the United States for nursing homes and home health agencies. Other types of long-term care providers in the United States often require much lower levels of training: for example, one-fifth of the states have no training requirements for personal care aides (PHI undated). The lack of training is believed by many observers to be a major cause of quality problems (Wiener et al. 2007a).

Strategies other than direct regulation are used in all five countries to improve the quality of care above the minimum set in the regulations. To varying degrees, these strategies rely on market forces and incentivize providers to improve their quality to remain competitive. In theory, the success of such strategies depends on the extent to which the long-term care supply exceeds demand, since the assumption is that consumers have numerous choices of providers. In practice, evidence on the effectiveness of these strategies is mixed (Totten et al. 2012). Some countries mandate the participation of providers in these market-based strategies, such as public reporting of quality scores in the United States (Stevenson and Bramson 2014). Some countries make such strategies voluntary, which typically results in lower participation rates. For instance, Japanese welfare facilities for the elderly can choose to work with an external agency for quality evaluation (which follows national guidelines set by the government) and report data publicly. Only 7.5 percent of the special nursing homes for the elderly and 3.2 percent of the group homes for elderly people with dementia participated in the voluntary assessment and reporting in 2011 (OECD/European Union 2013). In Finland, the use of standardized assessment tools to collect and report data is voluntary, with about 40 percent of institutional care and 30 percent of home care being covered by public reporting (OECD/European Union 2013).

Systematic and uniform data—including standardized individual assessment tools, training and support systems to ensure providers collect data in a consistent way, and a data repository—play a major role in quality assurance in the United States. The use of standardized individual assessment tools is gaining popularity in many economies, although the collection and use of this data remain relatively rare. In particular, the interRAI Long-Term Care Facilities Assessment System (interRAI LTCF) is currently available and used to some extent in Canada, Europe (Belgium, England, Finland, France, Germany, Iceland, Italy, the Netherlands, Norway, Spain, Sweden, and Switzerland), Asia (Hong Kong SAR, China, the Republic of Korea, and Japan), and the Pacific Rim (Australia and New Zealand) (InterRAI.org). The standardized individual-level information can be used for eligibility determination, care planning, needs assessment, and development of quality measures.

The experiences of Organisation for Economic Co-operation and Development (OECD) countries suggest that the degree of regulatory oversight and quality assurance in long-term care varies by setting, with greater focus on institutional care settings than home- and community-based care settings. In the United States, for example, nursing homes are among the most tightly regulated health sectors and must comply with a set of minimal standards mandated by the federal government (Stevenson and Bramson 2014) in order to receive government funding. In contrast, the various types of home- and community-based providers (such as assisted living facilities, board-and-care homes, and adult day services) are subject only to some basic licensure requirements and regulations established within individual states (Mollica, Sims-Kastelein, and O'Keeffe 2007). Indeed, in many countries, long-term care services rendered in home- and community-based settings are subject to little or no regulation. This relates to the fact that much of the home- and community-based care is mostly provided in individual homes, which makes inspection and data collection difficult, and includes a broad array of services, which makes the establishment of standards difficult.

Ensuring Quality of Care and Quality of Life: International Experiences

Internationally, the most common approach to ensuring the quality of long-term care is regulation—that is, ensuring that providers meet quality standards established by government agencies. These quality standards typically reflect the minimum quality level to be met for providers to be licensed to operate or to receive government funding. The role of government regulation in long-term care quality assurance is critical because long-term care consumers and their families are typically too disabled and vulnerable—physically, mentally, and/or socially—to change providers when they receive suboptimal quality of care and thus cannot effectively use their exit from the provider to motivate improvements in quality. Moreover, in many countries, supply constraints mean that consumers have difficulty changing providers even if they are unhappy with the quality of the care they are receiving, because alternative providers are not available.

Regulations

The regulatory process typically has three components: (1) rules that establish the standards or norms that providers must meet; (2) inspections or other means of collecting data to assess whether the providers are meeting the rules or performance norms; and (3) enforcement or other remedies to address problems identified during the inspection or other monitoring process.

Standards

A key issue in setting minimum acceptable standards is how to define the quality of long-term care. Two major domains that define quality are *quality of care* and *quality of life*. *Quality of care* refers to the technical competency of medical and nonmedical services (Wiener et al. 2007) and is typically measured by using structure, process, or outcome indicators (Donabedian 2005). Structure refers to professional and organizational resources that enable a provider or facility to provide quality care. Structural variables encompass the level, mix, education, and training of staff; characteristics of the facility, such as ownership and size; and accreditation. Process aspects include the care and services actually provided or administered, encompassing such deficiencies as overuse of potentially harmful procedures (e.g., physical restraints and antipsychotic medications), underuse of care consistent with practice guidelines (e.g., preventive services), or poor technical performance of procedures. Outcomes represent changes in health status or functional ability that are attributable to care provided or not provided. *Quality of life* refers to factors such as consumer choice and autonomy, dignity, individuality, comfort, and meaningful activity (Wiener et al. 2007). Government standards focus mostly on quality of care rather than quality of life and tend to emphasize structural requirements rather than process and outcomes. The relatively lesser attention to quality-of-life issues is partly due to the difficulty and challenges in conceptualizing and measuring quality of life.

In the United States, nursing homes and home health agencies (in some states) must be licensed by the states in which they are located in order to operate. In addition, nursing homes and home health agencies must meet federal quality standards in order to receive federal Medicare and federal-state Medicaid reimbursement (certification). Federal regulatory requirements cover a wide range of items, from inputs and structural capacity to care processes such as initial and periodic assessments for nursing home residents and home health consumers (Centers for Medicare and Medicaid Services 2015a). For example, nursing homes certified for Medicare must comply with requirements in resident rights, quality of life, resident assessment, quality of care, nursing services, dietary services, physician services, specialized rehabilitative services, pharmacy services, dental services, infection control, physical environment, and administration (Centers for Medicare and Medicaid Services 2015b). Licensing and other standards for home- and community-based services such as assisted living and personal care agencies are a state responsibility. These standards vary widely and are nonexistent in many cases (PHI undated).

In England, all providers must register with the Ministry of Health Care Quality Commission and meet minimum quality standards. These consist of 28 "Essential Standards of Quality and Safety" related to the regulations, grouped into six key areas (OECD/European Union 2013): (1) involvement and information (respecting and involving service users, consent, fees); (2) personalized care, treatment, and support (care and welfare of users, nutrition, cooperating with other providers); (3) safeguarding (abuse prevention, cleanliness and infection control, management of medicine, safety and sustainability of premises and equipment); (4) staffing (sustainability, recruiting, supporting workers); (5) quality and management (complaints, notifications of death and incidents and records); and (6) sustainability of management (registration of managers). Moreover, the managers of care homes and long-term care home service agencies must register separately with the Care Quality Commission and meet certain standards (e.g., pass a criminal background check and obtain a certificate to prove qualification in administrative roles).

Different from licensure, accreditation refers to the process in which providers are evaluated by third-party, nongovernmental organizations against their quality standards. Although done by nongovernmental organizations, accreditations sometimes are deemed by governments as compliant with regulatory inspections or certification requirements.

Australia requires residential and home care providers to be formally accredited by the Aged Care Standards and Accreditation Agency, which is also a condition for receiving public funding (OECD/European Union 2013). For residential care, the standards consist of a total of 44 expected outcomes ranging from physical environment, staffing, and management systems to resident lifestyle. For home care, the standards consist of 18 expected outcomes such as appropriate access and service delivery and users' rights. These standards are general statements with no detailed standards and give providers flexibility in how to meet the expected outcomes. The consensus in Australia is that these broad standards work better than more specific standards because they allow inspectors and providers to focus on the broad issues rather than less important details. Moreover, the general nature of the standards forces assessors to engage in conversation with providers to determine whether and how the expected outcomes have been achieved. Critics, however, argue that the standards are too general to be meaningful and are not enforceable.

In Germany, coverage of long-term care is universal, and the main purchasers in the long-term care sector are long-term care funds (statutory long-term care insurers). The power of regulating the long-term care sector is shared between the governments (both federal and state levels) and delegated decision-making entities (e.g., corporate entities) representing long-term care purchasers and providers through negotiations of the contracts (Garms-Homolova and Busse 2014). The government at the federal level determines the scope and general national rules for long-term care service provision. The Guidelines on Quality Evaluation (guidelines for LTCF) specify 82 criteria that capture structures and processes of care but do not address outcomes (Garms-Homolova and Busse 2014). Home care providers are subject to similar guidelines. Required qualifications for nursing personnel are also regulated at the federal level (Garms-Homolova and Busse 2014; OECD/European Union 2013). Based on requirements defined by the federal law, the delegated decision-making entities determine the details on quality measures, implementation, and enforcement during contract negotiations.

Japan mandates the accreditation of residential and home care providers. Accreditation of residential providers is also a condition for reimbursement. The prefectures certify providers, and the municipalities supervise and audit providers to ensure proper management. The standards for certification relate to staffing, complaint-handling procedures and elder protection, management and administration, and services provided (OECD/European Union 2013). The national government issues highly detailed structural requirements for staffing (which vary by facility type and size) for institutional providers and imposes high skill requirements on long-term care workers (Ikegami, Ishibashi, and Amano 2014). In addition, institutional care providers are subject to requirements on staff full-time equivalents (FTE) to resident ratios, which must be met both on a daily basis and per calendar month.

Monitoring

Once standards are established, regulators must monitor whether providers meet those standards. Two major strategies employed are inspection and periodic submission of data by providers. Although providers commonly complain about the frequency of inspections, few countries inspect nursing homes and other providers even once a year. Inspections of home- and community-based services providers are far less common than inspections of nursing homes.

In the United States, nursing homes and home health agencies that participate in government payment programs are inspected by the states in which they operate on behalf of the federal government and are evaluated against federal standards. The frequency of the inspection is roughly annually for all providers, but nursing homes that receive severe deficiency citations during the inspection are subject to revisits to confirm that deficiencies have been corrected. States also conduct unscheduled inspections in response to consumer complaints. Moreover, nursing homes and home health agencies certified to receive government reimbursement are also required to collect individual-level health and functional information using standard individual assessment tools—the Minimum Data Set (MDS) for nursing homes and the Outcome and Assessment Information Set (OASIS) for home health agencies—and submit data to the federal Centers for Medicare and Medicaid Services (CMS). Quantitative quality measures using assessment data—many focusing on resident outcomes—have been developed (and are reviewed by third-party independent organizations to ensure reliability and validity) and can be used to monitor provider quality.

In England, each provider is inspected at least once a year. Since 2006, the Care Quality Commission makes unannounced inspections, both on a regular basis (scheduled inspections) and in response to concerns (responsive inspections). The Care Quality Commission also conducts continuous assessments to determine each provider's risk of non-compliance. A key source is the "Quality and Risk Profile" which covers both qualitative and quantitative information about a provider, gathered from a variety of sources and converted to a common scale to generate a single risk estimate for each standard (Malley et al. 2014). Unfavorable continuous assessment results can lead to an inspection. In order to gain the perspective of consumers and to engage services users more during the inspection, the Care Quality Commission sometimes includes "experts by experience" (either services users or caregivers) on the inspection teams. Although this in theory should improve the transparency of inspection, there is no empirical evidence that the quality of inspection is improved by including these "experts by experience" (Malley et al. 2014). The Care Quality Commission encourages providers to ensure compliance through self-assessment and expects them to collect information to demonstrate performance to consumers. However, it does not require providers to collect individual outcome data and gives flexibility in the types of instruments and methods providers consider useful in self-assessing compliance. As a result, providers adopt a variety of instruments and collect unstandardized data, making cross-provider comparisons challenging (Malley et al. 2014).

Australia, Germany, and Japan inspect long-term care providers at varying frequencies. In Australia, the Aged Care Standards and Accreditation Agency monitors residential care providers' compliance with standards through announced and unannounced visits and review of a range of administrative and other information. Each provider is visited at least once a year. Home- and community-based care providers are required to self-report against standards and complete a quality review at least once during a three-year cycle (Gray, Cullen, and Lomas 2014). Following the self-assessment, the Aged Care Standards and Accreditation Agency reviews the providers' reports and conducts site visits. In Germany, quality assessment of nursing homes and home care agencies is done by the Medical Review Boards through annual quality inspections (Garms-Homolova and Busse 2014). Facilities are also inspected without prior notice by the Local Residential Homes Authorities (a government agency) at least yearly, unless they have been inspected by the Medical Review Boards. The Medical Review Boards and the Local Residential Homes Authorities are thus required to collaborate closely to prevent duplicate inspections (OECD/European Union 2013). Japan inspects institutional care providers annually, although the inspection is deemed completed in alternate years by submission of documentation rather than in-person inspections unless serious problems are identified (Ikegami, Ishibashi, and Amano 2014).

Enforcement

After standards are established and providers are determined as compliant/non-compliant through monitoring, enforcement is supposed to ensure that non-compliant providers come into compliance. However, enforcement of regulations is weak in the five countries this study focused on and in other OECD countries. Strong enforcement strategies such as suspending admissions or revoking licenses or certifications are only infrequently used in the most serious/hazardous cases, partly because such strategies may have unfavorable consequences for consumers such as service interruption for current consumers and longer wait times for prospective consumers (particularly in markets where long-term care supply is limited).

Market Mechanisms

Government regulations typically set the minimum level of quality that providers must meet, but without additional mechanisms, providers have little incentive to exceed the minimum and deliver higher-quality care. Recognizing this, several countries have structured programs to encourage market competition on quality dimensions.

Public Reporting

Public reporting helps provide quality information or other provider information to consumers, payers, and health care providers. The goal of public reporting is to facilitate informed decisions by consumers in selecting providers, which in turn incentivizes providers to improve performance. Public reporting has the advantage of being relatively low-cost, particularly when the data are already collected through the monitoring process (e.g., inspection results, deficiency citations, individual assessment data).

The United States collects the most individual-level quality information with regard to health and functional status as well as care process for nursing home residents and home health patients. Data on home health patients' experience/satisfaction are also collected through post-service surveys. Quantitative quality measures and indicators are developed using these data and posted on the Internet (https://data.medicare.gov/). Most of these quality measures concern outcomes such as pain, pressure ulcers, and falls. Inspection results such as staffing, deficiency citations, and penalties are also posted on the Internet. Some other counties also publish quality data (e.g., basic provider information, inspection results, accreditation reports) on the Internet, but none of these countries focuses on outcomes to the extent that the United States does. However, even in the United States, quality data are not available for nonmedical home- and community-based care services, partly due to the challenges and costs of collecting standardized data.

Since 2008, in order to simplify the interpretation of data, the United States added a nursing home star-rating score to the public reporting website (http://www.medicare.gov/nursinghomecompare). Each nursing home is rated between one and five stars based on health inspection results, quality measures, and staffing levels. This star-rating is designed to help consumers and their families compare nursing homes more easily.

However, little evidence is available on the effectiveness of the star-rating system on quality improvement over public reporting of quality data and individual quality measures. Moreover, some observers express concern that nursing homes may focus on quality areas covered by the star-rating at the cost of those not covered (Werner, Konetzka, and Kruse 2009). While it is receiving increased attention in the United States, a star-rating system was discontinued in England where data showed fewer than one in six consumers were aware of the availability of publicly reported quality data and even fewer were actually using it (Commission for Social Care Inspection 2009). More generally, a recent systematic review by the Agency for Healthcare Research and Quality examined published studies focusing on public reporting of health care quality information and found mixed evidence to support its effectiveness in improving quality of care (Totten et al. 2012). The review also found evidence suggesting that many long-term care consumers and families may not use the information (Castle 2009).

Pay-for-Performance

Pay-for-performance, or value-based purchasing (VBP), is a payment model in which good quality of care or substantial improvement in care is rewarded financially. Many countries, including China (Yip et al. 2014), are using or testing pay-for-performance models in health care systems. However, its application in long-term care is still rare.

In the United States, several state Medicaid programs have adopted pay-for-performance strategies in nursing homes. The targeted performance areas typically include care process-based and outcome-based quality measures and staffing. Evidence on the effectiveness of these pay-for-performance programs on quality improvement is inconsistent across quality areas and geographic areas (Werner, Konetzka, and Polsky 2013). In 2009, CMS initiated the Nursing Home Value-Based Purchasing (NHVBP) Demonstration in three states. In addition to quality measures and staffing, this demonstration targets inappropriate hospitalizations and deficiency citations from inspections. However, the evidence does not show that the demonstration promoted meaningful quality improvement, partly due to the design of the demonstration and the challenges in measuring quality outcomes (White et al. 2013). For example, the nursing home resident assessment tool, the MDS, changed during the demonstration period, which compromised the demonstration evaluators' ability to compare pre- and post-demonstration resident outcomes. In 2014, a VBP program was established which focuses on nursing homes that provide skilled nursing services (often temporarily needed by long-term care recipients to restore function and health after an acute hospitalization episode). The VBP program, to be implemented in 2019, will tie Medicare payments for skilled nursing facilities to their performance metrics, such as hospital readmission rates (Centers for Medicare and Medicaid Services 2015c).

In Japan, the government sets a fee schedule for each service covered under the public long-term care insurance (LTCI) program. Additional financial rewards are given to providers who perform better than the minimum requirements—for example, those providers who have more users with functional improvement over a pre-determined threshold. For institutional care providers, the conditions for financial rewards also include the rate of discharge to the community and having comprehensive care planning for end-of-life care and rehabilitation. Moreover, both institutional and home- and community-based care providers are rewarded financially for hiring staff with better qualifications, more experience, or specialty training (e.g., dementia care), which is consistent with Japan's overall quality assurance strategy of relying on highly skilled and qualified long-term care workers.

Controlling Supply versus Unlimited Entry

For market mechanisms to maximize their effectiveness in improving quality, long-term care supply should exceed demand so consumers can choose alternative providers. Under these circumstances, providers with suboptimal quality of care would lose business to those with good quality of care, which would either drive them out of the market or force them to improve quality.

In reality, however, evidence on the effectiveness of market mechanisms in improving quality is inconsistent, partly due to government control over long-term care supply. When supply is controlled and tight, consumers often have limited alternative providers to choose from and sometimes must stay with providers of suboptimal quality. Thus, providers do not have strong incentives for quality improvement.

Supply constraints are important in countries where the government pays for long-term care. Greater supply may induce higher demand, which government programs would have to cover. Given population aging and the decrease in supply of informal care, a lack of supply controls may greatly increase government expenditures.

Voluntary Initiatives

Provider and Professional Associations

Provider and professional associations can play a role in quality assurance and improvement. For example, in the United States, the American Health Care Association, an association of mostly for-profit nursing homes and residential care providers with about 12,000 members, provides information or guidelines about best practice, tool kits, and education to enhance their quality of care.

However, the main function of provider associations is to represent members before government agencies and legislators, and they are not in a position to take enforcement measures to ensure compliance. Moreover, provider associations do not necessarily contribute to—and may even lobby against—quality improvement goals that are not consistent with their business interests. For example, nursing home associations in the United States have opposed establishing minimum staff-resident ratios at the federal level due to the potential costs.

Accreditation or Quality Evaluation by Nongovernmental Agencies

In addition to mandatory licensure and certification to participate in long-term care funding programs by government agencies, some countries encourage—and in some cases require—providers to acquire accreditation, as well. In the United States, nursing homes and home care providers may choose to be accredited by the Joint Commission (http://www.jointcommission.org/), an independent, not-for-profit organization that accredits more than 20,000 health care organizations and programs in the United States but relatively few nursing homes and other long-term care providers. This voluntary accreditation is widely viewed as weaker than regular certification. Efforts by provider associations to have accreditation substitute for certification are strongly opposed by consumer groups in the United States.

The Japanese national government recommends but does not require third-party evaluations of long-term care providers (except for Alzheimer's group homes for which such evaluation is mandatory). Providers may gain knowledge about quality improvement through the evaluation process, and the results are posted on the Internet. However, only 7.5 percent of special nursing homes for the elderly and 3.2 percent of group homes for elderly people with dementia participated in the voluntary assessment and reporting in 2011 (OECD/European Union 2013).

The Role of Leading Providers or Organizations

Sometimes leading providers or organizations may undertake additional quality assurance or improvement initiatives, which provide the opportunity to test the effectiveness of innovative initiatives in improving quality. In the United States, a "culture change" movement to transform nursing homes from medical/health care-focused institutions to more home-like places has been underway for two decades (Rabig et al. 2006; Thomas 2003). The two most well-known examples are the "Eden Alternative" and the "Green House" models. Both models aim to improve the quality of life for residents with regard to their dignity, privacy, and autonomy and food enjoyment through changes in both the physical and psychosocial environments of nursing homes. Such changes include smaller homes, a facility layout that encourages social activities, and allowing residents to make their schedules. Although the empirical evidence is mixed, culture change is believed to improve residents' quality of life and the working environment for staff (thus reducing turnover). The CMS supports culture change adoption, and Medicaid programs in several states have pay-for-performance strategies in which culture change adoption is considered a plus (Miller et al. 2013).

In Japan, some large corporate chains providing home- and community-based care and assisted living are interested in implementing the interRAI assessment tool in their agencies. This can help the large chains expand management control over their agencies by having standardized individual-level outcome data to compare quality across the agencies. They can also publicize this quality assurance activity outside the government's regulatory framework to gain competitiveness (Ikegami, Ishibashi, and Amano 2014).

Recent Developments in Quality Assurance in China

Setting Standards and Instituting Regulatory Oversight

The quality assurance system in China is still in its infancy. China currently has three sets of national standards: the *Code for the Design of Buildings for Elderly Persons (1999)*, *Basic Standards for Social Welfare Institutions for the Elderly (2001)*, and *National Occupational Standards for Aged-Care Workers (2002)*. To further formalize the licensure process, the Ministry of Civil Affairs issued two new regulations, *Procedures for Licensing Senior Care Facilities* and *Measures for the Management of Senior Care Facilities*, both promulgated in June 2013. Several additional sets of national standards governing senior care services are in the pipeline. These national standards are general principles and provide local governments with the flexibility to establish enforceable standards under the national principles. In January 2014, the Ministry of Civil Affairs, Ministry of Commerce, and several other government agencies co-issued a policy document entitled *Guiding Opinions on Promoting the Standardization of Senior Care Services*, which states that comprehensive standards on a whole range of institutional and home- and community-based senior care services will be established by 2020.

Recently, various provinces in China have tried to adopt new practices in setting quality standards and regulations for both institutional and home- and community-based services. For example, Zhejiang Province established provincial standards for home-based aged care service and management in 2011, covering the areas of service target groups, service content, credentials and competencies of the service staff, and agency quality rating. Hangzhou, the capital city of Zhejiang Province, implemented "two standards, two methods"—the standard for home-based elderly services and the method for evaluating home-based elderly service needs, and the standard for nursing home services and the method for evaluating the eligibility for state-run nursing homes—as a way to standardize and normalize elderly services. Heilongjiang Province established standards for aged care service quality in 2013.

Tianjin published industry standards in 2013. In Tianjin, standards for services provided in the community specify the requirements for elderly nurseries (adult day care services), community dining centers, service organizations, emergency safeguard systems, service content, and service quality rating. The standards for home care specify the requirements for staffing, service content, service quality monitoring, and improvement. Eight additional sets of criteria are under revision, including criteria for nursing home care and hospice services.

Shanghai promulgated more detailed industry standards in 2013, and it subsidizes the cost for providers to meet those standards. Specifically, if the proposed one-time investment for a facility to meet the standards is higher than RMB

1.5 million (approximately US$242,000), the Shanghai municipal government subsidizes 30 percent of the investment using its social welfare lottery fund, and the district/county level government also provides the same amount of subsidy. Less-developed districts/counties and facilities that focus on providing care for disabled elders have priority for receiving the subsidies.

Building an Information System

In 2011, the Ministry of Civil Affairs began to develop the National Aged Care Information System, a major initiative to build a national aged care system during China's Twelfth Five-Year Plan (2011–15) period. The National Aged Care Information System has many functions and sub-systems, three of which have profound implications on quality assurance for aged care (China Society News 2010). First, the aged care information management system will include an aged care facility assessment system, a consumer assessment system, service quality monitoring and management system, facility annual inspection query system, and professional training system. Second, the aged care database will include characteristics and other information about aged care facilities and their residents, community-based services, and aged care professionals. Third, the public system will include an aged care complaint management system, service information posting system, online service reservation system, and aged care products promotion system. Overall, the National Aged Care Information System will provide the central, provincial, and local governments with the tools and data to regulate the industry and providers. Making the data available to the public will likely incentivize service providers to improve care quality and efficiency.

The National Aged Care Information System will facilitate the standardization of many non-regulatory quality assurance strategies that have already been utilized in major provinces and cities. For instance, Beijing's Municipal Bureau of Civil Affairs implemented a voluntary facility-rating system (similar to the hotel rating system) that assesses institutional care providers between one and five stars based on the locally devised *Star-Rating Standard of Institutional Care for the Aged* (Beijing Municipal Administration of Quality and Technology Supervision 2005). The standard not only covers structural capacities (such as physical environment and facilities, management and staffing, and qualifications of the staff) but also includes outcomes such as incidence rate of stage II pressure ulcers and consumer satisfaction rate. Facilities will be reassessed every three years. Between 2005 and the first half of 2011, only 13 providers participated in the star-rating system (Chinanews 2012). To incentivize providers, in 2011, the Beijing Municipal Bureau of Civil Affairs began to offer financial rewards to providers based on the stars they receive (Chinanews 2012). By the end of 2012, about 300 facilities went through the rating but only some showed adequate quality and received star(s). Specifically, 29 facilities received one star, 21 received two stars, 3 received three stars, 2 received four stars, and 2 received five stars (Chinanews 2012).

Similar systems are used in some other provinces and cities, including Jiangsu, Zhejiang, Tianjin, Shanghai, and Hebei, several of which also include home- and community-based service providers in the rating system. Jiangsu Province assesses and subsidizes aged care providers that meet a certain level of quality. The *Jiangsu Regulation for Elderly Rights Protection*, the first of its kind in China, was promulgated in 2011 and used to certify and subsidize aged care providers with certain experience and to reward enterprises for good quality, use of standardization, and a consistently good reputation/brand. Shanghai rates providers based on assessments, service coverage, and senior care satisfaction and also financially rewards some providers based on their rating. Hangzhou (capital city of Zhejiang Province) relies on third-party assessors to assess the quality of home- and community-based service providers and aims to assure quality by brand quality certification for providers (Zhu 2012). Since 2010, Hebei Province allocates provincial bonus and subsidy funding to prefectures based on a formula that takes into account prefectural-level financial capability, difficulty in implementing aging work, and performance appraisal based on star-ratings of aged care institutions.

One important component of the National Aged Care Information System is a database of older people who receive aged care and those who need aged care, for which a standardized individual-level assessment tool to collect health, function, self-care ability, and other useful information is crucial. The *Ability Assessment for Older Adults*, which is largely based on interRAI, was posted by the Ministry of Civil Affairs in June 2013 to solicit public comments. The assessment tool was tested among 581 seniors with varying degrees of dependency in six facilities in Beijing, Guangzhou (capital city of Guangdong Province), and Suzhou (in Jiangsu Province). Based on the testing results, the tool was revised and re-tested in 10 facilities in Beijing (MOCA 2013). The tool was tentatively proposed as a recommended (but not required) standard.

Several cities such as Guangzhou, Shanghai, Nanjing (capital city of Jiangsu Province), and Beijing have begun using standardized tools—similar to the *Ability Assessment for Older Adults*—to assess function and self-care ability for seniors who apply for aged care services. The primary goal of individual assessment is to determine care needs and thus appropriately allocate resources. The assessment varies across regions, but it provides a foundation for potential standardized data collection in the future that could be used for quality assurance.

Upgrading the Aged Care Workforce

For both institutional and home- and community-based services, the skills and competencies of caregivers have critical impacts on the quality of care. Aged care is a "high-touch" industry involving close relationships and interactions between direct care workers and elderly care recipients (many of whom are frail and vulnerable) on a daily or even round-the-clock basis.

The Ministry of Civil Affairs published *National Professional Standards for Aged-Care Workers* in 2007 and a revision in 2011, stipulating the training requirement for basic certification to be a minimum of 180 credit hours. More training is required to get more advanced certification (MOCA 2007, 2011).

The number of formal caregivers providing aged care services is estimated to exceed 300,000, among whom less than 100,000 have certification (China Philanthropy Research Institute 2015). The China Philanthropy Research Institute also reports that about 200,000 caregivers received aged care training in recent years—these data together suggest that many people who received training do not remain in the industry.

Recently, a few provinces and cities have begun subsidizing caregivers who receive professional training and who work in the aged care industry. For example, the *Options of Building a Home-Based Aged Care System in Suzhou, Jiangsu* in 2013 requires local Bureaus of Civil Affairs to offer free professional training for caregivers, gives awards to professional caregivers who receive certain levels of training and acquire certificates, and subsidizes the wages of those professional caregivers who work with the same service agency for more than one year. Liaoning Province and Tianjin city also subsidize caregivers' wages.

The Future of Quality Assurance in China: Prospects and Challenges

As in the countries reviewed in this chapter, regulatory oversight should be the primary approach to quality assurance for aged care in China, moving toward a more uniform approach that builds upon successful regional and local experiences. Most of the recent developments in quality assurance discussed in this chapter were initiated by provincial and municipal governments under the overall guidelines from the central government. While this approach promotes innovation and provides the opportunity for provinces and cities to learn from each other's experiences, there is considerable variation across geographic areas, and some areas may have inadequate standards and enforcement. Greater uniformity could strengthen the national quality assurance system and help eliminate geographical disparities in quality.

However, since formal long-term care services in China are still at an early stage of development, very strict regulations may not be advisable for two reasons. First, it can be too costly to be financially feasible or appealing to policy makers. This is particularly so in the current policy environment in which the overwhelming goal is to increase supply and build service capacity quickly, which seems to sideline concerns over quality assurance and regulatory oversight (Feng et al. 2011). Second, it may have the unintended effect of stifling private sector initiatives to further the growth of the industry. Instead, the current regulations should be made consistent and transparent, which would appeal to investors and facilitate their entry into the aged care market. The government could then gradually implement tighter regulations and stronger enforcement.

The review of international experiences in long-term care quality assurance highlights the importance of building a standardized information system for measuring, monitoring, and improving the quality of care. This kind of information infrastructure can foster an evidence-based approach to policy making, quality improvements, and regulation. It entails the periodic collection of good-quality information on long-term care providers and service users.

However, China has little publicly available information on the characteristics of and quality of care provided by senior care service providers to aid quality monitoring or inform consumer choices (Feng et al. 2014). As in other countries, it would be more feasible to start with collecting such information from institutional care providers and their residents, then expand the data collection to home- and community-based service providers and their customers. Standardized tools to assess aged care providers (both institutional and home- and community-based) nationwide need to be developed and implemented.

In the United States, all Medicare or Medicaid certified nursing homes are mandated to report both facility- and resident-level data electronically and on a regular basis. This is achieved through a uniform survey instrument for annual facility inspections and a standardized resident-level assessment instrument, the MDS (Version 3.0).

It will also be important to further develop and implement standardized individual assessment tools to regularly assess seniors, particularly aged care recipients' function and other health-related conditions. The *Ability Assessment for Older Adults* proposed by the Ministry of Civil Affairs and similar tools adopted by several provinces and cities provide a solid foundation for further development of a standardized tool. The National Commission on Aging and 24 national government agencies issued the *Opinions on Promoting Preferential Treatments for Seniors* in 2013, which requires that all health care institutions build health records for seniors age 65 years or older in their service regions and provide free annual physical exams and health consultations for them. These requirements provide opportunities for standardized assessment of seniors, which may generate valuable data useful for quality assurance.

To accelerate the process, Chinese policy makers might consider launching a demonstration project in a few advanced provinces or major cities to pilot a "reduced" form of data collection process. In the long run, the ultimate goal of the demonstration would be to build a standardized data collection process and make data easily accessible to both LTCF and home- and community-based care providers across the country. It could generate data to feed into the National Aged Care Information System, following a two-step strategy as described below.

- As an initial step, it would be easier to start a facility-level data collection process. All prospective and existing residential care facilities participating in the demonstration would be mandated by the local government authority to report some basic facility-level information (e.g., ownership, size, services provided, staffing levels and mix, and demographic profile and aggregate health conditions of current residents) on a regular basis (e.g., once a year). Facilitated by the National Aged Care Information System, information on all individual facilities could be made available to both the central government authority and local regulatory agencies on a

timely and ongoing basis. With this type of information, the government would be able to implement targeted monitoring and interventions focusing on a small number of facilities where problems are most likely to occur, such as facilities that house much-sicker-than-average patients yet have much lower-than-average staffing levels (Liu, Feng, and Mor 2014). In essence, this targeted approach mirrors the "Quality and Risk Profile" method currently used in England.
- As a second step, a similar pilot program could be initiated to test a resident-level assessment instrument designed to obtain key information on individual residents' functional status and care needs. This information could be used for care planning and quality assurance purposes. This step can be accelerated now that several provinces and cities have adopted the standardized assessment tool proposed by the Ministry of Civil Affairs.

Given the importance of the skills and competencies of aged care professionals in delivering high-quality care, policies supporting aged care as a profession could have a profound impact on quality of care. In addition to the policies adopted by a few provinces and cities to subsidize aged care training and award caregivers who remain in the profession, further raising compensation (higher pay and better benefits) will attract more people with better education to enter this profession. This would improve the social status of people working in this industry, which in turn would improve the reputation of the profession, thereby creating a virtuous circle for the growth of aged care professionals.

Better compensation for the aged care industry will not only attract more people to become trained caregivers but will also attract more clinicians to work in aged care. Based on provincial reports in response to *Several Opinions of the State Council on Accelerating Development of the Aged Care Industry* (2013), 14 provinces view the shortage of caregivers capable of providing skilled care services as one of the main issues faced by the aged care industry (China Philanthropy Research Institute 2015). In particular, aged care facilities face shortages of clinicians such as medical staff, skilled nurses, social workers, dietitians, rehabilitation therapists, and counseling psychologists. Home- and community-based service agencies face the same challenge; most of them only focus on non-skilled services such as homemaking and meal delivery.

Finally, policy makers in China could act more forcefully on the "power of the purse" which, if used creatively, could be effective in incentivizing providers in regulatory compliance and quality improvements. The review of international experiences revealed that quality assurance for aged care is particularly challenging where public financing of such care is limited and the government thus has little stake or incentive to strengthen regulatory oversight and where providers have little reason to comply with government requirements. Therefore, the more the Chinese government has at stake (with increased public financing in the aged care service sector), the better positioned it will be to demand greater quality assurance and more effective regulatory oversight.

References

Beijing Municipal Administration of Quality and Technology Supervision. 2005. *Star-Rating Standard of Institution for the Aged* 养老机构星级划分与评定. Beijing Municipal Administration of Quality and Technology Supervision 北京市质量技术监督局, Beijing, China (accessed March 8, 2014), http://www.bjtsb.gov.cn/UPLOAD/20130220/201322083320422.pdf.

Castle, N. 2009. "The Nursing Home Compare Report Card: Consumers' Use and Understanding." *Journal of Aging & Social Policy* 21 (2): 187–208.

Centers for Medicare and Medicaid Services. 2015a. *Proposed Fiscal Year 2016 Payment and Policy Changes for Medicare Skilled Nursing Facilities* (accessed May 23, 2015), http://www.cms.gov/Newsroom/MediaReleaseDatabase/Fact-sheets/2015-Fact-sheets-items/2015-04-15.html.

———. 2015b. *State Operations Manual Appendix PP—Guidance to Surveyors for Long Term Care Facilities* (accessed March 16, 2014), http://www.cms.gov/Regulations-and-Guidance/Guidance/Manuals/downloads/som107ap_pp_guidelines_ltcf.pdf.

———. 2015c. *State Operations Manual Chapter 2—The Certification Process* (accessed March 16, 2014), http://www.cms.gov/Regulations-and-Guidance/Guidance/Manuals/downloads/som107c02.pdf.

Chen, Q. 2011. "京养老机构开展星级评定 分五级最高奖32万元." Sohu News (accessed March 8, 2014), http://news.sohu.com/20110604/n309303595.shtml.

China Philanthropy Research Institute. 2015. "The Demand on Elderly Care Service Is Large; Policy Improvement and Practice Is Urgently Needed." ("老年照护服务需求巨大，亟待政策完善与行动力") (accessed May 9, 2015), http://www.pubchn.com/news/show.php?itemid=84761.

China Society News. 2010. "Promote the Development of Elderly Service Industry by Informatization—Introduction to Contruction Project of National Social Elderly Service Information System 冯晓丽:" ("以信息化带动养老服务业发展—《国家社会养老服务信息系统建设项目》介绍"). China Society News (accessed May 9, 2015), http://shfl.mca.gov.cn/article/xgbd/201011/20101100115932.shtml.

Chinanews. 2012. "Beijing Selects Five-Star Elderly Care Institute for the First Time, the Winners Are Given 320,000 RMB as Bonus" ("北京评选首批五星级养老院 获奖金32–万元"). Chinanews (accessed March 8, 2014), http://www.chinanews.com/sh/2012/10-23/4270838.shtml.

Commission for Social Care Inspection. 2009. *Commission for Social Care Inspection Annual Report and Accounts* 2008–09. Care Quality Commission (CQC), London, U.K. (accessed March 8, 2014), https://www.gov.uk/government/uploads/system/uploads/attachment_data/file/250486/0664.pdf.

Donabedian, A. 2005. "Evaluating the Quality of Medical Care." *Milbank Quarterly* 83 (4): 691–729.

Feng, Z., X. Guan, X. Feng, C. Liu, H. Zhan, and V. Mor. 2014. "Long-Term Care in China: Reining in Market Forces through Regulatory Oversight." In *Regulating Long-Term Care Quality: An International Comparison*, edited by V. Mor, T. Leone, and A. Maresso. Cambridge, U.K.: Cambridge University Press.

Feng, Z., H. J. Zhan, X. Feng, C. Liu, M. Sun, and V. Mor. 2011. "An Industry in the Making: The Emergence of Institutional Elder Care in Urban China." *Journal of American Geriatrics Society* 59 (4): 738–44.

Garms-Homolova, V., and R. Busse. 2014. "Monitoring the Quality of Long-Term Care in Germany." In *Regulating Long-Term Care Quality: An International Comparison*, edited by V. Mor, T. Leone, and A. Maresso. Cambridge, U.K.: Cambridge University Press.

Gray, L., D. Cullen, and H. Lomas. 2014. "Regulating Long-Term Care Quality in Australia." In *Regulating Long-Term Care Quality: An International Comparison*, edited by V. Mor, T. Leone, and A. Maresso. Cambridge, U.K.: Cambridge University Press.

Ikegami, N., T. Ishibashi, and T. Amano. 2014. "Japan's Long-Term Care Regulations Focused on Structure—Rationale and Future Prospects." In *Regulating Long-Term Care Quality: An International Comparison*. V. Mor, T. Leone, and A. Maresso. Cambridge, U.K.: Cambridge University Press.

Liu, C., Z. Feng, and V. Mor. 2014. "Case-Mix and Quality Indicators in Chinese Elder Care Homes: Are there Differences between Government-Owned and Private-Sector Facilities?" *Journal of American Geriatrics Society* 62 (2): 371–77.

Malley, J., J. Holder, R. Dodgson, and S. Booth. 2014. "Regulating the Quality and Safety of Long-Term Care in England." In *Regulating Long-Term Care Quality: An International Comparison*. V. Mor, T. Leone, and A. Maresso. Cambridge, U.K.: Cambridge University Press.

Miller, S., J. Looze, R. Shield, M. Clark, M. Lepore, D. Tyler, S. Sterns, and V. Mor. 2013. "Culture Change Practice in U.S. Nursing Homes: Prevalence and Variation by State Medicaid Reimbursement Policies." *The Gerontologist* 54 (3): 434–45.

MOCA (Ministry of Civil Affairs of the PRC). 2007. *National Professional Standards for Senior Care Caregivers 养老护理员国家职业标准* (accessed May 9, 2015), http://fss.mca.gov.cn/article/ywbz/200712/20071200005097.shtml.

———. 2011. *National Professional Standards for Senior Care Caregivers 2011 养老护理员国家职业标准 2011年版* (accessed May 9, 2015), http://www.sdmz.gov.cn/articles/ch00237/201210/376eaf1e-2b1b-47ed-b121-03bc24186160.htm.

———. 2013. *Ability Assessment for Older Adults ("老年人能力评估")* (accessed March 8, 2014) http://www.mca.gov.cn/article/zwgk/tzl/201306/20130600473269.shtml.

Mollica, R., K. Sims-Kastelein, and J. O'Keeffe. 2007. *Residential Care and Assisted Living Compendium: 2007* (accessed May 20, 2015), http://aspe.hhs.gov/daltcp/reports/2007/07alcom.pdf.

OECD/European Union. 2013. *A Good Life in Old Age? Monitoring and Improving Quality in Long-Term Care, OECD Health Policy Studies*. Paris: OECD Publishing.

PHI. Undated. "Quality Care Through Quality Jobs." (accessed May 22, 2015), http://phinational.org/policy/issues/training-credentialing/training-requirements-state/personal-care-aide-training.

Rabig, J., W. Thomas, R. Kane, L. Cutler, and S. McAlilly. 2006. "Radical Redesign of Nursing Homes: Applying the Green House Concept in Tupelo, Mississippi." *The Gerontologist* 46 (4): 533–39.

Stevenson, D., and J. Bramson. 2014. "Regulation of Long-Term Care in the United States." In *Regulating Long-Term Care Quality: An International Comparison*, edited by V. Mor, T. Leone, and A. Maresso. Cambridge, U.K.: Cambridge University Press.

Thomas, W. 2003. "Evolution of Eden." In *Culture Change in Long-Term Care*, edited by A. S. Weiner and J. L. Ronch. New York: Hawthorn Press.

Totten, A. M., J. Wagner, A. Tiwari, C. O'Haire, J. Griffin, and M. Walker 2012. "Public Reporting as a Quality Improvement Strategy. Closing the Quality Gap: Revisiting the

State of the Science." Rockville, MD: Agency for Healthcare Research and Quality. http://www.effectivehealthcare.ahrq.gov/search-for-guides-reviews-and-reports/?pageaction=displayproduct&productID=1198.

Werner, R., R. Konetzka, and G. Kruse. 2009. "Impact of Public Reporting on Unreported Quality of Care." *Health Services Research* 44 (2 Pt 1): 379–98.

Werner, R., R. Konetzka, and D. Polsky. 2013. "The Effect of Pay-for-Performance in Nursing Homes: Evidence from State Medicaid Programs." *Health Services Research* 48 (4): 1393–414.

White, A., A. Laberge, E. Axelrod, and A. Edwards. 2013. *Implementation of Nursing Home Value Based Purchasing Demonstration—Year 2 Experience*. AcademyHealth Annual Research Meeting, Baltimore, MD.

Wiener, J. M. 2011. "Long-Term Care Financing, Service Delivery and Quality Assurance: The International Experience." In *Handbook of Aging and the Social Sciences*, edited by R. Binstock and L. George. London: Elsevier, Washington, DC.

Wiener, J. M., M. P. Freiman, and D. Brown. 2007a. *Strategies for Improving the Quality of Long-Term Care*. Washington, DC: National Commission for Quality Long-Term Care. http://www.newschool.edu/ltcc/pdf/NCQLTC_QualityReport_RTI_Final.pdf.

Wiener, J., J. Tilly, A. Howe, C. Doyle, A. Cuellar, J. Campbell, and N. Ikegami. 2007b. *Quality Assurance for Long-Term Care: The Experiences of England, Australia, Germany and Japan*. Prepared for American Association of Retired Persons, Washington, DC.

Xinhua Net. 2013. "Retiree Entertainment Center Arson Kills 2 in E China." Xinhua (accessed March 8, 2014), http://usa.chinadaily.com.cn/china/2013-07/28/content_16842715.htm.

Yip, W., T. Powell-Jackson, W. Chen, M. Hu, E. Fe, M. Hu, W. Jian, M. Lu, W. Han, and W. Hsiao. 2014. "Capitation Combined with Pay-for-Performance Improves Antibiotic Prescribing Practices in Rural China." *Health Affairs* 33 (3): 502–10.

Zhu, H. 2012. "Private Organizations and Home and Community Based Aged Care—Examples from Shanghai and Hangzhou 民营机构介入社区老年照护服务的经验研究." *Journal of Zhejiang Shuren University: Humanities and Social Science* (3): 1671–2714.

CHAPTER 8

Coordination of Services within Long-Term Care and between Medical Care and Long-Term Care

Chang Liu

In November 2015, the Chinese central government issued national guidelines for integrating medical and social care. The guidelines set an ambitious goal of making all elder care facilities capable of providing medical/health care by 2020. This gives rise to a number of questions: How can China move from the current situation of having very little medical care available in most elder care facilities to a coordinated and integrated elder care system? What are the major challenges in terms of financing, workforce development, and system engineering? Even in countries with well-developed long-term care systems, fragmentation of services and lack of coordination across service providers remain common problems.

This chapter focuses on the coordination and integration of services, both within the long-term care sector and between medical/health care and long-term care services. It begins by introducing the concept of care coordination and describing international experiences. The chapter then discusses the main challenges and constraints China faces in building an integrated care system for the elderly at this early stage of development, particularly in the long-term care sector.

Care Coordination: The Characteristics of Integrated Care Systems

According to the U.S. Agency for Healthcare Research and Quality (AHRQ), care coordination is defined as "deliberately organizing patient care activities and sharing information among all of the participants concerned with a patient's care to achieve safer and more effective care." For both primary care and elder care practice, this means that "the patient's needs and preferences are known ahead

---

Chang Liu is a Managing Director for East and Southeast Asia at ACCESS Health International and an Assistant Professor at Duke-NUS Graduate Medical School.

of time and communicated at the right time to the right people, and that this information is used to provide safe, appropriate, and effective care to the patient" (U.S. Department of Health and Human Services 2015).

The concepts of integrated care and continuity of care are closely related to care coordination (Armitage et al. 2009; Shaw, Rosen, and Rumbold 2011). The World Health Organization (WHO) defines integrated care as "a concept bringing together inputs, delivery, management and organization of services related to diagnosis, treatment, care, rehabilitation, and health promotion." (WHO 2012). There are at least two levels of integrated care: integrated health care for the whole population (macro-level integration) and coordinating care for individual patients when the care team involves two or more participants (micro-level integration) (Pike and Mongan 2014). Care coordination and integration are means to achieving patient-centered care and to improving services in terms of access, quality, user satisfaction, and efficiency. Continuity of care is defined along three dimensions: (1) informational (through information exchange); (2) management (delivering consistent and apt care to the patient spanning across different care settings as needed); and (3) relational (ensuring that the necessary provider-patient relationship is maintained across the health care settings).

Curry and Ham (2010) identify nine characteristics of a macro-level integrated system of health care (box 8.1). These characteristics are relevant to the broad integrative processes around clinical services, organization, finance, information and communication technologies, and norms.

Box 8.1 Characteristics of an Integrated Care System

- Multispecialty medical groups in which generalists work alongside specialists to deliver integrated care
- Aligned financial incentives that avoid the perverse effects of fee-for-service reimbursement, encouraging the prudent use of resources and promoting quality improvement
- Information technology that supports the delivery of integrated care, especially via the electronic medical record and the use of clinical decision support systems
- The use of guidelines to promote best practice and reduce unwarranted variations in care
- Accountability for performance through the use of data to improve quality and account to stakeholders through public reporting
- Defined populations that enable doctors and the wider health care team to develop a relationship over time with a "registered" population
- A physician-management partnership that links the clinical skills of health care professionals and the organizational skills of executives
- Effective leadership at all levels, with a focus on continuous quality improvement
- A collaborative culture that emphasizes teamwork and the delivery of patient-centred care

Source: Curry and Ham 2010.

Care Coordination for an Aging Population

Reasons for Care Coordination

An aging population is one of the key drivers reshaping health care systems all over the world. The presence of multiple disease conditions and frailty of their physical being makes the elderly complex cases, which require treatment and care at various health care and social service settings and specialties (Leichsenring 2004). Ensuring care coordination and continuity of care in medical care and long-term care is necessary for the elderly as it enhances the quality of care and patient experience and is more cost-effective, as described below.

- First, care coordination improves the quality of care. Providing transitional and long-term care services in the community and promoting primary care and preventive care are necessary for proper disease management. Sometimes the elderly need specialized care, and failure to get timely treatment can lead to scenarios like unnecessary hospitalization for a prolonged duration or deterioration in the quality of life. Fragmentation of care—whether primary, secondary, or even social—adversely affects the care delivered to the elderly with complex needs, and it poses a serious deterrent to treating patients appropriately at health care settings other than acute care hospitals. (Spoorenberg et al. 2013). Integrating health and social care services is necessary to reduce the fragmentation of services that leads to gaps in care and to replace this with a system in which services are coordinated around the patient. Care coordination programs have been shown to have a positive impact on health outcomes (including quality of life, independence, functionality, and general well-being) as well as patient satisfaction and user experiences.
- Second, care coordination improves the quality of life for both elders and their caregivers. Taking care of an elderly person is a stressful proposition, as it is usually associated with appointments with multiple health professionals and caring locations and lasts a long period of time. The number of elderly living alone is increasing while the availability of informal caregivers is decreasing. Even when there is a family to look after the elderly, the family may not be able to devote as much time and resources as are necessary to care for them. This means that the demand for elder care services as well as the stress level for caregivers are both rising (Coyte, Goodwin, and Laporte 2008). Care coordination supports safer and more effective care, relieves caregiver pressure, and improves communication among elders, family caregivers, and professional service providers. Empirically, Curry and Ham (2010) report evidence that care coordination is beneficial for individual service users and caregivers, especially when several different approaches are used together.
- Third, service coordination and integration relieves pressure on acute hospitals and reduces financial costs placed on public resources. In the United States, around 20 percent of Medicare patients are re-admitted within one month of being discharged from the hospital (Rennke, Nguyen, and Shoeb 2013). In Singapore, the proportion of public hospital admissions

from the elderly, age 65 and older, has increased from 28.6 percent in 2006, to 33.4 percent in 2013 (Ministry of Health 2014). The majority of these hospitalizations are preventable, but it is very common that patients were not discharged due to the absence of a caregiver at home or lack of an appropriate facility to which the elderly could be handed. These avoidable hospitalizations put very high pressure on current acute hospital-centric health care systems and contribute to soaring health care expenditures. Better-coordinated care allows the elderly to receive timely treatment to avoid unnecessary hospitalization or other adverse events as well as improves the efficiency of the health care system.

Challenges for Care Coordination among Aged Care Services

Nolte and McKee (2008) describe the relationship between the level of needs of a target population and the ideal type and intensity of care integration. For elderly care users who are more likely to have long-term, severe, and unstable conditions, "a fully integrated system that would assume responsibility for all services, resources and funding, which may be subsumed in one managed structure or through contractual agreements between different organizations" would be beneficial.

While aged care requires the highest level of integration, a common challenge in many countries' health care systems and long-term care delivery systems is lack of integration of different services across different programs or settings, both within long-term care and across acute medical care and long-term care. This leads to fragmented care for older people for whom both may be necessary. One of the main reasons is that in most countries, the provision and regulation of long-term care is separate from the health care system, even though the lines are not always clear-cut (King's Fund 2014). For example, in China, the main regulatory body of long-term care services is the Ministry of Civil Affairs, while health care services are under the supervision of the National Health and Family Planning Commission.

For elder care financing, the fragmentation of programs, services, and benefits for long-term care recipients contributes to misaligned incentives such as cost shifting between payers and providers. It also increases the cost to the individuals and to society. Among the few countries that offer public long-term care insurance (Germany, Japan, and the Republic of Korea), long-term care insurance is operated separately from the health insurance system.

Care Integrative Processes and International Experiences

The Integrative Processes

Integration of different kinds of services is usually rather complex. First, services and manpower should be available. Second, these services must be able to be connected somehow through both physical and informational links and financial incentives. Third, systematic and normative goals and values are necessary so that

Box 8.2 Six Categories of Care Integrative Processes

1. Systemic—The coordinating and aligning policies, rules, and regulatory frameworks
2. Organizational—The coordinating structures, governance systems, and relationships across different organizations
3. Clinical/service—How care services are coordinated
4. Informational—The clinical and managerial information systems to support practice across different care settings
5. Financial—The budgetary and payment systems in place across the participating organizations
6. Normative—The extent to which mission, work values, etc. are shared within a system

important system engineering can be implemented. It is even more challenging when the task is to coordinate between social care and health care services, which usually have totally different regulatory frameworks, are under different organizations, are provided by different professionals, and use different financing and payment models.

Previous published studies describe the general guidelines for integrating health and social care services. At the macro level, the Nuffield Trust, King's Fund, the European Observatory, and the Canadian Policy Research Networks have all identified the same broad categories of integrative processes (box 8.2) and similar broad approaches—by merging systems, sharing clinical standards or values, or bringing structures, services, or some functions together (Nolte and McKee 2008; Curry and Ham 2010; Shaw, Rosen, and Rumbold 2011; Pike and Mongan 2014).

The Nuffield Trust report also found interactions among organizational, clinical, informational, and financial integrative processes. The interactions among governance arrangements, financial incentives, and clinical information were particularly notable (figure 8.1).

At the micro level, when coordinating care for individual patients, a "person-centered" focus is even more important than the structures, organizations, or pathways. The "experiential" dimension needs to receive the same attention as the dimensions of quality and cost-effectiveness (Frontier Economics 2012).

In translating the general guidelines to real practice to achieve both macro- and micro-level care integration, usually the normative integrative mission and person-centered emphasis need to come first. At the same time, strong leadership, consistent communication, and very practical procedures are needed.

International Experience and Case Studies

Most Organisation for Economic Co-operation and Development (OECD) countries have created coordination tasks or assigned responsibilities to guide

Figure 8.1 Interplay among the Six Integrative Processes

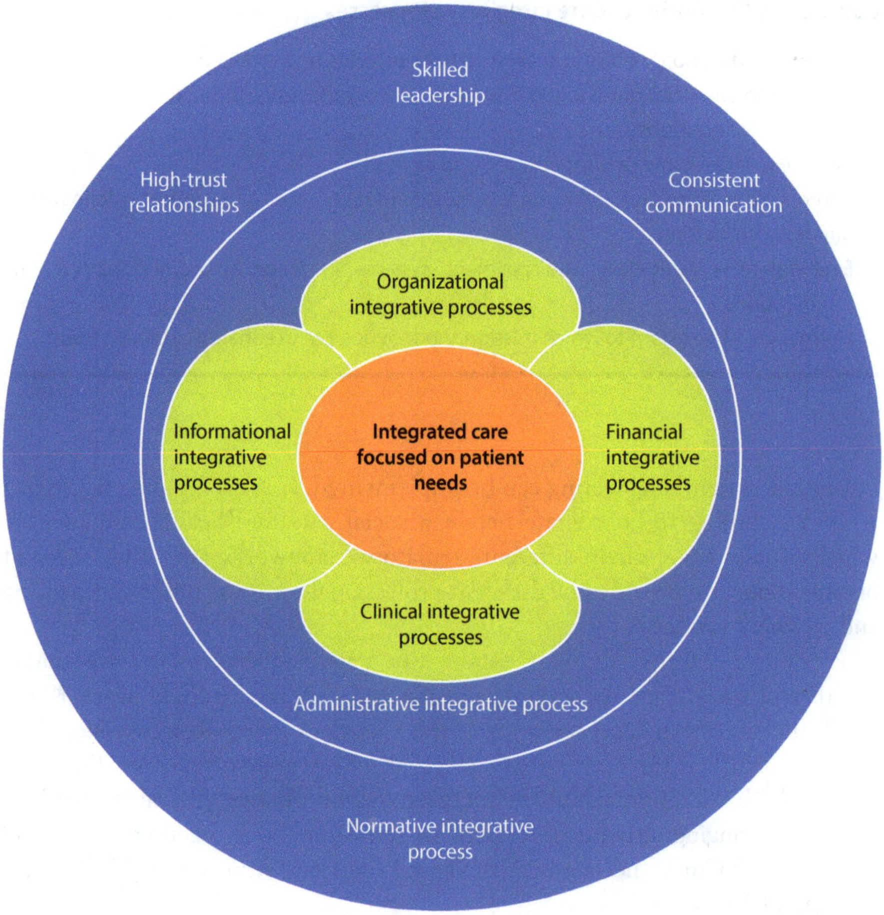

users through the care process, including different categories of care integrative processes (OECD 2011):

- *Systemic*: initiating national mechanisms or centrally set regulations or guidelines (e.g., Norway, the United Kingdom, the United States);
- *Organizational*: the use of dedicated governance structures for care coordination (e.g., Belgium, France, Singapore, Japan)
- *Clinical/service*: the allocation of care coordination responsibilities to providers (e.g., Australia, France, Sweden) or care managers (e.g., Japan, Germany, Denmark, the United Kingdom)
- *Informational*: mechanisms (websites or agencies) to provide individuals with single points of access to long-term care information (e.g., Canada, Singapore)
- *Financial*: coordination between payment systems across the participating organizations (e.g., United States under the Affordable Care Act)

This section briefly describes relevant international examples of care coordination within long-term care services or between long-term care and medical care services. The six categories of care integrative processes are used as a framework for these case studies.

United States (Medicare and Medicaid)

In the United States, the federal Medicare program, which provides health insurance (including hospital insurance, medical insurance, and prescription drug coverage) for people aged 65 or older and younger people with certain disabilities, covers limited post-acute care at nursing homes and home health agencies. Medicaid, a federal-state jointly funded, means-tested insurance program for low-income people, covers a broad array of long-term care services, although the coverage varies by state (Grabowski 2007, 2012). For dually eligible individuals, Medicare pays for acute care services, while Medicaid pays for long-term care services.

For low-income elderly or disabled, the medical and social services are actually both reimbursed by the government. However, the services are not well-integrated due to the misaligned incentives created by different payment schemes. In the past, the health care providers and long-term care providers in the United States did not need to coordinate their work. Under the Affordable Care Act, to reduce costs and improve care coordination for this population group, several "integration" interventions have been suggested (table 8.1).

An important feature of the Affordable Care Act is the creation of Accountable Care Organizations (ACOs). This is an important transformation in organizational structure and models of care, aimed at improving care coordination among a broad range of health care providers, benefiting patients, and minimizing inefficiencies. It also creates financial incentives for providers to collaborate with private insurers and specifically focus on preventing chronic diseases, improving transitions between caregivers, and avoiding preventable hospital re-admissions. Under the new reimbursement models, providers would share savings achieved by eliminating unnecessary expenses and improving quality (OECD 2011).

Table 8.1 "Integration" Interventions for Medicare and Medicaid (United States)

Systemic	Affordable Care Act
Organizational	The creation of a new Medicare-Medicaid Coordination Office under the Affordable Care Act, with the express purpose of aligning the two programs
Clinical/service	Federal managed care initiatives: Social Health Maintenance Organization (S/HMO), Programs of All-Inclusive Care for the Elderly (PACE); Medicare Advantage Special Needs Plans (SNPs) like the Evercare Program; Accountable Care Organizations (ACOs)
Informational	—
Financial	The creation of a new Medicare-Medicaid Coordination Office; ACOs
Normative	—

Note: — indicates not applicable.

United States (Veterans Health Administration—VA)

The Veterans Health Administration (VA) employs physicians, owns and runs hospitals and medical offices, and manages services within a budget allocated by the federal government. The VA focuses on older people, often with complex needs. The setup of the VA system has the benefit of a very clearly defined patient population and a powerful organizational structure overseeing different kinds of services in the region. The strong culture of providing all-inclusive care for the patients, as well as measurement and reporting powered by one of the best and integrated health care IT systems, and the capitation payment models are also key elements of providing coordinated health and social care to the population (table 8.2).

United Kingdom

In the United Kingdom, long-term care services coordination is primarily at the national level, where regulations are put in place. Local authorities are also making improvements and shaping new developments based on the needs of each community.

Established in 2005, Torbay Care Trust in England is contracted by the Torbay Council to provide all social care functions for the local council. The objective is to improve the integration and coordination of older people's health and social care. The target population is the highest-risk individuals who require intensive support from community matrons and integrated teams. As shown in table 8.3, the Torbay Care Trust uses most of the key processes in creating coordinated services for the population to which it caters.

In a formal evaluation study with a before-and-after comparison of resource use and comparison with other areas, Torbay had the lowest use of hospital bed days in the region and the best performance in terms of length of stay. The use of residential care and of nursing homes was reduced, while the use of home care services increased.

Table 8.2 Veterans Health Administration (United States)

Systemic	Comprised of regionally based integrated service networks rather than a fragmented hospital-centered system
Organizational	21 networks, each having its own responsibility for resources across all care settings; network managers are held accountable through a rigorous accountability structure and performance regimen
Clinical/service	Introduced patient-centered care coordination, which has sought to rationalize and unify care and to ensure that care is provided when the patient requires it
Informational	Investment in IT has enabled effective data sharing; promotion of consistent high-quality care through the dissemination of evidence-based guidelines, decision support tools, and physician alerts
Financial	Resources allocated on a capitation basis to each network
Normative	A strong culture of measurement and reporting has been developed, allowing for comparison between regional networks

Source: Curry and Ham 2010.

Norway

The Norwegian government issued policy suggestions to improve long-term care coordination, including better defining priorities, focusing on early intervention, changing the funding system, developing specialist health care services, and introducing new information technology and education for long-term care professionals.

Specifically, in order to increase patient involvement and improve efficiency and quality of care (both medical and social), the Norwegian government introduced a law on individuals having the right to an individual care plan (table 8.4). At a national level, this enables patients to get their own individualized care plan, managed and coordinated by health professionals. The law is directed at improving the care continuum for patients with difficult conditions, so it typically involves individuals with co-morbidities, elderly patients, or people with severe psychiatric diagnoses.

Sweden

In Sweden, county councils had responsibility for general hospitals, primary health care, and psychiatric care, while responsibility for care of the elderly rested with the municipalities. The different administrations and budgets created challenges for coordinating health and social care services. In the 1980s, "chains of care" were introduced, with the objective of improving integration between the

Table 8.3 Torbay Care Trust (United Kingdom)

Systemic	—
Organizational	Five integrated health and social care teams organized in zones or localities aligned with general practices
Clinical/service	Each of the five teams is co-located and has a single manager and single point of contact and uses a single assessment process
Informational	Patient-held records are accessible to any professional involved in the patient's care, which helps in coordinating care across care settings
Financial	A pooled health and social care budget is used to commission whatever care is required to provide packages of care for service users
Normative	The key focus for all teams is knowing their population and proactively managing the care of the most vulnerable in partnership with general practitioners

Source: Thistlethwaite 2011.
Note: — indicates not applicable.

Table 8.4 Individual Care Plan (Norway)

Systemic	Law on individuals having the right to an individual care plan
Organizational	—
Clinical/service	The plan is created through a collaborative process involving the patient and his/her social and medical provider and could also involve other key individuals
Informational	—
Financial	—
Normative	—

Source: Bjerkan et al. 2011.

health services of the county councils and the social services of the municipalities (table 8.5). Defined as "a concept of integration and collaboration in health care, which includes all the services provided for a specific group of patients within a defined geographical area," "chains of care" were also designed to improve the collaboration between health professionals and social workers.

In recent years, the Swedish government has developed a safe-care continuum especially for elderly with complex health problems and severe needs. As this group of frail elderly is a major user of long-term care services, targeting this group is a key element of a cost-effective strategy.

Finland

The municipality is the main provider of social services for the Finnish population, while private home care providers serve a small population on a local scale. Their services are now tax-deductible to reach underserved elderly. The elderly have always needed to contact both public and private home care providers to get all the care services they needed. The Finnish city of Tampere initiated a program called "Kotitori," translating to *home market,* as a model of integrating public and private home care for the elderly (table 8.6).

Table 8.5 Chains of Care (Sweden)

Systemic	—
Organizational	A "coordinated network" in which financial and clinical responsibilities of the different parties remain separate, and there are not usually binding contracts regulating the activities performed; the "chain" involves several responsible authorities and medical providers for a specific patient group within a county council area
Clinical/service	Chains of care are based on evidence-based health care and clinical guidelines, that is, agreements on distribution of medical work, within a county council area, between different providers of health care
Informational	—
Financial	—
Normative	Chains of care have become the building blocks of local health care, while benefiting from being embedded in such an integrative context

Sources: Ahgren 2003; Karlberg 2008; Ahgren and Axelsson 2011.
Note: — indicates not applicable.

Table 8.6 Home Market (Finland)

Systemic	—
Organizational	A hub connecting public and private home care providers is created, which acts as an accessible one-stop shop for elderly and their spouses to get a clear overview of the available options
Clinical/service	The elderly then get assistance from Kotitori case managers in choosing the most appropriate home care service(s)
Informational	The home market; regional health information exchange systems (RHIE)
Financial	—
Normative	Instead of getting standardized care packages, the elderly are guaranteed a personalized care service package based on their needs

Sources: Tynkkynen et al. 2012; Hyppönen et al. 2013.
Note: — indicates not applicable.

Singapore

Laid down in the National Health Plan of Singapore are the virtues of individual responsibility and familial piety. The government has designed policies to encourage and drive the message that individuals need to take care of themselves. Acute care hospitals have received the greatest attention thus far, while health care settings like nursing homes, community hospitals, and residential settings had been left within the purview of private and voluntary welfare organizations.

With the realization that the population is rapidly aging and that integration of care and continuity of care are crucial to ensuring the delivery of good care to the elderly, the government has undertaken a number of steps in this direction. While acute care must remain a significant part of the health care delivery system, the growing demands of an aging population have made the current hospital-centric model unsustainable. Currently, all six public hospital clusters in Singapore are under a system-wide transformation into a Regional Healthcare Systems model, described in table 8.7, to better integrate care services under one roof.

Singapore's Agency for Integrated Care (AIC), also described in table 8.7, was created in 2009 to bring about a patient-focused integration of primary, intermediate, and long-term care. The agency operates at all levels: patient, provider, and system. It works to have the providers at all levels coordinate their efforts on behalf of the patient. The agency provides advice to patients and families regarding appropriate health care services and helps them navigate the system. An example of the issues it is addressing is the follow-up treatment of chronic disease patients after discharge from the hospital. In addition, one of the agency's main initiatives seeks to expand and improve health care capabilities at the community level.

Another significant role for the AIC is ensuring integration of health and social care services for elderly and disabled populations. The agency coordinates and facilitates the placement of sick elderly people in nursing homes, with community providers, in day rehabilitation centers, and in long-term care facilities, as well as facilitating treatment in their own homes by managing referrals to home care services. The agency also actively helps people in this "vulnerable" population apply for available financial assistance. The relevant funding sources are pooled and administered under the Health Ministry and AIC.

Table 8.7 Regional Health Care System and Agency for Integrated Care (Singapore)

Systemic	The Agency for Integrated Care (AIC) was created in 2009 to bring about a patient-focused integration of primary, intermediate, and long-term care
Organizational	Under the regional health care systems (RHS) model, hospitals will work in close partnership with other health care providers within the region such as community hospitals, nursing homes, general practitioners, and home care providers
Clinical/service	Regional hospitals are developing care coordination programs with care coordinators to connect to other health care settings spanning the care spectrum
Informational	AIC; the Agency maintains a website called "the silver page" as an integrated information hub for elder care services
Financial	—
Normative	—

Sources: Haseltine 2013; Liu and Haseltine 2014; Liu, Bhasker, and Haseltine 2014.
Note: — indicates not applicable.

Currently, special grants are available for health and social care providers to work together and try out new solutions. Policy makers are also considering models of bundled or capitated payment.

Japan and Thailand

The Japanese government tries to integrate long-term care and health care, with a primary emphasis on community-based care. A general practitioner's assessment is required as part of the long-term care triage process. There are maximum separate monthly out-of-pocket payment ceilings for long-term care and health care but also another ceiling for those with high expenditures in both long-term care and medical care combined (OECD 2011).

Thailand has also piloted service models that integrate health and social care: the "Bangkok Model" and the "Community-Based Integrated Services of Health Care and Social Welfare" for the elderly. These pilots involve collaboration between local authorities, volunteers, and older people. The "home health care" scheme is another pilot through 26 local hospitals targeted at older people living at home. Services provided include health promotion, treatment, and rehabilitation.

Characteristics of Successful Systems

Alltimes et al. (2012) interviewed patients, caregivers, commissioners, and providers in the United Kingdom and described what characteristics a successful integrated system should have (box 8.3). It emphasizes the importance of micro-level integration—to provide patient-centric care systems and improve

---

Box 8.3 Characteristics of Successful Integrated Systems

- Integrate around people, not pathways—Integration is only valuable if it improves experience and outcomes for the individual.
- Patients and caregivers are key drivers of integration—Patients and caregivers are often the most passionate advocates of integration and the most effective agents for delivering it.
- Patients and communities are part of the solution—Local communities need to be supported to design and deliver their own solutions to local needs. When communities feel empowered to make the most of their own resources, they can provide highly innovative solutions to plug gaps in existing services, reduce inequalities, and help more people receive care closer to home.
- Make it easier to navigate and coordinate care—From the patient's perspective, the biggest obstacle to receiving excellent care is the challenge of navigating the health and social care system and coordinating multiple different services.
- Information is a key enabler of integration—Full and accurate information about a patient's needs and care must be available throughout the care journey to everyone involved, including the patient.

Source: Alltimes 2012.

---

the experiences of both patients and caregivers. While systemic, organizational, clinical, informational, financial, and normative measures are crucial, the ultimate measures of a successful coordinated system are always patient experiences and outcomes.

Care Coordination in Chinese Medical Care and Long-Term Care Systems

China is aging at an unprecedented rate, and the increasing numbers of elderly will bring with them more chronic diseases—diabetes, cardiovascular conditions, Parkinson's, dementia, and many more—and the need to treat and care for them on an ongoing basis. There will be an increasing need for rehabilitation care, intermediate and long-term care, and palliative care, supported by various types of elder care facilities in both institutional and community settings. More medical professionals and allied health care staff will be needed to support the infrastructure. Moreover, this will put great financial and emotional stress on the elderly's family members and society.

The Chinese health care systems, which have focused primarily on treating episodic acute care ailments in hospitals, are not well suited for treating the elderly. Currently, long-term care and social services for the elderly are still in early development, while the medical care system is undergoing a major reform process. To achieve higher care quality and efficiency in the aged care system, huge gaps in coordination of services, both within long-term care and across medical care and long-term care, need to be addressed.

Strengthening Primary Care and Care Integration

The concept of care integration is often based on the strong role of primary care as the driver of coordination functions, including gatekeeping. Recent OECD experience suggests an emerging delivery model in which considerable emphasis is placed on primary care (as a gatekeeper and a "case manager"), defined links among providers, and specialized outpatient and day surgical treatment, which reduces the need for inpatient beds. The international trend is toward the transfer of services currently provided in hospitals to community-based ambulatory centers or telemedicine clinics. Rapid advances in information and communication technologies are facilitating this trend. Many of the models described in the previous section (i.e., the United States, the United Kingdom, Sweden, Singapore, Norway, and Japan) have a core focus on the aging population.

Continuity of care, a major tenet of coordinated care, is still in its infancy in China, and there is still very limited cross-referral to ensure that health conditions are managed at the most appropriate and cost-effective level. Competition among hospitals for revenues provides few incentives to coordinate care with primary care units or other hospitals, contributing to "disintegrated" behaviors, such as lack of referrals and follow-up care. The well-recognized poor quality of primary care providers also leads patients to seek care in hospitals.

In 2009, the Chinese government launched a national health care reform program, committing to raise health spending significantly, with the goal of providing affordable, equitable, and effective health care for all by 2020. From coverage of only about 55 percent of the urban population and 21 percent of the rural population in 2003, urban and rural health insurance coverage soared to 89 and 97.5 percent, respectively, by 2011. Significant increases in government subsidies for health insurance have contributed to less out-of-pocket spending, which is a major cause of impoverishment. Benefits have also been expanded gradually. The New Rural Cooperative Medical Scheme (NRCMS) which targets the rural population has become more comprehensive, incrementally adding outpatient benefits while including coverage for specific diseases (e.g., certain cancers, diabetes, hemophilia).

The health care reform is also a realignment of the health care delivery system away from the current hospital-centric model to one that manages care across levels of the system, with primary care providers playing the key role in care coordination. Three key elements of health reform include: re-orienting the delivery system with a greater emphasis on primary and preventive care; reforming health care financing and incentive systems; and deepening reforms of the hospital system. These reforms are needed in light of population aging and the increasing burden of chronic diseases and demand for care. If these reforms succeed, they will help China moving toward a coordinated care approach to the delivery of health services.

Currently, innovative models of integrated care models are being developed and tested as local pilot programs. For example, the "Hospital-Community Healthcare Center (CHC) consortium" model, which establishes a cooperation mechanism between public hospitals and primary health care facilities such as CHCs, has been piloted in several big cities in China, including Beijing, Shenzhen, Zhejiang, and Wuhan (some renowned cases include Beijing Chaoyang Hospital Alliance and Zhenjiang Kangfu Hospital Groups). The objective of this model is to achieve more efficient service utilization through better coordination and clear division of responsibilities between hospitals and CHCs. In 2012, Chengdu government supported a pilot program, the Internet of Things Clinics Project, which focuses on introducing specialty clinics to provide convenient and rapid access to specialized outpatient care for patients residing in urban neighborhoods. This service delivery model provides an alternative to patients seeking outpatient care in hospitals and could potentially improve the capacity of the community-based health care system by making outpatient care more responsive and cost-effective for patients.

Aged care services have two elements, health and social, both of which are important factors to be addressed for ensuring delivery of integrated care to the elderly. Medical care integration is already a huge challenge in China, and on top of overcoming this challenge, policy makers need to think about adding one more layer of integration: integration with social care services. To be affordable and sustainable, the development of aged care services should proceed in close coordination with the ongoing reforms that shape health services provision and utilization. Conversely, the health care reform should take into account expected demographic changes and the fact that the increasing share of elderly in the population will lead to increasing demand for health services.

Interactions with Medical Care or Vertical Integration with Medical Care Services

Vertical integration refers to the coming together of care services at different levels—for example, hospitals, long-term care facilities, rehabilitation, and community-based organizations—to create a single geographically based system for all health and social care services (Kodner and Spreeuwenberg 2002; Nolte and McKee 2008).

To foster vertical integration, the Chinese central government issued government guidelines for integrating medical and social care in the fall of 2015. Important tasks under these national guidelines include: establish and complete collaborative models between the health care and social aged care sectors, support aged care facilities to provide health care services, push health care services to the community and to the households, incentivize the private sector to develop health and social integrated service projects, encourage the development of facilities that provide both health and social services, implement preferable tax and land policies to cultivate the sector, and support manpower development.

On the national level, there will be many systematic and operational challenges in achieving the goals described in the guidelines. For example, one major problem is that there is so little medical/health care currently available in most elder care facilities. Building the infrastructure and providing the necessary devices might not be difficult, but the challenge will be to find and retain qualified medical professionals (physicians and non-physician practitioners). Without substantial financial incentives or career advancement opportunities, diverting health professionals to non-hospital settings will remain extremely difficult. Another challenge is financing and regulation: currently, social and health care services are in general regulated by different governmental functions and under different insurance/public funding schemes. The coordination of health and elder care financing has important implications for how well the services can be integrated.

At the local level, some encouraging regional efforts have been made. For example, the official implementation plan for accelerating development of the aged care industry in Anhui Province specifies several measures to facilitate convergence of aged and health care services, including: (1) health facility mapping process to include the aged care service needs of local residents; (2) new aged care facilities with more than 100 beds can apply for approval to provide medical care services like nursing and rehabilitation care as long as they have dedicated beds for such services, and other aged care facilities with enough resources can also apply for a permit to operate a clinic; (3) development of demonstration areas where aged care, health care, rehabilitation, and hospice care service providers work side by side to encourage the development of integrated care providers; (4) information sharing arrangements among aged care, community service, housekeeping service, health care, and nursing service providers; (5) if their health facilities meet the policy criteria of basic health insurance schemes for urban wage-based workers/urban residents or the NRCMS, they can apply to be a designated service provider so their residents can enjoy the reimbursement policies of these schemes; and (6) health facilities should provide health management services and establish health records for the elderly in their catchment area who are 65 years old and above, giving priority and offering preferential services to the elderly.

Chongqing also facilitates coordination by encouraging aged care institutions to establish facilities that provide the necessary health, medical, and rehabilitation services. Such qualified medical institutions (as in Anhui) are then permitted to apply for inclusion in the Urban Employee Basic Medical Insurance Program (UEBMI), the Urban Resident Basic Medical Insurance Program (URBMI), and the NRCMS.

In Shanghai, the local health department and social services bureau work together closely and with other government agencies like the National Development and Reform Commission and local pension fund office in promoting aged care development and integration into the health care systems. For example, Shanghai piloted a universal needs assessment toolkit, which was developed according to international InterRAI standards in two districts in 2014 then expanded the assessment tool into a citywide policy. It is very useful as it created a unified patient assessment in hospital, community, and elderly home settings and can be used for triage patients, service referrals, and financial assistance or reimbursement.

Horizontal Integration across the Mix of Elder Care Services

Horizontal integration refers to the coordination of care for an individual across different care settings that are at the same level—for example, community-based services such as general practices, community nursing services and social services, mergers of acute hospitals, or the formation of organizations such as care trusts that bring together health and social care (MacAdam 2008; Curry and Ham 2010).

Unique to China, some elder care centers (e.g., in Hangzhou) are not purely residential homes or day care centers but a mixture of these, with elements of "sheltered accommodation" (i.e., housing for older people in a collective setting, with a warden and some shared facilities) as well as outreach services for residents living nearby. This model has not yet reached full development anywhere in China, but the idea is to provide a comprehensive range of services: day care, respite care, meals in house and/or meals on wheels to older people's houses, home care, occupational therapy, physiotherapy, exercise classes, education and social activities, and call in service ("12349" national hotline to provide call-in service, already established in three cities of Henan Province and 11 prefectures/172 counties in Hebei). If it did so, the Chinese model of social care would operate as "a neighborhood resource center" or "support unit" for older people, with some respite beds, specialist nursing provision for people with dementia, and outreach services such as home care, nutrition, and public health advice (physical and mental exercises, falls prevention, hygiene). These facilities would provide a good example for developing a "hub and spoke" model design in which residential facilities are also resource and outreach centers for community-based facilities and home-based programs.

Another recent trend is that many grassroots medical institutions are being converted to community health centers to serve this purpose. By 2005, over 15,000 community health service centers had been set up in Chinese cities, and urban community health services were available in 95 percent of the cities at or above the prefectural level and in 86 percent of the districts under municipal jurisdiction and the county-level cities. These community health centers can also be used to create awareness about health care and hygiene.

By the end of 2005, China had 195,000 urban community service and 8,479 comprehensive social service centers. Family visits, regular service provided at fixed venues, and mobile service are available in most places, providing care and housekeeping services, emergency aid, and other free or reduced-payment services for the aged.

Another major trend in the provision of horizontally integrated elderly services is being driven by the private real estate sector. Real estate developers, insurance companies, and commercial banks are investing in Continued Care Retirement Communities (CCRCs) across major Chinese cities to provide integrated services for the elderly from middle-class and high-income families. Within these large-scale developments (which usually have the capacity to house at least 1,000 and sometimes over 5,000 elderly), a range of aged care social and medical services is provided. As traditional real estate developers usually do not necessarily have the capacity and resources to develop and operate all the needed services, models of collaboration with different service providers and operators within these retirement communities are emerging (also see chapter 4).

Urbanization and Opportunities for Care Integration

Two major shifts are taking place all over the world and will especially be seen in developing economies in the coming decades: urbanization and demographic changes. These two shifts have raised a myriad of issues such as serious environmental pollution and increasing numbers of elderly with chronic diseases.

While China is enjoying rapid economic growth and social progress, the health and well-being of its people and the livability of its urban environment are seriously challenged by urbanization and demographic changes. Rapid industrialization and urbanization have led to increasing urban population density and pollution. In addition, rapid population aging has resulted in an increasing number of chronic disease patients who require constant and lifelong care. This creates a challenge and an opportunity to plan future cities that are designed to accommodate increasing numbers of elderly.

While health care systems are crucial in dealing with the elder care crisis, just focusing on health care is far from enough to ensure that seniors are well cared for and enabled to lead fulfilling lives. Sound urban infrastructure and social services could play vital roles in dealing with these issues. As China is building new cities and expanding its cities in the form of opening "new development zones," it offers unique opportunities to design and implement new infrastructure and organizations, service provision models, financing, and IT systems for providing integrated health care and elder care.

China has many interesting cases in which the private sector partnered with local government to develop a whole new urban area. When building these new cities, local policy makers and stakeholders have the opportunity to test new policies such as innovative land and reimbursement systems, develop the building and IT infrastructures that will facilitate the integration of health and social services, redesign training and human resources, and plan urban environment and transportation designs for "a city for all ages." While there would be many challenges to realizing this vision, the experiences and lessons learned from China's development process would shed light for many other developing economies.

Implications for China's Future

While China is building its aged care sector, ensuring care coordination and continuity both within and across the medical care and long-term care systems is a crucial consideration. Integrated care for the elderly and "person-centered care" put older people themselves in the central role and ask what they need in order to remain at home and autonomous and to raise the quality of their lives. It enhances the quality of care and patient experience and is more cost-effective than the current segregated aged care systems, which tend to operate in their own interest and in ways that are most convenient for the service provider rather than the service user.

Using the six categories of the care integrative process framework, some key points and policy suggestions emerging from the discussion in this chapter are summarized below.

- *Systemic*: Coordinating policies among the various involved ministries and government divisions is crucial for setting up rules and regulatory frameworks and ensuring care integration. In China, the National Development and Reform Commission is in a special position to serve the function of aligning policies and coordinating across ministries. This coordination and long-term thinking are especially important if China wants to seize opportunities for care integration during its urbanization process.
- *Organizational*: The Chinese government might consider different types of vertical and horizontal coordinating structures and governance systems. It can leverage existing resources and programs of services provided to the elderly (e.g., converting grassroots medical institutions into community health centres) as well as the new aged care developments (e.g., CCRCs).
- *Clinical/service*: As the Chinese national health care reform is addressing the need to improve the capacity and quality of primary care providers and general practitioners, it is important to incorporate gatekeeping and case management skills into this workforce development. Creating financial and other

incentives to divert health professionals to non-hospital settings is also critical.

- *Informational*: An integrated information and assessment system is crucial for care coordination for the elderly. As health care information technology innovation is booming in the private sector, the government should direct these new developments in a coordinated and integrated fashion and set national standards. Uniform elderly needs assessments (both health and social) across medical care, long-term care, and community settings (like the Shanghai model) are also useful and should be developed into a national policy.
- *Financial*: China can test new population-based payment models as well as budgetary and payment systems across the participating organizations.
- *Normative*: Instead of just taking the top-down approach, it is important to develop a participatory process to incorporate the feedback and needs of the elderly and caregivers into policy making and new practice model development. Ensuring that older people are treated with dignity and respect is central to person-cantered care, as is the aim of ensuring that older people have a voice in what services are provided.

References

Ahgren, Bengt. 2003. "Chain of Care Development in Sweden: Results of a National Study." *International Journal of Integrated Care* 3: e01. http://www.ncbi.nlm.nih.gov/pmc/articles/PMC1483939/pdf/ijic2003-200301.pdf.

Ahgren, Bengt, and Runo Axelsson. 2011. "A Decade of Integration and Collaboration: The Development of Integrated Health Care in Sweden 2000–2010." *International Journal of Integrated Care* 11: 7.

Alltimes, Geoff. 2012. *Integration: A Report from the NHS Future Forum*. NHS Future Forum, Department of Health, London. www.gov.uk/government/uploads/system/uploads/attachment_data/file/152172/dh_132023.pdf.pdf.

Alltimes, Geoff, and Klaske Wynia. 2013. "Embrace A Model for Integrated Elderly Care: Study Protocol of a Randomized Controlled Trial on the Effectiveness Regarding Patient Outcomes, Service Use, Costs, and Quality of Care." http://www.biomedcentral.com/1471-2318/13/62#B5.

Armitage, Gail D., Esther Suter, Nelly D. Oelke, and Carol E. Adair. 2009. "Health Systems Integration: State of the Evidence." *International Journal of Integrated Care* 9: e82. http://www.ncbi.nlm.nih.gov/pmc/articles/PMC2707589/pdf/ijic2009-200982.pdf.

Bjerkan, Jorunn, Marie Richter, Anders Grimsmo, Ragnhild Helles, and Jytte Brender. 2011. "Integrated Care in Norway: The State of Affairs Years after Regulation by Law." *International Journal of Integrated Care* 11.

Coyte, Peter C., Nick Goodwin, and Audrey Laporte. 2008. "How Can the Settings Used to Provide Care to Older People be Balanced?" Policy brief, WHO Regional Office for Europe, Denmark. www.euro.who.int/__data/assets/pdf_file/0006/73284/E93418.pdf.

Curry, Natasha, and Chris Ham. 2010. *Clinical and Service Integration: The Route to Improved Outcomes*. London: King's Fund. http://www.kingsfund.org.uk/sites/files/kf/Clinical-and-service-integration-Natasha-Curry-Chris-Ham-22-November-2010.pdf.

Frontier Economics. 2012. *Enablers and Barriers to Integrated Care and Implications for Monitor*. A report prepared for Monitor, London. http://www.monitornhsft.gov.uk/sites/default/files/Enablers%20and%20barriers%20to%20integrated%20care%20report%20June%202012.pdf.

Grabowski, D. C. 2007. "Medicare and Medicaid: Conflicting Incentives for Long-Term Care." *Milbank* Q 85(4): 579-610.

Grabowski, D. C. 2012. "Care Coordination for Dually Eligible Medicare-Medicaid Beneficiaries Under the Affordable Care Act." *Journal of Aging and Social Policy* 24(2): 221-32.

Haseltine, William A. 2013. *Affordable Excellence: The Singapore Healthcare Story*. Washington, DC: Brookings Institution Press, April 30. http://www.goodreads.com/book/show/15864076-affordable-excellence.

Hyppönen, Hannele, Jarmo Reponen, Tinja Lääveri, and Johanna Kaipio. 2013. "User Experiences with Different Regional Health Information Exchange Systems in Finland." *International Journal of medical informatics* 83 (1): 1–18. doi:10.1016/j.ijmedinf.2013.10.002.

Karlberg, I. 2008. "Sweden." In *Managing Chronic Conditions: Experience in Eight Countries*. edited by Ellen Nolte, Cécile Knai, and Martin McKee. Copenhagen: World Health Organization on behalf of the European Observatory on Health Systems and Policies. http://www.euro.who.int/__data/assets/pdf_file/0008/98414/E92058.pdf.

Kodner, D., and C. Spreeuwenberg. 2002. "Integrated Care: Meaning, Logic, Applications, and Implications—A Discussion Paper." *International Journal of Integrated Care* 2: e12. http://www.ncbi.nlm.nih.gov/pmc/articles/PMC1480401/pdf/ijic2002-200212.pdf.

Leichsenring, Kai. 2004."Developing Integrated Health and Social Care Services for Older Persons in Europe." *International Journal of Integrated Care.*

Liu, C., and W. A. Haseltine. 2014. "He Singaporean Health System." In *2014 International Profiles for Health Care Systems*, edited by S. Thomson, R. Osborn, and D. Squires. Commonwealth Fund Press.

Liu C., E. Bhasker, and W. A. Haseltine. 2014. "Singapore Healthcare Today: Progress Toward Sustainable High Quality Healthcare, 2013–2104." In *Affordable Excellence: The Singapore Healthcare Story*. Brookings Institution Press with the National University of Singapore Press, November 18.

MacAdam, Margaret. 2008. *Frameworks of Integrated Care for the Elderly: A Systematic Review*. Ottawa: Canadian Policy Research Networks. http://www.cprn.org/documents/49813_EN.pdf.

Ministry of Health. 2014. Press release on "Bed crunch," https://www.moh.gov.sg/content/moh_web/home/pressRoom/Parliamentary_QA/2014/bed-crunch.html.

Nolte, Ellen, and Martin Mckee. 2008. *Caring for People with Chronic Conditions: A Health System Perspective*. Copenhagen: World Health Organization on behalf of the European Observatory on Health Systems and Policies. www.euro.who.int/document/e91878.pdf.

OECD (Organisation for Economic Co-operation and Development) 2011. *Health at a Glance 2011: OECD Indicators*. Paris: OECD.

Pike, Brigid, and Deirdre Mongan. 2014. *The Integration of Health and Social Care Services*. Dublin: Health Research Board. http://www.lenus.ie/hse/handle/10147/315536.

Rennke, S., O. K. Nguyen, M. H. Shoeb, Y. Magan, R. M. Wachter, and S. R. Ranji. 2013. "Hospital-Initiated Transitional Care Interventions as a Patient Safety Strategy." A Systematic Review. *Annals of Internal Medicine* 158 (5, Pt 2): 433–40.

Shaw, Sara, Rebecca Rosen, and Benedict Rumbold. 2011. *An Overview of Integrated Care in the NHS: What Is Integrated Care?* London: Nuffield Trust. http://www.nuffieldtrust.org.uk/sites/files/nuffield/publication/what_is_integrated_care_research_report_june11_0.pdf.

Spoorenberg, Sophie LW, Ronald J Uittenbroek, Berrie Middel, Berry PH Kremer, Sijmen A Reijneveld, and Klaske Wynia. 2013. "Embrace, A Model for Integrated Elderly Care: Study Protocol of a Randomized Controlled Trial on the Effectiveness Regarding Patient Outcomes, Service Use, Costs, and Quality of Care." http://www.biomedcentral.com/1471-2318/13/62#B5.

The King's Fund. 2014. *Providing Integrated Care for Older People with Complex Needs, Lessons from Seven International Case Studies*. Page 2. https://www.kingsfund.org.uk/sites/files/kf/field/field_publication_file/providing-integrated-care-for-older-people-with-complex-needs-kingsfund-jan14.pdf.

Thistlethwaite, Peter. 2011. "Integrating Health and Social Care in Torbay: Improving Care for Mrs Smith." The King's Fund, 11–13 Cavendish Square, London W1G OAN.

Tynkkynen, L-K., K. Hakari, T. Koistinen, J. Lehto, and S. Miettinen. 2012. "Integrating Public and Private Home Care Services: the Kotitori Model in Tampere, Finland." *Journal of Integrated Care* 20(5) 284-95. Doi:10.1108/14769011211270738

U.S. Department of Health and Human Services. 2015. "Prevention and Chronic Care." Agency for Health Care Research and Quality, Washington, DC. http://www.ahrq.gov/professionals/prevention-chronic-care/improve/coordination/index.html.

WHO (World Health Organization). 2012. *Modern Health Care Delivery Systems, Care Coordination and the Role of Hospitals*. Copenhagen: Regional WHO Office for Europe, Copenhagen. http://www.euro.who.int/__data/assets/pdf_file/0008/158885/BRU-report-Modern-health-care-delivery-systems.pdf.

CHAPTER 9

Long-Term Care Workforce Issues

Jiahui Zhang, Elena Glinskaya, Gong Sen, and Shuo Zhang

Introduction

Many countries face a chronic shortage of long-term care workers. Recruiting and retaining direct-care workers in long-term care settings is particularly challenging due to numerous factors, including low pay, low job prestige, few fringe benefits, and a lack of career paths. These positions are often viewed as dead-end jobs characterized by high turnover, low retention, and job dissatisfaction. These workforce challenges are common across Organisation for Economic Co-operation and Development (OECD) countries, and policy efforts aimed to address them abound (Colombo et al. 2011). Unfortunately, there are few successes thus far that can be readily shared and replicated in different countries.

The majority of the long-term care workforce are front-line workers who provide hands-on help with basic activities of daily living such as eating, bathing, dressing, and using the toilet. In all countries, women comprise the majority of these workers, including certified nurse's aides, home health care aides, and home/personal care workers. These front-line workers are generally low-skilled, with minimal training requirements in most countries. In the United States, for example, federal law requires a minimum 75 hours of training or passing a certification exam for a certified nurse aide, although some states have additional requirements.

At the higher end of the skills spectrum, the long-term care workforce also includes a group of licensed health professionals. They include registered nurses, licensed practical/vocational nurses, social workers, physical therapists, occupational therapists, physician assistants/aides, and long-term care facility administrators, who often assume supervising or managerial responsibilities rather than providing direct, hands-on care (Stone and Harahan 2010). Physicians are directly involved in the provision of long-term care in only a few countries, such as the Netherlands.

Jiahui Zhang is a senior researcher at the Development Research Center, State Council, China. Elena Glinskaya is a Lead Economist and Program Leader for Human Development for China, Mongolia, and the Republic of Korea at the World Bank. Gong Sen is an Executive Vice-President, Center for International Knowledge on Development (CIKD), Development Research Center, State Council, China. Shuo Zhang is a Senior Health Specialist at the World Bank.

In China, the shortage of qualified and skilled labor in its current long-term care workforce is particularly acute. The China National Committee on Aging reports that about 80 percent of families seeking long-term care have unmet need. According to national research, the elder care industry needs 10 million care workers, of which a great majority would provide care in institutional care facilities. However, by 2015, China only had roughly 1 million elder care workers and among them, merely 20,000 had received official training. These gaps have major implications for the quantity and quality of care provided, particularly because long-term care is labor-intensive in nature.

This chapter discusses key issues and challenges in developing the long-term care workforce in China, including frontline caregivers as well as health care workers and social workers. It concludes by proposing some priority areas where further effort is needed to strengthen China's long-term care workforce in order to provide quality services that can meet the country's growing demand for elder care.

Current Long-Term Care Workforce Challenges in China

Elder Care Labor Shortages

China is facing a shortage of low-skilled workers in all industries due to a decline in the overall working-age population and rapid urbanization and industrialization of the western and central regions. Surveys of rural workers suggest that only 11 percent would be interested in working in the elder care industry, while most prefer to work in factories or engage in other forms of blue-collar services.

Large disparities exist between the long-term care workforces in rural and urban areas, although labor shortages are a common concern. In urban areas, most skilled care workers work in elder care institutions, while home- and community-based care is provided mainly by non-professional staff. In cities and towns where home- and community-based care is underdeveloped, local community organizations, party members and cadres, and community volunteers often play a role in providing care for the elderly.

The development of elder care in rural areas lags far behind that in urban areas. Few, if any, skilled care workers are found even in rural elder care facilities, much less in home- and community care. Most elder care facilities and welfare centers in rural areas only provide sheltering, food, and basic care, and many elderly residents rely mainly on themselves or mutual help with peers. The staff shortage is even more serious in remote areas with poorer economic conditions. In economically more developed areas, home- and community-based care has been developed to some degree, but most are pilot projects supported by the local government. Most villages do not have specialized home- and community-based care for the elderly, who must instead depend on informal care from family members, relatives, and neighbors.

Low Qualifications of Elder Care Workers

In general, elder care workers in China have low levels of education and training. According to recent research by the Ministry of Civil Affairs on 2,158 elder care workers in approximately 120 care facilities across 15 provinces, these workers are predominantly older females with low levels of education, mostly from rural areas, and highly mobile (MOCA 2012). Around 83.5 percent of them were female. About 51 percent of them are in the 40–49 age group, and 28 percent in the 50 and older group. Very basic levels of education and training were required to qualify as elder care workers, with about 45.2 percent of them being junior middle school graduates. With respect to experience, 14.8 percent of these workers had less than one year of experience, while 25.9 percent had 1–2 years of experience.

Although training opportunities for elder care workers have increased, the effectiveness of the training appears to be limited. China has promulgated the National Occupational Standards for Elderly Care Workers. The central government's Plan for the Development of Social Services for the Aged (2011–15) also stipulates higher requirements in terms of the percentage of elder care workers who are certified as having received formal training. Free training for elder care workers is offered in some localities. However, because the examinations are held locally, local accreditation agencies may not follow the standards consistently. Aside from the formal training held by the Ministry of Civil Affairs and Ministry of Labor, some other organizations also offer training, which varies in vigor and quality.

Low Status and Pay and Limited Career Prospects

Elder care workers generally have a low social status in China. The job of elder care workers is to serve others, and according to traditional notions, such service jobs are not considered "decent" or respectable. Furthermore, taking care of the elderly is arduous, especially of those who are functionally disabled.

Elder care workers also have less stability in employment. A study by the Ministry of Civil Affairs of the PRC (MOCA) estimates that only 65 percent of elder care workers had signed labor contracts (MOCA 2012). Many elder care workers, especially those who work in home- and community-based care settings, are not covered by labor market regulations and labor laws. Their only resort in case of any grievances is the "China Home Service Association," which is a nonprofit organization affiliated with MOCA (http://www.chsa.com.cn/). However, most of the council members of the association are affiliated with service agencies, so decisions are usually not in favor of the workers in disputes over wages and working conditions.

The high mobility and low skills of elder care workers have much to do with their low wages. A study by Dong et al. (2014) reveals that elder care workers earn about 28 percent less than other domestic workers do in Shanghai. The reference wage set by the Shanghai Municipal Bureau of Labor in 2012 was RMB 2,200 for elder care workers, compared to RMB 4,600 for child care workers. The study shows that domestic workers in general belong to the lowest strata of society and the lowest category of income earners, and domestic elder care workers are the most disadvantaged subgroup of the domestic worker social class.

In order to attract workers to the elder care industry, some localities have raised the salaries for elder care workers. For example, Hangzhou (capital of Zhejiang Province) adopted a regulation stipulating that for welfare institutions and non-profit elder care facilities, the salaries for elder care workers who hold primary, intermediate, and advanced certificates should be no less than 1.3, 1.4, and 1.6 times the local minimum income level, respectively (not including insurance and other fringe benefits).[1]

One impediment to increasing incomes for elder care workers is the difficulty of raising the charges for elder care services. Currently, the average retirement income for urban retirees is only RMB 2,000, and living in an elder care facility would cost half or even a full month of retirement income. As most retirees must set aside some money for medical services, they are very sensitive to the amounts charged by care facilities. Some believe that public elder care institutions should serve the people without charging too much. Occasionally, the elderly held demonstrations or sit-ins in front of municipal government compounds to protest against raising residence fees by elder care institutions. To maintain social stability, local governments are also reluctant to increase charges for elder care services. In addition, home- and community-based care providers, which are currently less popular with elders due to their limited services and narrow coverage, tend to lower prices to attract more customers, which could in turn restrict pay raises for elder care workers there.

Health Care Labor Shortages and Challenges

Imbalances also exist in the distribution of Chinese health workforce, with critical shortages at the primary health care (PHC) level. Although the overall health workforce has increased in recent years, the share of health professionals working in PHC settings (including township health centers in rural areas and community health centers/stations in urban areas) declined from more than 40 percent in 2009 to just under 30 percent in 2013. Thus, the PHC workforce has weakened rather than grown relative to the hospital workforce. The percentage was even lower for registered nurses, at 20.7 percent in 2013. A survey commissioned by the National Health and Family Planning Commission (NHFPC) in 2013 revealed that nearly 50 percent of assistant physicians and registered nurses in the Township Health Centers left to work in county-level hospitals or above. Moreover, the educational level of health professionals at the PHC level is low.

Imbalances can also be seen between the health workforces in urban and rural areas. Although the number of health workers practicing in rural areas has increased, the supply gap between rural and urban areas has widened over time: the urban-rural ratio increased from 2.16 in 2003 to 2.52 in 2013 (figure 9.1). The number of health professionals per 1,000 population in urban areas was 9.18 in 2013, 2.5 times higher than in rural areas. Disparities in education levels also exist: health professionals with a bachelor's degree or above accounted for 20 percent of the health care workforce in urban areas in 2012, but only 6.1 percent in rural areas.[2] Most PHC workers in

Figure 9.1 Health Professionals per 1,000 Population in Rural and Urban China, 2003–13

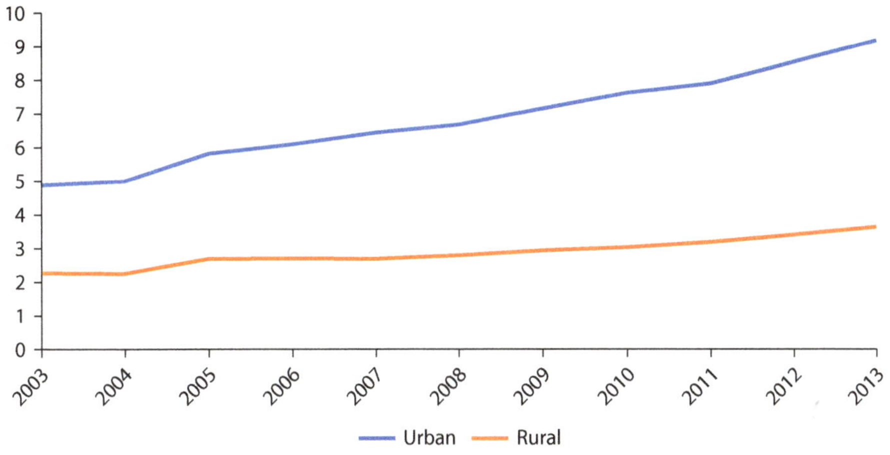

Source: Liu 2015.

Community Health Centers and Township Health Centers have received only post-high school and secondary school training, respectively. The lack of qualified health professionals at the PHC level, particularly in rural areas, is the major cause of patients bypassing PHC and seeking care directly at higher-level hospitals.

Although China's health care workforce has expanded steadily since 2003, the overall density is still low compared with developed economies. The total number of health care workers rose from 6.2 million in 2011 to 7.2 million in 2013, a 16 percent increase in approximately 3 years. As shown in figure 9.2, the number of licensed physicians per 1,000 population increased from 1.19 in 2003 to 1.68 in 2013 (41 percent increase), while the number of registered nurses per 1,000 population increased rapidly from 0.98 per 1,000 population in 2003 to 2.04 in 2013 (108 percent increase), thanks in large part to the massive expansion of nursing education.[3] By 2013, the number of health care professionals per 1,000 population in China was 5.3, including 2 licensed physicians (and assistant physicians) and 2 registered nurses per 1,000 population (NHFPC 2014). Nonetheless, these numbers are still low compared with the OECD averages of 3.2 doctors and 8.8 nurses per 1,000 population (OECD 2014).

Moreover, critical challenges remain in the composition and skill mix of the health care workforce. China has a severe shortage of pediatricians, psychiatrists, and general practitioners (GPs), whose percentage share of all licensed physicians is very low, at 4.3 percent, 1 percent, and 4.5 percent, respectively. These specialties are associated with relatively lower incomes and higher occupational risks and therefore are less attractive than other specialties. In contrast to the 4.5 percent of total licensed physicians in China who are GPs, the percentage in other countries ranges from 30 percent to 60 percent.

Figure 9.2 Number of Health Care Professionals per 1,000 Population in China, 2003–13

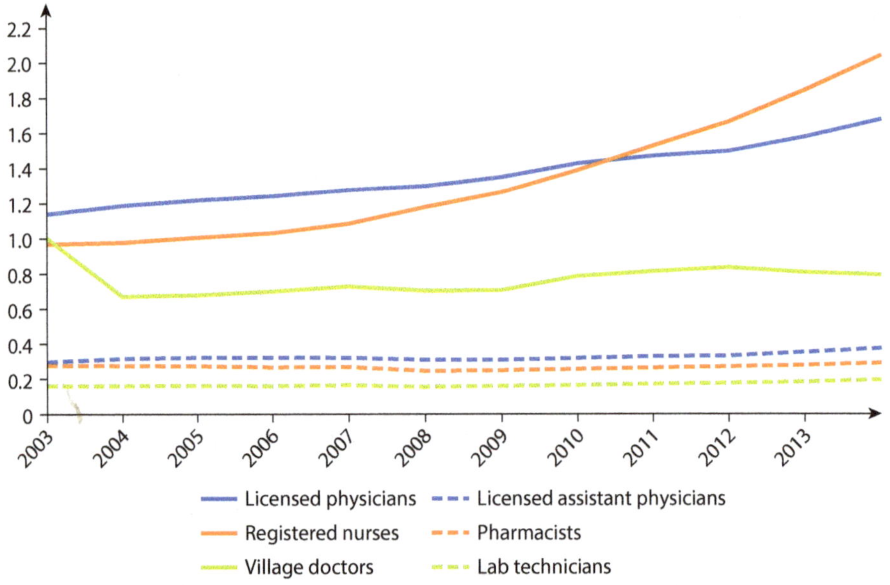

Source: Liu 2015.

A State Council policy issued in 2011[4] proposed the establishment of a GP-based PHC service delivery system with 2–3 GPs per 10,000 population (international best practice is 5 GPs per 10,000). To meet this target, China needs at least 300,000–400,000 GPs nationwide, more than double its current GP workforce (146,000 in 2013) (State Council 2011).

China also has a long history of nurse shortages. Unlike other countries, China has more physicians than nurses. The ratio of nurses to doctors reached 1:1 in 2013, compared to 3–4 nurses per physician in OECD countries (Qin et al. 2013) (figure 9.3). The shortage of nurses is more severe in rural China and at the PHC level, where the ratio of nurses to physicians is 0.82:1 and 0.55:1, respectively.

The shortage of health care professionals has important implications for elder care institutions, which need medical support. Some urban elder care institutions are staffed with professional medical personnel, while community, home-based, and rural elder care rely mainly on existing medical resources within the locality. One estimate suggests a shortfall of around 600,000 nurses for the 3.1 million occupied beds in senior care facilities across the country. The shortage of nursing staff for elder care is more acute during holiday periods such as the Chinese New Year, when staffing can fall by one-third (an estimate from the facility director at Beijing's largest senior care complex, the Shisanling Senior Living Community). When choosing elder care institutions, many elders prioritize the availability of full-time physicians and timely access to medical services. Therefore, facilities in proximity to large medical institutions or staffed with professional medical personnel are more desirable to the elderly.

Figure 9.3 Ratio of Nurses to Physicians, 2009 (or Nearest Year)

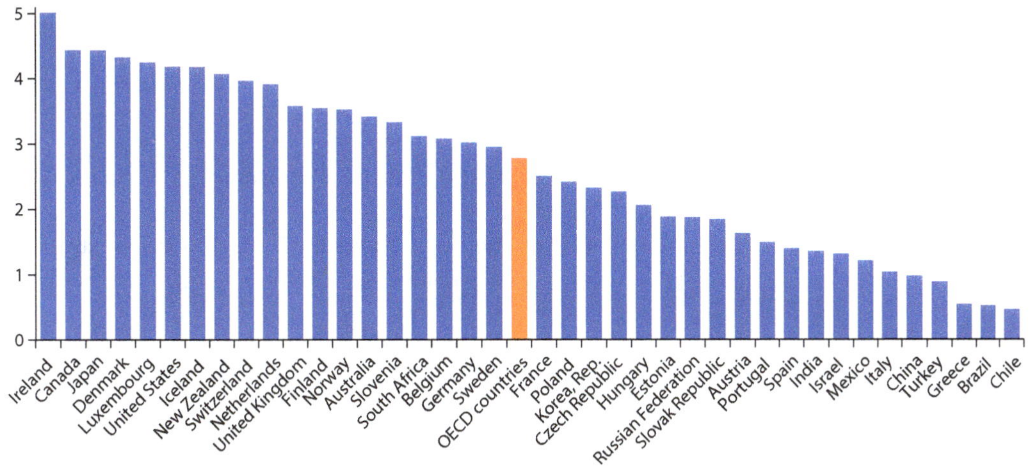

Source: OECD 2009.

Having no one to resort to in times of illness concerns the elderly who live at home the most.

The medical staff of elder care institutions, in particular, suffer from poor compensation and lack of stability. Compared with those working in hospitals, medical personnel working in elder care institutions earn far lower salaries. According to physicians in a residential home covered by the survey, attending physicians in residential homes earn half of what those working in hospitals earn, while nurses earn one-third of what their hospital counterparts earn. Senior physicians earn much more in hospitals and would not even consider working in residential care homes. The situation also varies between medical staff in public elder care institutions versus private institutions: public elder care institutions can often provide permanent staff status (and thus offer more stability) and even household registration (*hu kou*) and higher social status, so they are more attractive to specialized technicians. Few private institutions offer such advantages.

Medical workers in elder care homes may also face greater constraints in career advancement. Positions for various specialized technicians in public elder care institutions are limited, with a very low proportion of staff holding mid-level professional titles, let alone those holding senior professional titles. This leaves limited room for promotions for medical personnel. Moreover, the professional title assessment standards are often very strict, and in some cases, there are explicit stipulations that those who are not practicing in specialized medical institutions are not eligible for professional title assessment. In the research, some nurses revealed that work experience in elder care institutions is not counted when applying for certified nurse examinations. In addition, the assessment for senior professional titles includes requirements such as publishing papers and undertaking research projects, but physicians working in elder care institutions can seldom engage in scientific research. As a result, medical personnel working in elder care institutions tend to have low professional self-identity and low job satisfaction.

Shortages of Qualified Social Workers

Social workers can also play a critical role in elder care. In countries with developed long-term care systems, social workers and psychologists often take care of the destitute and those who need counseling and emotional support. In Hong Kong SAR, China, social workers and psychologists must undergo rigorous studies and obtain licenses, and they are well-versed to provide counseling as well as help seniors access different social services.

At present, China has few qualified social workers in the elder care sector. Only a small number of elder care facilities in major cities have social workers. Moreover, professional social workers in elder care institutions and communities are generally young. Although they have passions for work and good reserve of theoretical knowledge, they often lack the ability to translate theory into practical skills. Due to these constraints, the functions of social workers in elder care institutions and communities are limited to organizing some cultural and recreational activities for the elderly.

Challenges for Informal Caregivers

Under the current senior service system, home-based care is still the top choice for most elders, but family members often lack caregiving abilities or professional care skills. According to data from the Study on China's Urban and Rural Disabled Elderly in 2010, only 1.87 percent of the 33 million disabled and semi-disabled elders receive services from professional institutions. The vast majority of these people with disabilities are being taken care of by family members (or nannies) at home. However, most family caregivers have not received professional training or guidance, so they are under tremendous pressure when caring for loved ones at home.

While live-in nannies can help meet the needs for personal care services and have become an indispensable part of the elder care market, they are also in short supply. As mentioned above, at the low end of the labor market, demand is now exceeding supply. Insufficient supply, high cost, and ineffective supervision of live-in nannies have become major reasons for some elders to live in elder care institutions. Research shows that most elders had been cared for by nannies before moving into an elder care facility.

Although community volunteers also play an important role in elder care, they often lack professional training and care abilities. In many developed economies, social organizations have become an important support for seniors who receive home- and community-based care. However, the development of social organizations in China lags behind and they play a limited role in the provision of elder care services. In some localities and communities, mutual-help groups organized by seniors and other volunteers provide some basic services such as visits to elders who live alone.

Recent Government Policies and Reforms

In order to address the shortage of elder care workers, the Medium and Long Term Development Plan for Civil Affairs Personnel (2010–20) aims to add China's Medium and Long Term Development Plan for Civil Affairs Personnel (2010–20) aims to strengthen human resources and address the shortage of elder care workforce. Recognizing the importance of improving the quality of the elder care workforce, the State Council's Accelerating the Development of Services for the Aged calls for improvement in staff training and employment policies. Universities/vocational schools are to set up curriculum courses while providing opportunities for continuous learning and remote education. The Ministry of Civil Affairs recently rolled out a vocational school training program to prepare more senior care professionals, financed with RMB 40 million from a national lottery (Caixin Online 2013). Hands-on training is to be promoted, and subsidies are to be given to those who attend trainings for aged care. Attention is also to be paid to working conditions of staff and staff welfare, including social insurance and pensions.

A few local governments (including Anhui, Chongqing, Ningxia) have made similar policy announcements in line with the State Council's directions, including the announcement of financial support/subsidies to encourage uptake of training and certification for the long-term care workforce. In Anhui, for example, graduates of tertiary and secondary vocational-technical institutes are offered funding support to repay or reimburse student loans and tuitions if they work in an aged care facility for three years. Those who have worked for four years and have passed professional certification will receive rewards. Subsidies are also offered to those meeting certain eligibility criteria when they enroll in occupational training programs for aged care or undertake skills certification. Finally, graduates from disadvantaged groups taking on jobs in the aged care industry will be given allowances and subsidies for social insurance programs. In Yuzhong district of Chongqing city, the district-level government also subsidizes up to half (but no more than RMB 500) of the training fee for aged care institution staff who participate in short-term business training, vocational training, and moral training organized or commissioned by the city/district level civil affairs bureau.

Examples of local efforts to provide training opportunities for long-term care workers can be found across the country. The city of Shizuishan (in Ningxia) has established an aged care training base at Suizuishan Social Welfare Institute which provides a 21-day training course and issues the national entrance-level aged care provider certificate. Similarly, the city of Luzhou (Sichuan Province) trains aged care workers by starting aged care related training courses in colleges and technical schools. Henan Province has set up training bases in several colleges and vocational schools and has also adopted distance learning. In Gansu Province, the 15–20 aged care training institutions established in 2013 enabled the trained service providers to earn RMB 2,000, which was double their income in the last three years. Shandong Province specifies one enterprise as the aged care vocational training base in Jinan, and the local government requires all aged care institutions to get their staff trained. Institutions with certification rates of less than 85 percent are ineligible for receiving public subsidies.

Policies to mandate certification for the long-term care workforce have also been introduced. For professionals working in aged care institutions, licensing and registration requirements shall be the same as for those working in medical institutions or public welfare institutions. The State Council also released the Plan for the Development of Social Service System (2011–15) with an ambitious goal of reaching 100 percent certification of the long-term care workforce by 2015.

Other policies address the need to improve the supply and quality of social workers, who as noted above can play an important role in the elder care system. The Provisional Regulations on the System of Assessing the Professional Level of Social Workers and the Methods for Implementing Professional Proficiency Tests for Social Workers encourage professional social workers and college graduates majoring in social work to work in social welfare institutions. Guangzhou (and Chongqing) established a Department of Social Work in nursing homes as early as 2005. Guangzhou Province has even set up professional organizations like the Hong Kong SAR, China Anglican Church to include professional social workers in the elderly care service profession. The government has also set the standards and qualifications for professional nurses for the elderly, and by the end of 2005, nearly 20,000 people had obtained such qualifications.

Recommendations

Strengthening the Elder Care Workforce

Given the shortage of high-quality workers in long-term care, stabilizing and elevating the status of elder care workers is a critical priority going forward. In particular, it will be important to prioritize the stability and quality of mid- and high-ranking elder care workers. To attract more workers to this sector, the economic status of elder care workers as well as their social status should be improved. Both the industry and government should acknowledge the importance of caregivers and encourage more people to join their ranks, for example through public education and campaigns on how elder care is a high-impact profession and how they can progress in their career.

A key concern in China's elder care industry is the low rate of compensation and the lack of social security among elder care workers. Policy makers must focus on finding ways to raise the wages of these workers, and local governments must eventually increase the minimum wages of elder care workers. Balanced against the costs are the facts that improving the pay and conditions of the workforce and prioritizing permanent, formal staff over temporary staff will improve morale, reduce staff turnover, and improve the quality of care. Policies to improve promotion possibilities could also improve retention rates in the industry.

Another labor-related need is *hukou* reform, which would allow more workers to migrate from low-income areas to cities where they can learn caregiving skills and serve the growing ranks of senior citizens. Most new urban *hukous* are issued to high-end talent such as information technology (IT) or management professionals, with the glaring absence of workers at the other end of the spectrum (Caixin Online 2013).

More medical staff and social workers also need to be brought into the elder care sector. In particular, the industry needs to create a good environment for nurses, raise their pay level, and encourage them to be case managers and managers of nursing homes. In other countries, doctors remain in hospitals while nurses become nursing home administrators or chief nurses for the facilities. Nurses therefore have a large amount of autonomy in running the daily operations. Along with retired doctors, Chinese nurses must be empowered to become nursing home managers to meet the need for skilled professionals.

Investing in Workforce Education and Training

Investment in education and training of new and experienced personnel is the most important determinant of a high-quality workforce. Low-grade, low-paid care staff cannot provide high-quality care. Care staff need to be professionalized to raise their status and to equip them with the skills necessary to respond flexibly to a wide range of needs. Notably, while some of the required skills will be nursing skills, the vast majority are social care skills. Such skills include providing support to older people with basic needs (e.g., washing, cooking, shopping) and giving them advice on diet, exercise, and remaining healthy. These care workers need basic vocational training with continuous training in key areas such as nutrition and preventing falls.

In order to address the long-term demand for elder care, the formal system of education for elder care needs to be reformed. First, an evaluation and assessment of the effectiveness of teaching and training programs and schools is needed. Courses and curricula should be structured such that more emphasis is placed on practice rather than theory and on how care can be delivered in homes and communities. The quality of education also depends to a large extent on the faculty, so the government could look into expanding incentives (particularly financial incentives) to recruit high-quality teachers and staff who are equipped to impart the knowledge and skills needed to produce well-trained elder care providers.

At the same time, education and technical support are needed for providers—including welfare homes, nursing homes, skilled nursing homes, community centers, and hospitals—to help them improve the quality of care and meet established government standards. Training is needed in both the formal and informal private sectors as well as publicly managed homes. Funding for new training institutes may be needed. Moreover, policies to promote training for service staff must be encouraged and employment with certificates made mandatory. Competency and technical training are very important, but service providers should also be encouraged to go beyond just technical care to develop an understanding of the mental, emotional, and social needs of the elderly to help facilitate better communication between caregivers and the care recipients.

Even for professionals such as doctors and nurses, it will be important for them to gain knowledge of gerontology and other special needs care in order to provide better services for the elderly. Special needs care includes areas such as dementia care, rehabilitation, mental and physical rehabilitation combined through psycho-motor therapy, and traditional Chinese medicine for health management. The government could promulgate policies that allow public hospital doctors to provide services in private practices and even at home. Such forms of training for nurses, caregivers and other specialists could be added to curriculums at universities, vocational schools, or online education.

Training could also be geared toward improving the management of elder care services. The care manager, which is still a relatively new concept in China, is responsible for doing a needs assessment and helping to coordinate among health and other services, which is vital to delivering the appropriate products and services to the elderly. Although most institutions do not have such positions, China can prepare early by educating a new generation of care plan managers now.

Utilizing More Technology for Care Services

To relieve some of the demands for human labor, the government could encourage and guide enterprises to accelerate research and development (R&D) and promote information technology and auxiliary equipment for elder care. Information technology and auxiliary equipment can enable elderly people to live more independently and thus lighten the workloads of caregivers and lessen the demand for professional elder care support. For example, products for the elderly such as the "wristwatch" have been developed to collect and pass back health information on individuals. Real-time monitoring of the health situations of high-risk elderly people can enable timely rescue and treatment. In Hangzhou and Guangzhou, an emergency call system has been installed in the homes of elderly people so help can be provided quickly if needed. In France, sliding rails have been installed in the rooms of elder care institutions so disabled elderly can walk inside their rooms and complete simple activities such as using the bathroom.

Supporting Informal Caregivers

At the same time, informal caregivers should be given more support. This could be accomplished through measures such as:

- *Strengthening professional instruction for family members and community volunteers*. Giving basic training to the elderly and their family caregivers to help them understand key symptoms, master basic aged care and self-care techniques, and be aware of methods to avoid incidents would empower them to look after their own health more effectively. Elder care institutions and community care service organizations could be encouraged to provide home instruction to family members, or they could arrange for family members and community volunteers to visit and learn in professional elderly care institutions to gain basic knowledge of elderly nursing. Another option might be for communities to organize massive video training, since communities have such resources and have easy access to households. It could be done in community care centers while the elderly and family members get together and could even develop into a regular community center activity.

- *Providing appropriate subsidies for the services of family members and community volunteers*. For family members who provide full-time care for disabled or semi-disabled elderly people, the government could purchase the service to provide the subsidies, encourage enterprises to provide paid vacation for the employees' convenience to care for elders at home, give service coupons to community volunteers, and promote the experience of a "time bank" to accumulate service time for community volunteers or incorporate it into the integrity and ethical credits.

Notes

1. The current actual wages for elder care workers in Hangzhou have already exceeded those levels, making the government guidance less relevant.
2. This reflects a broader picture of the health workforce in China. Only 28.6 percent have a university or higher degree (more than five years of medical education), and the largest share (38.8 percent) has only three years of junior college or even less education.
3. In 2013, nursing schools recruited 0.56 million nursing students, 62 percent of them in vocational nursing schools (3-year program).
4. *Guiding Opinions of the State Council on the Establishment of a General Practitioner System in China*, July 2nd, 2011.

References

Caixin Online. 2013. "Blues for Gray Hair: What's Wrong with China's Elder Care Section." *Caixin Online*, March 6. http://english.caixin.com/2013-06-03/100536498.html.

Colombo, F., A. Llena-Nozal, J. Mercier, and F. Tjadens. 2011. *Help Wanted? Providing and Paying for Long-Term Care*. Paris: OECD.

Dong, Xiao-yuan, Jin Feng, and Yangyang Yu. 2017. "Relative Pay of Domestic Eldercare Workers in Shanghai, China." *Feminist Economics* 23.1: 135–59.

Liu, Gordon. 2015. "Quality of Hospital Management Practices in China". China Hospital Management Survey (CHMS), Unpublished manuscript.

MOCA., 2012. Quoted from the China Education Daily article and a website of of a consulting firm: http://renzx.com/news/current/84.html.

NHFPC. 2014. "2013 Statistical Communique on the Development of Health and Family Planning in China."

OECD (Organisation for Economic Co-operation and Development). 2013. *Health at a Glance 2009*. http://www.oecd-ilibrary.org/content/book/health_glance-2009-en.

———. 2014. "OECD Health Statistics 2014 How Does China Compare?" http://www.oecd.org/els/health-systems/Briefing-Note-CHINA-2014.pdf.

Qin, Xuezheng, Lixing Li, and Chee-Ruey Hsieh. 2013. "Too few doctors or too low wages? Labor supply of health care professionals in China." China Economic Review 24: 150–64.

State Council. 2011. *Guiding Opinions of the State Council on the Establishment of a General Practitioner System in China*. July 2. http://www.gov.cn/zwgk/2011-07/07/content_1901099.htm.

Stone, Robyn, and Mary F. Harahan. 2010. "Improving the Long-Term Care Workforce Serving Older Adults." *Health Affairs* 29: 109–15.

CHAPTER 10

Learning and Policy Formulation: International Experience and Implications for China's Policy

Jan M. Bauer and Du Peng

Introduction

Long-term care (LTC) is an imminent concern for policy makers in all aging societies. Even though governments have been aware of the rising challenge for a long time, LTC policies to ensure the dignified aging of the population are still underdeveloped in most countries and are subject to frequent reforms. Modern policy making emphasizes the importance of knowledge and evidence-based policies, but particularly if there is a lack of certainty about the right approach, experimentation and learning-by-doing become important mechanisms for improving policy making (Nauwelaers and Wintjes 2008). The design of an innovative LTC system requires innovation in the policy making process itself. The complexity of an efficient LTC system makes development from scratch difficult. However, sensitivity to cultural and social norms does not allow for mere copy-and-paste of international best practice (Dolowitz and David 2000; Heilmann 2008). Policy intelligence is required to promote, implement, and evaluate policy learning activities.

Executing the role of market steward and running an efficient LTC system greatly depends on the government's ability to understand market dynamics and steer provider activity. This new role of government requires active capacity building and learning by public employees (Gash et al. 2013). Learning from one's own experience, whether successes or mistakes, is probably most effective for improving policy performance. However, external lessons can complement this learning process in many areas, ranging from identifying policy needs to policy design, implementation, and policy evaluation (Nauwelaers and Wintjes 2008).

Jan M Bauer is an Assistant Professor, Department of Management, Society and Communication, Copenhagen Business School, Denmark. Du Peng is a Professor and Director, Institute of Gerontology, Renmin University of China.

It is useful to look not only at international LTC policies but also at the procedures used to develop these policies.

In order to develop a sustainable and innovative LTC system, China can benefit from international experience with LTC and explore best practices to formulate better polices. China has recently acknowledged the need for action on the 12th Five-Year Plan for the Development of China's Undertakings for the Aged and set up a Development Plan for the Social Old-Age Care System. As China is aging rapidly, a comprehensive LTC system needs to be implemented to improve the situation for the elderly. This requires an agile government which can benefit from the advancements of other more developed LTC systems but needs to adapt and test those ideas in the Chinese context. This approach can only be mastered by a governmental structure that is designed to learn and willing to do so.

This chapter outlines the important aspects of policy learning in LTC. This learning requires the collection of information and government structures to foster policy learning. Based on the European experience, a toolbox for policy learning and exchange is provided that can improve policy making at the national and local levels. The chapter concludes with a set of recommendations specific to the Chinese context.

The Chinese Government Network in Aging and Aging Policy Research Agencies

To coordinate the implementation and evaluation of aging-related policies, the Chinese government has created different specialized agencies. In October 1990, the China National Committee on Aging (CNCA) was approved and established by the State Council as a deliberation and coordination agency. It consists of 32 political entities (members), which are often strongly involved in the undertakings on aging, such as the Ministry of Civil Affairs, the Ministry of Finance, the Ministry of Culture, the Ministry of Human Resources and Social Security, the Ministry of Commerce, the National Development and Reform Commission, and China Association on Aging (figure 10.1). The CNCA has five main duties: (1) conducting research and developing elderly care strategies, as well as major policies; (2) protecting elders' legitimate rights and interests; (3) providing guidance and management of undertakings on aging, and promoting activities to improve elders' physical and mental health; (4) supervising the work of local governments on aging; and (5) coordinating with the United Nations and other international organizations on aging.

The Committee has set up its office in the Ministry of Civil Affairs, which is co-located with the China Association on Aging. The CNCA Office is the coordination agency for the Committee and carries out its work within China, but also promotes international exchanges and cooperation in the name of the China Association on Aging. The CNCA also has five main duties: (1) implementing the decisions made by the CNCA; (2) researching and proposing national aging policies, including planning and measuring the implementation process;

Figure 10.1 China National Committee on Aging Office and Its Members

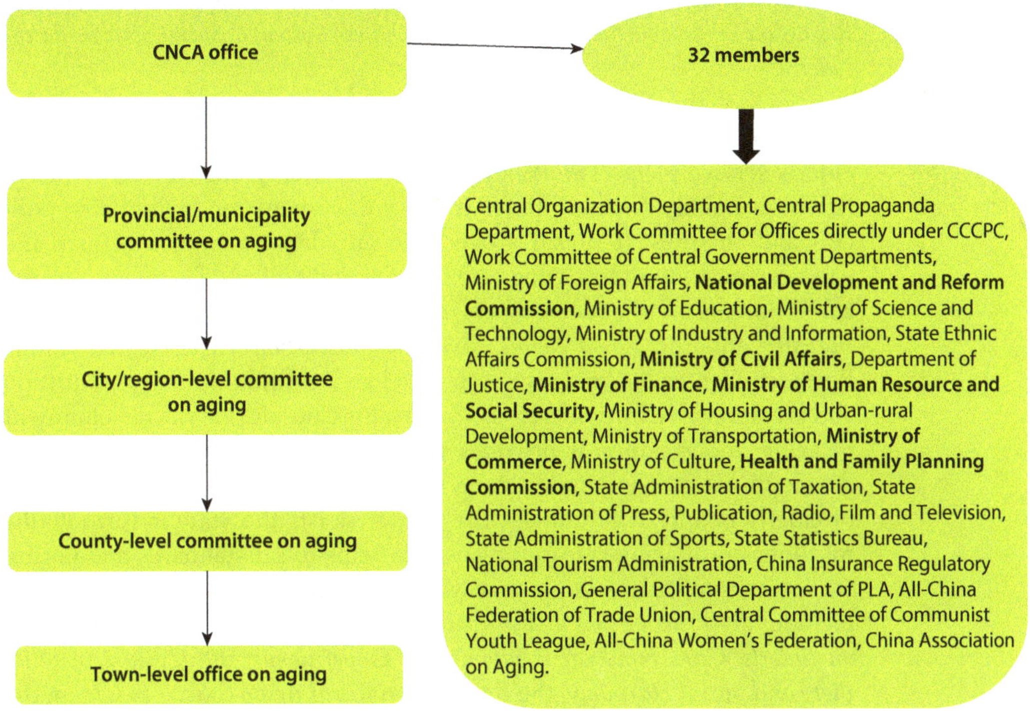

(3) supervising and inspecting projects implemented by the National Committee on Aging in local areas; (4) connecting and coordinating the work of the Committee's members; (5) creating and collecting knowledge on the work on aging from different source and disseminating the results.

There are also a number of agencies involved in knowledge building in the area of research, policy development, and evaluation. These include government agencies, as well as academic institutions.

- Relevant divisions of the State Council are responsible for the development of policy planning, formulation, and implementation for the elderly. The Research Institute of the State Council provides opinions on the respective policies and advises the decision-making process. It is responsible for drafting the *Report on the Work of the Government* and manages the preparation of important meeting documents of the State Council. The institute also assists in drafting relevant meeting documents of Communist Party of China's (CPC) Central Committee. The Development Research Center of the State Council (DRC) is mainly responsible for studying global, comprehensive, strategic, and long-term matters with regards to national economic and social development, as well as reformation and the opening-up process. The DRC provides the CPC Central Committee and the State Council with suggestive and consultative opinions for policy formulation; and provides suggestions on the formulation of national mid/long-term plans and regional development policies. Documents relevant for development of elderly care policy include the *Compilation of Research Results on Enhancing the Construction of Chinese System of Social Services for the Elderly*.

- Agencies of the Ministry of Civil Affairs are responsible for performing comprehensive and proactive research to provide a basis for developing elderly service plans. The Policy Research Center of the Ministry of Civil Affairs is mainly responsible for drafting documents on civil affairs' policies and theories. It presides over relevant departmental meetings and works on mid/long-term aging care theories and policies. The main research achievements are the *Research on Admission to Chinese Elderly Care Service Industry* and the *Research on Civil Administration Theories*. The China Research Center on Aging is a state-level and multidisciplinary institution and is responsible for research on important issues during the development of aging undertakings. It provides theoretical support for promoting the development of aging undertaking and, thereby, improves the life quality of elderly people. Additionally, the Center assists the State in formulating mid/long-term aging research plans and helps to set standards and norms, while performing large-scale surveys on aging. Main research achievements include: the *Practice and Consideration in Aging-Specific Work*, the *Research on Elderly Care Function Positioning of Government*, the *Culture of Filial Piety and Social Harmony*, the *Research on Rural Aging Policies in China*, the *Self Evaluation of Elderly Health and Independent Living Abilities*, the *Research on Elderly Care Pattern with Chinese Characteristics*, the *Report on Development of Chinese Aging Undertaking (2013)*, the *Report on Development of Chinese Elderly Service Industry (2014)*.
- The Chinese Academy of Social Sciences is responsible for creating health and elderly care think pieces and promulgates relevant industrial standards for elderly care services. In 2015, CASS set up the China Elderly Care and Health Research Center to undertake the national elderly care and health research projects and cooperate, among others, with the Ministry of Civil Affairs, the Health and Family Planning Committee, the National Development and Investment Corporation, and the China Development Bank to develop industry standards and proposals in order to formulate and implement an elderly care industry standards system and create the national elderly care and health think tank. Main research achievements are the *International Investment and Operation Management for Elderly Care and Health Industry*, the *Typical Cases of International Elderly Care Services* and the *Bluebook of Chinese Elderly Care and Health Industry*. Additionally, the Population Research Institute of the Chinese Academy of Social Sciences (CASS) has conducted relevant research activities from the economic perspective.
- A number of leading universities participate and lead research projects, academic conferences, government-sponsored forums and similar means to disseminate their results among policy makers with the aim to improve policies on aging issues.

- The Renmin University of China focuses on gerontology studies and policy research. The Renmin University is the earliest domestic university to focus on aging issues in China and the sole university awarding gerontology Ph.D degrees. Specifically, Renmin studies gerontological theories, development of aging society, aging policies, population aging trends and characteristics, and the impact of population aging on society and economy. So far, Renmin Univeristy has trained over 100 gerontological masters and doctoral students. It successfully hosted the 11th China Gerontology Forum, which as greatly promoted the teaching and research development of gerontology in China. It has published several Chinese textbooks, such as the *Social Gerontology*, the *Aging of Chinese Population*, the *Research on Population Aging Process of China*, the *Research on Family Provision of Elderly Care Services in China*, the *Introduction to Social Security* and translated many foreign textbooks on gerontology such as the *Gerontology: Multidiscipline Perspectives*, the *Aging Theory Handbook*, the *Social Gerontology: Multidiscipline Perspectives*.
- Peking University focuses on the interdisciplinary research on aging and elderly heath and has conducted two nationwide large-scale aging surveys, that is, the Chinese Longitudinal Healthy Longevity Survey and the China Health and Retirement Longitudinal Study. The aging research institutions affiliated to this university are the Elderly Health and Family Research Center of Peking University, the Research Center on Aging of Peking University and the Gerontological Research Institute of Peking University. Main research achievements include the *Analysis on Factors Affecting Health and Longevity*, the *Research on Aging and Family* and the *Research on Elderly Care and Filial Piety Awareness during Social Transition*. Main textbooks on gerontology are the *Introduction to Gerontology*, the *Geriatric Sociology*, the *Geriatric Psychology*, the *Elderly Cognition Science* and the *Aging Biology*.
- Tsinghua University—focusing on evaluation of elderly health status and LTC development, placing emphasis on fundamental research. Tsinghua University has set up a Gerontology Research Center. Its research team is mainly devoted to research on LTC and evaluation of health among the elderly. Main research achievements are the *Introduction to Long-Term Elderly Care* and the *Economics of Aging* (translation). Its School of Architecture is mainly engaged in elderly housing research and related research articles mainly include the *Analysis and Design Suggestions on Chinese Urban Elderly Care Facilities*, the *New Design Tendency of Japanese Amalgamated Houses and Elderly Living Facilities*.

Policy Framework and International Experience

Internationally, policy learning in LTC increasingly takes place on the supranational level to foster the exchange of knowledge. As one example, the European Union (EU) has included LTC in its social protection and social inclusion agenda to help national governments dealing with this increasingly relevant and complex domain. Now part of the Europe2020 strategy, the European Commission (EC) uses an

Open Method for Coordination (OMC) as a tool to promote international learning, create a substantial knowledge base, and enhance national efforts in LTC.

The EC is using the OMC as an innovative approach to foster policy learning and intelligence in LTC. The OMC offers an alternative to the usual regulatory process within the EU, which is based on binding agreements that involve a long decision-making process (Dehousse 2003; Humburg 2008). This model of governance is based on non-binding agreements—so-called soft laws—to achieve convergence of the EU member states in areas of economics and social policies (Szyszczak 2006; Trubek and Trubek 2005). The idea of the OMC is to work through peer pressure by regular public evaluation of the member states, which should ultimately lead to national efforts toward a common goal even without enforcement measures and sanctions. It is also meant to encourage an exchange between countries and foster an environment for innovation (Dehousse 2003). By setting up procedural routines of monitoring and exchange, member countries are expected to emulate their neighbors' best practices, which should ultimately lead to better policies.

In its most sophisticated form, the OMC uses the following instruments (Radaelli 2003):

- Guidelines,
- Benchmarking and sharing of best practices,
- Multi-lateral surveillance,
- Indicators,
- Iterative process, and
- Implementation through domestic policy and legislation.

The OMC has been advocated as a promising instrument to reach common EU goals while accounting for the diversity of its member states. This feature became particularly crucial, as the 12 new member states are characterized by great heterogeneity among them and particularly when compared to the old members. This great diversity, however, is seen as an asset rather than an obstacle and ought to provide an opportunity for policy experimentation and mutual learning (Zeitlin 2005). The OMC is flexible, as the suggested guidelines can be adapted to the individual characteristics of a member country. This more decentralized method allows for a less hierarchical approach and brings together member states as well as social partners and civil society at the local level.

Coordination of the supranational efforts starts with the formulation of common goals. For the EU, the Council has established a framework for future advancements and sees the main goal of health care reforms in these three objectives (Social Protection Committee 2002):

- ***Accessibility***: People need the opportunity to have access to up-to-date health and care services, and countries need to ensure sufficient access to these services for the poor. For LTC, these issues are extended to various components for a good overall care strategy including the family, technology, and a supportive environment.

- ***Quality***: People require the best possible standards for the quality of health and LTC. This objective includes topics such as the development and control of standards, cost-effectiveness, licensing and accreditation, and the definition of patient's rights.
- ***Financial sustainability***: The rise in health care expenditures is recognized to become a major burden on member states. Therefore, sustainability and cost containment are an important aspect of the reform and design of the health and LTC systems. This includes not only rationing and cost-effectiveness but also the establishment of appropriate incentive structures for users and providers.

To foster a more multidisciplinary and integrated approach toward aging, the EC merged the formerly separated OMCs on social inclusion, health care, and pension into one "Social OMC." The EU launched a European Innovation Partnership on Active and Healthy Ageing (AHA) (European Commission 2011a) which aims to improve the average healthy lifespan by two years by 2020. It focuses on three pillars: (1) prevention, screening, and early diagnosis; (2) care and cure; and (3) active aging and independent living. Within these pillars, the AHA has started with six Action Groups that work on specific issues (e.g., "Helping to prevent functional decline and frailty") and try to gather public (EU, national, or local level) and private stakeholders to share knowledge and find innovative solutions that meet the needs of the elderly (European Commission 2011b). The purpose of the AHA is to provide a platform that combines existing EU structures and helps facilitate combined research and mutual exchange of best practices (Social Protection Committee 2014). However, the design and financing of LTC remain the responsibility of each member state, and the EU restricts its activities to the tools of the OMC.

To provide efficient and high-quality LTC services, the European OMC highlights knowledge building through data collection as one crucial aspect of meeting the needs of the population. The government must collect data that provides sufficient information to make smart choices in LTC and adjust current policies if needed. This section focuses on the process of capacity planning as well as performance evaluation and outlines the information that is commonly used to improve policy making for the elderly within selected countries.

Capacity Planning, Needs Assessment, and Forecasting

A main government objective is to ensure an adequate supply of LTC services. Apart from equity issues regulating access for the poor, the responsible public entity must ensure that providers satisfy the effective demand for services. For capacity planning, the government needs to collect sufficient data to assess local demand. In addition, providing a timely care infrastructure requires a certain foresight to build capacity or change service models. Many countries use forecast methods to estimate future changes in demand, which allows for adjustment of regulations and incentives for the private sector.

In particular, residential care requires long-term planning since supply is much less responsive than the home care market. However, both markets share the often scarce resource of qualified care workers, who require time for training before entering the labor market. The capacity for residential care is often reported in available beds per 1,000 elderly.[1] The present demand for residential LTC in the current system can be derived from waiting lists or the number of unoccupied beds. A large number of people on a waiting list for admission to a residential care facility or long average waiting times indicate that the LTC sector does not satisfy the needs of the population. Hence, an expansion of service supply should be considered. In contrast, many empty beds may point to an oversupply of care services in the area but could also indicate that the services do not match the needs of the population. If there is no regulation ensuring quality of services or if prices are too high, beds remain empty despite a genuine need within the population.

However, such measures should be viewed in the context of the underlying LTC system and demographic dynamics of a country. The effective demand for care services does not simply represent the need for care. Institutional care is generally the last resort for elderly and used only when no alternatives are available. Therefore, effective demand for residential care is determined by (1) the need for care, (2) the availability of informal alternatives, (3) social attitudes toward institutionalization, (4) the availability and price of suitable home care alternatives, and (5) the costs and quality of such institutions (Zhan et al. 2006).

Against this backdrop, the political agenda is an important factor that determines the effective demand for care. For instance, expanding subsidies for providers and voucher to consumers can lower user fees and increase the effective demand for those services, so equity considerations are part of capacity planning. In addition, if public funding or access to residential care facilities is based on individuals' limited functional ability level, strict policies not only reduce admittance but also reduce the average length of stay, as more severe cases have short survival rates so beds are needed for a shorter period (Zhang et al. 2012).

International experience highlights the challenge of providing sufficient access to residential care within a limited budget for social services. A number of EU countries spend a considerable amount of their gross domestic product (GDP) on LTC to ensure that every elderly person receives a minimum level of care to maintain human dignity despite physical or mental deterioration. Due to the elaborate social welfare and safety net, the link between care needs and residential care demand is more direct and therefore more predictable. If progressing care needs make a home-centered care arrangement unfeasible, people will certainly be institutionalized. Even though it is common that residential care is paid by the elderly or other family members, LTC insurance or public benefits typically cover a substantial part of the costs; and ultimately, most European social welfare systems will ensure adequate accommodations for those elderly without means.

Despite the multiple determinants of residential care needs, capacity planning in European countries often uses the development of care needs—namely, the demographic transition—as the major determinant. This is a somewhat reasonable assumption, as the ability to pay, social norms, and governmental framework are not likely to change in the near future. In Germany, the responsibility for capacity planning is at the federal state level, but forecasts are done for each municipality separately. Based on census data, the statistical offices provide different scenarios for future needs. The most simplistic status-quo model assumes a constant probability of becoming disabled at a certain age over time. Alternative models incorporate additional trends into the prediction, such as changes in limited functional ability rates within certain age groups or decreasing preferences for home-care arrangements. Those forecasts create an upper and lower bound of care demand that are used to improve the decision making of local authorities (Burger, Weber, and Landkreisen 2011).

The Personal Social Services Research Unit (PSSRU) in England uses a model that projects four different outcomes: the future numbers of disabled older people, the likely level of demand for LTC services and limited functional ability benefits for older people, the costs associated with meeting this demand, and the social care workforce required (Wittenberg et al. 2006). The models rely on data from different sources to account for household composition, divorce rates, and informal care supply. A detailed description of the model is provided in box 10.1.

Box 10.1 The Base Case of the Personal Social Services Research Unit Macro Model

The Personal Social Service Research Unit model uses several steps to predict the demand for formal care from 2002 to 2041:

- The model uses population survey data (here the General Household Survey [GHS]) to categorize the elderly by age and gender into six classes depending on their problems with Activities of Daily Living (ADL) or Instrumental Activities of Daily Living (IADL). The categories range from 1 (people without any problems) to 6 (people living in the community who cannot perform two or more ADL tasks without help, and people who are in care homes or long-stay hospitals).
- The model includes public statistics and GHS data about household composition and informal care. People are put into two groups depending on their marital status (i.e., married and cohabitating or single, widowed, divorced, separated) then separates them again by cohabitation with children and receipt of informal care (based on GHS estimates), resulting in a total of eight groups. Home ownership is also included in the model as it helps capture socioeconomic status and public entitlement for the means test. Based on those categories, the model divides the population into 1,000 cells.
- The predictions from above are used to assess the demand for formal care. Using census information and data on the care infrastructure, the model estimates the relationship between the population in each cell and the demand for formal care. The model estimates

box continues next page

Box 10.1 The Base Case of the Personal Social Services Research Unit Macro Model *(continued)*

the demand for residential and home care separately using a logistic regression. In further steps, this projected demand is translated into estimates of expenditures and demand for the nursing workforce.

The predictions of the basic model rely on several assumptions. First, the model assumes that some relationships remain constant over time (e.g., the propensity to receive informal care from a child). Second, some non-constant components of the model follow the predictions (e.g., the change in the age distribution of the population), which drives the changes in LTC needs over time. As both developments are uncertain, the model is used to test the sensitivity of the results to misspecification. For instance, how does the result change if the supply of informal care declines by 1 percent annually compared to the baseline proportion from 2002? The results of such sensitivity analysis provide a corridor of possible outcomes and allow adjustments to the predictions in light of new data over time.

Source: Based on Wittenberg et al. 2006.

Notably, the development of care demand is more consistent in England than in the fast-changing care sector of China. If changes in the supply and demand for care are large and idiosyncratic, the predictions of the model will be less precise.

In addition, the English Care Quality Commission (CQC) has performed the duty of market oversight since mid-2015, assessing the financial sustainability of providers that are considered difficult to replace. To ensure the continuous provision of all demanded care services, the CQC timely informs local authorities when a provider under the scheme is likely to fail. Providers are considered to be difficult to replace when they are either very large, dominant in a scarcely populated region, or provide very specialized services. In this case, providers must transfer confidential information to the CQC that allows assessment of their current financial situation (CQC 2015b).

Monitoring System Performance

Beyond the first step of providing sufficient capacity, monitoring the quality of LTC services is another important step toward a comprehensive LTC system. Even though state-of-the-art provision should be individualized and adjusted to regional differences, the experience from the EU shows that in some parts of the policy process, more harmonization and centralized decision-making are required. Local efforts should focus on clear national (or supranational) targets, which can be developed and formulated by a broad range of stakeholders, as benchmarks for assessing policy effectiveness.

A clear set of indicators needs to be developed and monitored to measure the progress of regional authorities toward the common goals. The collection of reliable data makes it possible to identify deficiencies in specific areas as well as enables evaluation of policy interventions and assessment of their cost-effectiveness. However, a review of the Organisation for Economic Co-operation and Development (OECD) countries shows that there is still little experience in the field of LTC in finding good indicators. Moreover, evaluating the effect of one specific intervention is difficult, particularly as the increasingly integrated approach of LTC impedes the measurement of isolated outcomes (Zeitlin 2005).

The availability of reliable and valid data on care quality helps stakeholder in several ways (OECD/European Union 2013):

- It helps providers manage care services and workers.
- It helps care workers decide where they may wish to work.
- It offers consumers information for choosing among different care providers.
- It helps purchasers make informed resource allocation decisions.
- It helps policy makers set benchmarks for providers.
- It enables cross-national comparisons of performance.

The trend in data collection is moving away from measuring inputs toward measuring outputs and most recently outcomes. This shift has been influenced by experience from the general health care sector. Since the ultimate goal of LTC is to improve the situation of disabled elderly and their families, good performance should make those stakeholders better off and improve their well-being.

However, the nature of LTC makes outcomes assessment more difficult than in acute care. Elderly in need often face a decline in physical or mental health that cannot be cured, and good care increases the quality of life despite declining health. In addition, for people suffering from severe dementia, subjective assessments may not be feasible. Therefore, the clinical quality of care services and the assurance of minimum input standards are still commonly used as indicators in LTC. However, the introduction of overall quality-of-life measures has been promoted increasingly to capture the multiple dimensions of objective and subjective components to enable a holistic assessment of LTC to ensure dignified aging (OECD/European Union 2013). The current EU position on LTC has also necessitated a more global performance indicator, as the integrated approach for LTC makes the assessment of single inputs or outputs less meaningful.

The measurement of LTC is still severely underdeveloped in most countries and lags behind general health care. Following EU guidelines, social indicators should build on existing data. However, the indicator portfolio for the particular stream of the social OMC (i.e., health and LTC) needs to be a comprehensive and efficient tool to monitor the commonly agreed-on objectives and should also fulfill a minimum set of methodological requirements (European Commission 2009). To date, the social strand of health and LTC has around 30 indicators, categorized as primary and secondary indicators for each of the three objectives (Accessibility, Quality, and Sustainability) as well as a set of context indicators.[2] However, some of those indicators are still under preparation, and relevant indicators to measure quality of care and quality of life are lacking (European Commission 2015; OECD/European Union 2013).

To help develop better indicators, the EU funded a project on Quality Management by Result-oriented Indicators—Towards Benchmarking in Residential Care for Older People. The project had two main objectives: "to collect, sift and validate result-oriented quality indicators at the organizational level of care homes, based on an exchange of experiences in selected Member States" and "to investigate and gain experience in methods on how to work with result-oriented indicators and how to train care home managers in dealing with the respective challenges" (Leichsenring 2011). The project developed a set of 94 indicators in five categories (table 10.1), published in a handbook (Maas et al. 2010).

These results-oriented indicators were selected based on five criteria:

- Feasibility: Is it feasible to gather the relevant data in a relatively easy way in the daily practice of care homes?
- Validity/Soundness: Is the indicator appropriate and useful for measuring a defined quality aspect?
- Comparability: Can data be compared within and between care homes, over time, and across different providers?
- Ability to steer change: Is the indicator an appropriate instrument to steer improvement processes in care homes?
- Quantifiability: Can the indicator be expressed in a quantifiable manner (number, index, mark, etc.)?

Each indicator is presented in the handbook with an exact definition, a definition of operationalization, and the method of measurement (examples are provided in table 10.2). Practitioners should choose the most relevant indicators from the list but not use more than 10–15 indicators at once. The use of these results-oriented indicators should help foster cost-efficiency and improve quality of care by working with relevant stakeholders toward measurable success. Introducing these measures has relatively low costs but requires sufficient training and a management appreciation of the performance on these indicators (Leichsenring 2010).

At the national level, some countries have started applying the idea of outcome measures in their LTC system. England, for instance, recently passed a new Care Act in 2014 that puts local authorities in charge to ensure the "well-being" of elderly. To do so, providers need to register according to the

Table 10.1 Overview of Indicator Categories for Residential Care for Older People

	Domain	*Perspectives*	*Indicators*
1	Quality of care	Residents, staff	1–24
2	Quality of life	Residents, family, friends, staff	25–70
3	Leadership	Management, staff	71–87
4	Economic performance	Management, funder	88–91
5	Context	Funder, legislator, suppliers, general public	92–94

Table 10.2 Examples of Indicators

Indicator	*No. 20*	*No. 38*
Definition	Percentage of residents suffering from thromboses	Percentage of relatives/friends who feel their resident has adequate access to health care services
Operationalization	This indicator is measured on a defined day once a year as a prevalence measure or can be based on continuous care documentation	This indicator is generated as an item, constructed for its purpose, on annual satisfaction surveys or qualitative interviews with relatives/friends
Measurement/calculation formula	Numerator: Number of residents suffering from thromboses Denominator: Number of residents who have been assessed	Numerator: Number of relatives/friends feeling their resident has access to health care Denominator: Total number of relatives/friends surveyed
Use/purpose	The purpose of this indicator is to move toward the prevention of thromboses	This indicator gives an alternative perspective on whether residents are receiving necessary health care services that can improve overall functioning and health, ultimately enhancing quality of life
Perspective	Residents	Relatives/friends
Theme	Quality and safety of care	Quality of life, health promotion
Source	PROGRESS, 2010	NCHR&D Forum, 2007

national standards of the CQC and are subject to continuous monitoring. Inspection follows the guidelines of the CQC general quality assurance scheme, which assesses facilities using the following questions (CQC 2015a):

- Are they safe? Meaning that people are protected from abuse and avoidable harm.
- Are they effective? Meaning that people are protected from abuse and avoidable harm.
- Are they caring? Meaning that staff involve and treat people with compassion, kindness, dignity, and respect.
- Are they responsive to people's needs? Meaning that services are organized so they meet people's needs.
- Are they well-led? Meaning that the leadership, management, and governance of the organization assures the delivery of high-quality person-centered care, supports learning and innovation, and promotes an open and fair culture.

To answer those questions, the inspection teams use different sources of information as outlined in figure 10.2. The four areas combine different types of data collection such as databases, interviews, and observation to gather information from all stakeholders involved. A handbook published by the CQC provides transparent information to providers (CQC 2015a). The evaluation of provider performance is based on consistent principles to ensure comparability of results. The information is used to inform local authorities and improve user choice through a public rating system (grading homes from outstanding to inadequate).

Figure 10.2 Sources of Information for Quality Assessment Based on CQC 2015a

However, in contrast to the health care sector, the use of indicators from the Adult Social Care Intelligent Monitoring (ASCIM) program is still under development. To date, the indicators do not cover all five key dimensions, and the CQC lacks sufficient and reliable data to publish indicator performance on individual facilities. The current set of indicators mostly covers the dimensions of safety and leadership.[3]

To address the lack of a full set of indicators, particularly for the quality-of-life assessment, the PSSRU developed and tested the Adult Social Care Outcome Toolkit (ASCOT) to measure social care outcomes. The toolkit consists of eight domains of social care-related quality-of-life (SCRQoL) measures that are considered the care equivalent to the widely used outcome measure of quality adjusted life-years (QALY) in health care (Netten et al. 2012). The ASCOT provides a flexible baseline tool that can be used in a range of circumstances. An adapted version of the ASCOT for the purpose of monitoring residential care quality was recently introduced and is still at a preliminary stage of testing (Towers et al. 2015). The adapted eight domains from the ASCOT are presented in table 10.3.

The quality assessment was adjusted to the demands of residential home inspections by local authorities and relies on a personal inspection team to observe and interview stakeholders of the particular residential home. The first results regarding feasibility and usefulness appeared to be positive for local authorities. The toolkit is based on onsite visits and interviews by the authorities, and it is recommended to:

- Conduct a 2-hour structured observation,
- Interview at least five residents (2–3 each),
- Interview up to five staff members (2–3 each),
- Speak to family member and visitors, if available, and
- Interview the home manager.

Outside Europe, efforts are also being made to assess and monitor LTC service performance. Following a series of scandals, LTC services became one of the most regulated sectors within the United States (OECD/European Union 2013). The states are responsible for ensuring the performance of LTC facilities and regularly conducting unannounced site visits, although this practice has been criticized as overly expensive and inefficient. Further efforts aim to improve consumer choice, make information more easily available, and let a more market-based approach incentivize providers to improve

Table 10.3 Domains and Definitions of the Adjusted ASCOT

Care home domains	*Definitions*
Accommodation—living in a clean and comfortable home	Residents live in a clean and comfortable home and like how it looks and feels. Bedrooms and shared areas are well-designed, easy to get around, and meet residents' health and social care needs.
Personal cleanliness and comfort—being clean and presentable	Residents are clean and comfortable. They are dressed in ways that meet their individual needs and wishes.
Food and drink—eating and drinking well	Residents eat and drink well. They get a balanced and varied diet, including food they like and need.
Personal safety—feeling safe and free from fear	Residents feel safe and free from fear of physical and psychological harm and are supported to manage risks.
Being sociable—spending time with people	Residents spend time socializing with people they like and taking part in social activities. Close relationships with family, friends (from inside and outside the home), caregivers, and people from the wider community are supported.
Being occupied—having things to do	Residents spend time doing things they like, value, and enjoy on their own or with others. They are supported in continuing activities that they have been involved in the past.
Choice and control over daily life—having choices, feeling in control	Residents have choice and control over their daily life. They feel that they "have a say" in their care, daily routine, and activities and that their views are respected.
Dignity—being treated with dignity and respect by staff	Residents are treated with compassion, dignity, and respect. Staff think about what they say and how they say it and consider the feelings of residents when giving care and support.

Source: Based on Towers et al. 2015.

the quality of care. On a public website,[4] nursing homes are compared and rated on a five-star scale, based on data from three categories: health inspections, staffing, and quality measures. These quality measures are composed of different indicators (e.g., percentage of long-stay residents with a urinary tract infection) that are assessed separately for long- and short-term stays.[5] The website, however, does not cover all LTC facilities and allows comparisons only among certified Medicare and Medicaid providers.

In Korea, LTC facilities have been part of the quality assessment scheme since 2008. All institutions are subject to quality assessment that follows an annual procedure. The assessment plan is publicly available and includes the period of assessment as well as the relevant indicators, and providers receive briefing sessions before the assessment to ensure a fair and transparent inspection. The Health Insurance Review and Assessment Services (HIRA) uses administrative data, insurance claims, and survey data consisting of 36 quality indicators that assess structure, processes, and outcomes. The performance on all indicators is condensed into one composite indicator score, and results are published in an annual report. The assessment results for selected indicators are presented in table 10.4. Based on this comprehensive assessment, the HIRA and the public can easily monitor the quality of individual providers and also the development of the whole sector (HIRA 2011).

Policy Innovation and Methods of Modern Governance

Today, policy makers and practitioner agree that the design of a LTC system should be based on tailor-made home- and community care services. These include: (1) home medical visits, home nursing, home assistance, and home adjustment; (2) day or short-stay hospitals, day care and transportation, night care centers, service housing; and (3) tele-assistance (European Commission 2007).

However, this perspective on active aging and consumer-centered solutions is still relatively new, and international experience with effectiveness is limited.

Table 10.4 Example of Assessment Results for Long-Term-Care Hospitals in Korea

Classification indicator	*Indicator name*	*Total average (variation from 2009)*		
Patient safety	Rate of non-slip floor installed (bathrooms, toilets, stairs)	'10	75.7	(25.0↑)
		'09	50.7	
Medical care workforce	Presence of duty doctor at night/on holidays	'10	36.4	(6.2↑)
		'09	30.2	
Other human resources	No. of patients attended by one physical therapist	'10	65.2	
Medical devices	No. of oxygen supply equipment per bed	'10	24.2	(2.0↑)
		'09	22.2	
Processes	Rate of patients with indwelling catheter (in high risk group)	'10	22.7	(1.4↓)
		'09	24.1	
Outcome	Rate of patients with newly appeared bedsore—high-risk group	'10	1.5	(1.2↓)
		'09	2.7	

Source: Based on HIRA 2011.

In addition, the success of such solutions is likely to be sensitive to the environment of implementation and could benefit from more iterative policy making and mutual exchange. In the case of such complex and interdependent systems, leaving the duty of finding innovative solutions to the decentralized market will most likely not generate optimal solutions (Marengo and Dosi 2005).

Hence, policy learning and experimentation is an important aspect of modern policy formulation. To foster a large variety of LTC projects, local governments require funding and sufficient leeway in order to cooperate with the private sector to find innovative solutions. A culture of innovation that allows for failure and ensures recognition of successful ideas is also essential. Proper policy experimentation requires sufficient *ex-ante* planning and a sophisticated monitoring framework that allows the *ex-post* evaluation of the intervention. This section outlines the framework for successful policy experimentation and provides international examples of how knowledge can be distributed to improve policy making on a large scale.

Policy Experimentation and Randomized Controlled Trials

The design of small-scale programs is often influenced by positive past or foreign experiences, but uncertainty about the efficiency of the specific intervention remains. While experiments benefit from creativity and local variation, the monitoring framework should be highly standardized to make the results comparable and ensure a reliable impact assessment. The latter is often difficult, and the identification of causal relationships usually requires a certain study design that often conflicts with ethical considerations or short-term political interests.

The best way to obtain causal effects is the application of a randomized controlled trial (RCT) framework. The idea of RCTs was originally used in medicine and relies on a random selection of treatment and control groups to identify a causal effect of a drug—a detailed description of how to conduct a RCT can be found in White, Sabarwaland, and Hoop (2014). This approach has spilled over into the field of political science but often faces problems in application. Many evaluations failed due to public pressure or people's reactions to presumably unfair behavior toward the control groups. The long-run benefits of clear policy evaluation are often not enough to overcome the short-term problems of such experiments.

To avoid the dilemmas that arise with RCTs, alternative methods have been developed that require the collection of more sophisticated data to assess a treatment effect but allow for a less restrictive study design (King et al. 2007). Even when an RCT framework is not feasible, small-scale experimental approaches at the local level can help assess whether an intervention works (WeDO 2012). The experience from such local approaches should be evaluated in a standardized way to make results comparable. Such information helps determine which ideas have the best chances of success when scaled up more broadly. However, since scaling up might require the implementation of such projects in a significantly different environment, local authorities need a platform for exchange. They must discuss the design with private and public stakeholders on the local and national levels to allow for smart and locally adapted solutions. For this purpose, the EU founded the AHA which streamlines efforts to promote efficient solutions by including all relevant social domains.

Peer Reviews

To help disseminate knowledge from local experience, the OMC uses peer reviews as an instrument for fostering mutual exchange and learning. For a peer review, host countries invite other member states and important stakeholders to a meeting in order to receive feedback and discuss upcoming policy plans. Since 2008, more than 10 peer reviews have been conducted in the field of health and LTC, focusing on topics such as migration of LTC staff, care quality, and priority setting in care policies.[6]

The latest peer review meeting was held by Slovenia and focused on "Long-term care—the problem of sustainable financing."[7] In advance of the meeting, countries and stakeholder groups submitted answers to the main questions asked by the Slovenian government. The essence of the peer review was synthesized in a report that is publicly available on the EU website. The knowledge created through the review is expected to not only influence Slovenian LTC policy but also improve the European understanding of important issues in financing LTC. Through this process, many learning documents and case studies are available and can be translated into best-practice guidelines.

The European Semester

While peer review is a demand-driven and project-centered instrument for improving policies, the EC also benchmarks national efforts toward the common Europe 2020 targets[8] in a more formalized manner. Based on the collection of comparable data, the EC evaluates regional performance and assesses the need to take action. Even though LTC is not a direct Europe 2020 target, the topic is addressed through the flagship initiative Platform against Poverty and Social Exclusion.

The iterative report-and-recommendation process is structured in an annual "European Semester." At the beginning of each year, the EC publishes a country report that highlights progress and domains needing specific attention from the national governments, not only assessing the performance on indicators but also pointing out structural issues. Thereafter, countries submit a National Reform Program (NRP) that outlines national efforts toward smart, sustainable, and inclusive growth. Based on the analytical framework of the country report and the content of the NRP, the EC gives Country Specific Recommendations (CSRs) containing achievable goals for the next 12–18 months. While not following these recommendations allows for sanctions in the area of public finance, the EC has no legal basis for enforcing reforms in social policies. The countries discuss the CSRs before the EC adopts a final version. To achieve the goals of the CSRs, the EC supports the member states through close monitoring and exchange with other countries.

The learning of best practice is then facilitated through peer reviews and another instrument of the OMC.

Implications for China

Going forward, the design of China's LTC sector needs to focus on efficiency and provide a sustainable solution for the benefit of the entire Chinese population. Until today, China has had no national health insurance system or comprehensive public LTC program for the elderly. Although some pilot projects have emerged, most elderly people have insufficient access to LTC services, which are often based on fee-for-service with little quality control (Feng et al. 2012; Li et al. 2013). In light of the demographic and economic transition, the Chinese national government is set to take action to make LTC available to a larger share of the population and to enable access for the less affluent. However, expanding large-scale LTC service provision will be challenging, as demographic projections suggest particularly rapid growth of the oldest-old population, the group most likely to be in need of LTC (Li et al. 2009).

As China has little experience with LTC policies, it is worth exploring knowledge from other countries and incorporating international best practices into the design of a national system. However, simply adopting policies from other countries is unlikely to succeed, as they need to be embedded in the national framework and adjusted to the country-specific context (Heilmann 2008). Therefore, the international examples described above can only be viewed as trend-setting and sources of ideas worth testing in China.

Progress in social policies has been closely tied to the development of clear goals and corresponding indicators, while clear responsibilities within the governmental hierarchy are needed to ensure accountability for progress of the system (Gash et al. 2013). In the 12th Five-Year Plan for the Development of China's Undertakings for the Aged, the Chinese national government outlined the direction for future advances in LTC and declared some specific goals, but the plan does not outline clear responsibilities and remains vague in many areas. A document on Preferential Policies for the Elderly from 2013[9] provides equally little specifics. The Opinions of the State Council on Accelerating the Development of Services for the Aged, also published in 2013, provides a more detailed agenda for LTC until 2020. In addition, the Chinese central government has implemented the newly revised Law on Protection of Rights and Interests of Seniors, which clearly outlines the responsibilities of departments related to aging.

The State Council is responsible for issuing national plans related to aging, while local governments (above the town level) are responsible for local planning and developing annual programs according to the national plans. For system building, the State Council and relevant ministries set the standards for elderly care service facilities, elderly care service quality, and service practitioners. Local governments at all levels must make plans to guarantee the elderly's rights to access basic medical services, encourage and support social forces to provide home-based care services, and develop community services. Local governments also need to incorporate the construction of elderly care service facilities into urban-rural development planning and make comprehensive arrangements for construction land and materials.

In recent years, China has made strong efforts at capacity building. Following the 12th Five-Year Plan, the government wants to increase beds in old-age institutions by 3.42 million nationwide during the period 2011 to 2015. This would increase China's coverage to around 30 beds per 1,000 elderly (Feng et al. 2012), which is comparable to other Asian economies. By 2020, capacity should be increased to 35–40 beds per 1,000 elderly, and the development of service coverage shall be included in social and economic development plans (State Council 2013).

However, there seems to be little information about the effective demand for services, a fact closely related to an underdeveloped system of population statistics. Currently, China mostly relies on data from the census, which is carried out every ten years and "hardly meet[s] the government's need to understand population dynamics and to make forecasts to better guide decision-making and public service management" (Juan 2014).

To develop a demand-driven LTC industry, the government needs better data and statistical tools. Existing sources should be complemented with new data to assess the existing supply as well as local needs and demands. Against this backdrop, China's National Committee on Aging recently announced a survey of more than 200,000 elderly (Wang 2015) and there are multiple data sources available that might be helpful for understanding the remaining gaps between the supply and demand of care services (box 10.2). The data sets could be matched with provider information, similar to the PSSRU approach, to estimate the relationship between the supply and demand for care services.

Box 10.2 Possible Data Sources on LTC

In China, information on the aging population is collected through the population census and sample survey of population carried out by the State Statistics Bureau. Some aging research institutions and universities also conduct social surveys related to the aging population. These surveys provide comprehensive basic data for understanding the aging population situation, elderly care needs, and future development trends in China.

- **The Sampling Survey of the Aged Population in Urban/Rural China** The Sampling Survey of the Aged Population in Urban/Rural China aims to provide a basis for aging policy decision making, planning, and promoting construction of the aging service system. It also offers basic data support for aging scientific research. This survey, which is organized and carried out by the China National Committee on Aging Office, was conducted in the years 2000, 2006, 2010, and 2015 thus far. Survey respondents are the elderly aged 60 and over. Investigation contents include aging population basic information, employment, pension coverage, housing, community service, social participation, aging service demand, medical security, and health condition.

box continues next page

Box 10.2 Possible Data Sources on LTC *(continued)*

- **China Health and Retirement Longitudinal Study (CHARLS)** The China Health and Retirement Longitudinal Study aims to collect a set of high-quality micro data on elders aged 45 and over and their families. It is implemented by the Institute of National Development of Peking University. The data is mainly used to analyze China's aging population and promote interdisciplinary research on aging. Investigation contents include individual basic information, family structure and economic support, health condition, physical measurement, health service utilization and medical insurance, employment, retirement and pension, income, consumption, property, and community basic situation.
- **Chinese Longitudinal Healthy Longevity Survey (CLHLS)** The Chinese Longitudinal Healthy Longevity Survey aims to better understand the social, behavioral, environmental, and biological factors affecting the longevity and health of humans. It was first carried out by Peking University in 1998 and was supported by the National Institute on Aging in America. Follow-up surveys were implemented in 2000, 2002, 2005, 2008, 2011, and 2013. This survey focuses on the elderly aged 60 and over.
- **China Longitudinal Aging Social Survey (CLASS)** The China Longitudinal Aging Social Survey aims to collect basic information on the aging population and aging problems in China and provide data support for the government to revise population policy and social security policy. It is implemented by the Institute of Gerontology of Renmin University of China. Survey respondents are the elderly aged 60 and over in 29 provinces. Investigation contents include the elderly's basic information, health and medical condition, social and economic situation, daily lifestyle, pension level and living arrangement, and family and community resources for the elderly.

National statistics on waiting time for existing services could also help in understanding the demand for care.

Getting precise estimates will be particularly challenging given China's massive transition, as the rise of new care alternatives such as comprehensive home care will alter the demand for institutional care. Nevertheless, these market dynamics should be consistently monitored at the national level, and information needs to be accessible to the public. Such knowledge would be essential for allocating funds to local commissioners and helping to ensure the efficient use of public money.

In terms of care quality, data collection and evaluation should become part of local commissioning, guided by national standards. This information is vital for monitoring providers and also enables comparison of local government performance at the national level. However, as shown by international experience, finding good indicators is difficult. Even though the use of outcome measures is preferred in theory, many countries (including the EU) still rely on input and output indicators. The types of indicators that are selected depend on a trade-off between costs of data collection and value added to public planners.

To provide a comprehensive overview, data should be collected with broad coverage. As this is costly for providers, they have little incentive to collect such data and transmit them to public officials. Therefore, quality assessment should become part of procurement contracts or a requirement for receiving an LTC provider license. An alternative is to collect data from the public side through regular quality inspections. If feasible, an automated routine of data collection is preferable. Different indicators could be used to measure home and residential care, but research should test the validity of international examples for application in China.

Similar to the European approach, local progress toward commonly defined LTC goals should be channeled through one institution. The creation of a platform for collecting and analyzing information on the elderly is outlined in the Five-Year Plan. The Office of the CNCA is assigned similar tasks as the AHA and could be a helpful point of contact for international exchange and national knowledge creation. Many nongovernmental institutions have also become involved in the research on aging and provide policy consultations, such as the Institute of Gerontology of Renmin University, the Institute of Population and Labor Economics at the CASS, the Institute of Gerontology of Peking University, and the Research Center of Gerontology of Tsinghua University. In recent years, so-called folk think-tanks have also contributed to the policy research on aging, including the China Planning Institute on Aging, Ownmind Management Consulting Group, the China Philanthropy Research Institute, and the China Silver Industry Association. Further incorporating their expertise might improve future policy making (Xia and Qian 2014).

As described in this chapter, the need for national coordination is high on several dimensions. First, integrated LTC systems rely on health care, social services, and pensions, which are usually administered in different governmental bodies. Second, national guidelines and quality standards need to be developed to harmonize the activities of local governments. Third, national statistics require consistent data collection to monitor and evaluate total sector performance. Fourth, consulting local governments and fostering an exchange between different stakeholders can provide important information for efficient policy formulation. The latter two tasks might benefit from tools used in the OMC, such as Peer Reviews or the more institutionalized design of the European Semester.

To develop innovative and efficient care solutions, modern governance suggests an iterative, bottom-up, experimental approach shaped by the experience of different stakeholders. In contrast to common prejudice about the Chinese policies of centrally directed top-down planning, experimental bottom-up policies are a commonly used tool by the national government (Heilmann, Shih, and Hofem 2013). This "experimentation under hierarchy" suggests an interactive process of policy experimentation and adjustment at the local level, with possible implementation of successful best practice at the national level. This approach shows great similarities to some core features of the European OMC and has been used successfully in some areas. Many pilot projects were scaled up into full operational programs that transformed economic regulations (e.g., transformation of state-owned enterprises) and the structure of the Communist Party. This promotion of minimally regulated experimentation can be regarded as an important contributor to China's economic rise (Heilmann 2008). The method of policy experimentation is promoted in the 2013 Opinions on the Development of Services for the Aged.

However, this approach has largely failed to influence national-level policies in the field of social protection. For instance, there have been several pilot projects to improve the health care system in rural areas, but none of those experiments managed to become a national program. As of 2003, about 80 percent of the rural population was still without health insurance (World Bank 2005). Reasons for difficulties particularly in the social domain can be found in the limited benefits for local elites, who have little incentive to make a pilot project successful if the program mainly helps the lower classes (Duflo, Fischer, and Chattopadhyay 2005).

To make social policy experiments work, local innovation is crucial but should operate in a coordinated framework under a central government that shows strong commitment, supervision, and enforcement. As highlighted above, a strict monitoring framework for evaluation is needed to assess the cost-effectiveness of such experiments and make their results comparable. As the design of policy experiments has important implications for evaluation opportunities, it should follow a standardized procedure. When the gold standard of fully randomized control trials are not feasible, alternative validated methods may be considered (Oliver et al. 2010; Stoker and John 2009).

In contrast to most Western countries, the Chinese government has little restrictions under the law to launch such programs freely. In the context of LTC, this can be seen as an advantage, as the process of implementation will face few institutional or juridical obstacles. Given the large public knowledge base on care provision and the strong implementation capacity, the Chinese government has all the external preconditions to close the coverage gap of LTC needs within the population.

However, as many elderly can rely on little own financial means, even the most efficient LTC sector would require considerable public funds to meet the needs of a steadily aging society. Therefore, establishing an adequate funding mechanism for LTC services for the elderly remains a major challenge.

Notes

1. People aged 65 and older. Alternative indicators assess beds per capita or population and sometimes measure the number of facilities.
2. The full set of indicators and the progress of collection can be found in (European Commission 2015).
3. The full set of ASCIM indicators is available from (CQC 2016).
4. Available at https://www.medicare.gov/nursinghomecompare/profile.html. Similarly, Canada provides a tool to compare LTC providers since 2015 (CIHI 2015).
5. Full set of indicators available at https://www.medicare.gov/NursingHomeCompare/About/Quality-Measures-Info.html.
6. http://ec.europa.eu/social/main.jsp?year=0&country=0&theme=9&catId=1024&langId=en&mode=searchSubmit#searchDiv.

7. http://ec.europa.eu/social/main.jsp?catId=1024&langId=en&newsId=2097&furtherNews=yes.
8. The overall EU targets are adjusted to the country-specific context.
9. http://www.ifa-fiv.org/wp-content/uploads/2014/10/Preferential-Policies-for-the-Elderly.doc.

References

Burger, F., M. Weber, and D. S. Landkreisen. 2011. "Vorausberechnung der Pflegebedürftigen und des Pflegepersonals für Baden-Württemberg bis 2030."

CIHI. 2015. *Canada Provides a Tool to Compare LTC Providers Since 2015.* Your Health System. http://yourhealthsystem.cihi.ca/.

CQC (Care Quality Commission). 2015a. *How CQC Regulates: Community Adult Social Care Services Provider Handbook.* http://www.cqc.org.uk/sites/default/files/20150327_asc_community_services_provider_handbook_march_15_update_01.pdf.

———. 2015b. *Market Oversight of "Difficult to Replace" Providers of Adult Social Care Guidance for Providers.* http://www.cqc.org.uk/sites/default/files/20150327_market_oversight_full_guide_providers.pdf.

———. 2016. *Intelligent Monitoring Adult social Care Indicators.* http://www.cqc.org.uk/sites/default/files/20160105_Adult_Social_Care_Intelligent_Monitoring_Indicators_and_Methodology_for_publication.pdf.

Dehousse, Renaud. 2003. *The Open Method of Coordination: A New Policy.* Les Cahiers européens de Sciences Po, 3. https://www.researchgate.net/publication/48854093_The_Open_Method_of_Coordination_a_New_Policy_Paradigm.

Dolowitz, David P., and Marsh David. 2000. "Learning from Abroad: The Role of Policy Transfer in Contemporary Policy-Making." *Governance* 13 (1): 5. doi:10.1111/0952-1895.00121.

Duflo, Esther, Greg Fischer, and Raghabendra Chattopadhyay. 2005. *Efficiency and Rent Seeking in Local Government : Evidence from Randomized Policy Experiments in India.* Department of Economics, Massachusetts Institute of Technology. https://www.povertyactionlab.org/sites/default/files/publications/107_Duflo_Efficiency_and_Rent_Seeking.pdf.

European Commission. n.d. "Employment." http://ec.europa.eu/social/main.jsp?year=0&country=0&theme=9&catId=1024&langId=en&mode=searchSubmit#searchDiv.

———. 2004. *Modernising Social Protection for the Development of High-Quality, Accessible and Sustainable Health Care and Long-Term Care: Support for the National Strategies using the "Open Method of Coordination."* http://ec.europa.eu/employment_social/soc-prot/healthcare/com_04_304_en.pdf.

———. 2007. *Joint Report on Social Protection and Social Inclusion 2007.* doi:ISBN 20978-92-79-05561-4.

———. 2009. *Portfolio of Indicators for the Monitoring of the European Strategy for Social Protection and Social Inclusion—2009 Update.* http://ec.europa.eu/social/BlobServlet?docId=3882&langId=en.

———. 2011a. *Operational Plan for the European Innovation Partnership on Active and Healthy Ageing.* http://ec.europa.eu/research/innovation-union/pdf/active-healthy-ageing/steering-group/operational_plan.pdf#view=fit&pagemode=none.

———. 2011b. *Strategic Implementation Plan for the European Innovation Partnership on Active and Healthy Ageing.* http://ec.europa.eu/research/innovation-union/pdf/active-healthy-ageing/steering-group/implementation_plan.pdf#view=fit&pagemode=none.

———. 2014. *Peer Review in Slovenia: Long-Term Care—The Problem of Sustainable Financing.* http://ec.europa.eu/social/main.jsp?catId=1024&langId=en&newsId=2097&furtherNews=yes.

———. 2015. *Social Protection Committee Indicators Sub-Group Portfolio of EU Social Indicators for the Monitoring of Progress towards the EU Objectives for Social Protection and Social Inclusion 2015 Update.* doi:10.2767/929097.

Feng, Zhanlian, Chang Liu, Xinping Guan, and Vincent Mor. 2012. "China's Rapidly Aging Population Creates Policy Challenges in Shaping a Viable Long-Term Care System." *Health Affairs* 31 (12): 2764–773.

Gash, Tom, Nehal Davison, Sam Sims, and Louisa Hotson. 2013. *Making Public Service Markets Work.* http://www.instituteforgovernment.org.uk/sites/default/files/publications/Making_public_service_markets_work_final_0.pdf.

Heilmann, Sebastian. 2008. "Policy Experimentation in China's Economic Rise." *Studies in Comparative International Development* 43 (1): 1–26. doi:10.1007/s12116-007-9014-4.

Heilmann, Sebastian, Lea Shih, and Andreas Hofem. 2013. "National Planning and Local Technology Zones: Experimental Governance in China's Torch Programme." *The China Quarterly* 216: 896–919. doi:10.1017/S0305741013001057.

HIRA (Health Insurance Review and Assessment Service). 2011. "Comprehensive Quality Report of National Health Insurance." HIRA, Seoul. http://www.hira.or.kr/eng/news/02/1212222_25619.html.

Nauwelaers, C. and R. Wintjes. 2008. "Innovation Policy, Innovation in Policy: Policy Learning within and across Systems and Clusters. *In Innovation Policy in Europe Measurement and Strategy.*

Humburg, Martin. 2008. "The Open Method of Coordination and European Integration—The Example of European Education Policy." Berlin Working Paper on European Integration (8). http://www.polsoz.fu berlin.de/polwiss/forschung/international/europa/arbeitspapiere/2008-8_Humburg_OpenMethodofCoordination.pdf.

Juan, Shan. 2014. "China to Improve Population Forecasting." 17573820. http://www.chinadaily.com.cn/china/2014npcandcppcc/2014-03/11/content_17340059.htm.

King, Gary, Emmanuela Gakido, Nirmala Ravishanka, Ryan T. Moore, Jason Lakin, Manett Vargas, Martha Maria Tellez-Rojo, Juan Eugenio Hernandez Avila, Mauricio. Hernandez Avila, and Hector Hernandez Llamas. 2007. "A 'Politically Robust' Experimental Design for Public Policy Evaluation, with Application to the Mexican Universal Health Insurance Program." *Journal of Policy Analysis and Management : [The Journal of the Association for Public Policy Analysis and Management]* 26 (3): 479–506. doi:10.1002/pam.

Leichsenring, Kai. 2010. "Quality Management in Residential Care by Result-Oriented Performance Iindicators." http://interlinks.euro.centre.org/model/example/QualityManagementInResidentialCareByResultOrientedPerformanceIndicators.

Leichsenring, Kai. 2011. "Quality Management by Result-Oriented Indicators: Towards Benchmarking in Residential Care for Older People." *Management* (June): 1–16.

Li, Mei, Yang Zhang, Zhenyu Zhang, Ying Zhang, Litao Zhou, and Kun Chen. 2013. "Rural-Urban Differences in the Long-Term Care of the Disabled Elderly in China." *PLoS ONE* 8 (11): 1–7. doi:10.1371/journal.pone.0079955.

Li, Qiang, Mieke Reuser, Cornelia Kraus, and Juha Alho. 2009. "Ageing of a Giant: A Stochastic Population Forecast for China, 2006–2060." *Journal of Population Research* 26 (1): 21–50. doi:10.1007/s12546-008-9004-z.

Maas, F., F. Hoffmann, R. Rodrigues, and A. Hovenier. 2010. "Measuring Progress: Indicators for Care Homes." doi:10.1086/454495.

Marengo, Luigi, and Giovanni Dosi. 2005. "Division of Labor, Organizational Coordination and Market Mechanisms in Collective Problem-Solving." *Journal of Economic Behavior and Organization* 58 (2): 303–26. doi:10.1016/j.jebo.2004.03.020.

Nauwelaers, Claire, and René Wintjes. 2008. "Innovation Policy, Innovation in Policy: Policy Learning within and across Systems and Clusters." In *Innovation Policy in Europe Measurement and Strategy*, 225–68. Cheltenham, UK: Edward Elgar Publishing.

Netten, Anne, Peter Burge, Juliette Malley, Dimitris Potoglou, Ann-Marie Towers, John E. Brazier, Terry Flynn, Julien Forder, and Beryl Wall. 2012. "Outcomes of Social Care for Adults: Developing a Preference Weighted Measure." *Health Technology Assessment* 16 (16) doi:10.3310/hta16160.

OECD/European Union. 2013. "A Good Life in Old Age? Monitoring and Improving Quality in Long-term Care." OECD Health Policy Studies, OECD. http://dx.doi.org/10.1787/9789264194564-en.

Oliver, Sandy, Anne-Marie Bagnall, James Thomas, Jonathan Shepherd, Amanda Sowden, Ian White, Jac Dinnes, Rebecca Rees, Jill L. Colquitt, Kathryn Oliver, and Zoe Garrett. 2010. "Randomised Controlled Trials for Policy Interventions: A Review of Reviews and Meta-Regression." *Health Technology Assessment* 14 (16): 1–192. doi:10.3310/hta14160.

Radaelli, Claudio M. 2003. *The Open Method of Coordination: A New Governance Architecture for the European Union.* http://www.sieps.se/sites/default/files/3-20031.pdf.

Social Protection Committee. 2014. "Adequate Social Protection for Long-Term Care Needs in an Ageing Society." doi:10.2767/32352.

———. 2002. *Joint EPC/SPC Draft for a Council Report in the Field of Health Care and Care for the Elderly.* http://europa.eu/epc/pdf/epcspchealth_en.pdf.

State Council. 2013. *Opinions of the State Council's on Accelerating the Development of Services for the Aged.* http://jnjd.mca.gov.cn/article/zyjd/zcwj/201310/20131000534003.shtml.

Stoker, Gerry, and Peter John. 2009. "Design Experiments: Engaging Policy Makers in the Search for Evidence about What Works." *Political Studies* 57 (2): 356–73. doi:10.1111/j.1467-9248.2008.00756.x.

Szyszczak, E. 2006. "Experimental Governance: The Open Method of Coordination." *European Law Journal* 12 (4): 486–502. doi:10.1111/j.1468-0386.2006.00329.x.

Towers, Ann-Marie, Jacquetta Holder, Nick Smith, Tanya Crowther, Ann Netten, Elizabeth Welch, and Grace Collins. 2015. "Adapting the Adult Social Care Outcomes Toolkit (ASCOT) for Use in Care Home Quality Monitoring: Conceptual Development and Testing." *BMC Health Services Research* 15 (1): 304. doi:10.1186/s12913-015-0942-9.

Trubek, David M., and Louise Trubek. 2005. "Hard and Soft Law in the Construction of Social Europe: The Role of the Open Method of Co-Ordination." *European Law Journal* 11 (3): 343–64. doi:10.1111/j.1468-0386.2005.00263.x.

Wang, Xiaodong. 2015. "Massive Survey to Focus on 223,000 Elderly." China Daily. http://www.chinadaily.com.cn/china/2015-07/29/content_21438901.htm.

WeDO. 2012. "Framework for Long-Term Care Services Principles and Guidelines for the Wellbeing and Dignity." http://wedo.tttp.eu/system/files/24171_WeDo_brochure_A4_48p_EN_WEB.pdf.

White, Sabarwaland Hoop. 2014. "Randomized Controlled Trials (RCTs): Methodological Briefs: Impact Evaluation 7." UNICEF Office of Research, Florence.

Wittenberg, Raphael, Adelina Comas-Herrera, Derek King, Juliette Malley, Linda Pickard, and Robin Darton. 2006. *Future Demand for Long-Term Care, 2002 to 2041: Projections of Demand for Long-Term Care for Older People in England*. http://eprints.lse.ac.uk/13245/.

World Bank. 2005. "China's Health Sector—Why Reform is Needed." Rural Health in China: Briefing Notes Series 3. http://www-wds.worldbank.org/external/default/WDSContentServer/WDSP/IB/2005/08/11/000090341_20050811151809/Rendered/PDF/332320ENGLISH0CHA0BN31en.pdf.

Xia, Cheng, and Chen Qian. 2014. "Research on the Participation of the Folk Think-Tanks in Chinese Government Policy." *Canadian Social Science* 10 (4): 125–29. doi:10.3968/4725.

Zeitlin, Jonathan. 2005. "Conclusion." In *The Open Method of Co-Ordination in Action. Theoretical Promise, Empirical Realities, Reform Strategy*, pp. 447–503. The European Employment and Social Inclusion Strategies. New York: Oxford University Press.

Zhan, Heying, Guangya Liu, Xinping Guan, and Hong-guang Bai. 2006. "Recent Developments in Institutional Elder Care in China: Changing Concepts and Attitudes." *Journal of Aging & Social Policy* 18 (2): 85–108. doi:10.1300/J031v18n02_06.

Zhang, Yue, Martin L. Puterman, Matthew Nelson, and Derek Richard Atkins. 2012. "A Simulation Optimization Approach to Long-Term Care Capacity Planning." *Operations Research* 60 (2): 249–61. doi:10.1287/opre.1110.1026.

www.ingramcontent.com/pod-product-compliance
Lightning Source LLC
Chambersburg PA
CBHW081428270326
41932CB00019B/3124